T0222362

Lecture Notes in Computer Science

Lecture Notes in Computer Science

Edited by G. Goos and J. Hartmanis

190

M.W. Alford J.P. Ansart G. Hommel
L. Lamport B. Liskov G.P. Mullery
F.B. Schneider

Distributed Systems

Methods and Tools for Specification
An Advanced Course

Edited by M. Paul and H.J. Siegert

Springer-Verlag
Berlin Heidelberg New York Tokyo

CR Subject Classification (1982): C.1.2, C.2, D.1.3, D.2, D.3, D.4

ISBN 3-540-15216-4 Springer-Verlag Berlin Heidelberg New York Tokyo
ISBN 0-387-15216-4 Springer-Verlag New York Heidelberg Berlin Tokyo

Printing and binding: Beltz Offsetdruck, Hemsbach/Bergstr.
2145/3140-543210

general specification methods and tools as well as architectural knowledge, modularization concepts and programming paradigms for distributed systems. A presentation of these topics was the major aim of the course. As said before, all aspects involved are still in a research stage to a very high degree. Therefore it is impossible to give a complete picture of all ideas, concepts, methods, and tools. Instead we have tried to show and discuss the range of possible solutions by presenting a specification system used by a commercial company, and in contrast, examples and basic principles for formal specification and verification. It is important of course to have an understanding of programming concepts and paradigms for distributed systems when specifying and designing them. Important concepts and paradigms are presented in chapter 4. As an example for a language for programming distributed systems we have selected the Argus language.

Finally we want to express our gratitude and appreciation

> to the lecturers, who have spent considerable time discussing the course contents during the preparation period and preparing the excellent lecture notes, and

> to all members of our staff, foremost Mrs. U. Weber and Dr. H. Halfar, who have helped with organizing this course and editing the lecture notes.

The authors and editors are confident, that both the course participants and the readers of these lecture notes will find an in-depth study of the material contained herein rewarding for their own work.

M. Paul
H.J. Siegert

Preface

The papers comprising this volume were prepared for and presented during the Advanced Course on Distributed Systems – Methods and Tools for Specification. The course was held from April 3 to April 12, 1984 at the Technische Universität München. Due to its success it was repeated from April 16 to April 25, 1985. The organization lay in the hands of the Institut für Informatik, and it was jointly financed by the Ministry for Research and Technology of the Federal Republic of Germany, and the Commission of the European Communities.

Research on distributed systems is in progress within universities as well as in industry and governmental organizations. Networks, particularly high speed local area networks, are often the spur to build distributed systems. In the past a certain agreement on some basic models has been achieved, e.g. on the ISO–OSI–Reference Model, on lower level protocols, and on some synchronization problems. However, concepts and programming paradigms pertinent to higher level protocol layers, to overall concepts for distributed systems, to design choices, and to higher level language support are still important research areas. A discussion and presentation concerning these issues can be found in [Lampson 81b].

Another important research area aimed at improving software quality and reducing software production costs is the support of the specification and design phases within the software life cycle. This problem has received more and more attention during the last decade. Looking at the relative cost or manpower for different phases in the life cycle of software one could see a definite shift of importance from the coding and implementation phase to the specification and design phase. A typical figure is, that about 40% of the total development costs are spent for specification and design. Again we have not yet an agreement on the direction or on the methods and tools to be used for specifying even simple systems.

For a successful specification of distributed systems one has to combine

Contents

Chapter 1
Introduction

Production of software for distributed systems, as any other production of industrial goods, requires different activities to be performed. Scanning the literature on software engineering we can find an enormous variety of models for the production of software using different notions for the activities in the production process. In spite of this variety of models and notions we try to filter out the essential activities:

- Acquisition and Analysis
  Gathering, structuring, and analysing informations on the feasibility of a project.
- Requirements Specification
  Specification and analysis *what* the software system should do.
- Design of System Architecture
  Specification and analysis *how* the logical structure of the system should be and *what* each module should do.
- Design of Components
  Specification *how* each module should be realized.
- Implementation
  Specification of the whole system in an executable programming language.
- Integration and Installation
  Make the system run.

An ordering of those activities in time with additional revision cycles is often called a *software life-cycle model* or a *phase model*.

Rapid prototyping means to produce a quick implementation of essential parts of the system in order to show important properties of the system to the user as early as possible. It is especially useful to agree upon requirements on the man–machine interface of a system and is therefore regarded to be a part of requirements engineering.

During all those activities a lot of specifications are produced. Our goal is to produce better quality software and to rationalize the software production process. This can be achieved if we try to find errors in those specifications as soon as possible. The cost for correcting an error made in some activity grows exponentially in time of error detection as can be seen from Figure 1.1.

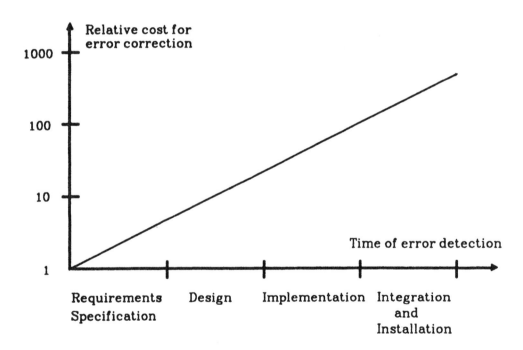

Figure 1.1:   Cost for error detection

The extent of how many errors can be detected by analytical tools depends on the degree of formality of a specification. As Figure 1.2 shows, the production of software would ideally start with a complete formal specification of the requirements. By formal specification we understand a specification formalized in syntax and semantics. In this case we could come to an implementation by using semantics-preserving transformations.

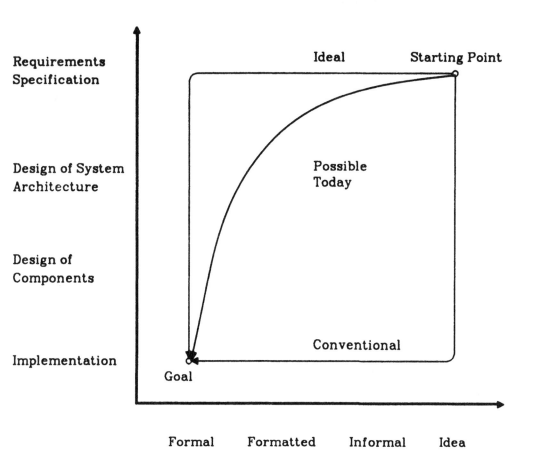

Figure 1.2:   Process of software production

Conventionally the specification of requirements, of the system architecture, and of components exists only as a vague idea in the head of the programmer who is starting with coding immediately.

Tools available today allow to go the third realistic way using also informal and formatted specifications. Informal specifications consist of natural language and arbitrary graphs. In formatted specifications there is a well-defined syntactical frame with some informal semantics in it.

Tools can be classified using the following criteria:

- Activities which are supported by a tool. Mostly a tool is applicable only for one or few activities.
- Underlying theoretical models. Those are typical the entity-relationship model, Petri net theory, the finite state machine, etc.
- Form of representation, either graphical or in a linear notation.
- Guidelines for the way to succeed. Some tools even claim not to restrict the user at all and support any way the user wants to take without giving any recommendation.
- Degree of formalization.
- Degree of computer support. Some tools even do without any computer support.
- Availability and cost of tools.
- Scope of intended application.

If we do not have the necessary methods and experience to design a system we cannot blame our tools for that. The most important methods used in software production are the reduction of complexity by decomposition and abstraction. In decomposing systems we try to identify well-known patterns, often called paradigms. Such paradigms may be algorithms (as for example sorting and searching algorithms in sequential programming) or high level language constructs. Successful application of methods is a mental, intuition-guided activity that can not be automized and needs a lot of exercise and experience.

After discussing methods and tools for specification we will take a look at the aspect of distribution. There are different reasons for using distributed systems:

- *Load sharing* to better exploit available processing capacity.
- *Resource sharing* to use expensive resources or scarcely used special equipment.
- *Data sharing* to access distributed databases.
- The *geographical structure* may be inherently distributed. The bandwidth of the communication lines or the weakness of analogue signals may force their processing in loco.

- The *logical structure* may be simpler e.g. if each parallel process is located in a separate processor.
- The *reliability* of a system can be enhanced by tailoring an appropriate structure.
- The *flexibility* of a system is increased having the possibility to add and delete single processors.

Let us have a closer look at the aspect of reliability. Reliability can be defined as the degree of suitability to perform well under specific operating conditions during a specific time. A probabilistic measure for reliability is the *availability* of a system. The mean value of the availability A of a system is usually defined as A = MTBF / (MTBF + MTTR), with MTBF meaning the meantime between failures and MTTR meaning the meantime to repair.

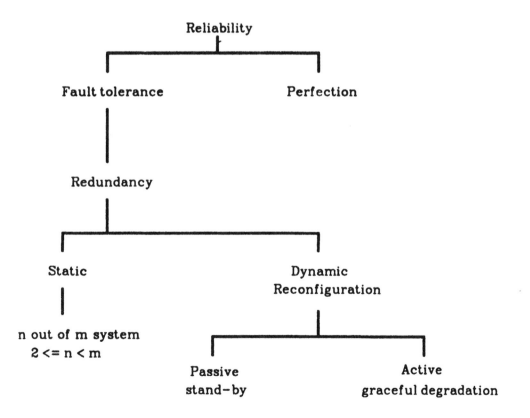

Figure 1.3: Reliability of a system

Figure 1.3 shows that reliability can either be achieved by *perfection*, that means constructing perfect hardware and software, or by *fault tolerance*. Fault tolerance can be achieved by *redundancy* which may either be static (n out of m system) or dynamic, requiring *reconfiguration*. Reconfiguration can be done either using passive *stand-by* processors or using already active processors giving up some of the less important functions of the system (*graceful degradation*).

The course material has been selected such that not only some methods and tools are presented for all activities of the software production process but also fundamentals to understand those methods and tools.

We also tried to present currently known thinking patterns in the field of distributed systems as to alleviate the decomposition process. We are shure that this course does not provide a closed theory or fool-proof recipes how to produce software for distributed systems and that a lot of research and development remains to be done.

Chapter 2
Basic Concepts

2.1. Introduction to Models

This section presents an overview of the models commonly used as the foundation for specifying properties of a distributed systems. This will of necessity only review a few selected models -- an review of all of the models used by different specification techniques is beyond the time and space limitations for this course.

Before examining individual models, it is useful to consider why one should be interested in the subject of models for specifications. The major motivation can be derived from the following observation: a model is used to precisely define desired characteristics of a system -- what is not specified cannot be verified, and what is not verified may be in error. The purpose of a model is to precisely define specific properties or characteristics of a system under consideration to be built or analyzed, and provides the foundation for verifying those properties. Different models are used to specify different properties; alternatively, to express a specific property of a system, one must select from a class of models which represent that property.

The kinds of properties necessary for the development of distributed systems include the following: sets, sequences, and structures of data; transformations of one data set into another, and the implied input/output relationships between the transformations and the data sets; sequences and concurrency of data sets which arrive or are generated at different points of time; transformations of one time sequence into another; sequences of transformations; data flow between transformations; concurrency of transformations; control of interactions between concurrent transformations; time to perform a transformation; and reliability/ availability of performing a transformation in an environment of faults.

If we compare the properties of a flow chart or pseudo-code to this list of desired characteristics, we see that a flow chart or pseudo-code (structured or otherwise) usually expresses sequence, selection, and iteration of processing steps; the characteristics of data flow, concurrency, and performance are not present. A program structure chart for a serial program usually identifies all subprograms CALLED by a subprogram, flow of control, and flow of data; but no concurrency would be represented.

Whether one thinks these representations to be sufficient for representing serial programs, clearly they are insufficient for addressing the problems of concurrent distributed software. To represent these properties, we will examine the following models: mathematical function; finite state machine; functional hierarchy; Petri Net; and graph model of computation.

2.1.1 Mathematical Function

To define a mathematical function, one must specify three things: an input domain (e.g., a set of input variables); an output domain (e.g., a set of output variables); and a rule for transforming the inputs into the outputs. For the transformation to be a function, it must always produce the same outputs for the same input data set.

There are several relevent aspects of mathematical function which affect its applicabilty as a model for specifying distributed systems. First, a mathematical function is not an algorithm -- a function can be specified by providing an algorithm, but it is a design issue to construct an algorithm which performs a transformation within a specified accuracy.

For example, one can specify a transformation by
$$y = \sin(x)$$
but any one of at least three algorithms can be used to accomplish it:

1) $y = x$ (for small values of x)

2) y = polynomial in x (different polynomials for different
desired accuracy); or

3) y = Taylor series (calculated iteratively).

A second relevent aspect of a mathematical function is that it can be "decomposed", i.e. specified by a combination of logic and lower level functions. For example, one can define the absolute value function by
$$ABS(g(x)) = x \quad \text{if } g(x) > 0$$
$$= -x \quad \text{if } g(x) < 0$$
This has the effect of specifying a function in terms of a structure of functions, and thus specifying an algorithm approach. The structure can be described in terms decision tables, pre-conditions and post-conditions, or flow-charts. Since one would like to specify a transformation and not an algorithm in order to separate requirements from design, use of a mathematical function appears to be very desirable.

The HOS specification approach [Hamilton 77] provides techniques for decomposing any arbitrary function in terms of logical operators JOIN, INCLUDE, and OR together with lower level functions, and repeating the decomposition until the lowest level arithmetic operators are encountered. This process decomposes both control flow and data flow simultaneously, and provides tools to check that the two are consistent.

However, a this approach is limited because a mathematical function inherently has no memory -- given an input, it produces an output but saves no data. This means that a collection of mathematical functions cannot be used to specify the required data contents of distributed computer systems. Attempts to use recursion (i.e., a function invoking another copy of itself to process a subsequent input) to overcome the lack of memory results drives the complexity of the function description exponentially.

In view of this limitation, it appears that a mathematical function is a necessary ingredient but not a sufficient model for specification of a distributed system. By itself, it can only be used to specify functions which require no memory; the model must be augmented to address the problems for which distributed systems are most widely used.

2.1.2 Finite State Machine

The concept of a Finite State Machine (FSM) seems to be tailor made for the specification of processing for a data processor. Essentially, an FSM is composed of a set of inputs X, a set of outputs Y, a set of states S, an initial state So, and a pair of functions which are used to specify the outputs and state transitions which occur as a result of an input. The transformation function specifies the outputs which result from an input when the FSM is in any of its possible states; and the state transition function specifies the next state which results from an input for each possible state. In other words,

X is the set [Xi] of inputs
Y is the set [Yi] of outputs
S is the set [Sj] of states
So is initial state
F maps Xi and Sj onto Yi
G maps Xi and Sj onto Sj+1, the next state.

Figure 2.1 provides an illustration of such a model.

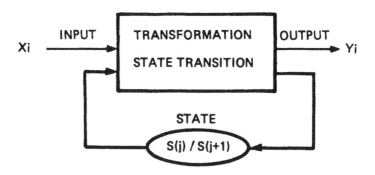

Figure 2.1: Finite State Machine Model

This model appears ideal for the specification of data processing because one can associate the inputs and outputs of the data processor with those of an FSM, and associate the contents of the data processor memory (including the processing registers) with the state, and the code with the transformations. The foundation for completeness analysis is that the transformations for all inputs should be specified for all output states, all outputs should be produced for some combination of input and state, and that the initial state should be specified.

The finite state machine model is one of the fundamental models of computer science. It has been used for the specification and validation of communication protocols. It is is at the heart of almost all program proof techniques. It has been incorporated into IBM's standard method for software development, and is the foundation for some techniques for Systems Analysis [Wymore 78].

However, there are two fundamental limitations for use of this model for specifying distributed processes. First, the finite state machine model inherently serializes away all of the underlying concurrency which one would like to exploit with multiple processors. The model explicitly assumes that all processing on an input is completed before the next input arrives. As a result, one of the most common errors in using the finite state machine model for the specification of concurrent processes is that clash states (i.e., states in which two arrivals occur at the same time) are neglected; this results in proofs of correctness for an inappropriate model. There have been attempts to extend the FSM model for the description of concurrency by using multiple parallel FSMs (e.g., with Cooperative Sequential Processes); the properties of such models are discussed later in Section 2.1.6.

A second fundamental limitation of the finite state machine model is that it presents has no inherent way of handling complexity: the model is "flat", i.e. if 2000 states are required to describe a process, the FSM description will not be understandable without additional structuring. The description of the function which maps an input and a state onto the output and the updated state can become extremely complex to specify even for small problems. Some mechanism is needed to decompose the transformation and state transition functions into smaller, more understandable pieces. Note that the FSM extend the concept of the mathematical function with the concept of state in order to describe how sequences of inputs are mapped onto sequences of outputs, and thus the problems of complexity found in the representation of mathematical functions still remain.

The above discussion suggests that the Finite State Machine model is not sufficient for the specification of distributed processing, but the model should be a necessary ingredient in such a descriptive technique. The FSM model provides the foundation for consistency and completeness properties linking inputs, outputs, state, and processing, and provides the link into program proof techniques. However, to provide a practical foundation for such specifications, the problems of complexity must be successfully addressed. One way to do this is to use the concept of a heirarchy of functions.

2.1.3 Hierarchy of Functions

The most common approach to specifying data processing requirements is to use the model of a hierarchy of functions. One starts by identifying a system function which has input domain consisting of all possible input data set sequences, and has output range of all possible sequences of output data. This system function is then "decomposed" into a collection of interacting functions which may have input/output relationships; these functions can in turn be "decomposed" into a collection of lower level interacting functions. Figure 2.2 illustrates such a representation. Note that both the data and the functions are decomposed: the input X is decomposed into the items (X1,X2,X3), the output Y is decomposed into (Y1,Y2), and the function A is decomposed into three interacting functions (A1,A2,A3), with intermediate data (Z1,Z2) not visible from the outside. Variations of this model are the foundation for many specification techniques, e.g., SADT [Ross 77], PSL/PSA [Teichroew 77], and N Squared Charts [Lano 77].

The benefits of this model arise from its ability to organize a large mass of data, and check the consistency of inputs and outputs between a top level function and its decomposition into a number of lower level interconnected functions (e.g., if X is input to F, it first be input to one of the Fi which decompose it). The process can be repeated as many times as necessary to obtain a hierarchy of functions with many levels, although the maximum number of levels is seldom more than 7 to 10. This

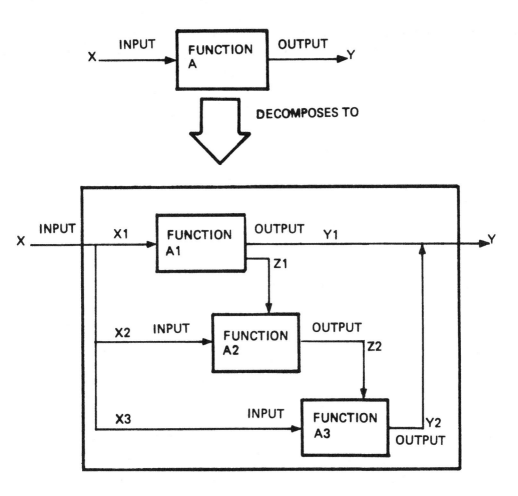

Figure 2.2:   Hierarchy of Functions Model

deals explicitly with the problems of representing concurrency and complexity, but at the cost of ambiguity -- only data flow is represented,
not control flow.

The fundamental limitation of this model is that it does not differen-
tiate between a function F inputting X and Z, X or Z, or X followed by Z.
Thus sequencing and condition information are not expressed by the model,
and cannot be verified using the model.   In a similar fashion, when a
function F is decomposed into functions F1, F2, and F3, the model does not
specify whether they are concurrent or executed in a specific sequence.
This limits the utility of this model for specifying conditions and
sequences of functions.

The above discussion suggests that any model used to describe complex distributed systems should have the hierarchy of functions as a necessary ingredient, but this model is insufficient to represent all of the required properties of such systems. In other words, the flat model of the Finite State Machine provides precision for describing processing of time sequences of inputs, but is difficult to use to describe large systems; while the Hierarchy of Functions can describe concurrency and provides visibility into the contents of large systems, but lacks precision. A precise method of describing concurrency is still needed, and this is addressed by the Petri Net.

2.1.4 Petri Net

A Petri Net [Peterson 81] provides a notation for formally representing sequencing and concurrency, and for identifying and resolving potential ambiguities. A Petri Net consists of a directed graph which alternates two kinds of nodes called places and transitions (See Figure 2.3). The places, represented by circles or boxes, define locations on the graph where tokens can reside. The are linked by arcs to transitions, represented as bars, which are locations on the graph which govern the movement of tokens from preceeding places to subsequent places if the condition of the transition are satisfied. The preconditions of the transition may specify that it may move tokens if a specified combination of tokens exist on the immediately preceeding places; the postcondition of the transition may specify to move tokens to some combination of the subsequent places. For simple Petri Nets, the preconditions are limited to the specification of all or one (i.e.the transition occurs if all places leading to the transition have a token, or if only one has a token); the postcondition is limited to specifying whether a token is generated for all places leading from the transition or only one. When the precondition is met, the transition is said to "fire", and tokens are removed from the preceeding places and generated for the subsequent places. More complex versions of Petri Nets allow arbitrary combinations of input arcs and output arcs to be specified as the preconditions and postconditions.

The Petri Net can be used to specify precisely concepts of sequence, selection, concurrency, and synchronization. Note that Petri Nets can be

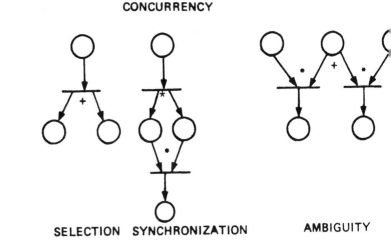

Figure 2.3: Example Petri Nets

specified which are ambiguous, i.e., when a place has more than one transition which follows it; in this case, rules must be established for
selecting the transition which is to take place (e.g., if random, then the
net is nondeterministic). Simulations can be automatically generated from
the Petri Net by defining a Petri Net Processor. This device examines the
status of all transitions, selects one which has met its input conditions,
and moves the tokens according to the postconditions. This step is
repeated until no preconditions are satisfied. This allows an analyst to
observe the movement of tokens and thus the behavior of a specified
process.

Many interesting properties of concurrent systems can be defined and
validated using the Petri Net. For example, a Petri Net can be analyzed
to determine whether correct termination will always occur (e.g, for a
single token entering, only one will exit, and no tokens will be left in
the graph when it exits), or whether the possibilty of deadlock exists
(e.g., the net may enter a state where no transitions are possible, or
where the net is cycling through an endless loop).

In spite of its advantages, there are two fundamental limitations for
using a Petri Net to describe distributed system. First, like the finite
state machine model, it is "flat", i.e., the Net appears in essentially
one level. However, several authors have independently developed the

concept of a Petri SubNet, thus using the concept of a hierarchy of Sub-nets to handle large complex networks. When done properly, this does not affect the semantics of the Petri Net, but does provide the ability to address a problem in pieces.

A more significant limitation to the Petri Net is that it specifies only control flow, not data flow. Even though conditions for the transitions can be specified in terms of data values, the semantics for changing or saving values of data variables is not an inherent part of the Petri Net, so we must look elsewhere for modeling such concepts. Attempts are being made to rectify this problem (e.g., see [Yau 83]), but the details have not yet been fully worked out. It is noted that Petri Nets are one of the tools used for the specification and validation of communication protocols.

2.1.5 Graph Model of Computation

The Graph Model of Computation [Cerf 71] is a directed graph nodes and arcs which is used to specify both control flow and data flow. The graph is quite similar to a Petri Net in which the transitions and places are effectively combined into one type of node. Each node of the graph represents a processing step, which has one or more input arcs and one or more output arcs. An input function is defined to specify whether all or only one input arc must be enabled in order for the transformation to take place; and an exit function specifies whether all or only one of the output arcs are enabled when the transformation is completed. This is effectively the same as the specification of the transitions of a Petri Net. However, unlike the Petri Net, each node has specified inputs and outputs from a defined alphabet of data items; this is used to specify the flow of data between nodes. This data flow can be represented graphically using dashed or dotted lines, while using solid lines for the arcs of the graph. Figure 2.4 provides a sample of such a graph model.

This model provides for the simultaneous specification of data flow and control flow (including the concepts of sequence, selection, iteration, concurrency, and synchronization of control flow), and hence provides the foundation for checking the consistency of the two. Because control flow is represented in a fashion similar to the Petri Net, the properties of correct termination and lack of deadlock can be analyzed,

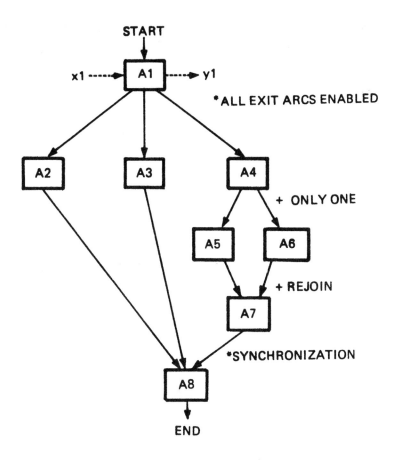

Figure 2.4: Example Graph Model of Computation

and the concept of a sub-net can be used to provide a heirarchy of decomposition. As with the data flow models, one can determine whether each data item input by the top level function is used, and each output data item is produced. However, because both data flow and control flow are specified, one can also analyze the consistency of the two (e.g., that each input to each node has been given a value before it is used).

The primary limitation of this model is that it can be used to describe the decomposition of a mathematical function, but does not inherently address transformation of time sequences of inputs, and does not incorporate the concept of a "state" which is saved from processing one input data set in order to process subsequent input data. To address these issues, the model would have to be extended as in Section 4.1.

2.1.6 Discussion

The point of the above discussion is that different properties are expressed by different models of requirements. Section 4 will show how these models can be extended to precisely define requirements in terms of time functions and finite state mechines.

2.2. Logical Foundation

2.2.1. Introduction

From the point of view of logical formalism, distributed systems are no different from any other kind of concurrent system. What distinguishes a distributed multi-computer system from a shared memory multiprocessor is the communication delay and the communication bandwidth. In the distributed system, information may take many milliseconds to go from one process to another, while in a multiprocessor it takes only microseconds. The bandwidth for message passing in the distributed system may be limited by telephone lines, while in the multiprocessor it is limited only by memory access delays. However, these differences are quantitative and not qualitative. In both cases, information received from another process represents that process's state when the information was sent, which is not necessarily the state when the information is received. The fact that the state of the system is changing while a process is viewing it is the fundamental problem in synchronizing any type of concurrent system. How one goes about dealing with this problem will be different for distributed and nondistributed systems, but the logical analysis of the problem is the same in both cases.

While there is no logical difference between distributed and nondistributed concurrent programs, there is a fundamental difference between concurrent and sequential programs. In sequential programs, one is concerned only with the relation between the starting and terminating state of program parts—the so-called *input/output behavior*.[1] Thus, the input/output behavior of $S_1; S_2$ depends only upon the input/output behavior of S_1 and S_2, not upon how this behavior is implemented.

Input/output behavior is not sufficient for talking about concurrent programs. The input/output behavior of

$$\textbf{cobegin } S_1 \, \mathbb{I} \, S_2 \textbf{ coend}$$

is not determined by the input/output behavior of S_1 and S_2, since the two statements can "interfere" with one another. To handle concurrent programs, we must talk about their complete behavior—what the program does throughout its execution—not just

---

[1] One should really be concerned with the output produced by the program, since all terminating programs are the same if they never produce any output. However, one usually considers the state of the output medium—for example, the state of the phosphors on a terminal screen—to be part of the program state.

what is true before and after the execution.

2.2.2. Sequential Programs

Since sequential programs are a very simple special case of concurrent ones, let us begin with them. The execution of a sequential program may be represented by a sequence of the form:

$$s_0 \xrightarrow{\alpha_1} s_1 \xrightarrow{\alpha_2} s_2 \xrightarrow{\alpha_3} \cdots \tag{2.1}$$

where s_i are *states* and the α_i are *atomic actions*. (The sequence is finite if and only if the execution terminates.) The state contains all information necessary to determine the possible future behavior of the program. (For a deterministic program, the state determines its precise behavior; for a nondeterministic one, it determines the set of all possible behaviors.)

The atomic actions are the actions that take the program from one state to the next. For example, an action α_i might be a particular instance of the program statement

$$\text{x} := \text{x+1}$$

Then the state s_i would be the same as state s_{i-1} except with the value of x increased by one. For sequential programs, it makes no difference how the program is divided into atomic actions, but for concurrent programs, this is crucial.

The actions and states are, in some sense, dual to one another. Different formalisms usually concentrate on just one of them, representing the above execution either as the sequence $s_0, s_1, s_2, \ldots$ of states or as the sequence $\alpha_1, \alpha_2, \alpha_3, \ldots$ of actions.

2.2.3. The Space-Time View

How do we generalize the above description of a sequential program's execution to the execution of a concurrent program, in which actions in the different processes are not naturally viewed as sequentially ordered? Perhaps the most natural approach is the *space-time* one, discussed at length in [Lamport 78a]. The execution is viewed as a partially ordered set of events, where the partial ordering is determined by the following constraints:

1. The events at a single physical location are totally ordered in time.

2. An event α that makes some physical change to the system must precede an event β which senses that change.

For distributed message-passing systems, these two types of orderings are interpreted as follows:

1. All the actions performed by a single process are totally ordered.

2. The sending of a message must precede its receipt.

This set of temporal orderings must be acyclic, so its transitive closure forms an irreflexive partial ordering.

2.2.4. The Interleaving View

The space-time view is very useful for understanding distributed systems. It represents the philosophy underlying most work on net theory. However, while our underlying view of the execution of a concurrent program may be a set of actions, experience has shown that we want to reason about programs—both sequential and concurrent programs—in terms of states. The space-time view is very strongly biased towards actions. To talk about states, we need the *interleaving view*.

In the interleaving view, we assume that, as in the case of a sequential program, the execution of a concurrent program consists of the sequence (2.1) of states s_i and atomic actions α_i. The justification for this view is that we could, in principle, determine the real order in which the actions took place. If two actions which don't influence one another are truly concurrent, then we may pretend that they occurred in either order. If two concurrent actions actions do influence one another, then they are not truly atomic, and must be subdivided into smaller actions.

By assuming that the actions are totally ordered, we are losing the ability to distinguish whether one action "really" preceded another, according to the precedence relations described above, or if the two actions were concurrent and were ordered just for convenience. This loss of information limits the type of question we can ask about the system. However, for those questions we can ask, the interleaving view provides a very convenient formalism for answering them.

2.2.5. Temporal Logic

In the interleaving view, an execution is a sequence of states and actions as in (2.1).
How do we talk about such a sequence? We could use ordinary logic. For example, we
can formally state that a property P holds of every state in the execution by writing

$$\forall i > 0 : P(s_i)$$

However, it turns out that one does not need the ability to write the kind of arbitrary
assertions about execution sequences that can be expressed in this way. Instead, a
special formalism called *temporal logic* has been developed for expressing properties of
execution sequences.

Temporal logic is a well-established branch of classical logic [Rescher 71]. Burstall
[Burstall 74] was the first to suggest using it for reasoning about programs, but the
application of temporal logic to concurrent programs is due to Pnueli [Pnueli 77].

Models and Semantics

We begin with the ordinary *linear time* temporal logic described in [Lamport 80a].
In this version of temporal logic, actions are ignored and only the states are used. Later,
I will describe an extension the takes the actions into consideration. The well-formed
formulas of temporal logic are called *assertions*. Formally, temporal logic assertions are
constructed from a set of atomic symbols, called *atomic predicates*, the usual logical
operators $\wedge$, $\vee$, $\neg$ and $\supset$, and certain temporal operators described below. To define a
semantics for temporal logic, we need to define a semantic model and what it means for
an assertion to be valid for a model.

We define a *state* to be a truth-valued function on the set of atomic predicates. We
write $s \models P$ to denote the value of the state s on the atomic predicate P. To see why
such a function represents what we ordinarily think of as a state, recall that an atomic
predicate is an uninterpreted symbol—for example, the string of characters a > 0. For
a program having a variable a, a state s can be interpreted as one in which a has the
value 1 if $s \models$ a > 0 $\equiv$ *true*, $s \models$ a > 1 $\equiv$ *false*, $s \models$ a > 2 $\equiv$ *false*, etc. Thus, the state
of the program is defined by the truth or falseness of each atomic predicate.

A *predicate* is a logical combination of atomic predicates. There is a natural way
to define a state s to be a truth-valued function on predicates. For example, for any

atomic predicates P and Q, we define

$$s \models (\neg P \wedge Q) \equiv \neg(s \models P) \wedge (s \models Q)$$

The generalization to arbitrary logical combinations should be obvious.

A *model* M is a pair $(\mathbf{S}, \Sigma)$, where $\mathbf{S}$ is a set of states and Σ is a set of sequences of states satisfying property E below. The set of states can be thought of as the set of all conceivable states of a program—for example, all possible combinations of values of variables and "program counter" values. A sequence $s_0, s_1, s_2, \ldots$ in Σ represents an execution that starts in state s_0, performs the first program step to reach state s_1, performs the next program step to reach state s_2, etc. The execution terminates if and only if the sequence is finite. The set Σ represents all possible executions of the program, starting in any possible state.

The one assumption we make about a model, expressed formally by property E below, is that the future behavior depends only upon the current state, and not upon how that state was reached. Before formally stating this property, we introduce some notation. For any element s of Σ, we write

$$s = s_0, s_1, s_2, \ldots$$

where the s_i are elements of $\mathbf{S}$. If s is a finite sequence, so

$$s = s_0, \ldots, s_n$$

for some n, then we define s_m to equal s_n for all $m > n$. Intuitively, s_i represents the state of the program at "time" i. The finite sequence $s_0, \ldots, s_n$ represents an execution in which the program halted at time n in state s_n. At all later times, it is still in state s_n.

If s is a sequence of length greater than one, then we define

$$s^+ = s_1, s_2, \ldots$$

which is the sequence obtained by deleting the first element of s. If s is of length one, then s^+ is defined to equal s. The equality

$$(s^+)_i = s_{i+1}$$

holds for all sequences s and nonnegative integers i. We also define

$$s^{+n} = s_n, s_{n+1}, \ldots$$

More precisely, for any sequence s in Σ, we define s^{+n} inductively by:

$$s^{+0} = s$$
$$s^{+n} = (s^{+(n-1)})^+ \quad \text{for } n > 0$$

We can now state our condition which the set Σ must satisfy as follows:

E. If $s \in \Sigma$ then $s^+ \in \Sigma$.

We are not assuming any preferred starting state for our program. The set Σ should be thought of as the set of all possible executions starting from all conceivable states. Condition E means that after the program reaches state s_1, its subsequent behavior is not affected by how that state was reached.

The semantics of our temporal logic are specified by defining how a temporal logic assertion is to be interpreted as a statement about a model. For any model $(\mathbf{S}, \Sigma)$ and any $s \in \Sigma$, we define what it means for an assertion A to be true for the sequence s. More precisely, we define the boolean $s \models A$, where $s \models A \equiv \textit{true}$ means that A is true for s.

The relation $s \models A$ asserts that A is true of the sequence s. We write

$$\Sigma \models A \quad \equiv \quad \forall s \in \Sigma : s \models A$$

When there is no chance of confusion, we write $\models A$ instead of $\Sigma \models A$. Thus, $\models A$ asserts that A is true for every sequence in Σ. Since Σ represents the set of all possible executions of a program, $\models A$ asserts that A is true for all possible program executions. The goal of reasoning about a program is to show that $\models A$ is true for a desired property A.

Unary Temporal Operators

In the simplest form of temporal logic, the only temporal operators are the unary operator $\square$ and its dual $\diamondsuit$, where

$$\diamondsuit A \equiv \neg \square \neg A$$

for any assertion A. We define $s \models A$ inductively as follows for all assertions A formed with the $\square$ operator.

- If A is an atomic predicate, then for any sequence s:

$$s \models A \equiv s_0 \models A$$

- If A is the logical combination of simpler assertions, then its interpretation is defined in the obvious way in terms of the interpretations of its components. For example,

$$s \models (C \vee D) \equiv (s \models C) \vee (s \models D)$$

- For any assertion A:

$$s \models \square A \equiv \forall n \geq 0 : s^{+n} \models A$$

It follows from these definitions that if A is a predicate, then

$$s \models \square A \equiv \forall n \geq 0 : s_n \models A$$

If we think of s_n to be the state at "time" n, then $\square A$ means that A is "always" true. In general, we regard $s^{+n} \models A$ to mean that A is true at time n, so, for any assertion A, $\square A$ means that A is always true.

It is easy to see that

$$s \models \Diamond A \equiv \exists n \geq 0 : s^{+n} \models A$$

so $\Diamond A$ means that A will eventually be true—where "eventually" includes the possibility that it is true now.

An important derived operator is the operator $\rightsquigarrow$, defined by

$$A \rightsquigarrow B \equiv \square(A \supset \Diamond B)$$

The assertion $A \rightsquigarrow B$ means that if A ever becomes true, then B must be true then or at some later time. Note that $\rightsquigarrow$ is a transitive relation:

$$(A \rightsquigarrow B) \wedge (B \rightsquigarrow C) \supset (A \rightsquigarrow C)$$

The Binary Temporal Operator

The unary operator $\Box$, with its derived operators $\Diamond$ and $\leadsto$, allows one to express a large number of properties. However, there are certain important properties of concurrent programs that cannot be expressed with it. To express these properties, we must generalize $\Box$ to a binary operator.

There are various binary operators which one can define, all of which are expressible in terms of the others. I will define the operator $\unlhd$ as follows. For any sequence s and assertions A and B,

$$s \models A \unlhd B \quad \equiv \quad \forall n \geq 0 : (\forall m \leq n : s^{+m} \models A) \supset s^{+n} \models B$$

Intuitively, $A \unlhd B$ asserts that B holds at least as long as A does—i.e., if A is true through time n, then B must also be true through time n. If A becomes false at any time t, then the truth of $A \unlhd B$ says nothing about the truth of B from time t onward. It is easy to see that

$$\Box A \quad \equiv \quad true \unlhd A$$

so $\unlhd$ generalizes $\Box$.

Note that $A \unlhd B$ means that B remains true until A becomes false, so $(\neg C) \unlhd D$ means that D is true until C is. The temporal operator *until*, which is often used, can therefore be defined by

$$A \; until \; B \quad \equiv \quad (\neg B) \unlhd A$$

We define the operator $\lhd$ by

$$A \lhd B \quad \equiv \quad (A \vee \neg B) \unlhd B$$

One can show that

$$s \models A \lhd B \quad \equiv \quad \forall n \geq 0 : (\forall m < n : s^{+m} \models A) \supset s^{+n} \models B$$

In other words, $A \lhd B$ asserts that B is true as long as A is and, if A becomes false, then B remains true at least one "step" longer than A. The operators $\unlhd$ and $\lhd$ obey the same transitivity relations as $\leq$ and $<$. For example,

$$(A \unlhd B) \wedge (B \lhd C) \supset (A \lhd C)$$

Temporal Properties of Programs

The temporal operators we have just defined can be used to express important properties about programs. A common property one wants to prove about a program is that some predicate is always true. For example, if a program is supposed to implement mutual exclusion, one wants to assert that it is always the case that at most one process is in its critical section.

Let P be the predicate which means that at most one process is in its critical section. Since Σ consists of the executions obtained from starting the program in all conceivable states, including states in which two processes are in their critical sections, $s \models \Box P$ cannot be true for all s in Σ. All that we can expect to be true is that P is always true for any execution that starts in a proper initial state. In other words, what we must show is that

$$\models \mathit{Init} \supset \Box P$$

where Init is a predicate which asserts that the program is in a proper initial state.

The assertion $\models \mathit{Init} \supset \Box P$ is an example of a *safety* property. Safety properties generally assert that something is always true of the program. However, one can characterize a safety property more generally as an assertion A satisfying the following condition:

If $s|_n \models A$ is true for every n then $s \models A$ is true, where

$$s|_n = s_0, ..., s_n$$

Thus, a safety property is one that holds for an infinite sequence if it holds for every finite prefix of it. Another way of saying the same thing is that a safety property is one such that, if it is false, then one can prove it false in a finite length of time.

The most important type of safety property one uses about concurrent programs is *invariance*, where a predicate I is said to be invariant if $\models I \supset \Box I$. Another important class of safety properties have the form

$$\mathit{Init} \supset \Box (A \supset B \unlhd C)$$

For example, first-come-first-served can be expressed in this form, with

$A \equiv$ Process i waiting and process j neither waiting nor being served.

$B \equiv$ Process i waiting.

$C \equiv$ Process j not being served.

Besides safety properties, the other large class of properties one uses about programs are *liveness* properties. Intuitively, whereas a safety property asserts that something is always true, a liveness property asserts that something eventually becomes true. The most common form of liveness property is $P \rightsquigarrow Q$, where P and Q are predicates. For example, the absence of starvation can be expressed in this form where P is the predicate which asserts that a process is waiting for service and Q is the predicate which asserts that the process is receiving service. We know of no formal definition of a liveness property corresponding to the above definition of a safety property.

Action Predicates

We now return to consider execution sequences of the form

$$s_0 \xrightarrow{\alpha_1} s_1 \xrightarrow{\alpha_2} s_2 \xrightarrow{\alpha_3} \cdots \tag{2.1}$$

with the actions α_i. We include two kinds of atomic predicates: *state* predicates and *action* predicates. A *state* is defined to be a boolean function on the set of state predicates, and an *action* is defined to be a boolean function on the set of action predicates. A model is defined to be a a triple $(\mathbf{S}, \mathbf{A}, \Sigma)$, where $\mathbf{S}$ is a set of states, $\mathbf{A}$ is a set of actions, and Σ is a set of sequences of the form (2.1) with each $s_i \in \mathbf{S}$ and $\alpha_i \in \mathbf{A}$. The set Σ must satisfy Condition E above, where s^+ is defined in essentially the same way as before.

Temporal logic assertions are formed from state and action predicates with the logical connectives and the temporal operator $\unlhd$. To define the semantics of these assertions, we can proceed as before. The only new thing that must be added is the definition of $s \models A$ when A is an action predicate. If $s = s_0 \xrightarrow{\alpha_1} \cdots$, then we define

$$s \models A \equiv \alpha_1 \models A$$

In other words, an action predicate is true of a sequence if and only if it is true of the first action of the sequence.

The only action predicates one needs have the form $atom(\pi)$, where π is part of a program. The action $atom(\pi)$ is true of an action α if and only if α is an atomic action in π. For example, suppose I is a predicate and π is a process in a concurrent program. The temporal logic formula

$$\Box(I \supset atom(\pi) \lhd I)$$

then asserts that if I is true, then any atomic action of process π leaves I true. In other words, it asserts that π leaves I invariant.

The ordinary temporal logic, without action predicates, suffices for talking about the program as a whole. However, action predicates are necessary for making assertions about individual parts of a program. Predicates of the form $atom(\pi)$ allow one to talk about the program component π by itself.

The Next-Time Operator

Many temporal formalisms employ a next-time operator, sometimes denoted by $\bigcirc$, whose semantics are defined by

$$s \models \bigcirc A \equiv s^+ \models A$$

The formula $\bigcirc A$ thus asserts that A will be true after the first action.

The $\bigcirc$ operator is not expressible in the temporal logic described above. This is most easily seen by observing that this logic is invariant under "stuttering". This means that if s' is the same as s except with some state and action repeated, for example if

$$s' \; = \; s_0 \xrightarrow{\alpha_1} s_0 \xrightarrow{\alpha_1} s_1 \xrightarrow{\alpha_2} s_2 \xrightarrow{\alpha_3} \cdots$$

then for any assertion A

$$s' \models A \equiv s \models A$$

This invariance under stuttering is the key to the use of temporal logic in the hierarchical description of a system. By not using the $\bigcirc$ operator, one avoids the trap of explicitly describing the granularity of time. Temporal logic formulas that are invariant under stuttering are meaningful assertions about the system when viewed at any level of abstraction. This is explained in [Lamport 83b].

2.2.6. Relating the Two Views

The space-time and the interleaving views are philosophically quite different. We now discuss how these two views are related. First, suppose we are give a space-time model of a distributed system—i.e., a set of events with a temporal partial order relation $\rightarrow$. We can extend the $\rightarrow$ relation to a total ordering of the events. Given this total ordering and an initial state, we can define the sequence of global states produced by this sequence of events, yielding an interleaving model.

In general, there are many ways of extending the partial ordering $\rightarrow$ to a total ordering. Thus, an interleaving obtained from a partial ordering is arbitrary. However, remember that in our semantics for temporal logic, a program is represented not by a single execution but by a set Σ of all possible executions. The set Σ will contain all possible interleavings obtained from any space-time model of an execution. Since the set of all possible interleavings derivable from $\rightarrow$ is logically equivalent to $\rightarrow$, no information is lost when we use the set Σ of interleavings.

When reasoning about a program, we are interested in temporal logic assertions A such that $\models A$ holds—in other words, for assertions that are true for all possible program executions Σ. Since Σ includes all possible interleavings, we cannot deduce any property of the program that depends upon an arbitrary choice of interleaving. Thus, any temporal logic assertion that we can prove about the program expresses a property of the program that makes sense in the space-time view. The only possible drawback of temporal logic is its restrictive expressiveness—there are interesting properties of the program that cannot be expressed in temporal logic.

2.3. Overview

2.3.1 Introduction

Computing has consistently followed two trends :

. movement towards better understanding and use of abstraction

. movement of the perceived root of system problems away from
the   hardware   and   software, towards various forms of
specification

Programming has moved from manipulation of hand switches through
to use of high level languages. Most developments have been based on
the idea of a compiler that processes language statements to produce
executable code. The concept of modularity and parameter passing and
the use of information hiding techniques in languages have reflected
the movement towards abstraction.

Other developments process a language, not to produce executable
code, but to make it practicable as a basis for a code production
activity. These operate on a specification language and make strong
use of abstraction. Most such developments have reflected the other
trend - to specify information which is less and less implementation
oriented.

This Course covers specification from the early stages of a
project through to the point of code generation. The Requirements
module of the course covers the early, pre-design stages. These are
summarised in section 2.3.2. The motivation for improving requirement
specifications is summarised in section 2.3.3.

Requirement Specification terminology is discussed in section

2.3.4 and section 2.3.5 briefly describes the types of support tools currently used. Finally, section 2.3.6 summarises the two methods (CORE and SREM) used in this course to illustrate principles of requirement specification.

2.3.2 Requirement Stages

Objectives

The earliest stage is evaluation of the objectives of the organisation the system is to serve. The aim is to discover whether a system is needed and if so, the objectives served and measures of effectiveness of the service provided.

This stage is frequently omitted. Often there is no clear means of identifying objectives of the organisation or of translating them into measures of effectiveness of the proposed system.

For this Course it is assumed that a decision that a system is needed has already been made and what remains is to decide the scope and form of support it must provide. This may be unduly optimistic, but if it is, there is little computer system oriented guidance available to help relieve the problem.

Environment Requirements

Any system must be viewed as being embedded in an environment. Major distinguishing criteria of quality for systems are :

. How well they match their environment

. How well they can adapt to changes in their environment

. How much they cause their environment to change

Hence it is necessary to achieve an understanding of the environment, the evolutionary forces acting on it and how far it is able and prepared to change.

A prerequisite to producing a valid System Requirement is specification of those aspects of the environment which permit assessment against these criteria.

There are problems which complicate the preparation of such a specification :

  . The environment is ill-understood; different parts interpret its behaviour differently

  . There are conflicting interests, some of which may be hostile to introduction or successful operation of the system

  . Authority for deciding disputes is often not clearly defined. Necessary decisions are often not made

  . The environment is continuously evolving, which modifies the system requirement, even as the system is developed

Some method is needed, to achieve a common understanding, or to illustrate the differences in understanding. It should help identify the authority for making decisions, make the authority aware of the need for each decision and the probable consequences of delay in making it. Finally, it should help identify the most likely areas of evolution and interference and assess how best to deal with the predicted problems.

System Requirement

A System Requirement is a statement of what the proposed system must do. Normally it avoids defining how the system is to do what is required. That is the business of System Design. In practice, freedom from imposed solutions (design or implementation influences) is frequently impossible. For example :

. The Environment Requirement often has embedded design. It describes what is in essence the design of the environment. This can easily lead to unnoticed expressions of System Design.

. It can be difficult to distinguish between the way the environment currently does its job and the requirement the job satisfies. User authorities unaware of technology available for the proposed system are likely to express "requirements" based on current practice, which is by definition about to become obsolete.

. There are sometimes reasons, not necessarily technical, for constraining design. For example existing hardware or software may pre-determine some of the hardware or software to be used.

. Practice might have shown that there is only one way to do some things (but note the above point about familiarity with available technology).

. Sometimes current practice is so established that a customer authority decides it would not be cost-effective to introduce a system that did other than support current practice.

Hence a System Requirement consists of "pure" requirements and required solutions. The two should be distinguishable, in case there is later infeasibility. There is a difference between absolute infeasibility (the "pure" requirement cannot be satisfied by current technology) and treatable infeasibility (a required solution prevents successful implementation).

System Requirements form a bridge between the customer/user view of the proposed system and the designer/implementor view. This means that the audience for a System Requirement Specification is often divided between people who understand abstraction and formal terminology and those with neither an understanding nor the motivation to achieve an understanding of such matters.

For the latter people, formal terminology is unacceptable. Yet without formal terminology the System Requirement Specification cannot seriously be the basis of a contract for development of the proposed system.

A method is required which distinguishes between "pure" requirements and imposed solutions. It must use a terminology capable of demonstrating coverage of the Environment Requirement Specification for an audience untrained in use of formalisms and yet capable of forming the basis of a contract for the development of the proposed system.

2.3.3 Motivation for Improving Requirements

There are two basic reasons for improving requirement specifications. First, end-user satisfaction is often low because what is implemented is inadequate, inaccurate and incomprehensible. Second, the requirements are often poorly expressed and much of the development and maintenance cost and schedule of the system is spent fixing problems from the Requirements Specification.

Improving User Satisfaction

Recurrent causes of the problems are:

- complexity of the required system

- high volume of information to be handled

- inconsistency, incompleteness and ambiguity in the recorded information

- poor communication of even the complete / consistent / unambiguous requirements

System complexity is often supplemented by complexity in the techniques and tools used. They make successful system realisation less probable. There is a need for techniqes and tools which assist handling genuine complexity without adding unnecessary complexity.

Dealing with high volumes of information requires systematic techniques for handling acquisition and expression of the information and reliable tool support for input, analysis and output of the information.

Inconsistency for large systems is unlikely to be removable without tool support. The problems arise from large volumes of information, coupled with poor performance of people in performing repetitive checking tasks.

Completeness of the Requirement Specifications can never be guaranteed. Adequate techniques for analysis and support tools should make it possible to guarantee analytic completeness - ie the absence of any analytically detectable evidence of incompleteness.

Ambiguity is a very difficult problem for Requirements. There are notations which dramatically reduce ambiguity from a technical viewpoint. People who understand the notations can very nearly guarantee that if the expressed requirement is feasible, it can be implemented correctly. The problem is that the notations are understandable only by few people. The statement of the requirement, though unambiguous, is not understood by the people whose need it represents. To them it remains ambiguous!

This latter difficulty is precisely the communication problem mentioned above. The Requirement Specification must not only be correct, it must be seen to be correct!

Cost and Schedule Reduction

It is not the intention here to argue the case for improvement based on measured evidence. Regardless of the measured evidence, the logic of attempting improvement is irrefutable.

The proposed system and its environment exhibit hierarchic properties (eg functional decomposition) and network properties (eg data flow relationships) and the combinatoric effects of an error made in the early stages and left undetected until later stages of development are demonstrably large.

For example, a data flow error in the Environment Specification may result in propogation of the error through several levels of Environment Requirement decomposition, several levels of System Requirement decomposition, several levels of Design decomposition and on to Implementation and the need to re-define and/or re-perform multiple tests for each implementation "module". At each level the error may propogate to more than one component. The growth of the error's effects will be exponential.

To effect repairs there would be new activities to be defined, changes to existing data definitions, data flows and operational states and new instances of each. There would be consequential effects on user and maintenance procedures, documentation and training. Finally, there would be problems of coordinating the changes with other changes such as other errors and system enhancements.

Getting it right early is clearly a sensible goal. What statistics may ultimately provide is an assessment of the cost to get it right compared to the cost of leaving it wrong. The comparison depends on the cost and effectiveness of the techniques and tools used. That is still a subject for experimental measurement.

2.3.4   Requirements Terminology

Representation Techniques

A notation may only express some "key" properties, such as data or control flow. It may, on the other hand, permit rigorous specification of all relevant aspects of the proposed system. In this paper, the two policies will be distinguished by use of the phrase quasi-formal in reference to a partial notation and formal, in reference to a complete notation. A basic axiom of this paper is that the absence of any defined notation is a recipe for disaster. What is to be decided is the role (if any) of quasi-formal and formal notations in successful Requirement Specification.

Use of Formal Notations. In general, the available formal notations are usually based on some kind of mathematical formalism which demands considerable training and discipline from its users and readers. A problem with use of formal notations is that the levels of expertise required are high, while the levels of relevant skills available are low. Hence, few non-research projects actually produce a formal specification.

This problem may disappear slowly, as training is improved and made more widely available. There is some possibility that, in terms of training enough people, the problems will never disappear.

Two factors must be addressed to achieve formal specifications :

. Available staff skills must be used to maximum effect

The task of developing a requirement specification should be layered, so that staff of different skill levels, or with different types of skill can be used on those aspects which are appropriate to their skills.

. Maximum use must be made of tools

Tools should be used to perform repetitive (boring) jobs, assist skilled jobs (eg perform complex analyses) and provide a good environment for skilled tasks (eg provide advanced interfaces to support use of formal notations).

Quasi-Formal Notations. Achieving a rigorous specification which can be used to guide the system development demands the use of formal notations. Their use conflicts (in current practice) with getting the specification understood and agreed by the customer community.

The customer community is not going to leap in its entirety into crash training programs in understanding formal notations, so an alternative is required. This requires translation between the formal notation and the customer - perhaps mapping parts of a formal specification onto simpler (quasi-formal) notations.

Examples of such notations have been in use for years - eg data flow diagrams. The simpler notations are not complete, and sometimes not rigorously defined. They should be treated as informative rather than definitive. Their job is to convey an understanding of some limited aspect of the full specification.

If such notations are used, they must be demonstrably mapped on to a formal notation. When used, it must be made clear that it is the formal representation which is definitive.

Expression v Acquisition

The existence of a notation does not solve the problems of specification of requirements. Problems arise from the inability of analysts to extract information from their customers and from their inability to cope with the volume of information that is extracted.

There is a need to promote the discovery of information and to organise its storage and analysis to achieve maximum effectiveness. This requires a strategy for analysis and guidelines on treatment of departures from the strategy (ie tactical guidelines). It also requires guidelines on interviewing and prompting techniques to extract information and decisions when required.

Much can be done to assist in this area for very little cost and most formal notations could be used to much greater effect if some effort was devoted to the relevant techniques. During this course indications will be given of techniques which have been applied to the activity of Environment Requirement Specification.

2.3.5 Use of Tools

Tools to support requirement specification could be subdivided in numerous ways. For the purposes of this overview the division chosen separates largely passive tools (database systems) and special purpose active tools (requirements exercisers) from conventional analysis tools. It should be noted that there is no reason why all the classes should not be used in combination.

Database Systems

Database systems have been in use for over a decade in support of requirement specification. Their purpose has been threefold. First, they provide a means of storing information and later retrieving it in various different forms for analysis, ad hoc enquiry and report generation. Second, they provide a means of automatic guarantee of consistency of cross reference between parts of the specification. Third, they provide a means of extending the terminology used to reflect special cases or improved understanding of what needs to be recorded.

The two most widely known examples are the RSL/REVS database associated with the SREM method [Bell 76] which is one of the example methods used in this Course and PSL/PSA [Teichroew 77a] which has been used in support of a number of methods, including CORE [Mullery 79], which is another of the examples methods used in this Course.

Exercisers

An exerciser, as used here, is a tool which operates on a Requirement Specification or on data derived from one to produce input to a simulation package which then provides an operating model of the behaviour of a system built to satisfy the given specification.

The technique was pioneered for Requirement Specification in SREM [Alford 79b] and has also been used in HOS [Hamilton 76].

This kind of tool, though little advertised at the moment may form a strong aid to transferring an understanding of problems, consequences of decisions and basic operational behaviour of a system produced from the requirement they have helped define. An important consequence of the need for such simulations might be the need to use example algorithms in the Requirement Specification, to permit full simulation. The danger of the examples being interpreted as design would require careful precautions.

Analysers

In addition to the special types of tool mentioned above, there is a large body of tools which support methods aimed at removal of ambiguity and proof of correctness. These normally exist in isolated clusters and are in a continuous state of evolution as the formal methods they support are enhanced or the support requirements are better understood. Published details of actual tools are not known to the author of this paper, but examples are mentioned for several methods in [Cheheyl 81].

2.3.6 Use of Examples

There are two methods for Requirement Specification which cover precisely the two types of requirement mentioned in this Course – namely Environment Requirements and System Requirements. The two methods are CORE (Environment) and SREM (System). SREM has been in development and practical use for a decade. CORE has been in development and practical use for over five years. Both are designed to be evolutionary, extending as our understanding of the Requirement Specification process increases.

CORE has concentrated on the earlier stages of requirements analysis and emphasises the use of a defined strategy, guidelines on tactical adjustment and use of prompting techniques and a simple but powerful diagrammatic notation to aid communication with the customer/user community. It has been used in conjunction with the PSL/PSA and other database systems and a number of special purpose tools are in process of construction for its support.

CORE has been adopted for use on major and minor projects by British Aerospace and is in process of adoption by several other major organisations.

SREM has concentrated on the development of System Requirements and their use for derivation of System Design. It defines guidelines on strategy and is a major contributor to demonstrating the utility of tool support, combining all three types of tools mentioned in section 2.3.5. It has been extended to bridge the stages of requirement and design so as to make a coherent development approach feasible. It goes some way towards the goal of defining a layered approach that facilitates practical use of staff of varying levels of skill.

SREM was developed by TRW for the US Army and has been used by the US Air Force. It is also in use by commercial organisations, in some cases just as a method and in others as the integrated method and tool set.

Chapter 3

Acquisition - Environment

The early stages of a system development project are characterised by the absence of clear information about the system. It frequently exists only as an amorphous set of ideas in people's minds. Often, though they agree on the need for a system and have convinced themselves that they all want the same system, they are in reality divided. The divisions occur over who or what the system is to serve and what service it is to provide.

An early task is to clarify who/what the system is to serve and the operations it is to serve. This requires discovery of information about the environment of the system, which involves :

- obtaining information from people who have as yet only half-formed ideas about the service required

- detecting and illustrating differences in perception of the required service

- getting decisions about whose view is to prevail or aiding the development of compromises

- illustrating the dangers of some practices they would like to carry over into use of the new system

- achieving completeness and consistency of the specified information, where possible, and a record of each instance where it is not achieved

. recording it in a form understandable by the customer and
user community and usable for developing a formal
specification of the System Requirement, suitable as the
basis of a contract to develop the proposed system.

This task is referred to here as Acquisition. Techniques for
acquisition are important at all stages, they are particularly so at
the start.

3.1. Start-Up

3.1.1 Introduction

Core Overview

CORE assists in meeting the objectives of environment analysis.
The assistance provided assists both technical / analytic skills and
psychological skills. The required skills are not complex. They
relate to systematic handling of large quantities of information and
use of accountability to encourage responsible behaviour.

The techniques discussed could be extended to provide a better
base for producing a high quality system requirement. A major
principle of the method is that of evolution. CORE has been used in
several environments (eg. avionics, communications systems, command
and control systems) and extended to meet the needs of specific
applications, organisations and staff skills.

The author has implemented a database system for support of
methods, including CORE, on anything from microcomputers through to
mainframes. The database is being used as part of a full, flexible
support environment under development in the UK by Imperial Software

Technology. This will provide advanced support tools to assist application of CORE or other methods and integration of their use (eg. use of CORE with more formal specification techniques). CORE-Specific support tools are also under development in the UK, by Systems Designers Plc. and British Aerospace.

Other basic principles underlying CORE are summarised in the next two sections. The initial stages of applying CORE are described in sections 3.1.2 to 3.1.6.

Strategy and Tactics

Strategy defines the general intentions of a plan. Tactics control the perturbing effects on the strategy of local disturbing influences. In methods for computer system specification, the concepts are barely recognised. The best one sees is use of "top down" methods (strategy) with "stepwise refinement" (tactics). There are many times for use of strategic and tactical planning. One such time is the stage of analysis of the environment's requirements.

CORE defines a strategy, based on "top down" and a "start-do-stop" sequence. It defines signals of perturbations and tactics for dealing them. The start-do-stop sequence is summarised as follows:

An approach to starting the analysis is defined. Indications are given to assist application of the approach to different types of system. Between starting and completion, there is a recursive application of a series of intermediate steps. Each intermediate step can be described in terms of its own "start - do - stop". The overall process is guided by clear scope bounds and "when to stop" criteria.

The subject of this first paper is the start-up step, which involves establishing an agreed scope and agreeing responsibilities and schedules for the analysis process. Later papers deal with the intermediate steps and with completion.

Acquisition and Expression

In the overview of the requirements process, the need was expressed for use of a means of expression which is accessible to untrained readers, but usable to generate formal specifications or to express parts of a formal specification. This is the "middle ground" which CORE attempts to bridge.

CORE has made use of a "simple" notation which can be used to generate a more formal representation. That notation will be used later to illustrate some techniques. Other notations could be used. One possible candidate would be CCITT's SDL notation. The criteria for selection of a notation are ease of understanding, coverage of necessary concepts and well defined scope. One benefit of use of a notation such as SDL is the fact that a number of tools are in process of development, or already exist, to support SDL for other purposes. Most of these tools could usefully be applied to analysis of environment requirements, thereby supplementing the normal CORE analyses.

Another problem described in the overview was that of acquisition of information. This is a notorious problem during requirements analysis. Customers and end-users are accused of not knowing what they want and not making up their minds about the requirements. Requirements are changed and extended repeatedly, during development and even during service life.

These problems are inevitable in many systems, but there are instances where analysis techniques could detect a problem and psychological techniques could force its removal, or make its continued existence the result of a recorded decision. This is where CORE has its strength. There are numerous techniques for the detection of omissions and problems. There are techniques for illustrating problems and for getting more information. There are techniques for provoking decisions or recording the need for them, so that they can not accidentally be forgotten. There is a clear definition of who has responsibility and who has authority in the decision making process.

3.1.2 Strategy

The principal aim of the start-up activity is to establish the scope of the information required about the environment. This is achieved by finding who and what, in the environment of the proposed system, is to be directly influenced by the system when it enters service.

A secondary aim of start-up is to establish the levels of detail at which the environment can be described and to agree a plan for its analysis, which addresses the higher (most abstract) levels before the lower (less abstract) levels. The plan includes assignment of responsibilities, authority and schedule for performing the analysis.

Depending on the nature of the environment, the levels identified may be based on "real world" concepts such as companies, departments, teams and job titles or on abstract "functional" concepts such as navigation, weapon control and attitude control. Ultimately, whether organised on real world or functional lines, the structure will target onto people and equipments who are the interface between the system and the environment.

Many embedded systems have little or no direct interaction with people, and in such cases there are likely to be few levels of abstraction in specifying the environment's requirements via organisational structure. Such systems are best dealt with by use of functional hierarchy, terminating in people and equipment operating in various functional "roles".

Systems involving direct provision of services to numerous people, perhaps in several different organisations (eg command and control systems, inventory systems) are best dealt with using real world hierarchies such as departments and teams, terminating in people and equipments operating in various organisational "roles".

It is strongly recommended that, where the analysis of the environment is performed as part of a contractual agreement, the start-up activity should be completed pre-contract and used as the basis for the scope of the contract. This will concentrate the customer's attention on the possible effects of warnings about damaging structures in the environment and will permit clear identification of what is to be covered, who is to be involved and when the work is to take place.

3.1.3 Prompts

At the start-up stage, there is a good possibility that the customer has a lot to say about what is required. Unfortunately, it is likely that what is said consists of a stream of unrelated or partially related "wish list" ideas, like "we want it all menu driven", "we want a fast, reliable turnround of accounting information", "we want an on-line enquiry service". How detailed the stream becomes may depend on how computer-literate the customer is.

It is a mistake to ignore the stream, or to suggest it is irrelevant. It is also a mistake to let the stream continue indefinately, without trying to guide it towards useful strategic goals. This is part of the aim of prompting techniques - to guide the customer towards discussing the requirements in the most (technically) productive order.

In any case, there is a high probability that the customer will eventually run out of ideas. To help in such cases is the other aim of prompting techniques. The analyst aims to steer the topic towards what is necessary at this stage, knowledge of the scope of the environment - ie what is the set of interests (called Viewpoints in CORE) to be supported/influenced by the proposed system.

This means picking out of the customer stream, all hints at Viewpoints. Any person, job title, department, equipment name or function should be noted and used to steer the conversation towards confirmation of their relevance and, if they are relevant, towards the discovery of other possible Viewpoints - eg "who does he work for?", "who works for her?", "who works in that department?", "who is responsible for that equipment?", "where do they get information from?".

Having discovered a Viewpoint, the customer should rule on whether it is to interact with the proposed system, or whether it causes one of the other Viewpoints to interact with the system. If a direct interaction is required, that is a Viewpoint relevant to the environment analysis. If a Viewpoint only causes another to interact with the proposed system, then that is considered in CORE as an Indirect Viewpoint. In the analyses, information to/from Indirect Viewpoints is considered, but their actions are not. Any other Viewpoints are not relevant and should nornally be excluded from further consideration (but see the later discussion on tactics).

If most interactions with the proposed system are predominantly via equipments in the environment, it is best treated as an embedded system. Rather than seeking "real world" entities (eg departments) it is better to seek functions and sub-functions to be supported.

Identification of functions and sub-functions is difficult, since the identification of what constitutes a "function" is vague, relying heavily on the experience of the customer and/or the analyst. In this sense, embedded systems are hard to analyse. A redeeming feature is that interfaces with the environment (in terms of input and output) and dependencies among external equipments are more likely to be written down, or at least known and thus analysable.

3.1.4 Analyses

Analyses at start-up concentrate on discovery of structural relationships among Viewpoints, indicating possible omissions or damaging organisational structures in the environment.

The basic test is for any Viewpoint which is either not part of another Viewpoint or contains no other Viewpoints. Three kinds of containment can be considered :

- . Reporting relationships - ie who reports to whom?

- . Membership relationships - ie which person belongs to which team?, which team belongs to which department?, etc.

- . Ownership relationships - ie which person supervises which equipment?, which department owns which equipment?

A Viewpoint may legitimately be without a superior, or be superior to no other Viewpoint, but this should be confirmed. In practice, other potential Viewpoints will usually be discovered - and some will be confirmed as relevant to the proposed system, while others will be explicitly excluded from further study.

A variant on the basic test is for a Viewpoint which contains only one other Viewpoint. It may be legitimate for a Viewpoint to control only one other but, what may be happening is that the

Viewpoint controls multiple instances of the same job title - eg a Supervisor controls several Assistants and the system must support them all. In fact, it is worth prompting for such cases as the Viewpoints are discovered.

A potentially damaging organisational structure is one which has one job title or one team contained in two or more other Viewpoints. This can arise either because a Viewpoint is actually responsible to several superiors, or because the same name is used for different purposes. The former is damaging because the system may need to include a means of detecting the context in which the user is currently working, to prevent corruption or leakage of sensitive information. The latter is damaging because of possible ambiguity in interpreting for which version of the name, particular facilities are required.

3.1.5 Tactical Issues

It is important to point out the cost and security implications of permitting the same person to fulfill more than one Viewpoint's responsibilities. It is worth prompting to determine whether any of the agreed Viewpoints could be performed by the same person. If they could, and the customer wishes to preserve that flexibility, the fact and the customer's decision should be recorded.

To deal with the problem, at least to avoid ambiguity when analysing the environment, a special form of Viewpoint, called a Role is used. Each "dangerous" Viewpoint is allocated a separate Role for each responsibility. Then each Viewpoint, when referred to is qualified by its Role - eg Design Consultant and Quality Control Consultant. The same kind of problem arises in functional hierarchies and can be addressed in the same way - eg Ship Navigation and Weapon Navigation.

On some occasions, though a Viewpoint interacts with the proposed system, it may be prohibited by the customer, or impractical to analyse the behaviour of the Viewpoint using someone's working knowledge of the behaviour. The most obvious case is a weapon system interaction with an enemy. The actual analyses performed in such cases must be recorded as areas of high risk of change.

In some cases, for non-technical reasons, the customer may require references to and even analysis of Viewpoints which do not interact with the proposed system - eg it may be that the Viewpoint is on a list for later take-over and inclusion in the environment of the system. It should be recorded that each such Viewpoint will not interact directly with the proposed system, or someone may make interaction occur - eg because he/she assumes that the inteaction was accidentally omitted.

Some customers do impose design constraints on the proposed system. These may include use of particular algorithms, use of particular equipments or even inclusion of whole existing systems, operators and all, in the proposed system. This forces an analysis of the behaviour of the imposed elements at some stage and may force "premature" design features in the rest of the proposed system. The probable consequences of such constraints should be pointed out to the customer and, if they are nevertheless retained, the probable consequences and the decision are recorded.

The customer is the final authority on what is required. Decisions may result, not from technical considerations, but from political or financial or some other considerations, which are not the business of the technical analyst, whose job is to record the requirement and warn of possible damaging consequences - not to censor it.

Though there is mention of the need to record damaging decisions and warn of the possible consequences, those records and warnings will not necessarily appear in the environment specification. CORE attempts to promote accountability, emphasising the analyst's responsibility to make the customer aware of the problems and to record the warnings. The customer decides whether to pass on or hide the warnings. Cases of safety related warnings or infringements of the law are a matter for guidelines on ethics rather than method, and are not covered by CORE.

Finally, if a need is discovered to extend the scope of the environment after it has been agreed contractually, there is a clear case for re-negotiation of the terms of the contract. However, such action is not necessarily recommended. It is a matter of local tactics as to whether new terms are negotiated or the extra cost/time are absorbed. Giving a little at one stage may be judged a good way of promoting future good will. That decision is beyond the scope of CORE. In any event, the extension should be pointed out to and authorised by the customer in a manner consistent with contractual terms.

3.1.6 Use of Start-Up Information

The product of the start-up activity can be thought of as a hierarchy of Viewpoints, together with a plan for the analysis of interactions between those Viewpoints, using information provided by agreed "user authorities". This can be used in two ways :

Control of Scope

A benefit during later analyses derives from the guidelines possible on what is relevant (ie within the scope of the environment analyses). People are highly prone to talk about things which are in their environment as well as the environment of the proposed system. There is a need to trap such cases and determine whether they should become relevant (ie the contract should be extended) or be dropped.

For example, any mention of a Viewpoint (person, job title, department, function) not in the set agreed during start-up is, by definition out of scope. Mention of inputs from or outputs to/from such Viewpoints are out of scope. Actions performed by out of scope Viewpoints are likewise out of scope.

If extensions of scope are clearly important to the customer, the decision on how to deal with the situation is the subject of tactical and contractual considerations, as described earlier.

Source of Prompts

During later analysis, start-up information can be used to direct effort and negotiate changes to schedule when problems arise. It can also be used to suggest possible interactions (eg "do you get inputs from there?", "do you send outputs to there?").

When analysis of interactions between Viewpoints is under way, start-up information can be used to prompt in other ways (eg "are you involved in doing that?", "do you use some of that information?").

These prompts are a considerable insurance against omissions.

3.1.6 Example

Overview of the Example

In the space available here, it is impossible to give a full tutorial overview on the use of CORE. Instead, an example taken from a CORE Workshop is used to illustrate some of the key points mentioned in the discussions on Environment Requirements. In particular, the example diagrams are not fully described. In practice they should be supported by notes which supply information not covered by the diagrammatic notation and which explain the intended interpretation of the diagrams for people not experienced in interpreting the notation.

The following brief description of the example environment is intended to give an idea of what the environment is like and to illustrate some of the recurrent problems with descriptions of environment requirements. It is used later to suggest how the various CORE analyses pick up and deal with problems. Hence, the reader should be warned that the description attempts to be plausible while at the same time containing the seeds of future problems.

The size of the description supplied here is very much smaller than one would normally be given. Hence the problems are relatively easy to detect and deal with, even without systematic analysis techniques. Remember that a specification of perhaps ten to a hundred times the amount of information contained in this example would normally contain many times the number of errors to be seen in this example. For such cases, systematic analysis is essential.

The example concerns a company involved in provision of security monitoring services for a number of clients. The monitoring covers a number of possible alarm indications – such as fire, flood and burglary. The current service is provided by hardware on the client's premises, which monitors alarm systems local to those premises, and reports changes of state in any of the systems via a direct line to a Central Station run by the security company.

At the Central Station the hardware includes a set of lights for each customer site, indicating the current alarm state for the customer. A red light indicates a fire alert, an orange light indicates a burglary, a blue light indicates flood and a green light indicates a safe state.

The Central Site Operators monitor the lights and, when they change from green, the Supervisor at the Central Station consults a schedule supplied by the company being monitored, to determine whether the alarm is genuine or just an exercise or the customer site is in process of opening or closing.

In the case of a genuine alarm, the Supervisor telephones a Customer Contact, whose name and phone number are stored in a separate file, to report the condition. It is the Customer representative's responsibility to check the condition and call in the police, fire service or other emergency services as appropriate. The customer must also later report to the Central Station to confirm clearance of the alarm state. The Central Station will not report further alarm states until the clearance has been received.

All transactions between the Central Station and their clients are logged in an archive, which contains date and time stamped tape recorded telephone conversations and records of opening schedules.

What is now required is a system which automates many of the manual tasks, reduces the hardware complexity and provides greater flexibility to monitor various types of alarm devices. This is thought to involve a microcomputer based at the customer's premises linked to a minicomputer based at the Central Station.

Schedules are to be entered by the client's staff via the microcomputer at their own site and transmitted to the host minicomputer. The microcomputer monitors the state of the customer's alarms and reports it to the minicomputer which tells the Security Company's staff of any significant change. Problem reporting is still to be via telephone.

The basic ideas relevant to preliminary establishment of the scope of the requirement are described below.

Start-Up

The first thing to do is to look at the example description for all "doers" (ie. potential Viewpoints). The list is long. It will not be completely covered here, but examples are :

Company; Client; Hardware; Central Station; Security Company; Supervisor; Central Site Operator; Customer Site; Customer Contact; Police; Fire Service; Emergency Services; Customer; Archive; System; Hardware at Client's Premises; Hardware at Central Station; Alarm Devices; Microcomputer; Minicomputer; Customer's Premises; Client's Staff; Security Company's Staff; Host Minicomputer.

Clearly a lot of these names are really just renaming of the same thing. For example : Client and Customer are the same thing as are Client's Premises and Customer's premises. In a description as small as this it is just about possible to distinguish all these from the context in which they are mentioned, but imagine the problems if the renaming occurred up to thirty or even a hundred pages after the first name was mentioned.

Another problem is that some of the names are not really relevant to the proposed system. For example, Police and Fire Service are just examples of Emergency Services. Even the latter is not strictly the business of the proposed system, since there is no direct connection with Emergency Services. It is possibly valid to include Emergency Services, since the eventual User Manuals will need to emphasise that the Central Station does not have responsibility to notify them, whereas the Customer Contact might. Hence, Emergency Services are an example of a CORE Indirect Viewpoint.

For this example, after various prompts and analyses, the

Viewpoint Hierarchy agreed is as shown in figure 3.1 : 1 which uses a special box-and-line notation.

The boxes are divided into an upper and lower section. The upper section contains a code indicating hierarchic position (V2 consists of V21 and V22). An "I" in the top section indicates that the Viewpoint is Indirect and hence will be mentioned only as a source of inputs or a destination of outputs.

The presence of "shadow" boxes indicates replication. For example, there are many Customer Sites (box V2) and many Local Alarms (box V22) in each Customer Site. Here, many could indicate two or more. For a complete specification the supporting text for this diagram should indicate the maximum to be supported in each case.

Note finally, that there is only one operator and one supervisor at the Central Site. In the fully expanded example, this is later detected to be a mistake, but that will not be shown on this course.

The Viewpoint hierarchy is also expanded to show the various roles in which the system will appear (boxes V212, V222, V412, V422 and V432). In such a case, the requirement is first expanded to show what the person or equipment must do (description at the level of boxes V21, V22, V41, V42 and V43) and then the division of those tasks between the person or equipment and the proposed system is considered.

In this course the analyses performed do not go down as far even as the level of V21, etc.. Instead, just the first level is analysed (interactions between V1 to V5, with only V2 and V4 being expanded in terms of the Actions they perform).

In practice, it is recommended at this stage that a timetable should be agreed with the customer authority for analysis of the

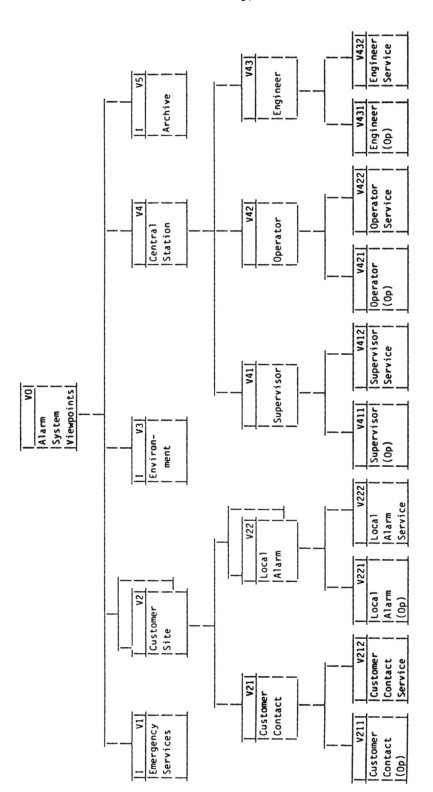

Figure 3.1 : 1 Example Viewpoint Hierarchy

various viewpoints, with the assistance of named user authorities. This permits progress measurement from the early stages of the project

3.2. Information Gathering

3.2.1 Introduction

Overview of a Recursive Step

After Start-Up, CORE analyses consist of the recursive application of a process called Viewpoint Decomposition. This takes a Viewpoint which has already been provisionally specified and re-specifies it in terms of information gathered about its subordinate Viewpoints (in the Hierarchy). When the two specifications are consistent, the "parent" Viewpoint Specification is considered to be confirmed and the subordinate Viewpoints are then themselves re-specified in terms of their subordinate Viewpoints.

Analysis at each level of recursion uses five intermediate substeps :

. Information Gathering

. Data Structuring

. Action Structuring (Isolated)

. Action Structuring (Combined)

. Reliability/Availability Analysis

Special features of the first and last levels of recursion and the main characteristics of the intermediate sub-steps are summarised in the next two sections. The main purpose of section 3.2 is to describe Information Gathering, which is described in more detail in sections 3.2.2 to 3.2.6. The other intermediate steps are described in greater detail in later sections.

The First and Last Recursive Steps

After Start-Up there is as yet no provisionally specified viewpoint to describe in terms of its subordinates. The top level could be taken to be "System + Environment", together with the Indirect Viewpoints which stimulate it or receive responses from it. A provisional specification of this top level would consist of an abstract Action - eg "Use stimuli to produce responses" and a definition of the stimuli and responses from all Indirect Viewpoints in the Viewpoint Hierarchy.

Taking this as the first Viewpoint to be analysed, the analysis would be to discover the intended stimuli and responses. This process can be performed as the first "real" Viewpoints are analysed.

For CORE the first Viewpoints analysed are those immediately below the top level. They are analysed in the stages mentioned in section 3.2.1, with the exception that consistency with the top level is ensured by the manner of their construction. Re-specification of Viewpoints in terms of their subordinates then follows the general recursive step, until the lowest level Viewpoints have been provisionally specified.

At this stage there is no lower level against which it can be verified. The CORE Viewpoint Hierarchy could be taken to the level at which the proposed system is a Viewpoint. Then one lowest level Viewpoint is a provisional System Requirement which can be verified against the eventual actual System Requirement Specification. If this is done the lowest level CORE Viewpoints also permit production of provisional User Manuals.

Overview of Intermediate Sub-Steps

Information Gathering takes information provided at a (technically) varying level of detail and relevance, records it, detects out of scope or apparently premature detail and marks it as such. The information is checked for consistency within and between related Viewpoints. Prompts are made to ensure completeness and consistency.

Data Structuring takes outputs, known from Information Gathering to be relevant for the Viewpoints currently under analysis, and establishes detectable dependencies and structural constraints. Prompts are based on Data structures from the parent Viewpoint, necessary structural relationships at the current level and relationships between Data and the known information about the Viewpoint which produces it.

Action Structuring (Isolated) takes Actions and Data, known from Information Gathering to be relevant to each Viewpoint currently under analysis, and establishes dependencies among the Actions performed by the Viewpoint. Prompts are based on Data dependencies for the current Viewpoints, Actions performed by the parent Viewpoint and detectable peculiarities in the known temporal, control and Data flow dependencies.

Action Structuring (Combined) takes the Actions performed by related Viewpoints and demonstrates that they and their dependencies are mutually consistent and are together consistent with the Actions and dependencies of the parent Viewpoint level. Prompts are the same as those for isolated Action Structuring, but extended in scope to cross Viewpoint boundaries.

Reliability/Availability Analysis takes the combined Viewpoints currently under analysis and adds any required new Actions and Data flows necessary to handle possible problems of reliability or availability of the service provided. Prompts are based on known causes of problems with Actions, or the mechanisms for their performance, Data and Data flows or the media for their storage or transfer.

3.2.2 Strategy

This intermediate sub-step is the start-up activity for a CORE recursive step. It takes technically unstructured information and sorts it into things to be pursued at this step, things to be postponed and things which are out of scope.

The main aim of Information Gathering is to record all "transactions" known to be performed by Viewpoints at the current level of analysis. In CORE, a "transaction" consists of an Action performed by the Viewpoint, together with the Data used and derived by the Action and the source/destination of the Data.

As a back-up to the mainstream of analysis, information is gathered about key Events and operational Conditions. A "transaction" concept associated with Events and Conditions requires that any Event should either trigger or terminate a Condition or an Action and any Condition should test Data or another Condition and select or limit the performance of an Action.

Information Gathering first considers each Viewpoint in isolation. Analysts interview a user authority for the Viewpoint to find which Actions performed require support which could be provided by the proposed system and/or which inputs and outputs could be supported by the proposed system, etc. When each user authority interview process is complete, communications between the Viewpoints are analysed for consistency / completeness.

3.2.3 Prompts

Prompts for this intermediate sub-step arise in three ways :

. Asking about "transactions" in general terms (What do you do? What data do you use? What Data do you derive? etc.)

. Analysis of what the user autority has said, for omissions (What Data does that Action use? Where does that Data come from? etc.)

. Use of information already available from other sources (the Viewpoint Hierarchy, previous levels of Viewpoint analysis, information from other user authorities at the same level)

This paper does not cover all the prompts, but the ideas are summarised below:

Consistency within Transactions

Each source must be associated with at least one item of Data input. Each input must be associated with at least one source and must be used by at least one Action. Each Action must have at least one input and at least one output. Each output must be derived by at least one Action and go to at least one destination. Each destination must be associated with at least one output.

Consistency between Transactions

Different Viewpoints must agree on their mutual transactions. For example, if Viewpoint "A" has Viewpoint "B" as one of its destinations, then Viewpoint "B" must have Viewpoint "A" as one of its sources. Moreover, if "A" claims to derive Data "X" for "B" then "B" must claim to use "X" from "A".

Viewpoint Hierarchy

Each Viewpoint which is part of the Viewpoint under decomposition is a potential source and/or destination for each other such Viewpoint. Hence, if no Data appears to be exchanged by any pair, the user authority should be prompted at least to confirm that no exchange occurs.

Premature information from previous levels

Premature information mentioned at any level is noted and reconsidered at the next level. At any level below the top, there may be premature details from previous levels. At this stage, it should be checked to see whether has been included or should be included or is still premature.

Previous level information

For the Viewpoint under decomposition (apart from at the top level) there exists a provisional specification. That is a source of prompts when considering its "child" Viewpoints at the current level. For instance, which parts of an Action performed by the "parent" are performed by which of its "child" Viewpoints.

3.2.4 Analyses

Analyses at each intermediate sub-step are predominantly aimed at detecting evidence of incompletion, which is then used to generate the prompts for the sub-step. Examples of such analyses for Information Gathering are suggested in the previous section.

Other analyses are recommended at each sub-step, for evidence of aspects of the information supplied which may adversely affect the cost or reliability of the proposed system or limit the ability of the environment to make best use of such a system. Examples of such analyses for Information Gathering are described below :

Source or destination not in the Viewpoint Hierarchy

This is, by agreement with the customer authority, out of scope, as are any inputs or outputs only mentioned in connection with it. Leaving it in may result unwanted system features.

Data derived by several Actions or received from several sources

This may be a valid specification of current practice, but should be questioned, because it may lead to the need for a significantly more expensive system, to cope with problems about where a particular instance came from and how it should be handled. It might lead to deadlock situations in either the environment or the proposed system.

Actions/Data not hierarchically below those of the previous level

These are evidence of omission at the previous level or of out of scope information at the current level. In the latter case, continued inclusion could lead to unwanted system features.

Data which is only feedback to the Viewpoint which produced it

This is evidence of information which is probably premature for the current level of analysis. Continued inclusion is necessary, so that it is not forgotten, but it should be marked as premature and considered at this level only if subsequent analyses show it to be necessary.

Actions which only communicate with other Actions of the same Viewpoint

This is a similar case to that just discussed. It should be marked as premature and considered at this level only if subsequent analyses show it to be necessary.

The same Action performed by more than one Viewpoint

This usually indicates use of the same name for two different actions. Sometimes it can be because of overlapping responsibilies. This could lead to an expensive or complex system, which has to recognise the relevant user context.

3.2.5 Tactical Issues

The "user authority" may be a person, documents or a combination of the two. Ideally there should be someone to consult about interpretation of documents and to supply omitted details. Unaided analysis of documents often permits only recording of the scope of the disaster rather than development of a good quality requirement. However, even that knowledge may help make decisions about whether to continue and how much contingency to allow if development proceeds.

Before prompting based on information already available the analyst should encourage the user authority to volunteer information. This may make the acquisition process appear to take longer than necessary. However, a new view on the environment unprejudiced by previous analyses is likely to mention information previously overlooked or to indicate differences in how different user authorities believe the environment behaves. For similar reasons, transactions for each user authority should be collected independently and then compared for consistency.

Hierarchic relationships between the "parent" level and the current level are sought, to help achieve complete coverage. Hierarchic relationships within the current level are not pursued at this stage, though if they are expressed it is encouraged that they should be recorded. This is an example of a regular tactic : never ignore information which is volunteered, even if it seems premature or irrelevant - it may be neither, and even if it is premature, it may be the last time the informant thinks to mention it.

An occasional problem arises in the form of Actions which the user authority claims either use or derive no Data. Typical examples are Actions which generate time signals or which perform an archiving service. Such claims are very rarely valid. A timer process is almost invariably provided with some kind of start-up signal and an archive is only of use if, at some time, things can be retrieved from it.

When faced with such claims the analyst should question their validity by asking the user authority to consider how the Action starts or stops. A frequent problem with requirement specifications is concentration on normal operations and neglect of aspects such as start-up, close-down and break-down. This is the cause of a number of peculiarities detectable by analyses recommended in CORE.

Another recurring problem with analysis of environment requirements is that of disagreement among user authorities about the requirements. The task of the analyst is to detect the problem and get it resolved. It is not the analyst's job make the decision, unless responsibility is delegated by the customer authority. Even then, the authority resides with the customer authority. If the customer avoids making a decision, it may be necessary for the analyst to provoke a decision.

The normal technique for doing that is formally to propose a decision (eg in a progress report) indicating the timescale in which the decision must be confirmed or rejected to avoid cost and schedule problems. For some contracts it may be possible to proceed as if the decision has been accepted if the customer authority does not respond. In any case, the problem and its consequences have been documented early and if the customer authority is accountable within his/her organisation there will be a strong incentive to resolve it as soon as possible.

Sometimes making an outright recommendation is politically very dangerous. In such cases it is often more constructive to list the advantages and disadvantages of each option, with particular emphasis on the points which make one option more sensible than the others.

The precise means of provoking a decision may require adjustment for the personalities involved. With some people, putting things in writing too early may be counter-productive. Some may be so disorganised that the longer the wait before the problem is documented, the more the analyst's position is at risk. Hence, when the techniques are used is a matter of subjective judgement. Nevertheless, the problem and the decision must be documented by the analyst and approved by the customer authority.

One valid documented decision by the customer authority is to postpone the actual resolution of the problem, with acceptance of the consequential risks to schedules and cost. This may prevent further work or require renegotiation of the schedule and costs or spawn a subcontract to perform a feasibility study on each of the options.

3.2.6 Use of Information Gathering Information

The product of Information Gathering is a consistent but unstructured body of information about the probable environment requirements at the current level of recursion. It is used later in

the same level to assist in deducing structural, temporal, control
and data flow relationships. Part of it is used in lower levels to
prompt in later Information Gathering activities. At the lowest level
of recursion part of it is used to indicate whether completion of the
agreed task corresponds to completion of Environment Specification.

Data Structuring

Outputs recorded during Information Gathering are used during
Data Structuring to prompt for hierarchic and derivation dependencies
among the Data relevant to the current recursive step.

Action Structuring

Actions, conditions, events, inputs and input/output
relationships recorded during Information Gathering, and Data
dependencies recorded during Data Structuring are used during Action
Structuring (Isolated) to prompt for hierarchic and temporal/control/
data flow relationships.

Next Level Information Gathering

Premature information carried over from the current recursive
level is used at the next level to prompt during Information
Gathering, as described earlier.

Completion

At the lowest level of recursion the absence or continued
presence of premature information helps demonstrate completion or
identify design constraints or to indicate deficiency in the
originally agreed scope.

3.2.6 Example

Information Gathering for the top level Viewpoints in the example started in section 3.1 is presented here. It is done, as if from two sources.

The Central Station Viewpoint information has been gathered from the example description in the previous paper. It is shown in a tabular form in figure 3.2 : 1. The Customer Site Viewpoint has been gathered from another source, possibly by another team of analysts. It is shown in figure 3.2 : 2.

First consider figure 3.2 : 1. The main lesson to be learned here is that the user authority is quite likely to say a lot about the current manually operated system (red, orange, blue and green lights, for example). In many cases, as with the lights here, the information as stated will have nothing to do with the proposed system. What might have been relevant would have been the alarm status each light indicates. In fact, at this level, the only distinction would be between the safe state and one of the alert states.

Note also the inputs and outputs which are "internal" to the Central Station. These should for the moment be treated as premature. They may be pulled in as relevant by later analyses at this level.

A third point is the mention of the Archive as a destination of outputs, but not as a source of inputs. This should be questioned. In this case, we will assume for the moment that the user authority is adamant that the Central Station makes no use of Archived information which is relevant to the proposed system. In the full workshop a later reliability analysis shows this to be a mistake. The mistake will not be detected on this Course.

In practice, this first set of information is largely wrong or

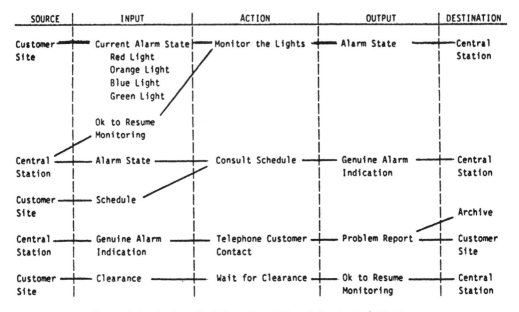

Figure 3.2 : 1   Example Information Gathered for Central Station

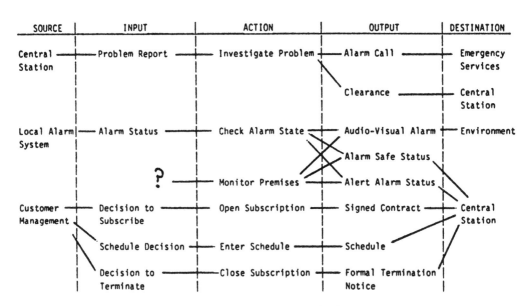

Figure 3.2 : 2   Example Information Gathered for Customer Site

out of scope or deficient. It will be assumed for the current exercise to be replaced by a better quality version.

The second table, in figure 3.2 : 2 refers to an out of scope Viewpoint (Customer Management). This should be questioned - first with the user authority and later, if the user authority is adamant about its relevance, with the customer authority. In this case, we will assume that the customer authority agrees it should have been included and the necessary contractual negotiations permit its inclusion as an Indirect Viewpoint.

The second point to note is the absence of inputs to the Action, Monitor Premises. The similarity of outputs compared with Check Alarm States gives a strong hint that this represents renaming. That should be checked. We will assume that it is indeed renaming.

A third point to note is the absence of inputs or outputs for the Archive. This should be questioned. There should in fact be outputs, at least to store copies of outputs to the Central Station.

Comparison with the Central Station table indicates a difference of opinion about the Data exchanged. The Central Station expects to receive the Current Alarm State from the Customer Site. The Customer Site expects to send an Alarm Safe Status and an Alert Alarm Status. Differences should be queried with the user authorities and resolved.

There are exchanges mentioned by the Customer Site, which are not confirmed by the Central Station (eg. Signed Contract, Formal Termination Notice). These should be checked with both user authorities to determine whether they are really relevant.

Finally, there are omissions from both. Some are detected later. They are found because of analyst experience causing the right prompts, because of CORE analyses and in some cases by luck.

3.3. Data Structuring

3.3.1 Introduction

This intermediate sub-step is the second in the general CORE recursive step. It is the first attempt at identifying structure in the (usually) unstructured information recorded during Information Gathering for the current level of analysis.

The purpose of Data Structuring is to identify any detectable hierarchic and derivation order constraints imposed by the environment on outputs from each Viewpoint at the current level of analysis. In so doing it may demonstrate that some Data, previously thought to be premature detail, is really needed to justify the stated constraints.

The process of Data Structuring is performed in isolation for each Viewpoint currently under analysis. Inputs and Actions are normally not used at this stage unless they can demonstrate a derivation dependency between outputs.

By the nature of construction of the Viewpoint Hierarchy, apart from Data exchanges with Indirect Viewpoints, the structured set of Viewpoint outputs forms also the structured set of Viewpoint inputs.

3.3.2 Strategy

Data Structuring for each Viewpoint is performed in three stages. First a provisional hierarchic structure is formed, based on analysis of "packets" of Data. A "packet" is basically Data which is at some time passed alone from one Viewpoint to another. Then the derivation order of the "packets" is determined and finally any constraints on the internal layout of the "packets" are recorded.

Technically unnecessary structural constraints are checked for and queried. Incompatibility with Data Structuring at the parent Viewpoint level is checked for and queried.

3.3.3 Prompts

As with the other intermediate sub-steps, there is insufficient room in this paper to explain fully all the prompts used at this stage, but the main ideas are summarised below :

Packets

The initial prompts are based on discovering which of the stated outputs for the Viewpoint under analysis are ever passed in isolation to another Viewpoint. These outputs are referred to as Packets of information. They are not the only Packets used in Data Structuring. Others are sometimes necessary as a result of hierarchic relationships among the Packets already known.

Dependent Packets

The next type of prompt is used to discover the need to refer to additional Packets. Some existing Packets are sometimes passed also as part of another Packet. In order to define completely the hierarchy among such Packets, it is sometimes necessary to identify additional information which does not ever go on its own to another Viewpoint. This is itself a Packet because it is part of the parent level Packet but is logically separate from the child level Packet.

Help in deducing separation of outputs into Packets can come from the Data structuring information produced at the previous level of Viewpoints (other than at the top level, of course).

Hidden Packets

A third type of prompt seeks to discover a third type of Packet. This is Data which is never passed alone from the Viewpoint under analysis to another Viewpoint, but which is passed as part of more than one existing Packet. The result of these first three types of prompt is a Packet Hierarchy which is then used to investigate the logical order of derivation of Data.

Hints at hidden Packets might come from a look at the Data which has been marked as premature. In making the decision (during Information Gathering) it should be marked as below some existing Data which is not premature. If it is below more than one Data name, it is probably a hidden Packet.

Derivation Dependencies

Having identified the basic Packets and hierarchic relationships among them, the user authority is prompted for any dependencies among the Packets. For example the contents of one are necessary to the derivation of another, or the contents of one determines whether another is produced at all, or whether it continues to be produced. This type of prompt is interlaced with prompts to discover the conditions of derivation.

Help with identifying derivation dependencies may come from the derivation dependencies identified among Data relevant at the parent Viewpoint level. That is likely to identify major dependencies among Data at the current level. Also, consideration of relationships between Events and Data may help discover Data dependencies.

Conditions of Derivation

The user authority is prompted to state whether each Packet, when it is derived, is derived unconditionally, whether more than one instance is derived before any dependent Packets are derived and, if so, whether the multiple instances are produced successively (iteration) or in parallel (replication) or a combination of the two.

Help with identifying conditions of derivation can come from relationships between Conditions and Data, identified during Information Gathering and from the known information about replication of Viewpoints, available from the Viewpoint Hierarchy agreed during Start-Up. Also, the apparent existence of Data loops (ie Data which appears to be both before and after other Data in the stated dependencies) is a strong indication of iteration.

Constraints on Format

Consideration of format is strictly a design issue, yet in the environment there frequently are format constraints. For example, use of public communications systems may well impose some protocol requirements. These are sought when all the other Data structuring is complete. Each Packet is considered individually to discover any such constraints.

The constraints are recorded and indicated as externally imposed design constraints.

3.3.4 Analyses

Examples of analyses aimed at detecting incompletion of Data specification are suggested in the previous section. Examples of analyses for peculiar or dubious Data relationships in what has been specified are described below:

Multiple contexts for packets

Any Packet which appears in more than one context is an indication of possible configuration management problems in the environment or in the proposed system. When a Packet is sent to several places or appears in other Packets, the need for such practices should be checked with the user authority. If the practice looks particularly damaging, the customer authority should be informed of the possible consequences (eg later changes may be performed on one occurrence but not on another).

Multiple times of derivation

This case is usually similar to that of multiple contexts or an instance of use of the same name for two different purposes or evidence of an undetected iteration. It should be checked with the user authority or customer authority as indicated for multiple contexts.

Data, Event or Condition not mentioned in Information Gathering

This can only occur if some previuosly undiscovered component has been mentioned or an existing name has been mis-spelled. The condition should be checked and the specification adjusted to complete/correct the component specification.

Recursive Data Structures

Occasionally recursive Data structures do occur, but just as often they appear to occur because of careless use of names. It is very similar in appearance to the case of multiple contexts. When it is detected it should be checked with the user authority for validity.

3.3.5 Tactical Issues

One of the biggest problems of application of CORE without automated support is that of keeping up to date with all the new information and changes to existing information. This is particularly the case with the information collected during Information Gathering. Since it is mentioned during an informal interview process, it is highly likely later to require many changes/updates as structural and temporal relationships are investigated.

Data Structuring will normally cause large numbers of changes and Action Structuring will cause many more. Keeping an up to date and tidy copy of Information Gathering information is impractical for manual use of CORE. It is recommended that the information be kept in a tabular form and updated in handwriting until it can be shown to have been completely covered by the various Data and Action diagrams produced later. Given automated support, these limitations do not apply and the whole information base can and should be kept up to date.

The problems of volume of information and of changes are aggravated by another of the recommended CORE tactics - that of saving known information (in this case, about structure and derivation constraints) until the user authority has made an independent attempt to identify the constraints. The benefit of getting an independent opinion on how the environment behaves far outweighs the disadvantage of additional changes it generates.

Another serious problem can arise if the various dubious Data structures mentioned earlier are challenged rather than checked. There is a very large difference between the attitude generated by statements like "Can you tell me why that is not structured like this structured like that, it should be like this ...!". If a constructive attitude from the user authority is desired then confrontation should be a last resort.

Nevertheless, the analyst does have a duty to point out dubious practices and their possible consequences. The most constructive way to do so is to record the existence of the practice, the forseen consequences, the alternatives considered and later, if appropriate the reasons for rejection by the customer authority - and note that, in the case of detected damaging practices, it is the customer authority rather than the user authority who must authorise their continued use.

3.3.6 Use of Data Structuring Information

The products of Data Structuring are three types of Data structure. The first is a simple definition of hierarchic relationships among Packets of Data. It uses a simple box-and-line notation.

The second is a more complicated definition of derivation dependencies among Data Packets. This is usually expressed in a notation consisting of a modified form of the diagrammatic notation used in Jackson's JSP, which has extensions to cater for parallellism and indeterminate order.

The third type of Data structure is one which illustrates any imposed format constraints. It may use the extended JSP notation (eg to illustrate where format is and is not constrained), but it is likely also to include special-purpose layout descriptions supplied by the user or customer authority.

Of the three types of Data structure, only the derivation dependencies are normally used in performing later CORE analyses.

They are used to assist Action Structuring and, at the next level of Viewpoint analysis, to prompt during Data Structuring, as described above.

During Action Structuring (Isolated), the known derivation dependencies are used to prompt for discovery of dependencies among the Actions available from Information Gathering.

3.3.7 Example

From the example developed in previous papers on Environment Requirement, we will just take the outputs of Customer Site and perform Data Structuring on them. In practice, the outputs for Central Station should also be structured.

Looking at figure 3.2 : 2 in the section on Information Gathering, there are eight outputs defined. We will assume for simplicity that the user authority asserts that each of these is at some time passed alone to another Viewpoint and that none is contained in any of the others. The result is that there are eight "packets" whose order of derivation must be established. They are :

- Alarm Call
- Clearance
- Audio-Visual Alarm
- Alarm Safe Status
- Alert Alarm Status
- Signed Contract
- Schedule
- Formal Termination Notice

It is usually worth prompting on the basis of "start-do-stop" - ie. what comes first and what comes last? In this case, the user authority will confirm that nothing else can happn until a Signed

Contract has been sent by the Customer Site and nothing else happens after issue of a Formal Termination Notice. Hence, these would appear to be the first and last outputs.

In fact, this will later be shown to be a mistake, but that is the subject of later analyses. For the moment, we will assume that the analyst has no grounds for suspicion, and accepts the assertion.

For any one customer there is only one issue of a Signed Contract and a Formal Termination Notice. If a customer leaves and rejoins there could be reliabilty problems (eg. if the system keeps a record of all customer names - past and present), but for the moment we will assume that a rejoining customer will be treated just like any new customer.

There are, however many Customer Sites, as is indicated in the Viewpoint Hierarchy established in an earlier paper. Hence, there will be many Signed Contracts and many Formal Termination Notices - one pair for each Customer Site.

The next question is, which packet comes next? The answer is that no monitoring of the Customer Site can occur until a Schedule has been entered, defining the Customer Site operations such as opening and closing times. Hence that comes next, but can there be more than one schedule? The answer is, yes. For example a shop may change its opening hours during festivals such as Christmas. Then it would need to define a new schedule before and after Christmas.

What comes next?

After a Schedule is entered the user authority tells the analyst that the Customer Site's Local Alarm Systems are re-initialised and after any break in the normal (ie safe) alarm state a new Safe Alarm Status is to be transmitted to the Central Station. This then comes after each new Schedule is issued.

What comes next?

Hopefully, nothing else happens until the next Schedule is entered. In practice, something might. There might be one or more alarms. Hence, between each issue of a Schedule there might be one or more alarms, each to be followed by a new issue of the Safe Alarm Status or, if the alarm coincides with the arrival of a new schedule from Customer Management, by issue of the new Schedule followed by the Safe Alarm Status.

What is output during an alarm?

The first outputs will be an Alert Alarm Status to the Central Station and an Audio-Visual Alarm (ie. bells and flashing lights!) to the Environment. Note that this is the Environment around the Customer Site, not the CORE Environment of just the proposed system. These outputs may be considered as occuring in any order.

After the issue of the Alert Alarm Status, and in no way affected by the Audio-Visual Alarm, the Central Station should notify the Customer Contact for the Customer Site of the problem. This may cause the issue of an Alarm Call to the Emergency Services and must be followed by issue of a Clearance to the Central Station.

This accounts for all the identified packets and the established ordering relationships are summarised in figure 3.3 : 1.

As before, the shadow box indicates replication, the numbers in the top segment of the boxes indicate a temporal hierarchy (eg 22 consists of 221 and 222). Boxes below another box normally occur in the order of their appearance, from left (earlier) to right (later). The symbols in the top left of some boxes are used to modify the

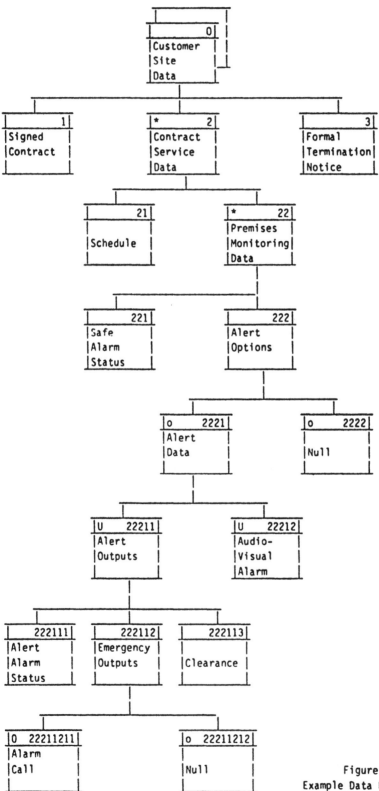

Figure 3.3 : 1
Example Data Derivation Order

normal order.

For example, the asterisk ("*") indicates iteration - eg there are numerous occurrences of "Contract Service Data" between issue of Signed Contract and Formal Termination Notice. The letter "o" indicates a selection among alternatives - eg "Emergency Outputs" consist of either an Alarm Call or "Null". Note that "Null" is a standard term in this notation to indicate that nothing is output. The letter "U" indicates that the outputs are issued in an undetermined order - eg "Alert Data" consists of both "Alert Outputs" and Audio-Visual Alarm in an undetermined order.

A final point to note about figure 3.3 : 1 is the appearance of new Data names (ie names which did not appear in the Information Gathering information. These names are necessary to indicate derivation relationships among the Packets. They are not themselves Packets. In practice there are frequently new Data names discovered at this stage, some of which are Packets. There are also frequently numerous changes to the originally agreed names, as the Data Structuring gives a better mutual understanding between the user authority and analyst about what is going on. None of these are shown here, and equivalent discoveries and changes occur later, during Action Structuring.

3.4. Action Structuring (Isolated)

3.4.1 Introduction

This intermediate sub-step is the third in the general CORE recursive step. It attempts to discover and record relationships between Actions in the environment, which may affect the required behaviour of the proposed system. They may even be relationships the proposed system is required to enforce when it is installed.

The relationships sought are temporal order (A occurs before B), control (a condition set by A determines whether B occurs or continues to occur) and data flow (an output from A is used by B).

The process of Action Structuring is performed in two stages. First, the Viewpoints at the current level of analysis are considered in isolation. Then the Actions of the current level Viewpoints are combined to form a set of relationships consistent with the isolated Viewpoint of the parent level. This paper describes the first of the two stages, consideration of the Viewpoints in isolation.

Given adequate tool support, it is probably more sensible to consider all the Viewpoints in combination at the first stage and then extract the isolated Viewpoints from the combiation. Without adequate tool support this could lead to the need to handle too much information at one time, so the manually applied approach is described here. There are some people who start with the combined Viewpoints, even for manual application.

3.4.2 Strategy

Action Structuring seeks three types of ordering relationship between Actions and attempts to demonstrate their compatibility. Once they have been demonstrated to be compatible the temporal order relationship is redundant. Until compatibility has been demonstrated, the expression of all these types of relationship provides numerous opportunities for detecting omissions and errors because of apparent incompatibilities between the stated relationships.

This is an illustration of another recurring theme in CORE: the use of apparent redundancy in the developing specification to detect problems with what has been said to date. In fact, the information is only redundant once all the forms of expression have been shown to be compatible. Until then the information is necessary to the acquisition of a complete and consistent specification of the environment behaviour to be supported.

The process of Action Structuring (Isolated) is driven by prompts based on the Data derivation relationships established at the previous intermediate sub-step. As with Data Structuring, hierarchic relationships are sought, often as a result of discovering iterative or control relationships among Actions which have a peculiar mixture of temporal and Data flow or control flow relationships expressed.

3.4.3 Prompts

The main ideas behind prompting at this intermediate sub-step are summarised below. The ideas discussed are not the only possible sources of prompts, but they indicate the types of analysis which can lead to automated detection ofthe need for more information.

Data derivation order

The main driving force behind Action Structuring is the information available from Data Structuring, about the derivation order of Data. Examples are :

If Data items are derived in a specific order, then the Actions which derive them must occur in similar order.

If Data items are mutually exclusive and are output by different Actions, then the Actions are likely (not certain) to be mutually exclusive.

If a Data item is produced iteratively then the Action which outputs it is likely (not certain) to be iterated.

Control relationships between Events, Conditions and Actions

Relationships between Events and Conditions and the Actions they "control", established during Information Gathering can be used to indicate probable time-ordering relationships among Actions.

Action Loops

An Action which appears to occur both before and after other Actions is a probable indication of an iterative relationship in which they all participate.

Absence of hierarchic relationships

An Action (below the highest level of Viewpoint analysis) is always part of another Action - at least at the parent Viewpoint level. If an Action at this stage is not part of another Action, there is an indication of the need for another level of Action hierarchy (ie there is a missing parent Action) or the "part of" relationship has been overlooked. If a parent Action is missing, it need not be performed wholly by the Viewpoint currently under analysis.

Temporal order with no corresponding Control or Data dependency

If one Action is said to occur after another and there is no corresponding Data or control flow dependency, then there almost certainly should be one, or the temporal dependency does not really exist.

Data flow which appears to contradict temporal order

If an Action derives Data which is used by another Action which is said to occur before the first, then there is probably an iterative relationship in which the Actions participate. Similarly, if an Action derives Data which it is also said to use, it is probably iterated or part of an iteration at a higher level.

Previous level Action Structuring

The ordering relationships among Actions established at the parent Viewpoint level, together with the mapping of Actions at the current level on to the parent level Actions can be used to suggest probable ordering constraints at the current level.

3.4.4 Analyses

Examples of analyses aimed at detecting incompletion at this intermediate sub-step are suggested in the previous section. Examples of analyses for peculiar or dubious Action relationships in what has been specified are described below :

Multiple contexts

This is similar to Data in multiple contexts, discussed during Data Structuring. It can lead to configuration management problems. It can be evidence of overlapping responsibilities. It can be evidence of re-use of the same name for different purposes. There is a valid interpretation, which is that two functionally identical Actions are performed at different times, operating on different Data. A special notation is used to record such cases. In any case, the analyst should query such instances to confirm the condition.

Recursion

Actions which directly or indirectly invoke themselves do occur, but usually require handling with special care. Sometimes such cases only appear to occur - usually because of an accepted practice in the environment of using the name of an Action as the name of one of its decomposed parts. For example, a "Quality Control" Action by a department may be implemented by several "Quality Control" Actions by the department's staff. Such naming conventions in a Requirement Specification are dangerous and should be avoided where possible.

Actions, Data, Events or Conditions not mentioned during Information Gathering or Data Structuring

A common problem at each successive intermediate sub-step after Information gathering is the discovery of new information which logically should have been discovered during Information Gathering. Failing to record and integrate them into those parts of the specification which logically reference them (eg new Data may have to be integrated into Information Gathering and into Data Structuring products) is a guarantee of an incomplete or inconsistent Requirement Specification.

3.4.5 Tactical Issues

As with earlier intermediate sub-steps, information available from previous levels is saved until the user authority for the current Viewpoint has indicated how the Viewpoint is understood to behave. This, as before, maximises the chance of a new look at the environment discovering new information.

A policy which might appear to contradict this is the use of Data Structuring information for the Viewpoint under analysis right from the start of this intermediate sub-step to prompt for probable ordering relationships. The reason for this policy is that the same user authority who indicated Data derivation order is the one who will now be discussing Action ordering and much the same ground is now covered again, just looking for confirming Data and control flow relationships. People are strongly opposed to repeatedly trying to derive the same information from scratch and so in this case, the maximum use is made of the information the user authority has already supplied.

If, for a particular application of CORE, there is not a separate authority for each Viewpoint at each level, the policy of saving previously collected information for later prompting might have to be modified in more places. However, that would be because of a failure to apply the full CORE method as recommended. There would be attendant dangers of missing vital information about how the environment behaves.

One of the reasons for getting the Viewpoint Hierarchy agreed and the customer and user authorities agreed during Start-Up is to ensure early warning of danger signals which might prevent successful analysis.

A common problem at all stages of Requirement Specification is the re-use of the same name for different purposes. It is usually assumed that, perhaps because of some notational convention, readers of the specification will be able to distinguish from the context which interpretation of the name is intended. In the later, design and implementation stages this may sometimes be true. Though it is worth noting the need in some coding languages for notations which explicitly indicate context (eg "with xyz do name := ..." or "xyz.name := ...".

The assumption that the intended use will be recognised implicitly from the context is particularly dangerous at the Environment Requirements stage. Often, people's ability to communicate is severely inhibited by unknown, different uses of the same words. There must either be unique names or some explicit means must be used to indicate the version and context of the name currently in use at any place in the specification. Hence, such cases should be queried and, if necessary, a versioning policy agreed with the customer authority.

A problem which exists at all stages becomes particularly difficult at the time of Action Structuring. That is the means of communication between the user authority and the analyst. The analyst needs to show the user authority that some problems exist or that some information is missing or to explain his/her (the analyst's) understanding of how the user authority said the environment behaves. Also, different user authorities and possibly the customer authority must be shown the description of a related Viewpoint, to facilitate discussion of disagreements.

This problem requires the use of a notation which is capable of expressing as much or as little as is necessary for the problem and audience concerned. The CORE diagrammatic notation has been quite successful for that purpose, since it is usually explained by the analyst and can be queried by the user authorities as discussion proceeds.

Some people go further and use the notation as the principal notation for the final Requirement Specification. Whether this is a sensible policy is largely dependent on the skill of the design team, whether they were involved in its production and how good are the words that go with the diagrams. It is well to remember that the CORE notation does not completely cover the information necessary to express a requirement unambiguously.

For very high quality Requirement Specifications it will certainly be necessary to use a more formal notation for the System Requirement and it is probably advisable to do so even for the Environment Requirement. For the moment, it must remain a matter of individual project tactics how formal to make the Requirement Specification at each stage.

3.4.6 Use of Action Structuring (Isolated) Information

Information recorded during Action Structuring (Isolated) is used later at the current Viewpoint level to assist the construction of the Action Structuring (Combined) representation. It is also used at the next Viewpoint level (if there is one) to confirm that the combined Viewpoints at that level are consistent with the Isolated representation at this level.

If the proposed system is one of the lowest level Viewpoints, the Isolated representation at the lowest level of the Viewpoint Hierarchy can also be used to aid production of user manuals for the system and the system Viewpoint can be used as a provisional System Requirement, against which the full System Requirement can be checked for consistency/coverage.

3.4.7 Example

Taking the Data derivation order established for the Customer Site in the previous paper on the Environment Requirement, it is possible to demonstrate the result of Action Structuring analyses as a series of diagrams which represent Data, control and temporal flow simultaneously.

What is shown here is the result of what might typically be quite a time consuming process. The diagrams shown would be the result of several meetings, each lasting from one hour to half a day and each followed by perhaps half a day of analysis and drawing effort.

It is worth noting that, at the end of such a period, there is still an omission in the representation, as will be shown in the later process of Action Structuring (Combined). It is in fact quite probable that in a more complex example incorrect temporal relationships will be carried forward to later analyses.

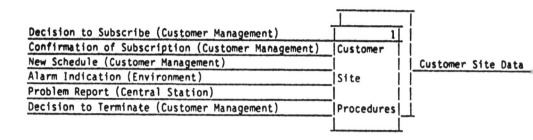

Figure 3.4 : 1   Top Level Isolated Viewpoint for Customer Site

As a first step, consider the top level Data item in figure 3.3 : 1. This was called Customer Site Data and was replicated (once for each Customer Site). This suggests a top level Action for the Customer Site, as shown in figure 3.4 : 1.

This diagram has included all the known inputs to Customer Site and shows the one composite output, Customer Site Data. The Action is confirmed as being replicated.

Next, consider the next level of the Data diagram. This consisted of a time ordered sequence : Signed Contract followed by iterated instances of Contract Service Data, followed by Formal Termination Notice.

In trying to draw this, the Action Diagram notation demands identification of the Condition for termination of the iteration.

This identifies some Data which has not previously been mentioned. The Condition is "Termination Date is reached" and the Data is "Termination Date".

Examination shows Termination Date to be recorded as part of the Formal Termination Notice, which was previously said to be the last output. This means that some Contract Service Data could be output after issue of the Formal Termination Notice and before the expiry of Termination Date. In practice it very rarely is, hence the original mistake. Now, the Data diagram needs revision (not shown here) and the Action diagram which decomposes figure 3.4 : 1 is shown in figure 3.4 : 2.

In Action diagrams, Actions are represented by named boxes. Time ordering is shown by left to right order of appearance. Indeterminate order is shown by vertical alignment. The asterisk ("*") in the top segment of box 2 again indicates iteration.

Inputs are shown by named lines with an arrow pointing into the box. Outputs are shown by named lines with no arrow pointing into the box. A Condition for termination of an iteration is shown by a named line with an arrow pointing at the top of the box. A name in brackets is the source or destination of the Data. For composite names like Contract Service Data, different parts may go to different destinations, as will be shown in lower level diagrams.

Figure 3.4 : 2 shows no explicit Data dependency to justify the time ordering of box 1 followed by boxes 2 and 3 in indeterminate order. This should be queried with the user authority. In this case the justification is an interaction with the Customer Site, which can only be confirmed when the two Viewpoints are combined at the next intermediate sub-step.

Looking now at the next level of the Data diagram, it consists of

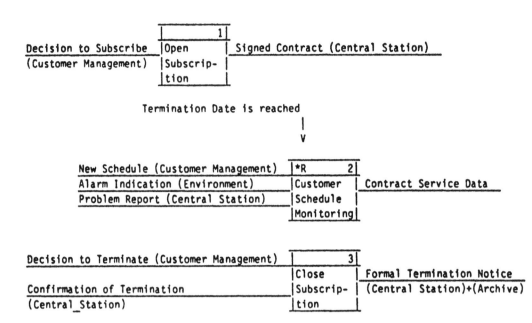

Figure 3.4 : 2   Customer Site Procedures

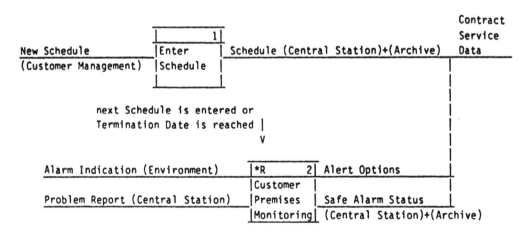

Figure 3.4 : 3   Customer Schedule Monitoring

the time ordered sequence of Schedule followed by iterated instances of Premises Monitoring Data. Is there a corresponding Action structure? The answer is yes, as is shown by figure 3.4 : 3.

In the top segment of box 2 in figure 3.4 : 3, the letter "R" means that the iteration is re-entrant. That is, the next iteration can start before the current iteration has completed. The reason this particular iteration is re-entrant is that in normal circumstances another iteration, internal to this one, can be terminated by the entry of the next Schedule.

The remaining diagrams for this Viewpoint is figure 3.4 : 4. There, vertically aligned boxes with the letter "o" in the top segment are mutually exclusive options. The Condition for the selection of each is shown by the Condition line pointing at the top of the box. Minor variations in this notation are adopted by some CORE users, but there should be no difficulty in interpreting these other notations.

The diagrams for the Central Station Viewpoint are presented below, as figures 3.4 : 5 to 3.4 : 8. Only one additional comment is relevant.

In figure 3.4 : 8, box 2 has a temporal peculiarity in its inputs and outputs. The problem Clearance appears to arrive before the Problem Report is sent. Where such cases are noticed, they are usually the result of an unnoticed iteration, or of a need to further decompose the Action.

For the moment, it is assumed that the peculiarity is not noticed, because leaving it helps demonstrate in section 3.5 how the analyses at the next intermediate sub-step permit detection of such cases.

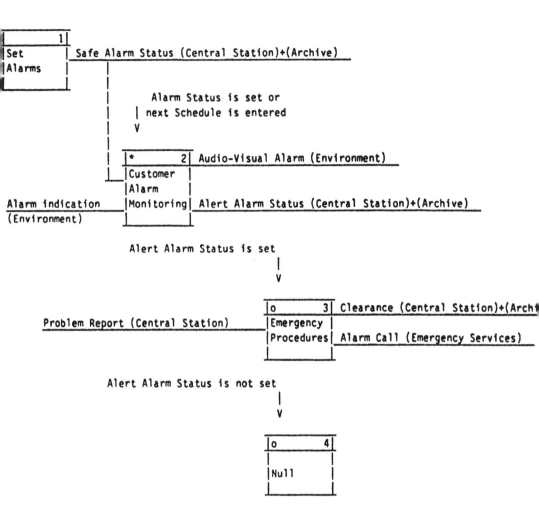

Figure 3.4 : 4   Customer Premises Monitoring

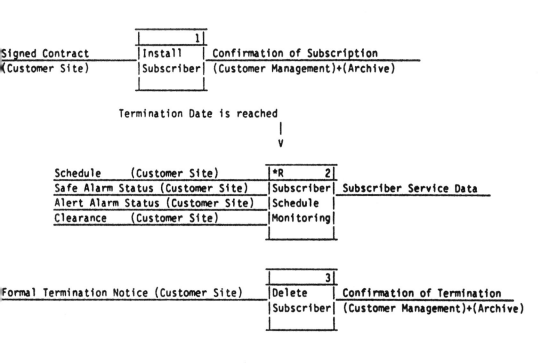

```
                                              ┌─────────────┐
Signed Contract          (Customer Site)      │          1│ │
Schedule                 (Customer Site)      │Central      │ │
Safe Alarm Status        (Customer Site)      │             │ │──── Central Station Data
Alert Alarm Status       (Customer Site)      │Station      │ │
Clearance                (Customer Site)      │             │ │
Formal Termination Notice (Customer Site)     │Procedures│ │
                                              └─────────────┘
```

Figure 3.4 : 5 Top Level Isolated Viewpoint for Central Station

```
                              ┌─────────┐
                              │        1│
Signed Contract               │Install  │  Confirmation of Subscription
(Customer Site)               │Subscriber│  (Customer Management)+(Archive)
                              └─────────┘
```

Termination Date is reached
|
V

```
Schedule        (Customer Site)       ┌─────────┐
                                      │*R      2│
Safe Alarm Status (Customer Site)     │Subscriber│  Subscriber Service Data
Alert Alarm Status (Customer Site)    │Schedule │
Clearance       (Customer Site)       │Monitoring│
                                      └─────────┘
```

```
                                      ┌─────────┐
                                      │        3│
Formal Termination Notice (Customer Site)  │Delete   │  Confirmation of Termination
                                      │Subscriber│  (Customer Management)+(Archive)
                                      └─────────┘
```

Figure 3.4 : 6 Central Station Procedures

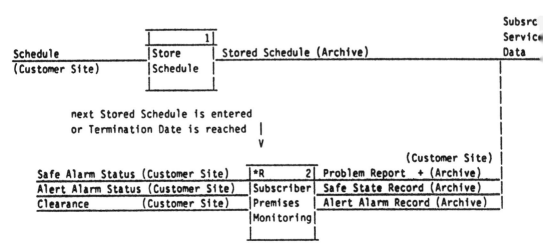

Figure 3.4 : 7 Subscriber Schedule Monitoring

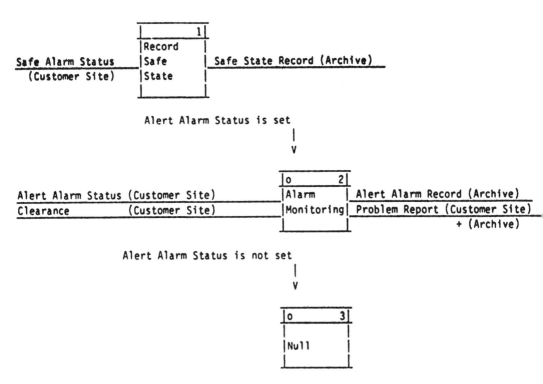

Figure 3.4 : 8 Subscriber Premises Monitoring

3.5. Action Structuring (Combined)

3.5.1 Introduction

This intermediate sub-step is the fourth in the general CORE recursive step. It attempts to combine the isolated Viewpoint information recorded at the previous intermediate sub-step into an integrated representation which is consistent with the isolated Viewpoint recorded for the parent Viewpoint at the previous recursive level.

The relationships sought are the same as those sought in establishing the isolated Viewpoints, but the analyses now cross the Viewpoint boundaries. At the end of this intermediate sub-step there should be no analytically detectable inconsistencies between or incompleteness of the Viewpoints being combined.

3.5.2 Strategy

The approach used is to take a known Data flow relationship between Viewpoints at the current level of recursion as the basis for a combined chain of Actions. To the first two Actions and the chosen Data flow, other known Data flows are added. The linked Actions (which may be performed by one of the first two Viewpoints or by other Viewpoints at the current level of recursion) are then added, preserving known temporal and control constraints known from Action Structuring (Isolated). The process is then repeated, bringing in more known Data flows and preserving constraints, until the Viewpoint combination is complete.

Then the combined Viewpoint representation is compared with the representation of the parent level Isolated Viewpoint to demonstrate consistency of decomposition, Data flow and temporal and control constraints between the levels.

When consistency has been demonstrated, the current level of recursion is near completion. What remains is to analyse for potential problems of reliability or availability of the service provided by the Viewpoints under consideration. That is one of the subjects of the final paper on Environment Requirements.

3.5.3 Prompts

The basic ideas behind prompting at this intermediate sub-step are based on derivation order and Data flow between Actions. The difference between this stage and Action Structuring (Isolated) is that the derivation order information from Data Structuring drives Action Structuring (Isolated), whereas at the current stage, the driving force is the derivation order between Actions produced during Action Structuring (Isolated).

The main ideas behind prompts based on existing Action derivation order and Data flow relationships are summarised below :

Confirmation of Correspondence Between Data Flow and Time-Order

Two Actions, performed by different Viewpoints, which have a connecting Data flow normally occur in the order indicated by the Data flow (ie the producing Action occurs first). There are complications to this simple concept (see (d) below), so it has to be confirmed.

Common Condition for Performance of Actions

If the performance or continued performance (where iteration is involved) of two Actions performed by different Viewpoints is controlled by the same Condition and both appear after the same integrated Actions (ie Actions which have already been integrated into the chain of Actions under analysis) their performance may in practice both be controlled by one test.

Mutually Exclusive Conditions for Performance of Actions

If the occurrence of two Actions performed by different Viewpoints is controlled by opposite values of the same Condition and both appear after the same integrated Actions, they may in practice be mutually exclusive Actions selected by one test.

Actions which Exchange Data

If two Actions, performed by different Viewpoints, each derive Data for the other, there may be a previously unmentioned iteration involved (with both feed-forward and feed-back of information) or the real operation of the environment may be more complicated than it appears from either Viewpoint in isolation. It may be necessary to decompose one or more of the Actions to demonstrate the validity of the interaction. It may also be necessary to decompose the Data to demonstrate the validity of the interactions.

Unordered Actions which have a Data Relationship

If two Actions, performed by different Viewpoints, have a Data relationship, but are agreed by the user authorities to occur in parallel or at least in an undetermined order, there may either be a mistake in their joint perception of how the environment operates or the Data flow may be one of several special types - eg it may be long-lived Data, such as exists in a shared library, where a user does not care whether the Data changes, so long as there is Data available when required.

In the case of special types of Data flow, it is important to establish the precise nature of the flow - eg must it always be the latest Data which is used?; are past values queued and if so, is a FIFO (or LIFO, etc.) selection policy used?; what happens to "lost" Data flows?

Temporal Order with no corresponding Data or Control Relationship

If, in combining Viewpoints, two Actions are integrated into a chain of Actions in a particular time order, but no Data or control flow relationship has been stated between them, then there is probably a Data or control flow missing (or the time ordering relationship does not really exist). This was discussed under the heading of Action Structuring (Isolated) and is an illustration of the fact that all the analyses performed at that stage can be re-applied at this stage with a widened scope (ie crossing Viewpoint boundaries).

3.5.4 Analyses

Examples of analyses aimed at detecting incompletion at this intermediate sub-step are suggested in the previous section. Analyses for peculiar or dubious Action relationships can be divided into two types : those which are also applied during Action Structuring (Isolated) and those which seek to detect the need for special Actions, Data flows, etc. either in the environment or in the proposed system, to ensure continued and reliable provision of the service the system is to support.

The former types of analyses are not re-described here and the latter are considered so important and are normally so poorly covered in Requirement Specifications, that they are the subject of a separate intermediate sub-step in CORE, the last for each CORE recursive step. Those analyses are one of the subjects of the last paper on Environment Specification.

Hence, for the present paper, no special analyses are described. What must be emphasised, however, is that the analyses for hierarchic coverage between the parent Viewpoint and the current level must demonstrate complete coverage, both upward and downward, before proceeding to the reliability/availability analyses. If they do not, there is a danger of some reliability measures being missed and some being mentioned twice (or two types of measure to deal with the same problem).

3.5.5 Tactical Issues

In practice there may be recorded inconsistencies and omissions and there may be omissions arising from systematic failure to detect any pointers to the missing information. There may also be information, premature for the current level of Viewpoints, which indicates that there is more to be said at a lower level.

Only the analyst's experience can defend against systematic omission of pointers to vital information. The CORE prompts greatly reduce the chances of such omissions, because they gradually expose all links between known elements of interest in the environment. However, it is still possible that the user authority may never receive a prompt for some information and may assume that the need for it is self-evident.

Hence, it is important that the analyst should never apply the CORE techniques as a mindless ritual. Progress will be faster and systematic omission less probable if the analyst makes use of experience and common sense as the techniques are applied.

The analyses performed at this stage are quite likely to show differences of interpretation of how the environment behaves. This should first be queried with the differing user authorities but in the event of unresolved disagreements, it is not the analyst's job to referee.

The customer authority must deal with unresolved disagreements between user authorities, though the analyst may reasonably make recommendations or at least indicate the consequences of deciding in favour of each option.

Another possible source of differences, is the chance that there are differences of interpretation between Viewpoint levels. For example, it is quite common for department heads to think things happen one way (according to "the book") while the department staff actually do things another way (eg because "the book" way is wrong or too inefficient in practice).

Again, the relevant user authorities and possibly the customer authority will be needed to rule on which version is to be supported by the proposed system. This too will cause re-work, perhaps back at previous recursive levels.

Where the user authority agrees that what he/she said was in error, there need be no recourse to the customer authority, unless the error is embedded in the customer organisation's procedures manuals. If "the book" way is indeed wrong, the customer authority must be asked for a ruling on how the case is to be treated. It is not normally within the analyst's area of authority to rewrite the customer organisation's procedures manuals without explicit agreement.

In general, resolution of the differences will usually lead to re-work of previous intermediate sub-steps. The problems associated with re-work are particularly acute if use is made of diagrammatic notations, such as the CORE notation, without automated support. For even quite small systems, diagrammatic re-work can consume a large proportion of the project schedule. It is usually unacceptable to avoid using diagrams completely, but major dependence on them, without automated support, may well escalate the cost of producing the Environment Requirement.

One type of problem arises because of a facility permitted in use of the CORE diagrammatic notation. In order to permit the presentation of the Environment Requirement Viewpoints at a rate judged to be appropriate to various audiences, CORE permits the definition of "cosmetic" Actions. These are Actions which are defined solely to reduce the complexity of any one level of Action diagram complexity.

A cosmetic Action is simply a collection of Actions on a CORE diagram, replaced by one single named Action with inputs and outputs consistent with those of the Actions contained. The reasons and rules for use of such Actions are not covered here, but it is important to remember that if such Actions are introduced, it will complicate the process of establishing consistency between levels.

Whether and when to use cosmetic Actions is a matter for subjective judgement, weighing up the benefits in controlling the complexity of presentation against the complexity of analysis.

3.5.6 Use of Action Structuring (Combined) Information

Action Structuring (Combined) information is used in the final intermediate sub-step of the general CORE recursive step, where it is assessed for potential problems of reliability and availability of the service provided by the combined Viewpoints.

As with the products of all the other intermediate sub-steps (with the possible exception of the Information Gathering products when CORE is applied manually) the information recorded is part of the eventual Environment Requirement, which is used to aid development of the System Requirement and, possibly, of user manuals for the proposed system.

3.5.7 Example

The combination of the Customer Site and Central Station Viewpoints is presented here in the order it would be presented to readers after the exercise is complete. Hence, figures 3.5 : 1 to 3.5 : 4 would normally be presented and described in that order.

The process of deriving the diagrams most profitably starts at the lowest level of the Isolated Viewpoint diagrams (ie at figures 3.4 : 4 and 3.4 : 8 in the previous paper on Environment Requirements) and works up to the top. The order of derivation of the diagrams presented here was thus the reverse of the order of presentation — figure 3.5 : 4 was derived first, then figure 3.5 : 3 and so on. There were iterations in the process, so that some of the diagrams were re-drawn several times, as later diagrams showed the need.

Figure 3.5 : 1 shows a few interesting points. First, there is an additional notational convention used in Combined diagrams. An arrow pointing at the lower face of an Action box is labelled with the name of the Viewpoint which performs it. If no such arrow appears then the Action is performed by a combination of Viewpoints at the current level of interest and thus requires further decomposition. The corollary is that if the arrow does appear then the Action requires no further decomposition at the current level.

Hence, in figure 3.5 : 1 the Action "Open Subscription" is performed by Customer Site, the Action "Install Subscriber" is performed by Central Station and the Action "Schedule Monitoring" is performed by a combination of both, and is decomposed in figure 3.5 : 2.

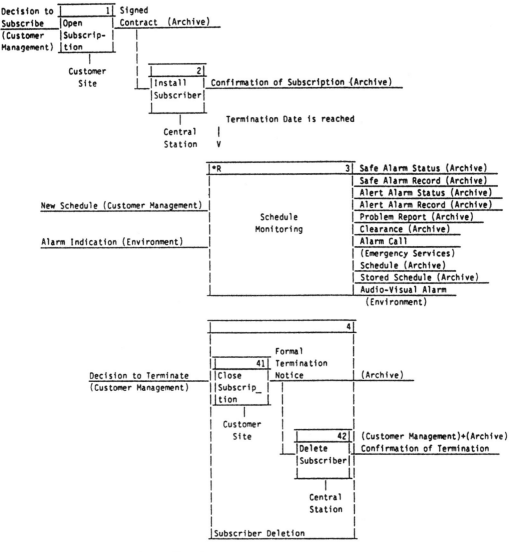

Figure 3.5 : 1 Alarm Procedures

A second point of interest is the Action "Schedule Monitoring". It is an iterated Action involving both Viewpoints. It is an example of the kind of Action whose parts (ie the sub-Actions performed by the individual Viewpoints) are often referred to by the same name by both individual Viewpoints.

Versioning or name qualification would be necessary to distinguish the various meanings. In this example name qualifiers have been used (Customer is a qualifier meaning the Action is that performed at the Customer Site, Subscriber means that it is performed for the Customer Site by the Central Station and no qualifier means it is the combined Action of both Viewpoints).

A third point of interest in figure 3.5 : 1 is the box labelled 4, which contains two other boxes. This is an example of decomposition of a box without going to another diagram. In this case, the Combined Action "Subscriber Deletion" consists of "Close Subscription" performed by Customer Site followed by "Delete Subscriber" performed by Central Station. It was judged to be most sensible to show the decomposition on the same diagram as its parent.

Whether the judgement was right is not a matter of concern for this paper. It is simply included to show that such decompositions can be done. They frequently are done as the diagrams are being built and discussed with user authorities. They should be used sparingly in the final product, as the resulting diagrams can be quite complex to draw and to interpret.

The fourth and final point of interest here is the absence of a Data flow justifying the temporal order between "Install Subscriber" and the subsequent Actions. This should be queried. There are other such cases in the remaining figures. This paper does not address the resolution of the cases detectable in the example.

Figure 3.5 : 2 represents the decomposition of "Schedule Monitoring". It contains one composite Action, "Premises Monitoring", which is a re-entrant iteration and is decomposed in figure 3.5 : 3.

Figure 3.5 : 3 contains two Actions ("Record Safe State" and "Customer Alarm Monitoring") which are performed by different Viewpoints and have no ordering relationship between them. This is information which was not evident from the Isolated Viewpoint diagrams. It was deduced as the diagrams were combined.

In figure 3.5 : 3 the composite Action, "Alarm Handling" is an instance of the combination of selections in each of the Isolated Viewpoints into a single selection in the Combined Viewpoints. This composite Action is decomposed in figure 3.5 : 4.

The final point of interest is in figure 3.5 : 4. It may be remembered that in the previous paper, a temporal peculiarity was pointed out in relation to the Action "Alarm Monitoring" in figure 3.4 : 8. The Clearance appears to arrive before the Problem Report is sent.

When attempting to combine the two Viewpoints, this shows as the apparent need for an explicit backward flow in time for the interaction between "Alarm Monitoring" and "Emergency Procedures" (figures 3.4:8 and 3.4:4). If "Alarm Monitoring" occurs first then "Clearance" flows backwards in time and if "Emergency Procedures" occurs first then "Problem Report" flows backwards in time.

The resolution of such anomalies is normally either mention of an iteration, with one of the Data flows being feedback to the start of the next iteration, or the decomposition of Actions and/or Data to demonstrate an additional tepmoral interaction not discovered for the Isolated Viewpoints. The latter is the case in this example. The Action "Alarm Monitoring" must be split into the part which sends the "Problem Report" and the part which "Waits for Clearance". The latter

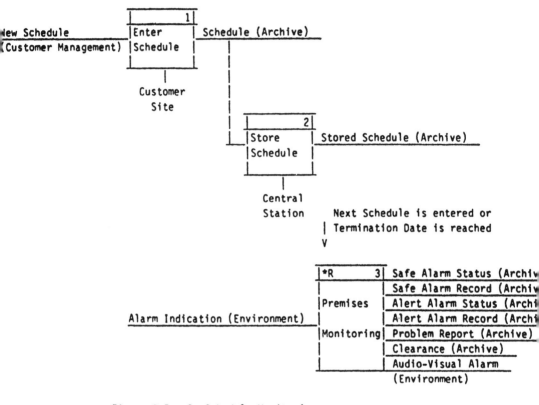

Figure 3.5 : 2   Schedule Monitoring

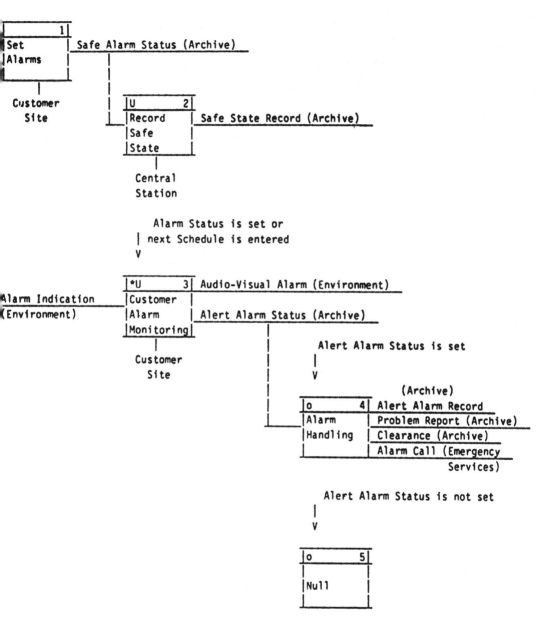

Figure 3.5 : 3 Premises Monitoring

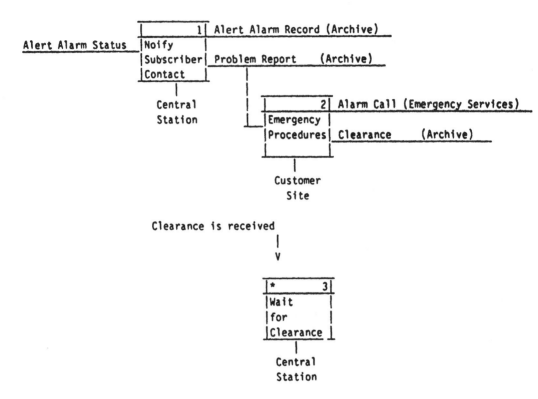

Figure 3.5 : 4 Alarm Handling

is just an idle loop (as far as current analyses have shown) which terminates as soon as the Customer Site issues the "Clearance".

Note that the "Clearance" is just a control on the continuation of the idle loop and arguably is not really an input to "Alarm Monitoring", in the sense of being used within "Wait for Clearance". In this case, "Alarm Monitoring" is a potential source of confusion when using the notation described here. This is a deficiency of the notation, not of the analyses.

3.6. Completion

3.6.1 Introduction

This final paper on the Environment Requirement covers the final intermediate sub-step of the general CORE recursive step, the final step of the overall CORE approach and the link to System Requirement.

The final intermediate sub-step is one which deals with potential problems with the reliability and availability of the service to be supported by the proposed system. Note that it may lead to modifications in the behaviour of the environment and/or to the identification of additional requirements on the proposed system.

Until the lowest level of recursion the decision on where the additional measures are to be implemented (in the environment or in the system) is left open. At the lowest level the relevant decisions are made.

The final step of the overall CORE approach deals with the relatively trivial process of demonstration of completion of the agreed scope of the task of producing an Environment Requirement and the more complex process of dealing with additional information, recorded but beyond the originally agreed scope.

Linking to the System Requirement deals with demonstrating that the information contained in the Environment can be used to guide development of the System Requirement and that the eventual System Requirement covers all the Environment Requirements in a manner consistent with the required Actions, Data flows and Conditions for their valid operation.

3.6.2 Completion of a Recursive Step

Strategy

The final recursive sub-step is primarily a subjective analysis process which may lead to the introduction of Actions, Data flows, Conditions and Events not previously identified. This in turn may lead to re-work of previous intermediate sub-steps at the current level of recursion. Occasionally it may lead to re-work of the higher level of recursion.

The basic strategy is to investigate each Action, Data flow and Condition to discover whether anything about it may cause a problem leading to break-down or failure to provide the required service within defined constraints.

If a problem is discovered, then an acceptable means of dealing with it is sought. This might involve use of preferred development techniques or modification of the environment or introduction of additional requirements to prevent the problem occurring. Alternatively, it might involve introduction of additional requirements to detect and possibly recover from the problem when it does occur. In practice there is no reason other than cost and schedule limitations why a combination of such measures should be excluded.

Prompts

The prompts used at this stage are based on a list of things that generally could go wrong with Actions, Data flows and Conditions and a list of possible techniques for handling such problems.

For each Action, the user authority is questioned about a number of possibilities. A few examples are included here to illustrate the intent of the questioning.

. If iteration is involved, could there be convergence problems or error build-up?

. What would happen if inputs were in error or out of expected range?

. If several Viewpoints communicate with one Action performed by another Viewpoint, could there be contention/deadlock problems?

. What happens if the mechanism (Viewpoint) which performs the Action breaks down or becomes overloaded?

. Could its outputs be out of range for Actions which use them, or could they be corrupted in transmission?

. Is there a danger of unauthorised interference in performance of the Action and if so, what would be the result?

. Could it be invoked by an unauthorised agent (Viewpoint)?

For each Data flow, the user authority is questioned about possibilities such as :

. Could it be inaccurate or out of bounds?

. Could it be corrupted in transmission?

. Could it cause any receiving Action to be unstable in operation?

. If the Data is iterated, could there be too many instances or could it take too long to process them all?

. Could it be subject to unauthorised access or modification?

For Conditions, the tests on Data evaluated for the Condition are much the same as for Data flows. Other possibilities exist, such as :

. Could the condition be evaluated incorrectly?

. What happens if the Condition changes while an Action it controls is in progress?

. Is there any selection not exhaustively covered by Conditions? (eg if P>Q do A if P<Q do B, what if P=Q?)

Having discovered the existence of a problem, the user authority is not necessarily going to be able to identify the best way of dealing with it. The choice may be between a low cost, low reliability change of procedures in the environment or use of expensive, high reliability development techniques or use of expensive, high reliabilty design constraints.

The analyst may prompt on possible measures to deal with the problem. Examples of measures which might be suggested are :

. Use of formal design and implementation techniques for all or selected parts of the development process

. Use of sampling techniques in a manually applied quality control process when the system is operating

. Use of replication either in the environment (eg two people monitoring equipment) or in the proposed system (eg design constraints demanding equipment replication) or in both (eg dual key control)

. Replication of Data or of communications channels

. Use of handshaking, encryption, checksumming, etc.

. Use of fault tolerance techniques (eg input checks, recovery measures)

. Use of limiters (either hardware or software design constraints or manual checking and emergency procedures in the environment)

. Use of filtering techniques (eg to reduce the volume of Data transfers)

. Use of priority techniques in the environment or the proposed system (eg to provide reduced service during peak load periods)

The full list of prompts is dependent on the experience put into producing the CORE guidelines and on the experience of the analysts applying CORE. This is an instance of the need for analysts to make use of their own experience rather than relying just on CORE.

A final form of prompt is for the cost of failure to deal with each problem and the amount the customer is prepared to spend on its avoidance. This may involve helping the customer authority perform risk evaluations and cost/benefit analyses. CORE provides no guidelines in this area, other than that it should be done.

Analyses

CORE analyses at this stage are fairly simple, though tedious. It must be demonstrated that each Action, Data flow, etc. has been considered from the point of view of reliability/availability and that for each problem identified a decision has been made on how to deal with it.

There remains the customer organisation's analysis of the current Viewpoint level. How this is done is not up to CORE, or to the analyst, but to the customer authority. It may be that the customer authority reviews the current level representation personally, or hands it over to the user authorities for review, or accepts their agreement with the analysts as the representation is produced, or calls in independent reviewers. CORE does not give guidelines on how the customer authority gains sufficient confidence to sign off the current level of representation.

Tactical Issues

Much of the information gathered for the purposes of reliability/ availability analysis consists of definitions of constraints. CORE does not demand the mention of literal constraints (eg. "Action XYZ must complete within 5 msec."). The use of literal constants such as "5 msec." is almost invariably a design constraint, rather than an absolute requirement. Even though it is common to include such numbers in Requirement Specifications, the design nature of the constant is illustrated by the fact that it is rarely true that a response time of, for example, 5.00001 msec. would be damaging. The number 5 is chosen because it is a "round" number and therefore easier to remember.

In CORE Environment Requirements, it is encouraged that constraints such as response times are expressed as parameters and the demanded literal constants should be attached to the parameter in an appendix to the main requirement. For example, in the case of "Action XYZ" above, the requirement is that "Action XYZ must complete within XYZ-Time-Limit" and in an appendix, the statement "XYZ-Time-Limit = 5 msec." would appear.

The benefit of this approach is that "XYZ-Time-Limit" is quite likely to be referenced from several places in the requirement and a later change of mind (eg to 6 msec.) requires a change only in one place. If the literal constant is embedded in the main requirement at each point of reference, it must be changed at each point. Moreover, if 5 msec. is a design constraint on more than one Action, the change cannot be a simple global edit of 5 msec. to 6 msec., because the new value does not necessarily apply to the other Actions.

Where possible, all design constraints are dealt with in a similar manner. The main body of the specification deals with the absolute requirement and references an appendix for the demanded design constraints.

One problem analysts sometimes suffer from is over-zealousness in pursuing reliability in some areas. It must be remembered that, having found a problem, a valid decision on how to deal with it is to ignore it. The customer is entitled to require an unreliable system, provided that the decision is recorded by the analyst and approved by the customer authority.

This leads to another issue which the analyst should bear in mind. The normal user authorities, particularly if they are later to become actual users of the system, will always opt for a reliable, efficient, easy to use system. Hence, faced with problems and suggestions for their solution, there will be a predisposition to select the suggestion which fits these goals best.

The problem is that the user authorities are frequently not constrained directly by consideration of cost. That is the business of the customer authority. The analyst should always consult the customer authority before introducing any measure to cope with a problem which would cause a change in the organisation or behaviour of the environment or which would significantly increase the cost of the proposed system. There is, of course an element of subjectivity in what constitutes a significant increase in cost. It might be best to agree a figure at the Start-Up step, or to consult the customer authority about every reliability/ availability decision.

One final issue to be resolved in the practical application of CORE is the contractual arrangement for approving or rejecting the products of any level of recursion. The things that must be pre-determined (preferably at Start-Up) are the form of expression which will be "signed off" by the customer authority, the time within which problems will be reported by the customer authority and the form in which problems must be reported in order to be dealt with by the analyst.

For example, if there is no timescale for signing-off, the analyst's schedule may be put at risk by continuing to the next level without approval. If there is no agreed form (standard) for expression of the requirement, it is always open to question whether the form actually used is "reasonable" for the intended audience. This could lead to major re-work just to re-present the same information according to a different standard. If the product is rejected with dramatic but meaningless comments such as "It's all rubbish" or "That's not how things happen", the analyst has no reliable means of improving it on a second pass. Hence, it should be agreed that rejection will be specific, indicating particular Actions, Data flows, etc., which are not correctly decomposed, constrained, etc.

Example

The example developed in the previous papers on Environment Requirements contain a large number of potential problem areas which should really be considered. In this Course there is time to indicate only a few examples.

First, consider figure 3.5 : 1 in the previous paper. What happens if the Customer Site issues a Formal Termination Notice with a Termination Date which is at or before the current date? It may be impossible to avoid some unwanted alarm processing if such a date is entered. Should there be a minimum notice period? Should the proposed system be involved in assisting checks on adherance to the minimum notice requirements? If so, how is it to know what is the current date?

Next, look at figure 3.5 : 2. What happens if the Customer Site issues an incorrect Schedule? Clearly there are likely to be a number of false alarms which may divert the Central Station's attention away from genuine alarms. Should semantic checks be required on the Schedule before it is transmitted? If so, that will be stored as premature information to be looked at when the Customer Site is decomposed at later Viewpoint levels. Would it be acceptable to require double entry of a Schedule to trap careless typing errors? If so the "Enter Schedule" Action should be iterated.

Next, look at figure 3.5 : 3. What happens if one of the Customer Site's Local Alarm Systems develops a fault and keeps indicating an alarm? What if the fault is cyclic? The Central Station could be overloaded by false alarm indications. What happens when the Customer Site is opening or closing? There may be temporary alarm indications each time this happens.

What happens if several hundred Customer Sites regularly open at 9.00, but others open at 9.30? How is the Central Station to distinguish the temporary false alarms from the occasional real ones between 8.50 and 9.30? The answer is probably to introduce some intelligence to the Customer Site "Alarm Monitoring", so that it inhibits alarm outputs ten minutes either side of opening and closing hours - but that is a gift to an enterprising burglar and a disaster if a fire starts during the dead period.

Finally, look at figure 3.5 : 4. What happens if the Central Station fails to spot an Alert Alarm Status transmission? Clearly, it might fail to issue a Problem Report and hence fail in its obligation to the Customer Site. Some form of acknowlwdgement should be introduced, and if it is not received, the Customer Site should re-transmit the Alert Alarm Status.

What if the Central Station notices the Alert Alarm Status, but forgets to issue a Problem Report, or cannot contact the Customer Contact for the Customer Site? In such cases, in the event of a burglary or fire, how can the distinction be made between Central Station negligence and Customer Contact negligence?

What if the Central Station takes a long time to notify the Customer Contact? What constitutes too long? What happens to prevent notification taking too long?

Clearly, the list of possible problems is longer than is shown here. What is evident is that problems can and should systematically be sought and dealt with. They should be the subject of additional measures at the current level or postponed for reconsideration at a lower level (ie marked as premature) or occasioally referred back to an earlier level or rejected as too improbable or not worth the cost of protecting against. Whatever happens, the possibility of the problem and the decision made should be recorded somewhere and referenced to any measures introduced to deal with the problem.

3.6.3 Completion of Environment Requirement

After performance of each agreed level of recursion in the CORE analysis process, the analyst will have completed the task agreed at Start-Up. Each Viewpoint in the agreed Viewpoint Hierarchy will have been analysed to a level agreed by the customer authority. Relative to the initial plans, the task is now complete. The situation is not that simple!

The typical situation will be that, in spite of having analysed the lowest agreed level, there is still "premature" information. Also, there will usually be information which could not be supplied in the timescales originally planned and which is now recorded as missing. There will be re-work in progress for previous levels because of agreed mistakes discovered at later levels. Finally there may be whole new Viewpoint structures discovered to be important, even though they were excluded at the Start-Up stage.

What actually happens at this point may be determined by a mixture of factors such as contractual constraints, current level of spend relative to budget, availability of staff and desire for future goodwill from the customer organisation (eg. to get future contracts). CORE cannot provide general guidelines on how to handle such situations. They are a matter for individual project or organisation strategy and tactics, rather than technical issues.

Contractually, as soon as the lowest level of Viewpoint has been represented and signed off and all re-work contractually required has been agreed and signed off, the task is complete. Technically, all important Viewpoints should be analysed and represented, all re-work completed and all omissions and inconsistencies removed. That being practically improbable, CORE recommends instead that the complete requirement is one in which everything which could be represented in the agreed schedule is represented and any analytically detectable omissions or inconsistencies are detected and recorded.

3.6.4 Linking to System Requirement

The most common application of CORE is to take the Viewpoint Hierarchy down to the point at which the proposed system appears as a Viewpoint. Then the system Viewpoint is in effect a provisional

System Requirement. Mapping between the CORE system Viewpoint and the eventual System Requirement is then relatively straightforward.

The CORE system Viewpoint identifies Actions and chains of Actions which must be performed by the proposed system. The system Actions are not normally expressed as algorithms unless the environment forces some algorithmic constraint. Such constraints are usually in the form of Action chains with necessary internal Data flows. Generally though, the CORE expression can be treated as a stimulus/response definition of the required system Actions, together with constraints on their occurrence.

Constraints on the occurrence of Actions are normally expressed in the form of a series of layers of Conditions extractable from the various levels of Viewpoint representation in the Environment Requirement. A danger inherant in the use of procedurally oriented notations for Requirement Specification can be controlled for CORE applications by recognising that for the purposes of System Requirement, extracting the stimulus / response view of Actions, limited by the extracted Conditions permits the expression of the System Requirement without forcing the appearance of algorithmic (ie. design oriented) specifications.

This is not to assert that algorithmic specifications are never of any value. If such expressions are deemed useful (eg. for the purposes of simulation of proposed system + environment behaviour) the original CORE representations still exist to assist in that area. They would certainly require supplementing by more detailed algorithms than are normally available from CORE analyses.

Either at the end of the CORE application or at the start of the System Requirement application, some decisions must be made about which of the Conditions controlling the performance of Actions by the proposed system are to be monitored by the system itself. These will require explicit representation in terms of Data entities known (perhaps via external sensor inputs) to the system. Conditions which are not to be monitored by the system must appear as procedural checks in the relevant user manuals.

Special information carried over from application of CORE into the development of the System Requirement is that which expresses design constraints and preferred development policies. A particular form of design constraint is any premature information left after analysis of the lowest level of the CORE Viewpoint Hierarchy. This is by nature unstructured and may either be structured during System Requirement or carried over as an unstructured list of preferred design policies. The particular policy adopted is a matter of System Requirement tactics.

3.6.5 Conclusions

The description of the process of producing an Environment has attempted to demonstrate systematic ways of extracting and analysing information about aspects of the environment to be supported by the proposed system.

It is advisable and possible to establish a strategy for analysis and tactics for control of perturbations to the strategy. The strategy and tactics should make use of prompting, analytic and psychological techniques to achieve maximum quality of specification and responsible attitudes through clear definition of responsibilties and accountability for decisions or lack of them. As far as is possible the techniques used should be well defined and easy to apply.

It is advisable and probably possible to use a simple notation which requires little training of the user community and yet which can aid analysis and demonstrate the existence of problems and the need for decisions. The notation should support the use of prompting techniques.

The selected notation should be capable of transformation into a more formally defined notation which might require more skills to interpret than are normally available in the user community. The reverse transformation should be possible, though it is to be expected that the more formal notation would contain greater and more precise expressive power than would be possible in the simple notation, so the reverse transformation would involve a filtering operation.

Use of tool support for prompting, analysis, expression, quality control and achievement of accountability is valuable for any system and probably essential for large systems or systems with a high cost of failure.

The CORE approach is an example of one which attempts to address many of these areas and is evolving to address them all. It is not a perfect answer to the problems of producing an Environment Requirement, but it does show that the task can be performed more systematically than analysts often think.

Chapter 4

A Graph Model Based Approach
to Specifications

This chapter presents an approach for defining the many levels of specifications of a distributed system which is based on a graph model for representing the decomposition of functions. The previous chapter focused on the procedures for systematically clarifying the initial poorly formulated concerns and goals of a system into a more precise definition of the system requirements. Although a method of representing this level of requirements was used to illustrate the procedures, the procedures are general enough to work with many different representation techniques.

The focus of this chapter is the definition of an approach for precisely defining required system level characteristics, then decomposing these requirements down to the specification of the units of code in the selected programming language. The underlying problem addressed is the identification of a unified model for representing all of the intermediate levels of requirements and design which preserves the properties specified at the system level. Of particular interest is the specification of the allowed concurrency of system functions, for it is this allowed concurrency which is exploited by a distributed processor.

Section 4.1 presents the graph model foundations on which the remainder of the chapter is based. Section 4.2 presents an overview of a method for developing system level requirements based on the graph model. Section 4.3 describes the process of further decomposing these requirements down to the finite state machine level1. Section 4.4 presents an overview of the problems to be addressed in the design of a distributed processor to satisfy these requirements. Section 4.5 defines an approach for transitioning the requirements into a distributed design.

4.1. The Graph Model of Decomposition

This section presents a graph model based approach for representing the concepts of decomposition, allocation, interface design, and exception handling in a way which defines and preserves system level requirements for sequencing and concurrency of system functions, their inputs, and their outputs. A way to incorporate these concepts into a language for expressing system requirements, and checking them for consistency is presented. This will provide the foundation for defining a Systems Requirements Engineering Methodology presented in the next section.

4.1.1 The Concept of Decomposition

The purpose of the Graph Model of Decomposition is to provide a quasi-formal definition of the conditions for decomposing a function into a structure of lower level functions. Previous requirements representation techniques which used the concept of decomposition have failed to capture simultaneously the characteristics of preserving input/output concurrency and structure, of preserving the criteria for completion of a function, and of preserving performance traceability and invariants of the transformations. An overview of how the Graph Model of Decomposition does this is presented in the following section; for details, see [Alford 79a].

First for background, a system function is defined as required transformation of inputs into outputs lasting over an interval of time which ceases its operation when one of its completion criteria is satisfied. We use the term "Item" to indicate a generic unit of input to or output from a function. An item may contain several concurrent subsequences of lower level items which occur over an interval of time. A completion criterion is a Boolean condition on the input which defines a reason for exiting a function; a function may have several completion criteria, and the next function to be perform usually depends on which completion criterion was used to exit the function. One may which to define the transformation in terms of preserving some specific invariants (e.g., for each element input, an output will be produced). To support top-down performance decomposition, we attach to the function a set of performance indices (e.g., accuracy, timing, etc.) which measure the effectiveness of the transformation.

A function can thus be viewed as a very large atomic action which operates over an interval of time, with the details of the transformation and internal states of the function not visible. To gain such visibility, the function may be decomposed into a set of lower level functions, some of which operate concurrently, some of which must occur in a specific sequence. As we shall see, these decompositions are not unique, and thus the selection of a specific decomposition constitutes a design decision.

The concept of decomposition requires careful definition if ambiguity is to be avoided. We define the concept in three steps. First sequences, concurrency, selection, and replication of functions are defined in terms of a graph whose nodes are functions; we call this a Function Net, or F-net. The solid arcs which connect the nodes of the F-Net represent time precedence relationships. If a function has two completion criteria, two arcs must exit the node representing the function. Special nodes of the F-Net indicate concurrency, replication (i.e., the a function is replicated a number of times, and all copies are operating concurrently), synchronization of completion of concurrent functions, and rejoin of selections. An F-Net may contain dotted arrows connecting the boxes to item names to represent the relationship between a function and the items which it inputs and outputs). Figure 4.1 presents the nomenclature.

Sequence and concurrency of input and output items are defined similarly by using a directed graph having items as nodes; this is called an Item Net, or I-Net. Such graphs have special nodes to indicate concurrency, iteration, and replication over an index set.

The second step to defining the concept of decomposition is to define a function composition by synthesizing the composition graph and its referenced functions into the characteristics of a system function. An I-Net of the items input by the functions on the F-Net is constructed; similarly, an I-Net of the outputs of the composition is constructed.
The overall completion criteria of the composition is constructed by combining the graph logic with the completion criteria of each of the functions on the F-Net. The set of performance indices of the composition is defined as the set of performance indices of the functions on the F-Net. Figure 4.2 presents a summary of this approach.

With these preliminaries, decomposition is now defined as a relationship between a function and a function composition if five criteria are

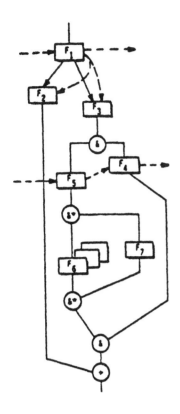

F-Net:
- NODES ARE FUNCTIONS WITH SINGLE ENTRANCE MULTIPLE EXIT
- ARCS REPRESENT PRECEDENCE (SEQUENCE)
- SPECIAL NODES
  & CONCURRENCY
  * ITERATION
  &* REPLICATION
  + REJOIN SELECTION

I-Net:
- NODES ARE ITEMS
- ARCS REPRESENT PRECEDENCE (SEQUENCE)
- SPECIAL NODES
  & CONCURRENCY
  * ITERATION
  &* REPLICATION (SUBSEQUENCES)
  + REJOIN SELECTION

Figure 4.1:   Graphs of F-Nets and I-Nets

A FUNCTION COMPOSITION IS A SYNTHESIS OF A COMPOSITION GRAPH AND ITS REFERRED FUNCTIONS F_I INTO A FUNCTION F_0.

$$F_0 = (I_0, O_0, D_0, C_0, P_0)$$

WHERE

I_0 = COMPOSITION OF INPUTS NEEDED

O_0 = COMPOSITION OF OUTPUTS PRODUCED
   NOTE: INTERMEDIATE INPUTS/OUTPUTS DELETED

D = $G(D_1, \ldots, D_N)$ GRAPH OF TRANSFORMATION

C_0 = $G(C_1, \ldots, C_N)$ GRAPH OF COMPLETION CRITERIA

P_0 = $(P_1, \ldots, P_M)$ SET OF PERFORMANCE INDICES

Figure 4.2:   Function Composition

satisfied (see Figure 4.3):

o   Input sequences and output sequences must be preserved where defined, although the function composition inputs and outputs may add more detail.

o   The completion criteria must match, in particular the number and type of exits.

o   Any invariants of the function transformations must be preserved.

o   The performance index of the function must be computable from those of the functions of the function composition.

This definition is transitive (i.e. the decomposition of a decomposition is a legal decomposition of the original function). Moreover, this definition of decomposition incorporates hierarchical control theory, generalized state space theory, decomposition by concurrent functions, and a version of the Michael Jackson Program Design Method as special cases. These are briefly discussed in the following subsections.

4.1.2 Decomposition by Object

Hierarchical Control Theory popularized by Mesarovic [Mesarovic 70] has as its fundamental theorem that any controller which handles subsequences of inputs (e.g., from different objects) can be expressed in terms

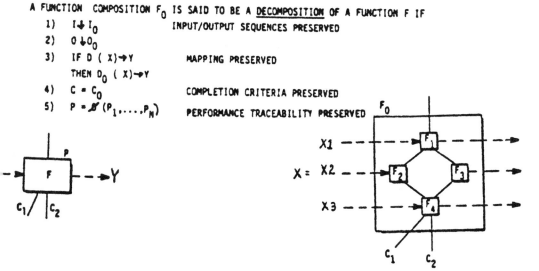

A FUNCTION COMPOSITION F_0 IS SAID TO BE A <u>DECOMPOSITION</u> OF A FUNCTION F IF

1) $I \downarrow I_0$ INPUT/OUTPUT SEQUENCES PRESERVED

2) $0 \downarrow 0_0$

3) IF $D (X) \rightarrow Y$ MAPPING PRESERVED
    THEN $D_0 (X) \rightarrow Y$

4) $C = C_0$ COMPLETION CRITERIA PRESERVED

5) $P = \mathscr{P} (P_1, \ldots, P_N)$ PERFORMANCE TRACEABILITY PRESERVED

Figure 4.3: Definition of Decomposition

of a set of controllers for each subsequence with a higher level control function. Figure 4.4 illustrates the approach. Assume that a system function F maps input item X into output item Y over an interval of time, and that the item X can be expressed as a set of concurrent subsequences (X1,...,Xn) and that the item Y can be defined as a set of concurrent subsequences (Y1,...,Yn); usually XI and YI are the inputs and outputs of the system related to the Ith object being addressed by the system. Then the theorem states that F can always be expressed as a replication of subfunctions, F_I, one for each input X_I, which maps X_I and a control C_I into Y_I. To produce the controls C_I, a status S_I is generated to summarize each XI, and the control rules of the function H are used to calculate all of the controls (C1,..,Cn) from all of the status items (S1,..,Sn). Mesarovic proves this can always be done, although the decomposition is not unique. Thus the problem of defining a control function is decomposed into two smaller problems: the problem defining how to deal with each input stream XI; and and the problem of defining the interactions between objects. The Graph Model of Decomposition provides the capability of expressing the fact that a function is replicated, one for each member of a domain (or indexing) set. The replication construct and requires that there always be a branch containing a function to provide the necessary coordination.

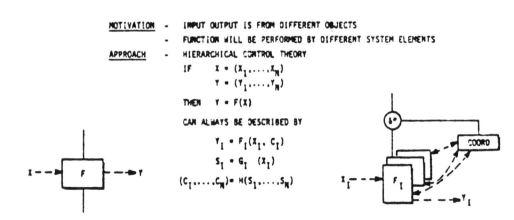

Figure 4.4: Decomposition by Object

4.1.3 Decomposition by Time Sequence

As discussed in Section 2.1.2, a finite state machine with initial state S0 can be viewed as a function which accepts a sequence of discrete inputs (X1,..,Xn) and generates a sequence of discrete outputs (Y1,...,Yn) plus a final state Sn. The weakness noted of this representation approach was that it produces a "flat" model, i.e., may require literally millions of states to represent a real system. The Graph Model of Decomposition provides a hierarchical approach for structuring these states which reduces to a strict state-space model when all sequences have been defined.

Figure 4.5 provides an overview of the approach. For example, suppose the input to a system function, F is the time sequence X_1 followed by X_2 followed by X_3. There are at least two ways F can be decomposed to deal with the time inputs: save up the inputs until all have arrived and then apply F; or perform partial transformations on intermediate inputs. In either case, F can always be represented as a graph of intermediate functions F_1, F_2, and F_3, each of which accepts only one external input Xi and produces not more than one external output plus the results of the processing so far, the Ai. Since the Fi can be viewed as large atomic actions, the Ai represent the instantaneous states when Fi has completed. The resulting decomposition is not unique; different decompositions result from different choices of the states Ai.

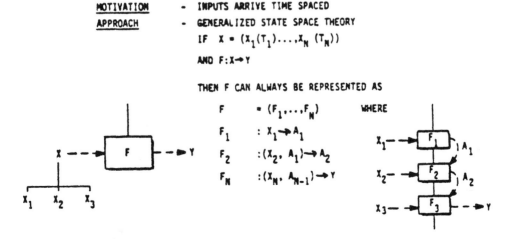

Figure 4.5:   Decomposition by Time Sequence

When the X_i are refined to the point that they represent discrete inputs rather than subsequences (e.g., data sets, where all data is logically input as one unit), then the composition function collapses into a strict state-space model where the completion criteria, C_i, become the state transition functions. Thus any time function accepting an input sequence can (non-uniquely!) be decomposed into a finite state machine.

4.1.4 Decomposition for Input/Output Modularity

When the approach described in the previous section is combined with the fact that inputs and outputs may be described in terms of sequences, selections, iterations, and concurrency, the principle of decomposing functions to preserve modularity with respect to inputs and outputs results. This concept was popularized in Michael Jackson's Program Design Methodology [Jackson 75].

Figure 4.6 presents an overview of the approach as represented by the Graph Model of Decomposition. Consider a function, F, which has input X consisting of the sequence X_1 followed by either X_2 or X_3 then X4, and the output Y consisting of Y_1 followed by Y_2 (note that the X_i and Y_i may themselves be subsequences). Then F can always be expressed in terms of

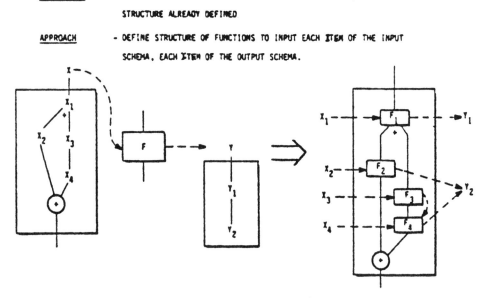

Figure 4.6: Decomposition by I/O Structure

a composition of functions which input and output the individual X_i and Y_i and intermediate values. The modularity considerations thus forces the function structure to be similar to the input/output structures. Thus the problem of transforming a structure of input items into a structure of output items can always reduced to the selection of a function composition plus the definition of the functions which accept no more than one external input and generate no more than one external output. As before, the decomposition is non-unique.

4.1.5 Decomposition by Concurrent Function

The final special case of decomposition is that of a concurrent function representation. The motivation is to decompose the definition of the transformation of input X to output Y by a sequence of transformations, with the output of one being the input to the next. Figure 4.7 presents the example where F is defined in terms of J acting on X, with H acting on the result, and G transforming the result into the output Y. If X is a time sequence, then J could be acting on one element of the input while G is transforming a previous element; hence J, H, and G can be represented as concurrent functions which input and output shared items. Thus a function can always be decomposed into a set of concurrent functions; as before, the decomposition is non-unique.

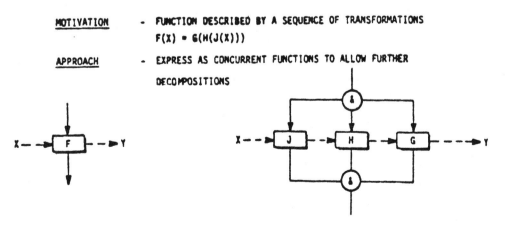

MOTIVATION   - FUNCTION DESCRIBED BY A SEQUENCE OF TRANSFORMATIONS
                 $F(X) = G(H(J(X)))$

APPROACH   - EXPRESS AS CONCURRENT FUNCTIONS TO ALLOW FURTHER
                 DECOMPOSITIONS

Figure 4.7: Decomposition by Concurrent Function

4.1.6 Allocation

A system can be viewed in two different ways. On the one hand, a
system can be viewed as an entity which performs a transformation of
inputs into outputs; on the other hand, a system is defined as a set of
interconnected components with a common goal (e.g., to perform the specified transformation). Allocation of function to component is the bridge
between the functional view and the component view of a system.

Figure 4.8 illustrates the result of combining the concept of allocation with the previously discussed concepts of decomposition. The use
of the different types of decomposition of a system function generally
results in a graph model which replicates functions for each input object,
which identifies time sequences of functions for each object, and expresses them in terms of concurrent functions. Allocation of functions to
subsystems can be expressed as a partitioning of these functions (i.e.,
each function assigned to exactly one partition), and each partition is
then assigned to be performed by exactly one system component. Note that
not only are the individual functions F_{ij} (and the coordination function)
allocated, but also the structure of sequences and concurrency across
objects, i.e., F_{13i} always happens before F_{23i}, but F_{13i} has no ordering

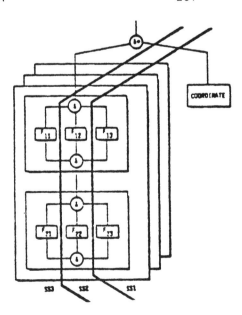

Figure 4.8: Allocation as a Partition of a Graph

and may occur before, after, or concurrent with F_{13j}. This removes the ambiguity with respect to sequences inherent in SADT and other requirements techniques which consider only data flow.

Thus the concepts of formal decomposition provide a foundation for the unambiguous expression of subsystem requirements in terms of allocation of decomposed system functions. This approach is explicitly hierarchical, and can be applied to any level of system component.

4.1.7. Interface Design

Figure 4.8 illustrates the fact that the boundary which separates the partitions of functions allocated to two different subsystems is pierced by arcs (indicating control is passed from one function in one subsystem to another), and dotted lines indicating items output by functions in one subsystem which are input to functions in another component. One interpretation of this boundary is that it represents the requirement to pass both control and items of information between the subsystems.

This concept can be formalized by associating with each boundary an interface function, whose purpose is to pass the required of control and items. This interface function satisfies all of the properties of a function: it has inputs, outputs, invariants of the transformation (i.e., it must pass the output of each function of one component to the corresponding function of the other subsystem), a completion criterion (i.e., it finishes when the last item is passed between the components), and natural performance indices (e.g., time and reliability to pass information).

The techniques of decomposition and allocation discussed above can be applied to the interface function to yield multiple layers of interface design. At each level of design, a the boundary separating the previous level of functions is associated with an interface function, which is decomposed and allocated, leaving a lower level boundary. Thus the top level interface may be decomposed into a pair of functions which merge all of the parallel inputs together into a serial string of messages with a common format (i.e., a multiplexor), and a function which distributes the messages to the appropriate processing functions; these are allocated to the sending and receiving components. The boundary between these functions is then associated with a lower level interface function, which might be decomposed into functions which organize the messages into packets, pass a string of packets, and then re-combine the packets into messages. Thus this approach provides a unified way to formally define both interface requirements and designs, including the derivation of communication protocols.

4.1.8 Layers of Requirements

The desire to express a methodology as a sequence of steps leads to an apparent contradiction when issues of resource management and fault tolerance are addressed. Classical Top-Down Systems Engineering theory suggests that one should decompose functions and then allocate them to components. A paradox arises from the fact that t is only after allocation that component resources needed to accomplish each function can be identified, total utilization estimated, and hence the need for resource management can be established. Since resource management is a control function which requires allocation, this must be represented back at the system level. Thus the functions must be allocated in order to determine whether control functions must be defined and allocated.

Similarly, classical systems engineering theory proposes that one first define system functions and allocations, then perform a Failure Mode Effects Analysis to identify potential problems, and then add functions to detect, avoid, isolate, and recover from the failures. These functions must also be decomposed and allocated to the components. This process has traditionally justified the concept of "iterating" the system design.

Our approach to handling this problem is illustrated in Figure 4.9. The composition graph is explicitly designed to be produced in several layers, with the first layer representing the standard flow (i.e., sufficient resources and no faults). Additional layers of functions and paths are added to address resource/fault exceptions by adding appropriate exits to the functions on the standard flow, and then identifying how the exception will be handled locally with entry back into the standard flow. If local recovery is not possible, an exception exit of the composition occurs which must match an exception exit of the function decomposed. Recovery from a fault is thus associated with re-entry to the standard flow level of requirements. Note that the original standard flow graph is left as an undisturbed, invariant subgraph of the combined graph. Although this concept is new to systems engineering, a version of the

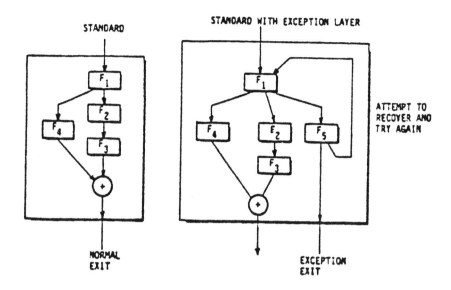

Figure 4.9: Layers of Requirements

approach was demonstrated by Liskov on the CLU operating system.

This approach has distinct advantages of providing a separation of concerns for handling complex problems. First the standard flow is defined, and then layers of requirements are added for each class of exception without disturbing previous layers. This separation of concerns promotes a systematic methodology for doing the system design and presenting the results of the design activity.

4.1.9 Discussion

This section has presented the basic concepts of a graph model approach for representing the concepts of decomposition, allocation, interface design, and addition of functions to provide tolerance to faults. The concepts of decomposition provide a way of specifying both sequence and concurrency of inputs and functions. The identification of concurrency at the system level is vital to the specification of distributed systems: at best, a distributed system can only exploit the concurrency available in the problem. In the next section, a systematic method for defining system requirements based on these graph model foundations will be presented.

4.2. System Requirements Definition

The previous section provided an overview of how the Graph Model of Decomposition is used to specify decomposition, allocation, interface design, and layers of requirements for fault detection and recovery.
In this section, we will show how these graph model foundations are used to derive a systems requirements and analysis methodology. The Systems Requirements Engineering Methodology (SYSREM) consists of the seven phases of activities presented in Table 4.1. Each phase is described below in terms of its role in the methodology, the specific steps necessary for completion, and the capabilities of automated tooflw which could aid the developer in doing the job.

4.2.1 Phase 1 - Define System

The system development process begins with a user requirement to do "something". This "something" is generally described in a system needs document which outlines overall objectives, performance requirements, and cost/schedule constraints. Phase 1 identifies the system inputs, outputs, performance indices, and potential constraints or guidelines for the system development. The user is required to state the system mission and objectives, system constraints (e.g., constraints on cost, schedule, special constraint on type of components to be used to build the system), The user is required to identify any special classes of input (e.g., the system has different classes of users) as well as standard scenarios of

PHASE 1   DEFINE SYSTEM
PHASE 2   IDENTIFY COMPONENTS
PHASE 3   DECOMPOSE TO SYSTEM LOGIC
PHASE 4   DECOMPOSE AND ALLOCATE
PHASE 5   ESTIMATE FEASIBILITY AND COST
PHASE 6   IDENTIFY CRITICAL ISSUES AND RESOURCES
PHASE 7   ADD RESOURCE MANAGEMENT AND FAULT TOLERANCE
PHASE 8   PLAN INTEGRATION AND TEST
PHASE 9   OPTIMIZE OVER DESIGNS

Figure 4.10:   Phases of Systems Requirements Engineering Methodology

of inputs. The performance indices of the system measure how well the system is operating, and is used to make the tradeoff decisions; this can include such factors as response times or efficiency of a transformation of inputs to outputs, as well as development cost and schedule.

4.2.2 Phase 2 -- Identify Components

Phase 2 identifies the potential classes of components or subsystems from which the system might be decomposed. There may be more than one potential combination of sensors, data processors, controllers, and communications components which might be used to build the system. The purpose of this phase is to identify potential combinations to which requirements might be allocated. These are system classes, because the exact details of the subsystems are subject to the allocation of system requirements to the subsystem. Thus, separate potential configurations will be identified for later analysis with respect to allocation of requirements to the subsystems of these configurations.

To support this phase, the capability is needed for identifying a number of subsystem class configurations, and their interfaces in block diagrammatic fashion, with a mechanism for naming and identifying these configurations. In addition, a mechanism is needed for associating subsystem design variables with the subsystem. These subsystem design variables will then be used to predict subfunction performance allocated to the subsystem, and be used with estimating rules to predict cost and schedules of manufacturing of subsystems. In addition, the cost estimating relationships themselves should be recorded for future reference.

4.2.3 Phase 3 -- Decompose to System Logic

In Phase 3, the decompositions of the system function down to the system logic level are identified. The system logic is defined by the time sequence of functions which deal with the inputs to the system. This system logic is simulated during this phase to predict system performance as a function of the design variables of the system function. Since more than one potential decomposition may exist, the system data base may hold many decompositions related by a graph structure of decomposition relationships.

To support this Phase, the user needs the following capabilities:

o Define composition and decomposition, and check them for consistency.

o Identify and manage a structure of alternative decompositions of functions. This includes the capability of defining potential system function configurations from a graph of possible decompositions.

o Provide the ability to define new system configurations in terms of old system configurations plus modifications.

o Provide the ability to extract all relevant information for a specific configuration in terms of functions and their decomposition hierarchy.

o Provide an on-line capability to portray graphically a composition and from that display to select functions for further display, or for identification of existing decomposition, or for display of decomposition to the indicated function.

4.2.4 Phase 4 -- Decompose and Allocate

The decomposition process is continued in order to get to the functions which might be allocated to specific subsystems of specific configurations. Again, simulators may be used to predict the system performance and frequencies of subsystem subfunctions as a function of scenario and design parameters.

More than one allocation will be examined for feasibility, cost, and schedule and different allocations of performance to the subsystems may be examined in order to reach balance points for a particular configuration.

For each allocation, a candidate allocation of performance index constraints is identified. This requires the following capabilities:

o Provide the ability to designate a specific allocation of subfunctions to particular subsystems of configuration. Provide the capability of color coding a specific allocation on a graphics terminal.

o Provide the capability of identifying and manipulating such an allocation configuration. This means to define such an allocation, and to define new allocations in terms of old allocations with modification.

o Provide the capability of analyzing potential allocations of specific system configurations for completeness, i.e., every subfunction being uniquely allocated to a specific subsystem.

o Provide the ability to specify performance bounds on performance indices of the subfunctions allocated to the subsystems. These performance allocations must also be specified such that several possible configurations can be considered simultaneously, and new ones can be specified in terms of old ones plus modifications.

4.2.5   Phase 5 -- Estimate Feasibility and Cost

Each subsystem allocations must now be analyzed for feasibility and cost. This involves definition of interfaces, summarizing the require- ments, identifying candidate DP distributed architecture classes, load estimation, and estimation of cost and feasibility. The following steps are performed.

Step 5a - Interface Design

An interface design must be postulated for each interface in order to estimate the required DP resources to service the interface i.e., memory space to store data and processing time to encode/decode the data. This requires the following capabilities:

o Provide the ability to extract and display the list of all input/ output pairs between subfunctions allocated to one subsystem and subfunctions allocated to another subsystem.

o Provide the ability to specify or allocate input/output (I/O) pairs to specific I/O links.

o Provide the ability to specify interfacing functions, and auto- matically generate specifications of interfacing across links consisting of I/O pairs plus interface sorting information.

o Provide the ability to describe alternate decompositions and allocations.

o The ability to specify performance requirements on these interface functions.

o If there is more than one interface link, the user should have the ability to call up on a graphics terminal the data to be passed across the interface, and to designate efficiently the interface link to which it is assigned. This information would be part of an interface configuration which would be designated by a specific name. More than one interface configuration might be held in the computer at a time.

Step 5b - Summarize

For a standard set of threat scenarios, the frequencies of the subfunctions are identified, as well as performance indices relating to response time and accuracy of computation. This summarization may occur several times -- once for each decomposition and allocation of interest. The following capabilities will therefore be needed:

o The ability to list a table of system functions allocated to the data processor, and the input/output relationships of these functions with other functions.

o The ability to make printer plots and/or graphics plots of a data flow diagram summarizing this information.

o The ability to summarize performance allocation, including those allocated parametrically.

Step 5c - Identify Maximum Concurrency

In this step the maximum concurrency of a potential data processor architecture is determined. The purpose of this step is to identify potential application of parallel or pipeline processing architectures. This does not attempt to give a true lower bound on the maximum concurrency, but to identify the maximum number of processors that might be possible without examining the impact of data conflicts. This is done by estimating the number of processors to support an object in each phase of the system logic, and attaching this estimated dimensionality to the subfunctions. The total dimensionality has been obtained by multiplying the number of objects in each phase of the system logic by the number of processors which could be used to support that object in that phase. This can be mechanized in a post-processor of the system simulator so that, as a simulator is run against various scenarios, a time history of maximum concurrency can be produced.

The result of this activity is the identification of those functions and phases of engagements where parallel processing might be able to exploit the natural parallelism of the problem. Unless this parallelism exists, a parallel processing architecture will run essentially no faster than a serial architecture.

To support these activities, the following capabilities are needed:

o Ability to specify algorithm concurrency per subfunction.

o Ability to translate this information into a simulation postprocessor, and use it to determine dimensionality as a function of scenario time.

Step 5d - Estimate Loads

In this step, the requirements for various DP resources are estimated as a function of their requirements and scenario. This is accomplished in the following way:

1. Identify the relevant resources. This might include instruction rate, memory requirements, communication rate between functions or processors.

2. These resource requirements are estimated for each function.

3. The resource requirements per object per system phase are estimated and attached to the subfunction.

4. These estimates are pulled out and used in a simulation postprocessor to estimate the resource utilization requirements as a function of scenario time.

To support these activities, the following capabilities are needed:

o Ability to specify resource requirements.

o Ability to construct a simulation post-processor and exercise it against the simulation.

o Ability to display the results of this analysis graphically.

o Ability to check (before simulation construction time) the completeness of the specification of these attributes for all of the functions allocated to the data processor.

o Ability to summarize (in tabular form) estimated instruction counts (average and peak) as a function of configuration and scenario. Other tables are to be produced for memory and communication requirements.

Step 5e - Postulate Architecture and Estimate Feasibility

In this step, the maximum dimensionality architecture is projected onto a potential functional architecture, which is then estimated for cost and feasibility. Several such architectures may be postulated, and the minimum cost solution identified.

The allocation of processing subfunctions to processors may require further decomposition, and may be accomplished statically or dynamically. Each configuration is defined in terms of processors and interconnects, and the resources of the processors and interconnects are identified. The mapping of the processing onto the new configuration is checked for consistency with the capacities of the processors and the interconnects, and the cost and feasibility of such architectures is then estimated from the architectures and the DP hardware data base.

The cost and schedule of developing the data base software and hardware is then defined in terms of sequences of steps, each with cost and schedules, for such development. Estimating rules used to approximate the cost should be made specific, with the references to the origin of such rules.

To support the above activities, the following capabilities are needed:

o Ability to specify a data processor/communications configuration in both textual and graphical forms.

o Ability to define additional decomposition of the allocated requirements to the data processor, and to identify potential allocation of these subfunctions to processors. The ability to specify whether this allocation is static or dynamic, contingent on DP resource management policies.

o The ability to estimate DP and communication sizes in terms of instruction rates and communication rates. These should be functions of specific configurations of the data processor and scenario.

o The ability to associate with processors in a specific configuration, and with communication lines in a specific configuration, particular processor and communication mechanisms which have specific costs and schedule guidelines. Thus, processors are assigned to specific existing hardware. These hardware elements have associated costs and schedules for development. The cost and schedule of the hardware development can thus be derived

o Ability to specify software costs and schedules. This again can be done in terms of development activities or development, integration, test tools, and testing.

Step 5f - Identify Critical DP/C Issues

In this step, the critical data processing communication resources are identified. These may be in terms of DP size, weight, power, scheules, dollars, instruction rates, and communication rates. This is primarily an analysis step, and no requirements on tools are currently envisioned.

Step 5g - DP/C Optimization

In this step, alternate data processing/ communication configurations are compared for a minimum cost/feasible solution. This involves top level trade-offs between communication costs and DP costs to support sophisticated communication protocols in order to achieve specified reliability and response times. The only capability to support is that those of providing a data base of alternate configurations and costs for comparison purposes.

4.2.6 Phase 6 -- Identify Critical Issues and Resources

In this hase, the results of Step 5 for each of the subsystems are combined to identify the system level critical issues and resources. This may require additional activations of Step 5 for different design points for different allocations of system performance requirements. Thus, the capability is provided of associating subsystem critical issues with allocated system performance requirements, scenarios, and allocated functions.

4.2.7 Phase 7 -- Add Resource Management and Fault Tolerance

Two issues are addressed in this phase: the implementation of resource allocation rules for correct system functioning in the presence of limited resources; and the identification of additional functions to support system level failure mode detection and system reconfiguration to meet reliability requirements. In both cases, additional functions and logic paths of the system logic may be identified, additional decompositions required of these functions, and additional allocation of these functions to subsystems may be required. This will necessitate the modification of the completion criteria of the system functions and the addition of input/output relationships of the functions to specify these additional system logic paths. Since these paths and functions are there specifically to address resource management and system reliability issues, they should be separately entered, identified, and bookkept.

Since there is more than one possible set of resource management rules and/or fault detection and recovery rules, these rules also must be specified in terms of specific configurations. Conceptually, these additional requirements and decompositions could be "color coded" to indicate the types of requirements: one color for the basic requirements, a second color for the resource management requirements, and a third color for the fault detection and recovery mechanisms. These resource management and fault detection recovery mechanisms then become subject to the same processes as the regular requirements in Phases 3, 4, and 5 for the identification of requirements to be allocated to subsystems, and the additional cost and schedules due to the addition of these requirements.

To support these activities, the following capabilities are needed:

o Ability to specify resource management and fault detection and recovery functions in a separable fashion.

o Ability to portray these graphically in a color coded fashion for comprehensibility.

o Ability to specify and manipulate resource management and fault detection and recovery functions as configurations which can be modified to yield new such configurations.

o Ability to parameterize such configurations as functions of input parameters, e.g., the values of the maximum amount of DP resource is a parameter whose value is specified at simulation run time.

o Ability to generate simulations from such configurations, in order to predict system performance as a function of resource values.

4.2.8 Phase 8 -- Plan Integration and Test

In this phase, the foundations for the development plans are laid, including identification of steps to develop subsystems, integrate them, develop test plans, test procedures, test tools, and test the integrated subsystems. The plans for developing the subsystems were identified in Phase 5 for each subsystem, but the costs, schedules, and detailed outputs of the integration and test-related activities must be developed as a function of the allocated subsystem configurations. The development activities can be considered as a different kind of system function, but with all of the attributes of system functions including performance indices (cost, schedule), inputs, outputs, completion criteria, decompositions, and resource requirements. Special analysis tools might be appropriate for the identification of critical paths and the simulation of the development plans to yield different kinds of resource requirements as functions of time, floor space, manpower, development machine time, etc. Further, the cost and schedule estimates of these steps may explicitly be functions of the functional and performance allocations of requirements subsystems. In addition, more than one possible integration and test approach may be feasible for a specified subsystem configuration. Mechanisms for manipulating these configurations must, therefore, be available.

To support these activities, the following capabilities are needed:

o Ability to specify development activities and their capabilities.

o Ability to identify configurations of such decompositions.

o Ability to display such configurations graphically, both on-line and hard copy.

o Ability to simulate the resource requirements of such configurations.

o Ability to identify critical paths of such development schedules.

o Ability to specify parametrically defined performance indices as a function of subsystem design parameter values. This provides the linkage between cost and performance.

Note that this requires an interface to the test planning activities.

4.2.9 Phase 9 -- Optimize Over Designs

In this Phase, alternative designs are compared for their cost/performance behavior. This is the central design management job of identifying how many decompositions and allocations to look at, pruning the design tree to search the system design space

4.2.10 Discussion

Note that this approach to system design performs a top down decomposition and allocation to components without knowledge of the issues of exceptions and system resources (i.e., Phase 1 thru 4). Drawing the system boundaries and identifying the inputs and outputs provides the motivation for decompositions of Phase 3, and the definition of the black box inputs and outputs provides the stopping point. The decomposition is then motivation by allocation questions.

The next phase is the bottoms-up response to the top down allocation. It is only after one identifies the technology for building the components that available resources can be compared to needs, and potential faults can be identified. Phases 6 and 7 then provide a synthesis of the top down and bottom up considerations. This provides a good example of how use of a formalism forces issues up to the surface (i.e., the problems of resource management and fault tolerance design cannot be done till you know both needs and capacities, but such requirements must be allocated form the system level.

The result of all of this activity is a set of functions allocated to the data processor, their inputs and outputs, their required performance (i.e., in terms of their contribution to the system performance indices), and the requirements for concurrencies and sequences of these functions. A preliminary design is also available which provides estimates of costs.

In the next section we will show how these requirements are reduced down to the finite state machine level where the techniques of SREM can be applied.

4.3. Software Requirements Decomposition and Analysis

The decomposition of the system level requirements down to the level of software requirements must first address the question: when do you stop? The approach that will be described here starts with the assumption that software requirements should be represented at the finite state machine level. To accomplish this for large projects, the finite state machine must be highly structured. Thus we will start by identifying an approach for expressing highly structured finite state machines which is based on extensions of the Graph Model of Computation: we call this the Graph Model of Performance Requirements.

4.3.1 Graph Model of Performance Requirements

The Graph Model of Performance Requirements is obtained by defining a Finite State Machine, structuring the inputs and outputs into messages with data contents which pass interfaces connected to external subsystems, structuring the STATE in terms of information kept about objects, using a version of the Graph Model of Computation to structure the specification of the transformation and state transition functions, and then adding features to specify accuracy and response time requirements. This Graph Model was developed specifically for the specification of functional and performance requirements for software in the Software Requirements Engineering Methodology (SREM) [Alford 77].

This model combines and extends the Finite State Machine model in several ways:

1. The input space X is structured into the set of messages Mi, each of which may can be passed by an input interface connected to only one external device. Each message is made up of a specific set of varibles.

2. the output space Y is structured in a similar fashion.

3. the state S is structured as the cartesian product of information associated with each object known by the data processor. There may be several classes of objects (called ENTITY_CLASSES), and each object may in a specific ENTITY_CLASS may be in exactly one of the distinct ENTITY_TYPEs which associate a unique set of data.

4. The transformation and state transition functions are expressed in term of Requirements Nets (or R_NETs) which are extensions of the Graph Model of Computation. The nomenclature of the R-Net is presented in Figure 4.11. The nodes are described as follows:

    (a) a START symbol, an an identification of the enablement criterion which is the arrival of a message or the setting of an EVENT by another R_NET.

    (b) an INPUT_INTERFACE, which inputs one of a specified number of messages from an external subsystem; and

    (c) an OUTPUT_INTERFACE, which passes a message to an external subsystem.

    (c) a SELECT node, which selects a specific member of an ENTITY_CLASS according to a selection criteria which is a function of the values of the data associated with the ENTITY.

    (d) an ALPHA, which is an elementary transformation whichs maps an input data set onto an output data set, producing values of all specified output data. An ALPHA can also be specified to CREATE or DESTROY a member of an ENTITY_CLASS, SET a member to a specific ENTITY_TYPE which associates a set of state data, INPUT and OUTPUT data, and FORM a specific message to be passed by an OUTPUT_INTERFACE which is a subsequent node on the graph.

    (e) an AND node which starts branches of processing which could be performed concurrently.

    (f) a REJOINING_AND node to indicate synchronization.

    (g) an OR node which evaluates data values specified criteria to select a specific branch of processing to be performed.

    (h) a REJOINING_OR node.

    (i) a TERMINATE node, which terminates processing on the current branch of processing. All DATA is specified as either LOCAL or GLOBAL. If GLOBAL, the data is specified to be part of the state data saved to process subsequent messages; if LOCAL, values will be discarded when the transformation function has completed for the current input message.

    (j) a SUBNET, specified by another graph.

(k) a VALIDATION_POINT, used to identify data recording points and to identify paths of processing.

(l) an EVENT, which is used to enable an R_NET after a specified delay time.

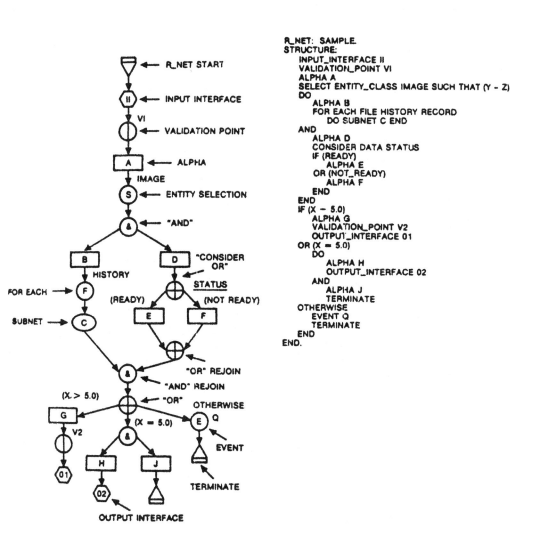

Figure 4.11: Example R_NET

The Graph of the R_NET is a restriction of the Graph Model of Computation discussed in Section 2.1, except that only well formed structures are allowed (e.g., IF case1 branch1 case2 branch2 ... caseN branchN otherwise branch(N+1) rejoin). The AND branches directly address the problems of logical complexity (i.e., for the specification of multiple state transitions and multiple output messages are to occur as a result of a specific input). The SUBNETs provide a mechanism for structuring the specification for understandability. Thus the R_NETs and their associated information represent a very highly structured finite state machine model of processing for the representation of the functional requirements of the processing. They can be used to specify the concurrency for processing a single input, but cannot specify how the processing of multiple inputs might be overlapped.

The performance requirements of accuracy and response times are expressed by linking them to the paths of processing specified by the R_NET graphs. This is done by first defining a PATH in terms of a sequence of VALIDATION_POINTs on an R_NET and its associated SUBNETs. A PATH can then be used to specify minimum and maximum response times. Accuracy requirements are specified by defining a PERFORMANCE_REQUIREMENT which CONSTRAIN one or more a PATHs by accepting the data recorded at each VALIDATION_POINT, processing it, and returning a value of PASS or FAIL. Note that the sequence of OR-NODE and SELECTIONS along a PATH are a specification of its pre-conditions; its post-conditions are the specified outputs, state updates, events set, and response time and accuracy conditions associated with the path. This thus provides the link between the graph model and the path-expression approaches to requirement specification. The graph model provides for an explicit integration of the paths in a way that the conditions can be checked for consistency and completeness of both control and data flow. The model can be used to assure that no data element is ever used before it has been given a value.

Thus the Graph Model of Performance Requirements can be used to define a highly structured finite state machine. The next question to be addressed is, how is the finite state machine level of requirements derived from the time functions expressed in the Graph Model of Decomposition, and what are the sequence of steps for doing so? This is the subject of the next section.

4.3.2 Software Requirements Engineering Methodology (SREM)

The purpose of the Software Requirements Engineering Methodology is to transform the data processing subsystem functional and performance requirements, previously expressed in system terminology and parameters, into a more detailed definition of requirements expressed in testable stimulus-response terms.   SREM is a formal, step by step process for defining data processing requirements. The basic elements of SREM are the methodology of application, its language, and the automated software tools to support the application, its language, and the automated software to support the application effort. The Requirements Statement Language (RSL) provides the user with the ability to define software requirements in a form which assures unambiguous communication of explicit, testable requirements, and combines the readability of English with the rigor of a computer-readable language. The Requirements Engineering and Validation System (REVS) provides the automated tools for translating, storing, analyzing, simulating, and documenting requirements written in RSL. Through the use of RSL and REVS, the engineer can verify the completeness and consistency of a software specification with a high degree of confidence.

The application of SREM is defined in terms of seven major phases of engineering activity as shown in Figure 4.12. The starting point is where the system definition phase has identified functions and operating rules; the interfaces between the subsystems; and the functions have been allocated to the data processor. SREM is completed when the point is reached where primarily software design/development expertise is required to continue, the interfaces have been defined at the element level, all processing steps identified with appropriate DP requirements levied, all actions of the DP in response to a stimulus determined in terms of sequences of processing steps, and the processing necessary to generate all required DP output interface messages specified. The steps required to reach completion are described in the following subsections.

Phase 1 -- Definition of Subsystem Elements

The first step in defining the subsystem elements is to assemble all available documentation about the system in order to ascertain the following type of information:

o System Definition: defines what the system does and how well.

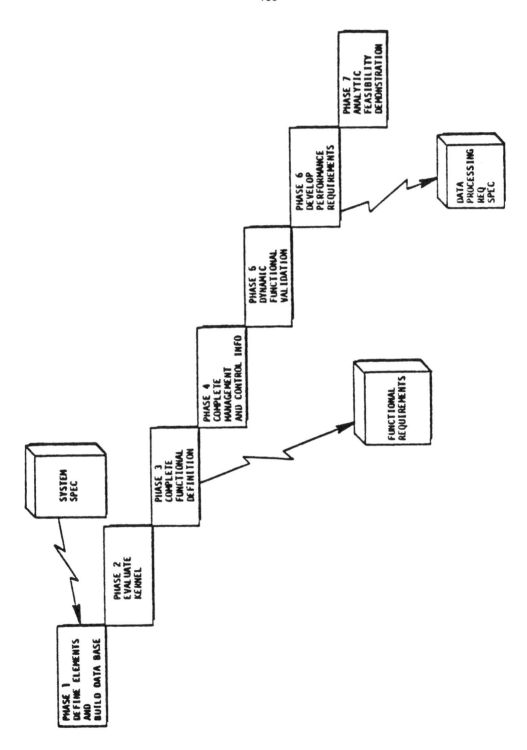

Figure 4.12: SREM Methodology Phases

o Subsystems and Interface Specifications: defines the pieces of the systems, their respective performance requirements, and how they communicate with each other.

o Operating Rules: define how the subsystems are to work together to achieve the system goals.

o Performance Requirements: allocation from system to subsystems.

o Analytical and/or function models.

All of this information, with the exception of the models is obtained from SYSREM discussed previously. The baseline methodology of SREM defined in 1975 required the identification of subsystems, interfaces, messages and their contents, and objects and their phases about which data must be kept in this phase, followed by the creation of a set of R-Nets to define the required processing. This set of steps still holds when transitioning from SSL to RSL with some amplification. The subsystems, interfaces, messages, and objects are already identified in SSL, together with the functions per object phase allocated to the Data Processor. The transition into RSL then proceeds as illustrated in Figure 4.13.

Invoking the axiom of generalized state space theory, and function F which inputs and outputs time sequences of messages can be represented as the repetition of a function which inputs a single message X_i, outputs one

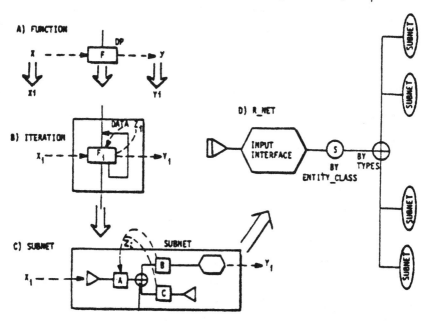

Figure 4.13: Transition from Functions to R_NETS in RSL

or more messages Y_i, and saves data Z_i for processing the next message X_i, or passes to the next state. Invoking the axiom again, we can represent the function F_i by a subnet of processing which inputs both X_i and Z_i, and then performs one of the following: produce the output message Y_i and the data Z_i; update Z_i with no message output; or transition to be next state. The set of all these subnets can then be collected into an R-Net which associates the message X_i with the ith member of the Entity Class, determines the type or phase of the object, and then applies the correct subnet of processing. Thus the system and software languages become integrated.

The capabilities provided for this and subsequent steps are the basic features that currently exist in RSL and REVS. Namely:

o The ability to define elements, attributes, relationships, and processing structures that allow a user to specify requirements traceability, subsystems, interfaces, messages and their contents, and sequences of processing steps.

o Translation of RSL into the system data base.

o Interactive generation of requirements networks.

o Static flow analysis -- detect deficiencies and inconsistencies in the flow of processing and data manipulation.

o Generalized extractor system -- subset the elements in the data base based on some condition (or combination of conditions) and display the elements of the subset with any appended information selected.

An addititonal capability, key and unique to this integrated methodology, is that where RSL and SSL address the same subjects, the languages must be fully compatible. The RSL and SSL data bases can be co-resident in a unified data base.

Phase 2 -- Evaluation of the Kernel

The first phase of SREM was concerned with representing the system in RSL and generating the associated data base. The second phase focuses on analysis of the data base, the modification and iteration of it, and in creation of documentation. The data base analysis is performed by the Requirements Analysis and Data Extraction (RADX) function of REVS. RADX provides commands that allow the performance of several functions: identification and listing of elements that do or do not meet some criterion; listing of elements in such a manner as to be suitable for inclusion in requirements documents; listing of RSL element, attribute, and relation definitions; and analysis to identify requirements that are ambiguous or inconsistent. A non-inclusive list of activities to be performed in this phase with RADX is as follows:

- o Identify free standing data and files. They should be analyzed to determine if they belong to entity group or if they are independent.
- o Identify input interfaces and their hierarchies to determine if all inputs to the computer are complete.
- o Identify output interfaces and their hierarchies to determine if all outputs from the computer are done.
- o Identify extraneous alphas (unit of processing), interfaces, subnets and validation points.

Phase 3 -- Completion of Functional Definition

Phase 3 is the final data definition and analysis. The work through Phase 2 provided definition of the higher-level elements of data hierarchies; definition of R-Nets and their enabling events; and declaration of the existence of processing steps (ALPHAs) and their place in R-Nets. This information has been entered into the data base and subjected to various forms of automated analysis and review. It now remains to complete the definition of these elements to provide a basis for construction of an executable simulation. Each ALPHA must be defined in terms of its data transactions, and definition of data known to the ALPHA must be completed. In general, the data which can be described at this stage are either those used by multiple R-Nets or those data which make messages. The need for additional data internal to the R-Nets will be discovered in the development of executable descriptions. At that time the need for definition of lower levels of the existing data hierarchies may be apparent.

Phase 4 -- Complete Management and Control Information

Phase 4 represents the inclusion in the data base of all remaining information related to management visibility. Traceability is the feature of the specification supporting this management function.

The originating_requirements for a software specification are most commonly contained in higher-level specifications. In general (depending on management decision) each identifiable software requirement in each higher-level specification will be identified as an originating requirement in the data base. The description attributed to an originating requirement may be a literal excerpt of the source, or may be an interpretation, against management discretion.

The process of developing the DPS requirements may expose system issues which cannot be resolved immediately in a formal manner, but which may have significant impact on the direction of further work. Each such issue is recorded in the data base as a decision which is traced from the originating_requirement(s) either directly or through other decisions. Each decision includes a statement of the problem.

A synonym may be declared and equated to any other element for clarity and convenience. There is an attribute ENTERED_BY which permits the author of information to record his name thus providing a log of changes.

The completion criteria for Phase 4 is as follows:

o All originating_requirements are represented in RSL.

o All originating_requirements are traced to RSL elements which satisfy them (RADX analysis).

o This traceability is printed by RADX and reviewed and baselined by a configuration control board.

Phase 5 -- Dynamic Functional Validation

At this point, the functional requirements for the processing are complete. The next step is Phase 5, which validates the dynamic properties of these functional requirements via simulation.

The purpose of the dynamic validation is to verify the completeness of the functional requirements, e.g., an object is detected, tracked, engaged, and then its data is purged from the system. For this reason, the interaction of the data processor and its environment (the system environment, the threat, and the actions of the other subsystems of the system) are modeled to simulate the sequences of messages in and out of the processor.

The first step toward developing a functional simulation is to define a BETA for each ALPHA on the R-Net structure in order of execution (first to last). This should be done for each R-Net in the same order as the R-Nets appear, e.g., initialization would probably be first.

A BETA is a PASCAL procedure which models the transformation of data and files input to an ALPHA into the data and files output from it. The purpose of a BETA is to implement the data flow required for functional simulation in order to determine the sufficiency of a functional specification. Thus, if the purpose of an ALPHA is to check message validity, the BETA is the functional simulation of how this should be accomplished.

To perform Step 5, an additional capability is required of REVS. That is the ability to operate on data base representation of the requirements and generate a discrete event simulator. These simulators are to be driven by externally generated stimuli.

Phase 6 -- Develop Performance Requirements

The top level approach to establishing the PERFORMANCE_REQUIREMENTS is shown in Figure 4.14. The system level requirements are used to derive the originating_requirements which specify performance criteria. Next, the performance originating_requirements are allocated to a particular processing path either directly or through the use of the decision path. If the mapping is one-to-one, then the performance originating_requirement can be traced directly to a performance requirement test. If the mapping is many-to-many, the DECISION must be used to allocate the higher level requirements that imply requirements to the individual performance requirements tests. Each performance_requirement test will constrain a

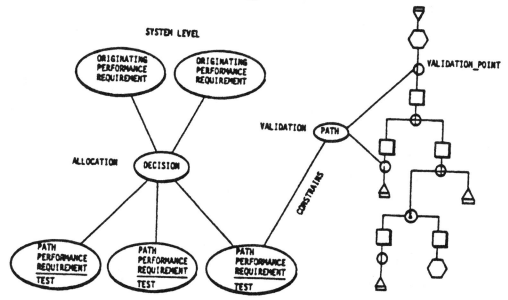

Figure 4.14: Performance Requirements Approach

validation_path or path(s). Validation_path(s) define the path of validation_points. These validation_points are inserted into the R-Net structure to record data needed to determine PASS/FAIL of the performance requirement test criteria.

There are six steps to perform Phase 6. They are discussed briefly as follows:

1. Collect Originating Performance Requirements. Documentation was initially assembled at the beginning of Phase 1, Definition of Subsystem Elements. It is collected again in this Phase because a period of time, weeks, months or a year has passed. Existing documents could have been updated and new documents created. Analysis of the originating_requirements contained in these documents will be necessary to identify the performance require- ments. Some may be stated directly, e.g., message processing timelines; others may be implicit.

2. Identify all processing paths. In this step, the originating_ requirements identified in Step 1 are mapped onto the functional requirement nets. That is, they are formulated in terms of data collected at various validation_points located on the R-Net structures. For each originating_requirement, the functional requirements defined by the R-Net structures are examined to determine those to which the originating_requirement applies.

The functional requirements defined by the R-Net structures are examined to identify the processing that the originating requirement will (or might) constrain, and to identify data available on the nets that can be used to determine whether the requirement is satisfied. An attempt is made to formulate a pass/ fail criterion for the originating_requirement in terms of data or files on the nets that can be recorded at validation_points during processing.

A validation_point is analogous to a test point in a piece of electronic hardware; it is a port through which information is collected in order to assess performance of the unit under test.

3. Assess Preliminary Traceability.   Three actions are necessary to perform preliminary traceability:

   (a) A top-down traceability starting with originating_ requirements and tracing down to the various validation_ paths. If paths cannot be found to satisfy the originating requirement, then a problem report shall be recorded in RSL through the use of DECISION element.

   (b) A bottom-up traceability starting with each validation_ path and tracing to the originating_requirements. If no originating_requirement can be found, a problem report is recorded in RSL using the DECISION element.

   (c) An evaluation and assessment of the first two approaches to determine if discrepancies exist. The iteration between top-down and bottom-up approaches will be repeated several times with eventually a traceability hierarchy taking shape.

4. Define allocation studies. To study the allocation of performance requirements to validation_paths, the types of traces that have a "Many" in them (i.e., one-to-many, many-to-one, or many-to-many) should be examined to determine if any erroneous relationships may exist. If there are some, then replace the traceability relation- ships to achieve as many correct "TRACES TO" as possible. The relationships that require studies should be noted through the use of the DECISION element.

5. Perform allocation studies. The objective of Step 5 is to derive a set of constraints for the paths that are traced from each origina- ting requirement. If these constraints are met, they must be allocated so that in concert they will ensure that the originating requirement is met. The various allocation alternatives that were considered, the analysis that was performed, and the allocation that resulted should be recorded via a DECISION element.

6. Define performance_requirements and validation_points. Performance requirements are defined by use of DESCRIPTION to give the English equivalent of the requirement that is to be tested. Validation

points are defined by identifying the data that is to be recorded by the validation point.

Phase 7 -- Analytic Feasibility Demonstration

Phase 7 of SREM provides for the demonstration of data processing subsystem analytic feasibility as a part of the overall requirements validation activity. The demonstration involves the design, implementation, integration, and test of a candidate design (including analytic algorithms) which meets all the requirements except those associated with timing. The objectives of the feasibility demonstration are to:

1. Provide a "breadboard" design under the same logical requirements as the real-time process,
2. Test this candidate design in a simulated environment,
3. Evaluate the performance of the candidate process against the specified validation criteria, and thus
4. Increase confidence in the feasibility of the requirements by illustrating a single-point (non-real-time) solution.

Results of formal testing of the candidate design against a predetermined set of test scenarios can be evaluated along with any applicable unit tests that were conducted for individual algorithm validation.

An extremely important goal satisfied by the development of a feasibility demonstration is the establishment that the software requirements are actually testable. Since the candidate design applies the performance requirement test criteria in the same manner as the real-time process, the performance evaluation associated with the candidate design will necessarily isolate any requirements which cannot be tested. If a requirement is found to be untestable or unverifiable through the testing of the candidate process, that particular requirement will be changed to a testable criterion.

Discussion

The result of all of these activities is a set of required paths of processing with response time and accuracy constraints, and required data flow. The potential concurrency is specified at the system requirements level. This then provides the starting point for the distributed design activities discussed later in this Section.

4.4. Overview of the Problems of Distributed Design

The decision to develop a distributed data processor (DDP) to solve a data processing problem is made with the expectation of a specific set of benefits: performance, cost effectiveness, extensibility or growth, survivability, robustness, and reduced communication costs. However, the designer of a distributed system should remember the famous maxim TANSTAFL (THERE AIN"T NO SUCH THING AS A FREE LUNCH). These benefits are not achieved without the the activity of design becoming substantially more complex. This shows up in two different ways: new problems arise for which new solution approaches must be derived; and previous solutions to old problems must be re-addressed to take new properties and implications into account.

In this section, we will review the set of decisions necessary to translate requirements into a design for non-distributed software. The sequence in which these decisions are made, and the techniques for representing the decisions are methodology specific; however, the overall set of decisions to be made appears to be methodology independent. The manner in which the criteria for these decisions is affected by a distributed design will be discussed, and the additional decisions necessary to accomplish the distribution will be identified. The new problems encountered, for which new technology is needed, will be identified, and thus provide a context for the methodology overview presented in Section 4.5.

4.4.1 A Taxonomy of Software Design Decisions

One of the difficult problems in structuring the software development activity is the separation of "requirements decisions" from "design decisions." Such a separation is necessary in order to structure the requirements/design activity for management reasons (i.e., first specify what is desired, then identify a design which satisfies it). Recently, there has been some concern that there is an inevitable intertwining of requirements and design, so that such separation is not even feasible (e.g., see for example [Balzer 83]). The taxonomy of software decisions which appears below provides one possible answer to such concerns.

Assume that the processing requirements have been defined to the level of a structured finite state machine represented by SREM (i.e., the inputs, outputs, state data, conditions for transforming input messages and current state into combinations of output messages and state updates, with performance requirements in terms of accuracies, response times, and arrival rates). This does not define a software design per se; for example, it does not do any of the following:

o identify a structure of sub-programs in a programming language,

o identify a method of mapping the required data onto the data structures provided by a programming language,

o establish timing or accuracy requirements for the sub-programs,

o establish the algorithm approach to be used to perform the required transformations.

Thus a number of design decisions are necessary to get to the point popularly attributed to a Preliminary Design (e.g., see for example [Boehm 81]).

One of the fundamental axioms of systems analysis is that any sub-system of a system can be considered as a system, and hence the procedures necessary to design a system can be used to design a subsystem. If this axiom is invoked, then the Systems Requirements Engineering Methodology leads to the identification of the decisions necessary to arrive at a software design. The following taxonomy of decisions results from such an analysis: selection of algorithms, establishing interfaces between algorithms, serializing the concurrency available at the system level and hence establishing the sequencing of the algorithms, grouping algorithms into compilable units of code, selection of mechanisms for transferring control and data between compilable units of code, selection of exceptional conditions to be identified in the code (e.g., resource overloads and/or failures), and selection of algorithms to accomplish the detection and recovery from such exceptions. The brief description each of these sets of decisions, and a discussion of why these decisions are differentiated from those at the requirements level, which appears below is summarized from [Alford 80].

1. Algorithm Selection

The definition of a required transformation of an input and state into output and state updates establishes the requirements for an algorithm, but does not define an algorithm per se. Thus a significant set of design decisions is the selection of algorithms, i.e., sequences of computational steps, to accomplish the required processing.

To illustrate the difference, consider the following examples:

o a requirement might specify a set of data are to be arranged in increasing order; it is a design decision to select a bubble-sort algorithm to perform the sorting.

o a requirement might specify calculation of $y = \sin(x)$ while a design might select the an algorithm which implements a sixth order polynomial.

o a requirement might specify prediction of an object's impact point on the earth, while algorithm design might select the coordinate system, a 4th order Runge-Kutta integration technique, time step to be used, and use of a spherical earth gravity model. Thus not one, but many algorithms must be specified to accomplish this single transformation.

The selection of algorithms to accomplish required transformations is performed to satisfy a number of potential constraints: satisfaction of accuracy and timing requirements, use of common utilities across the design in order to reduce software development cost, re-use of previously developed software, etc. The selection of algorithms occupies the bulk of the programmers during the preliminary and detailed design phases of software development, but is by no means the only decision made to perform the design of the software.

Note that the structure of the algorithms may be constrained by the decomposition of the requirements to the finite state machine level. If the processing requirement allocated to the data processor was to fit a straight line to 1,000,000 data points, there are various finite state machines which might solve the problem. Possible designs might include the following:

a) save all the raw input data, then fit the line when the last data point was received;

b) as each data point is added, increment the sums of the cross products, and invert the matrix when the last data point is received;

c) as each data point is added, revise an estimate of the straightline parameters (and output the estimate).

Each of these algorithms solves the problem, but each saves a different amount of state data, and each will have to address the problems of editing input data in a different manner. Thus the algorithm selection is actually accomplished in two stages: decomposition of the time functions to the finite state machine level, accomplished at the software requirements level; and selection of the algorithms to accomplish the transformations of the finite state machine function, accomplished for the software design.

The algorithm selection decisions are generally not affected by the decision to implement the processing on a distributed processor, with two possible exceptions: if an algorithm cannot be performed by a single processor due to execution time or memory constraints, a new algorithm might be selected which can be distributed; and additional algorithms must be defined to perform the additional processing caused by the distribution (e.g., to perform distributed data base concurrency control, or to implement a communications protocol).

2. Establishing Interfaces between Algorithms

An integral part of the algorithm design is the definition of the exact types of the data to be input and output by the algorithms. At the requirements level one might specify that "position" is to be calculated; at the design level, to select an algorithm, a specific coordinate system must be selected, and the units of distance established (e.g., East-North-Up, Earth-Surface-Earth-Fixed in Kilometers). The coordinate system and units for the inputs and outputs must be selected at requirements time; however, the selection of the data types for the intermediate algorithms is entirely a design decision. Note that these decisions are generally not affected by a decision to implement the processing in a distributed processor.

3. Serialization of Algorithms

A fundamental limitation of the finite state machine model is that it assumes that all processing on one input is completed before processing for the next input is initiated. It is for this reason that the maximum concurrency of processing needs to be identified at the system level, so that the serialization of the concurrency is an explicit decision. Even for non-real time processing to be performed by a serial processor, the serialization decision is made to optimize the operation of the software (e.g., queue up the inputs for processing in order to reduce overhead); for real time software, processing on one input may be suspended in order to process an arriving input with a short response time.

The serialization decisions are substantially impacted by the decision to implement the processing on a distributed processor. This is in fact one of the critical decisions of distributed software design -- to find a way to allocate the processing to processors in such a way that the processors can concurrently process their inputs, and to serialize the processing at each processor such that the overall set of response time will be satisfied. Note that this decision is usually made by defining units of code which are to be scheduled by a scheduler of the operating system; these might be called programs or "tasks" or "processes" in different languages, but are designated for concurrent operation, and this activity is generally the starting point of "process design".

4. Grouping algorithms into compilable units of code

To preserve modularity of the code with respect to the algorithms, each algorithm should be implemented as a as a separately compilable unit of source code in the programming language chosen. For software for which efficiency is a desired characteristic, this may be very undesirable due to the high overhead which results. For example, for modularity and re-usability reasons, the algorithm which implements a gravity calculation can be considered as a module of code; however, if a flat earth constant gravity approximation is used, it would be very inefficient to call a subroutine in order to return a constant value of the gravitational force. To reduce this type of overhead associated with subroutine calls, one design option is to incorporate subroutines directly in-line; this usually requires hand-crafting the code to fit (e.g., changing names of variables to provide compatable interfaces and avoid naming conflicts), although newer programming language features such as the Ada Pragma should reduce the effort necessary to accomplish this.

5. Selection of control and data transfer mechanisms

As a result of algorithms being allocated to compilable units of code, the interfaces between the units of code can be deduced. The standard mechanism to pass control in a serial HOL is that of CALL-RETURN; with HOLs which allow specification of concurrency (e.g., Ada, Concurrent Pascal), more than one mechanism may be allowed (e.g. invoking parallel processes, setting priorities of a task, setting variables used by the scheduler to determine whether a task can execute, or setting a semaphore before entering a critical region). The two standard HOL mechanisms for passing data are the specification of common storage and parameters of a subprogram CALL; other mechanisms include traditional file-oriented data management provided by an operating system, user defined utilities, or the definition of software to implement abstract data types.

Note that the selection of mechanisms to pass control and data between the compilable units of code is directly equivalent to the concept of interface design in the System Requirements Methodology. The selection of the interface mechanism may have to be changed if distribution takes place (e.g., if common storage is selected as the mechanism to pass information between two subprograms, and the subprograms are allocated to different processors, there may be no common storage accessible to both processors).

6. Selection of exceptional conditions to be detected

A Failure Modes Effects Analysis for the processor which is to execute the code and the software design will yield the processor failure modes and their probabilities of occurrence. It is then a design decision to examine the reliability requirements and determine the exceptional conditions to be detected, identified, and recovery paths selected. For example, most non-real time software will rely on hardware detected parity errors to determine if the hardware is working correctly, but may keep track of memory used to detect a condition of using too much memory. Real time software may be designed to detect if response times are being satisfied so that load shedding can be implemented.

The decision to implement the processing on a distributed processor results in a new set of failure modes to be considered (e.g., communication links may drop about 1 bit per million, may allow data to be corrupted, may drop messages, or lose contact for hours at a time; processing nodes may fail or go out of service for an hour or day at a time). In short, distributed processing gives the designer new failure modes to think about.

7. Selection of failure detection/recovery algorithms

There is more than one way to detect that a failure has occurred, and more than one way to recover from it (e.g., selection of checkpoint-restart points in the code, versus using an alternate algorithm to perform a calculation when the primary algorithm fails). The reliability require-ments and estimated probabilities of failure drive the selection of these algorithms. Since there are more failure modes for a distributed system, and many times the expected reliability is higher than for a centralized system, there are more fault detection/recovery algorithms to be selected for a distributed system.

4.4.2 Objectives for Distributed Processing

A decision to use a distributed processor to perform required computa-tions is made with the expectation that specific benefits can be achieved. These desire to achieve these benefits are the forcing function results in new problems be solved and require new decisions to be made to create a distributed design. A short list of those benefits are presented below.

1. Performance -- a DDP architecture can be used to achieve capacities of instruction execution rate, memory capacity, and the achievement of response times unavailable in single processor architectures due to either cost or technological feasibility (e.g., if the state of the art will support no more than 100 Million instructions per second execution, 10 of them would provide a composite rate of 1000 million instructions per second).

2. Cost Effectiveness -- A DDP architecture can be more cost effective than a single processor architecture due to the economies of scale in DP production.

3. Availability -- a DDP architecture can be made to detect errors in its components and reconfigure to replace a faulty component, thus increasing the probability that the DDP system will be available to perform the required processing when desired. In other words, faults are handled by providing spares at the processor level rather than at the internal circuitry level of an individual processor. This is another form of cost effectiveness.

4. Reliability -- a DDP architecture can be made to continue operating as a system in spite of failures of individual components. For example, if a processor performing a specific task stops due to an error, another processor might be reconfigured to perform the task within the specified response time.

The above benefits are processing oriented. In addition, there are a set of management benefits which are expected of distributed systems:

5. Extensibility/growth -- after the system has been developed and deployed, it is anticipated that additional capacity can be added by simply "plugging in" additional processing nodes, thus providing additional capacity at minimal cost (encompasses benefits of modularity and flexibility). This requires the ability to recon-figure the software to take advantage of the hardware capabilities.

These considerations apply whether the inputs and outputs are colocated or are geographically separated. If the inputs/output architecture is in-herently geographically distributed (e.g., inputs are geographically separated from the outputs), the processing could theoretically be per-formed by a centralized processor or by a distributed processor. The benefits expected from a distributed processor include the following:

6. Survivability -- the system as a whole may be required to continue to function even though individual nodes or communications links may be eliminated; this feature usually eliminates centralized processor designs (i.e., provides a single point failure).

7. Robustness to semi-transient failures -- communications links and processors may fail, be repaired, and be integrated back into the system in a manner which preserves maximum functionality (e.g., those inputs which do not require access to other nodes are handled locally even though communication links to other notes are not available).

8. Reduced communication costs/response time -- by distributing the processing to the locations of the inputs and/or outputs, the costs of communications to achieve required response times might be reduced (e.g., if a very tight response time is required at an input point, a designing including a hierarchy of control might provide fast response time locally while using lower communication rates to a central processor). This is another version of cost

effectiveness.

4.4.3 New Problems to be Addressed to Achieve the Expected Benefits

The new problems which must be addressed fall under the following categories:

1. Performance -- to achieve increased performance, the processing and data must be distributed between the processors in a way which satisfies three criteria:

   a) no resource is overloaded (i.e. processor, memory, communications);

   b) resources are scheduled such that response times are satisfied for all allowable loads for all time; and

   c) the processing is designed such that processors can be concurrently processing.

2. Response times -- to meet response times, the scheduling of processing on all processors and the communications scheduling must be coordinated (i.e., the problem of scheduling a processor to meet response times must be re-addressed for distributed systems).

3. Shared resources -- to utilize a shared resource, a synchronization mechanism must be designed to take distribution into account. The technique most commonly used in a central processor to synchronize the use of a common resource is that of mutual exclusion, which has the effect of serializing potentially concurrent processing. This approach is sufficient for a central processor, but has the effect of reducing substantially reducing the processing capacity of a distributed system. Thus the old problem of resource control must have new distributed solutions which preserve concurrency.

4. Increased availability -- to achieve increased availablity, additional software functions to test, detect potential errors, and perform reconfiguration to provide a complete functional architecture must be defined, designed, and implemented in the distributed software. It is noted that this software must achieve the desired results in an environment of faults.

5. Survivability -- to achieve the desired increased survivability, the design phase must identify the data and processing which must be replicated in the distributed nodes, and the procedures for

detecting, reconfiguring the processing responsibilities, and recovering the processing.

6. Reliability -- to achieve the reliability to transient processing failures, techniques for identifying and recovering from these failures must be incorporated into the design and implementation methodologies. This method must take into account the response time requirements (e.g., if response times are long, there may be time for check-pointing and restarting the calculations; if response times are short, the only potential solutions may involve masking the error by performing multiple copies of the processing and passing on results by majority voting).

7. Reliability -- to achieve reliabilty to transient communications errors, techniques must be used to either mask the failure by encoding the data for detection and recovery from errors, and/or by a protocol which involves the sending processor saving the data until an acknowledgement is received.

8. Robustness -- to achieve robustness to semi-transient errors, techniques must be developed and used to detect that a node is out of communication, reconfigure the processing to provide capability until the node is restored, and then provide the necessary actions to bring the node back "up to speed" so that subsequent processing can occur with fully up to date data.

4.4.4 Discussion

The problem description provided above identifies a large number of decisions which must be made in order to define a distributed design which are not present for a single program design, and identifies other single program design decisions which must interact with the distributed design decisions. The purpose of a methodology is to identify the sequence in which these decisions are made. In the next section, an overview of a requirements driven methodology for making these decisions is presented.

4.5. Transition to Design

The key issue to be addressed in this section is how the requirements for processing can be transitioned into a design. Assume that the requirements identify processing to be performed for each input under each possible condition (i.e., any combination of values of message variables anOd memory), the maximal processing concurrency, and performance requirements on accuracy, timing, rates, and reliability. A software design will define the units of compilable code, a set of data structures and their accessibility to the units of code, and a particular method of sequencing ?pthis processing. The code will have features to detect and recover from errors of the architecture of processors on which they execute. The key questions are:

o What is the mapping from requirements to design?

o What are the properties of the requirements which must be preserved in the design?

o What is a constructive technique for deriving the design from the requirements, so that the traceability is built-in rather than being added-on after the fact?

o Is there an overall context within which the various distributed design activities can be integrated and understood?

The discussion below presents a requirements-driven approach for deriving a distributed design from requirements. This approach is called requirements driven because it provides a constructive method for transforming a set of processing requirements into a design in such a way that specified properties of transformations and data are preserved. The approach naturally provides a separation of several different concerns: the problems of meeting accuracy requirements is separated from the problems of satisfying response times, and these are separated from the concerns of satisfying reliability/availability requirements. In addition, this approach lays the foundations for formalizing the relationships between the requirements, a rapid prototype, the real time design, and the test plans.

Figure 4.15 presents an overview of the approach. The primary thrust of design is from requirements to module design to distributed design to the fault tolerant distributed design. This approach is unusual in that

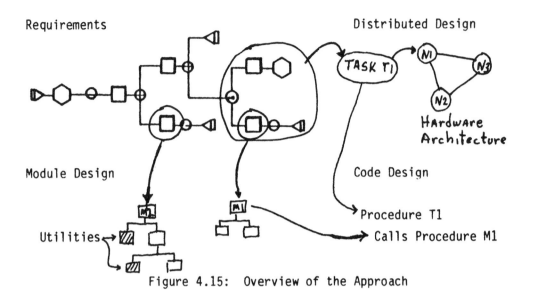

Figure 4.15:   Overview of the Approach

module design separated from the definition of tasks, data structures, and their allocation to processors.   There are two strong arguements for this:

1. The definition of the tasks can be considered as packaging, and packaging cannot be done without a good knowledge of the sizes of the things to be packaged; and

2. Many times the allocation of processing to tasks and tasks to processors is much more volatile than the design of the algorithms.

The packaging arguement arises from the fact that the final size of the processing cannot be determine until the algorithms are selected. Even though preliminary design analyses are performed during the time that the system and software requirements are being derived in order to assess feasibility, estimate costs, and identify critical issues, the final specification of the distributed design depends on the sizes and execution times of all of the algorithms which implement the specified processing. The preliminary analyses may provide information which is useful, but the final mapping of required processing onto the design can only be made when the requirements are finalized and the algorithms selected; it is only at this time that the final size and timing characteristics of the algorithms are known.   In a similar fashion, preliminary analyses can take place to determine requirements and feasibility designs for data base management software, communication protocols, operating system software, and fault detection and recovery software -- however, the final allocation of requirements must be performed in a specific sequence.

Considerations of volatility suggest that the problems of algorithm selection to satisfy accuracy requirements should be separated from their packaging for allocation to nodes of a distributed processor, satisfaction of response times, and implementation of detection of and recovery from hardware faults (e.g., using checkpoint-restart). If the computational rates change, or the software is to be ported onto a different sized processor (either larger or smaller), the packaging should change, but the algorithms may remain invariant. To take advantage of this, the mapping of processing onto modules should logically preceed the packaging of the processing for a specific distributed architecture.

In the discussion below, the steps for specifying a distributed design by this mapping process are discussed. The points at which the special problems associated with distributed processing are identified and resolved are highlighted.

4.5.1 Module Design

The portion of software design which concentrates on the definition of the algorithms to perform the required transformations we call "Module design." This provides an intermediate milestone between the requirement for a transformation and the definition of the subprograms in the programming language which implement these algorithms in code.

If one selects as a starting point the requirements derived using SREM, one is presented with the requirement for a large number of transformations (i.e., the ALPHAs which transform input message and state data into output message and updated state data), and accuracy requirement for paths of such required transformations. As previously discussed, the definition of a transformation is distinct from the definition of an algorithm: an algorithm is a sequence of steps which performs the required transformation; different algorithms perform the transformation with different degrees of accuracy, and using different amounts of memory and execution time. The module design phase of software development thus consists of the selection of algorithms to perform the required transformations with the required accuracy.

This approach to module design is derived by following the SYSREM approach discussed previously. The required transformations are allocated to a top level set of modules (i.e., logical units of code to perform the required transformation), and algorithms are designed and/or selected to perform these transformations. The act of allocation creates the need for establishing the interfaces between the modules; these interfaces are defined by definition of the data types to be input and output by the modules. When such interfaces are established, the many modules can be independently developed. Each module is then decomposed and expressed as an algorithm which uses a set of lower level modules to perform portions of the transformations. Since the failure modes are peculiar to the algorithmic approach used to perform the required transformations, a fault tolerance design can take place only after the algorithms have been selected. This is the final step in the algorith design process.

Module design thus consists of 5 kinds of activities: allocation of the processing to modules; definition of the data typing of the inputs and outputs; definition of algorithms which perform the required processing, including the definition of lower level modules; identification of utility modules; and fault tolerance design. These are discussed below.

Allocation

A Module can be conceived as a unit of work to be performed (this follows the definition of Parnas). To achieve traceability between requirements and design, the identification of modules can be achieved by allocation of ALPHA or SUBNET to Module. The allocation can be motivated by any number of considerations: reusability of previous design, identification of common modules, simplicity of traceability, etc.

Interface Design

The allocation of transformations to modules generates the need for an interface design between the modules. For module design, this takes the form of defining the variables to be passed between the modules. During requirements time, the content of the data passed between transformations is defined; a separate design decision must be made to define the representation of this data for the algorithm. For example, at requirements time one might define a required data element COLOR to contain the value of RED,GREEN, or BLUE; a data design might choose to represent the data item COLOR as an integer with range [1..3] to represent the three colors. For more complex examples, it is a design decision to select the coordinate system for a collection of variables to be passed between modules.

Note that the requirement for defining the data representation does not occur before an allocation forces the data into visibility; and that this interface design must be done in order for the modules to be developed separately.

Algorithm Design and Selection

When the transformation and interfaces are defined, and objectives in terms of execution time, memory, and accuracy, the algorithm can be designed. The design process is described as "design and selection" to emphasize that some algorithms are designed from scratch, while others are selected from known "algorithm families." If accuracy or resource utilization are not critical issues, then the first algorithm which solves the problem may be sufficient. If there are critical design issues, then the techniques discussed by Parnas and others may be necessary to achieve the desired performance within the constraints of the project. If an applicable algorithm data base is available which relates to the transformation, the objective of the algorithm design may be to use the lower level algorithms which already exist, in order to achieve an algorith with minimum cost.

The result of the algorithm design may be the identification of additional lower level modules (i.e. problems to be solved). This generates a hierarchy of modules, each of which may have more than one potential algorithm as a solution. The selection from of an algorithm set from these potential algorithms should be performed according to a consistent set of criteria across all modules.

Identification of Utility Modules

An explicit step must be included which cuts across the entire module design process to identify potential commonality of processing, and establish a set of utility modules (i.e., a set of modules which should be written only once and used throughout the software design). Note that this must occur at many levels of the design -- some might be identified at the requirements level (e.g., the prediction of a future state might occur under several different circumstances), while some utilities might show up only at the lower levels of design (e.g., gravity or string manipulation modules). The selection of the utility modules may then require a redesign of some algorithms to use these modules to perform the indicated transformation. Thus the benefit re-use of an algorithm may be achieved at additional design cost.

Fault Tolerance Design

When algorithms have been selected which meet the accuracy requirements within the resource constraints, a Failure Modes Effects Analysis can be performed on the selected algorithm set. The purpose of this analysis is to identify the potential failure modes of the algorithm, and potential approaches for detecting and recovering from these failures. For example, if an algorithm is developed for solving a set of non-linear equations by iteration, a poorly posed problem may have no solution, or the solution technique may not converge. The module design process completes by selecting the fault detection and recovery mechanisms for each algorithm set, and identifying potential failure exits of the modules.

Discussion

The end product of the module design phase is an identification of all of the algorithms necessary to perform the required transformations. Note that this is only a fraction of the total software -- a great deal of software is necessary to support the allocation of all of this code to the nodes of a distributed processor, and to support the data base management and communication. However, it is only after this design has been performed that reliable estimates can be given for the size of the code to perform these transformations can be made.

When scenario information is combined with algorithm estimates, estimates of required aggregate execution time and memory resources can be derived. This level of information can be incorporated into a design simulator in order to predict the resource implications of different allocations onto a distributed data processor architecture.

Several objective milestones exist for planning and controlling the algorithm design:

o by Preliminary Design Review, all of the modules are identified;

o by Critical Design Review, all of the modules have a design; and

o by end of Code and Unit Test, all of the modules have been coded and unit tested up to the level of the highest module.

Integration testing of the modules, including both thread tests and object level tests can occur without detailed knowledge of the data processor architecture, or knowledge of how the software is to be allocated to the nodes of this architecture.

4.5.2 Geographical Distribution

If the geographical locations of the inputs and/or outputs of the data processor are geographically separated, a geographical distributed design problem is defined.   The solution of this problem involves 4 sets of design decisions:

1) the allocation of processing to geographic locations;

2) the allocation of data to geographic locations;

3) the selection of communication mechanisms; and

4) the design of the distributed fault tolerance mechanisms.

These design decisions are not entirely independent of one another, and are not entirely independent of the decisions necessary to design the individual geographical nodes. One way of describing this dependence is show in the distributed design approach described by Mariani and Palmer. For each level of design, a sequence DECOMPOSITION-PARTITION-ALLOCATION-SYNTHESIS is followed, with these sequences overlapping.   Figure 4.16 illustrates this concept. The design decisions made at one level provide the context for the design decisions at the lower levels, and preliminary design information which affects feasibility and cost feeds back from lower levels to higher levels.

It is not clear whether there is a universally required sequence for making these decisions -- for any given hypothesized sequence, a counter example system can be constructed for which an alternate design decision sequence would be more efficient. However, as will be demonstrated below, some sequencing of the decisions is inherent.

Allocation of Processing

The allocation of processing to geographically separate locations can be expressed in terms of partitioning and allocating the Modules (or,

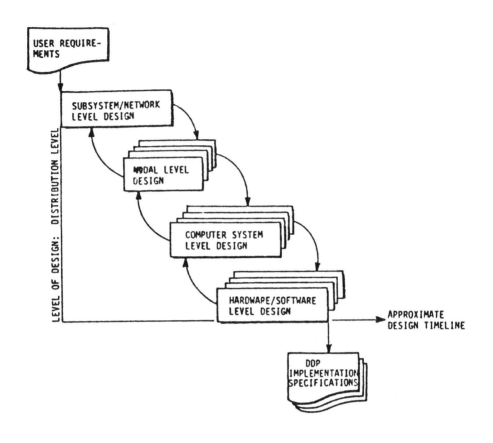

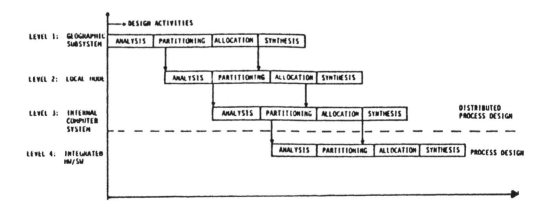

Figure 4.16: Levels of Distributed Design

alternatively, the ALPHAs and SUBNETs of the requirements) to geographic locations. Although the expression of this allocation is straightforward, the criteria for making the allocation decisions may involve several levels of tradeoff. Factors which motivate allocation include the following: tight response times, limitations on processor resources (e.g., execution rate and memory size), desire for autonomy of the distributed processors, and communication sizing implications of the data flow implied by the allocation.

Note that the allocation can be static or dynamic: if static, the allocation is defined at design time, or even at load time; if dynamic, then the designer must define the units of processing to be allocated, and the allocation rules.

Sometimes, a single partition of processing is to be allocated across several geographic locations (e.g., there may be an overall requirement to track aircraft, but the track processing is allocated over a number of geographically distinct processors rather than to a single processor). In this case, the techniques used at the system level for dealing with replicated transformations must be used: the partition of processing is defined as a time function, with concurrent inputs from several sources -- and a decomposition by object (i.e., hierarchical control) is used to define a set of concurrent functions plus a coordination/control function which implement it. These functions may in turn be allocated (or, in the case of the control function, further decomposed and allocated) to provide a fully distributed design. These decisions are sometimes dictated purely by sizing considerations -- the availability of the sizing simulators is invaluable here.

Allocation of Data

The allocation of data to the geographically separated nodes can be represented in much the same way as the allocation of the processing: the set of all state data is simply assigned to a location. The same kinds of considerations dictate the allocation of the state data to the locations as drive the allocation of processing: response time considerations will place the state data at the location with the smallest response time; memory size will serve as a constraint on such allocations; autonomy considerations will drive one towards allocation of sufficient state to conduct autonomous operation at the site where the data is used; and placement of data will affect the required communications rates.

These considerations may also provide a motivation for replicating some data in more than one location. This is generally done to implement distributed asynchronus control when response time is a critical issue, or to alleviate peak loading considerations on the communications mechanism. Note however that this type of data replication does not address the issues of graceful degradation due to communication or node failures -- these considerations are considered separately below.

Note that the allocation of both processing and data is necessary to define requirements for the communications mechanism, and even then the response time and scenario information must also be known.

Communication Mechanism Selection

As indicated previously, any time processing is allocated between units of hardware or software, requirements for an interface are defined. When processing functions are allocated between geographically separated nodes, the data flow between the functions allocated to different locations then result in requirements for flow of information between the locations. This is formalized by defining the interface function, decomposing it, and allocating these lower level functions between the two locations and a communication system. Several levels of interface design may result from this process:

1. If MODULE M1 sends data to MODULE M2, and these modules are allocated to different geographical locations, then an interface function is created between them. This interface function can be decomposed into functions to SEND (allocated to M1), RECEIVE (allocated to M2), and TRANSMIT the message. This provides the interface layer for indicating the transmission of data between modules of code. Note that a requirement for transparency (i.e., the interfaces between modules in the same location should look identical to those between modules in different locations) will force this first layer of communication to be identical for all inter-module communications. However, the decomposition of the TRANSMIT function will yield separate requirements to transmit information between local modules and modules which are geographically separated. The

collection of all TRANSMIT functions between modules in two locations becomes the requirement for the interface function between
the two locations.

2. The decomposition of the interface function to use a serial line
   generally results in the identification of pairs of merge-sort
   functions which merge potentially concurrent messages into a serial
   stream, with the requirement to provide a uniform format and add
   sufficient information to a transmitted message to route it to the
   appropriate function at the destination location. This provides
   the logical interface between processing at different locations.

3. When the merge/sort functions are allocated to the sending and
   receiving nodes, an additional interface is created between these
   two functions. This interface function may be decomposed into the
   actions for sending and receiving individual messages (e.g. by
   dividing the message into packets and sending individual packets),
   and allocated between the sending and the receiving node. This
   yields the layer of protocol which packetizes messages. The function of sending the individual packets is decomposed into a lower
   level protocol: requirements to encode and transmit packets, detect
   errors or missing packets, and re-send packets as required, are
   allocated to the sending and receiving nodes; functions which
   actually transmit the packets between the locations are allocated
   to a communications component (which may itself consist of collections of processors and communication components).

In a similar fashion, whenever state data is allocated to a location,
a requirement is generated to provide an interface between the code unit
which uses the data (i.e., creates, destroys, searches, access, and/or
updates it) and the data itself. If the module is in one location, and
the state data is in another, then requirements for an interface function
between them is generated. This interface function is decomposed and
allocated in much the same way as the module/module interface functions.
The first level interface design defines the ways in which the data will
be accessed: this corresponds to the definition of an Abstract Data Type.

A decision to keep copies of the data in multiple locations (e.g., to increase response time of the data access) is a valid second level decomposition of the interface function, and generates the need for a distributed data base management algorithm. The third level decomposition then leads to requirements being allocated to the communications system.

Fault Tolerance Design

When the processing and data have been allocated, and preliminary interface mechanisms have been established and characterized, a Failure Mode Effects Analysis can be performed. There are two major catagories of exceptions which can occur: resources of the system can be overloaded, or failures of the components can occur. The resources which can become overloaded include the instruction execution rates and memory capacities of each of the processors, and the communication rate between processors. The manner in which these are identified is left to the lower levels of design -- however, strategies for shifting processing and or data storage from heavily used to less used processors, or even instituting load shedding measures, must be addressed at this level. Similarly, there are several catagories of failures which are visible at this level: nodes can periodically fail, or fail and then return to service; communications links can lose bits due to transient noise, lose packets, lose messages, lose synch temporarily, or even go out all together for a period of time. When the frequencies and nature of these kinds of failures have been identified, strategies for adding functions to detect and recover from these failures can be identified, evaluated, and selected; the selected functions then become decomposed and allocated between the nodes and the communication hardware.

To illustrate this approach, suppose that the failure mode effects analysis identifies that communication lines are subject to failures which last for 2 hours at a time. Potential solution approaches might include the following:

o use an alternate communications path;

o deny processing of inputs which require access to remote data; or

o provide autonomous operation processing, and bring the data bases into agreement when communication is resumed.

Note that each of these approaches for recovering from a communication line failure requires additional data from the communications system (e.g., either the communication system assesses its status and notifies a node when the line status changes, or such functions are performed by the applications software), and additional processing functions. The amount of autonomous processing which can occur will depend on the manner in which the data is distributed -- fault recovery considerations might require additional data base distribution and concurrency control processing. This provides a mechanism for deriving requirements for the various layers of communication protocol to provide the interface between nodes which are subject to specific failure modes.

Discussion

The allocation of processing to the nodes of a geographically distributed data processing subsystem requires knowledge of several kinds:

1. Processing functions to be performed and required data interfaces of those functions;

2. Estimates of required rates of performing these functions;

3. Requirements on response times for the processing;

4. Estimates of resources required to perform the functions and store the data;

5. Estimates of resources limitations per node (perhaps as a function of cost);

6. Estimates of the costs and characteristics of the communications mechanisms; and

7. Objectives and the "non-functional" requirements (e.g., requirements for autonomy).

Some of this information is available from the requirements (e.g., processing functions, data, required response times, rates), some is a function of the module design (e.g, execution time estimates depend on the algorithms selected), while the remainder of the information is a function of the design of the local nodes (e.g., resource limitations due to size/ power or cost constraints) and communications mechanisms. This implies that several top level designs may be discovered to be infeasible when the details of the lower levels of design have been clarified; or alternatively, that the top level geographical design cannot be fixed until the feasibility of the lower levels of design have been established.

As with the module design process, there are a number of objective milestones which should occur in the geographical design process.

   o Since the purpose of the System Design Review is to establish over-all feasibility and cost, a preliminary geographic design is needed to establish the feasibility and cost of the data processor. This means that gross estimates of the instruction rates, memory size, communication rates, and required processor sizes, and the techniques for achieving the required non-functional requirements (e.g., availability, reliability, and autonomy). Thus a design analysis is required to estimate these factors, and potential designs which satisfy them must be identified. This will tend to set the technology and overall approach for the design even though the details will not yet be known (e.g., all response times will not yet be visible at this level).

   o During the software requirements phase, the response time requirements and data requirements become firmed up, and the feasibility analysis is updated.

   o For the Preliminary Design Review, allocation of processing to nodes is defined in terms of the requirements, and estimates of the algorithm sizes should be used to estimate the required sizing of the nodes and communication paths, and the units of code to implement the communication protocols, distributed control and data management are identified, together with budgets for execution time resources and code size.

   o For the Critical Design Review, designs of all this code are developed.

4.5.3 Local Node Design

The design of the data processor at a single geographical node may result in the definition of a data processing architecture which uses a local area network to link together a number of discrete processors. The same procedures are used to perform this design as to perform the geographically distributed design: the requirement processing and data are decomposed, allocated to the local nodes, interface designs are performed and allocated between the nodes and the communications mechanism (e.g., a bus or ring), and fault tolerance design is performed.

The same steps are performed but with a different set of issues, constraints, and tradeoffs. For example:

o communication between local nodes can be performed at a higher rate and with less noise than between two geographically separated nodes;

o aggregate memory and execution time rate requirements must be allocated to specific processors with discrete memory size and instruction rate characteristics;

o availability requirements lead to requirements for spare processors, and functions to perform testing and replace failed processors;

o reliability requirements lead to requirements for "hot spares" and multiple bus architectures, and functions to detect and replace the failed processors and communication paths;

o the problem of meeting response times must be resolved into response times for each of the processing nodes; and

o the resource management considerations may lead to duplication of code in processors, and functions to detect resource overloads and migrate work between processors to mitigate them.

The same set of milestones apply to this level of design as the previous level of design:

o A preliminary architecture of hardware and allocation of processing functions to the hardware must be available to establish feasibilty of the system design (note -- this does NOT need to be the final design), and this is updated to establish the feasibility of the data processing requirements.

o The data processor hardware architecture and allocation of processing to the architecture is established at the Preliminary Design Review. Note that the feasibility of this preliminary design cannot be verified until the process design is verified.

4.5.4 Process Design -- Logical Design

The Process Design activity provides the mapping of the required processing onto the scheduled units of code, the mapping of the required data onto the memory structure of the processing node, and defines the scheduling mechanism to serialize the concurrency such that the response times are met with adequate efficiency. The efficiency can be measured by the input rate which can be handled, or the monitary value of the computer time necessary to perform the processing.

We divide the process design into two parts: a logical design, which defines the logical units of concurrent processing and data structures; and the physical design, which maps these processing and data structures onto those provided by the programming language which will implement them. This two step approach separates the concerns of defining a design which meets the requirements (which is fundamentally HOL independent) from the concerns of using a set of utility routines to augment the HOL facilities to implement the design.

For example, a real time process design which used multiple concurrent tasks could be implemented using the facilities of Concurrent Pascal, or could be implemented as a single Pascal Program which has a scheduler as its main program which would sequence through the tasks implemented as procedures. Although the concurrent design could be implemented with either language, the facilities of Concurrent Pascal language and its run time support system would simplify the implementation; if sequential Pascal were used, additional effort would have to be devoted to defining and developing the scheduler. This approach is consistent with that advocated by the Michael Jackson Program Design Method -- a logical design is defined which uses concurrent processes in order to simplify the description of processing, and then this design is mapped onto a sequential higher order programming language (e.g., COBOL). In the remainder of this section, we will concentrate on the logical design.

The logical process design activity identifies the following:

o logical units of concurrent processing (which we call Tasks),

o the serialization rules (i.e., the rules for scheduling these Tasks and structure of iteration within the Tasks, if any) which will allow response times to be met,

o the mapping of variables which flow between modules onto abstract data types (i.e., data structures and the requirements to create, search, access, update, and destroy such data), and

o the design of the fault tolerance of the process.

Traceability to the requirements is achieved by addressing these design issues in terms of allocation, interface design, and fault tolerance design.

Allocation of Processing to Tasks

The problem of resolving concurrency arises because the system level requirements identifies required processing, its potential concurrency, and required interactions. In other words, there are a large number of processing actions which could be performed an any instant, and thus design decisions must be made to serialize this required processing. These design decisions can be expressed in terms of partitioning the required processing of the finite state machine onto a set of concurrent tasks. Each task can be viewed as a serial program which can be executed in parallel with other tasks. The representation of the tasks is straight-forward.

A more interesting question is, what criteria are used to select the task boundaries? A short answer is, the criteria of maximizing efficiency (or minimizing overhead) subject to satisfaction of response time. This corresponds to the problem of code optimization for program design, except that the process design (and demonstration of satisfaction of response times) must be assured as part of the Preliminary Design Review.

The first design decision to be made in serializing the processing is the form of the scheduler. At least three options exist:

1. Each task will run to completion without interruption by other tasks (this gives the programmer complete control of the scheduling of the tasks);

2. Any task may be preempted by a task of higher priority (this gives rise to problems of concurrent data access, deadlocks, etc.);

3. The tasks are performed concurrently by time slicing the processor execution (this is the approach taken in time share systems, and also gives rise to problems of concurrent data access, deadlocks, etc.).

If an objective of the design is to assure that response times are satisfied, then the run-to-completion approach provides the designer with more control and predictability of the response times; however, it may require the serialization decisions to be made during design time so that the satisfaction of the response times can be verified by the Preliminary Design Review.

A simple design might be to directly implement the finite state machine developed for the software requirements. This approach for serializing the potential concurrency is to require that all processing of one input message completed before the next one is accepted for processing. This design approach generally fails on two accounts:

- o it generally fails to meet response times (i.e., processing on one branch may exceed the time to detect and complete processing of a subsequent input within the specified response time); and
- o it generally fails to provide an efficient design (i.e., state data is stored into a global data base for each input message, and this may result in a high overhead for performing the software initialization of tasks and data manager calls).

At the other extreme, the approach of making each elementary transformation into a task also fails in most cases -- this results in an unacceptably high overhead for initialization of each task for each input, and generates a very difficult problem of controlling the serialization of the tasks to assure response times are met.

Since too few tasks may lead to high overhead and not enough granularity to allow response times to be met, but too many tasks lead to high overhead and too many tasks to find a schedule to meet response times, the trick is to establish a level of granularity which is just small enough to allow respose times to bet yet achieve efficiency. Note that the selection of the task boundaries requires knowledge of the size of the modules to be packaged, estimates of the overhead for initializing a task, estimates of the costs of the data management, estimates of the expected arrival rates of messages, estimates of the sizes of the data base, and the response time budgets.

Interface Design

Recall that the definition of the module interfaces establish the data structures of both state data and local data which flow between modules; and the processing requirements identify the conditions for creating, searching, accessing, updating, and destroying the state information. When the task boundaries are established, the need for an interface design is created. Two kinds of interfaces exist: task/task interfaces, and interfaces of the tasks to state data.

The task/task interface functions can be decomposed into three sets of functions:

1. The function of sending a message, allocated to the sending task (i.e., this establishes the mechanism to signal that a message is to be send, and identifies the contents of the message);

2. The function of receiving a message, allocated to the receiving task (i.e., this establishes the mechanism for signal a request for the next message from the task); and

3. The function of accepting the send and receive requests, and store the message in a data structure which can be mapped onto the memory structure of the machine (i.e., an abstract data type), which is allocated to the data management utilities (which may reside in the Application Operating System).

In the MASCOT system, such interfaces are implemented with a separate QUEUE for each task/task interface; the sending task might use a procedure PUTQUEUE, and the receiving task might use a procedure GETQUEUE. The PUTQUEUE and GETQUEUE procedures might then be entry points in the abstract data point which implement the QUEUE.

The task/state data interface design follow the same same approach. The requirement for each task to create, access, update, search, or delete data leads to the design of the data interface mechanisms; the collection of these mechanisms form the requirements for the abstract data type to hold and manipulate the state information, and these requirements are allocated to the data management utilities.

To illustrate this, consider a system which monitors the pulse rate and blood pressure of hospital patients. A Patient Admission task might create new patients. A measurement processing task might add blood pressure and pulse rate information. A display task might search the data base to identify the data for a specific patient, and then extract the information for display. A discharge task might record the data onto hard copy, and destroy the information. Each task would be allocated a specific interface routine (e.g., CREATE, SEARCH, ADD, and DESTROY), and a package of tasks and data structures would be designed to respond to these requests.

If the data access by the tasks is truly concurrent, then the servicing of one data access request by one task might conflict with that of another (e.g., a read/write conflict). This creates the need for a coordination function which receives status information and provides controls to detect and recover or avoid such conflicts. This coordination function can be allocated to the abstract data type (i.e. thereby hiding the concurrency conflict from the user), or it can be decomposed and allocated to the tasks (e.g., requirements for entering a critical segment of code or performing a rendevous before accessing data). Both kinds of designs can be derived from this approach.

Fault Tolerance Design

The Fault Tolerance design phase performs exactly the same activities as are performed for the other levels of design: classes of exceptions are identified, frequencies estimated, reliability calculated, and strategies for detection and recovery from these exceptions are selected, decomposed, allocated to elements of code, interface designed, and cost estimated.

For the Process Design, three classes of exceptions should be addressed: resource exceptions (e.g., overload of instruction execution rate, overload of memory), module exceptions (e.g., a module cannot complete its processing and satisfy its completion criterion), and hardware exceptions (e.g., memory parity error). The design decisions made here are the definition of the functions for detecting such errors (e.g., detecting exception exits from modules, detecting memory overload, or detecting parity errors) and selection of strategies for recovery (e.g., checkpoint/restart or invoking of a recovery block). The recovery strategies must match the exception detection mechanisms established at both the module and node levels of fault tolerance design.

Discussion

The same set of milestones are applicable to the process design as to the previous levels of distributed design.

o By software requirements review, a very preliminary design should establish the estimates of feasibility of meeting the response times in each processor.

o By the Preliminary Design Review, the set of Tasks are defined in terms of the required processing, the data base structures and processing is identified, and the satisfaction of the response times is demonstrated by simulation or analysis.

o By Critical Design Review, designs have been completed for each of the task control routines, data base utilities, and scheduler.

4.5.5 Process Design -- Physical Design

The final step in the design process is to map the logical design onto the physical design, i.e., mapping the logical units of code and data and serializing decisions onto the units of code and data provided by the implementation language. This set of design decisions establishes the final structure of the code in the selected higher order language, and can be distinguished from the logical design in the following ways:

1. The logical design identifies the logical units of concurrency and modules, while the physical design selects the independently compilable units of code in the programming language (e.g., determining that modules should be inserted in-line rather than invoked as procedures, or allocating two logically independent tasks plus scheduing rules to one serial program);

2. The logical design specifies the data structures input and output, while the physical design specifies the location of data structures in the code (e.g., for FORTRAN, identification of COMMON data structures and contents; for Pascal, the identification of the Procedure containing the variable declaration; for a procedure call, the selection of whether data is input/output by a parameter in the calling sequence or by common data);

3. The logical design specifies a particular scheduling mechanism, while the physical design would provide the tables of values for the table driven scheduler;

4. The logical design would specify the size of the data in common memory, while the physical design would specify all of the data declaration tables for the order and placement in memory or overlays; and

5. The logical design specifies the hierarchy of exception exits and exception handling, while the physical design provides the definition of the language mechanisms for their implementation (e.g., additional variables in the calling sequences to communicate the detection of a failure).

By its nature, the exact methodology is highly language dependent (e.g., the criteria for mapping the tasks onto concurrent task structures is not applicable to serial languages like FORTRAN). Since all modern high order programming languages have constructs for subprograms and common data, much of the physical design methodology is the same for all languages; the differences arise from the methods to take advantage of specific features of the language.

This approach provides a separation of concerns between the logical design necessary to solve the problem from the specific subprogram constructs provided by the implementation language, and thus leads to several advantages:

1. The logical design is language independent, so it can be implemented in any Higher Order programming Language, thereby providing re-usability of the design; and,

2. the logical design can use the principles of abstraction for creating many layers of design, while the physical design can implement the design in many fewer layers, thus increasing efficiency without loss of understanding.

The traditional approach for definition of this level of information is to define it very early in the preliminary design (i.e., to establish the physical units of code and their interfaces). As can been seen from the above, this can be considered as the last step of the detailed design, and thus must be established for the Critical Design Review. However, where the physical code structure affects the efficiency of the critical segments of code (e.g., when the cost of a subprogram "CALL" is a large fraction of the execution time budget), a preliminary version of the design must be available for the Preliminary Design Review.

4.6. Summary

Sections 4.1 and 4.2 presented an approach for defining system level requirements in a manner which identified and preserved the concurrency inherent in the overall system. Section 4.3 provided an approach for decomposing these requirements down to the finite state machine level, so that consistency and completeness of the processing requirements could be assessed; and the object-transition properties at the system level were preserved at the state machine level by construction.

Section 4.4 provided an overview of the problems of designing a distributed system to meet a set of requirements specified in terms of a structured finite state machines. Section 4.5 has provided an overview of a requirements driven methodology to drive this level of requirements into the design of concurrent distributed software. The overall problem of mapping required processing onto a structure of subprograms in a higher order programming language is seen to take place in three phases:

o processing is mapped onto modules;

o processing is mapped onto tasks allocated to the nodes of the distributed architecture; and

o the tasks and modules are then mapped onto the units of code of the programming language.

Each of these phases follows the overall approach of decomposition, allocation, interface design, and design of the exception handling mechanisms introduced in Section 4.1 and 4.2. The design phases are tied together at the major milestones of the Preliminary Design Review and Critical Design Review. The result is a method which preserves by construction the stimulus-response and data flow properties of the requirements.

This approach provides an overall context and a method for deriving the specialized problems of concurrency control, correct termination of distributed processes, communication protocols, and distributed operating system requirements and designs discussed in the other sections of the course.

Chapter 5

Formal Foundation for Specification and Verification

Over the past eight years, a significant body of theory and experience in concurrent program verification has emerged [Lamport 80b,Owicki 76,Owicki 82]. We have learned that even the simplest concurrent algorithms can have subtle timing-dependent errors, which are very hard to discover by testing. We can have little confidence in such an algorithm without a careful proof of its correctness.

Most computer scientists find it natural to reason about a concurrent program in terms of its behavior—the sequence of events generated by its execution. Experience has taught us that such reasoning is not reliable; we have seen too many convincing proofs of incorrect algorithms. This has led to assertional proof methods, in which one reasons about the program's state instead of its behavior. Unlike behavioral reasoning, assertional proofs can be formalized—*i.e.*, reduced to a series of precise steps that can, in principle, be machine-verified.

5.1. An Example

To illustrate and motivate assertional methods, we give an assertional correctness proof of an algorithm, due to Tajibnapis [Tajibnapis 77], that maintains message-routing tables for a network in which communication links can fail and be repaired. Although we recommend reading [Tajibnapis 77] for comparison, the presentation here is self-contained.

We will not attempt to give a very rigorous, formal correctness proof for this algorithm; the interested reader will find such a proof sketched in [Lamport 82c]. Instead,

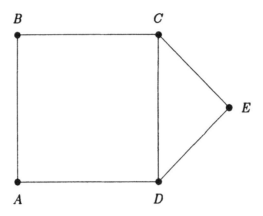

Figure 5.1: A Simple Network

we will give an informal proof which illustrates the basic ideas. It is a straightforward, though nontrivial, task to turn our informal proof into a formal one.

Informal Development of the Algorithm

We assume a network of computers communicating over two-way transmission lines, and we wish to devise a routing algorithm by which each computer can send messages to any another computer in the network, and each message travels over the smallest possible number of transmission lines. As an example, consider the network of Figure 5.1. Messages sent by computer B to computer E should go via computer C, not via A and D.

As we see, the network of computers can be represented by a graph in which each computer is a vertex and each transmission line is an edge. We must route messages along minimal-length paths, where the length of a path is the number of edges it contains.

Let $\delta(b,c)$ denote the distance between vertices b and c—i.e., the length of the shortest path joining them, or ∞ if there is no such path, with $\delta(b,b)$ defined to be 0. We say that two vertices are *neighbors* if they are joined by an edge, so the distance between them is 1. It is easy to see that if each computer x uses the following algorithm for relaying a message with destination y, then messages are always routed along a minimal length path.

if $x = y$
    then accept message
    else **if** $\delta(x, y) = \infty$
            then message undeliverable
            else send message to a neighbor p with the smallest value of $\delta(p, y)$
      fi
fi

In the network of Figure 5.1, B would send a message destined for E to C rather than to A because $\delta(C, E) = 1$ and $\delta(A, E) = 2$. The optimal routing of messages is therefore easy if each computer has the following information:

- Its distance to every other computer.

- Who its neighbors are.

- The distance from each of its neighbors to every other computer.

For now, we assume that a computer knows who its neighbors are, and consider the problem of computing the distances.

Suppose *dist* is any function satisfying the following relation for all vertices b and c, where $1 + \infty$ is defined to equal ∞:

$$dist(b, c) = \textbf{if } b = c$$
$$\textbf{then } 0$$
$$\textbf{else } 1 + \min\{dist(p, c) : p \text{ a neighbor of } b\}$$

It is easy to show that this implies $dist(b, c) = \delta(b, c)$ for all b and c.

This observation suggests the following iterative procedure for computing the distances, where assignment and equality of arrays is defined in the obvious way, and the **for all** statement is similar to a **for** statement, except that the different "iterations" may be performed in any order—or concurrently.

```
repeat
    olddist := dist ;
    for all computers b and c
        do if b = c
            then  dist(b, c) := 0
            else  dist(b, c) := 1 + min{olddist(p, c) : p a neighbor of b}
        fi
    od
until dist = olddist
```

Unfortunately, this program will not terminate for all initial values of *dist*. In particular, if $\delta(b, c) = \infty$ and initially $dist(b, c) < \infty$, then the value of $dist(b, c)$ will just keep increasing. To overcome this difficulty, we observe that if NN is the number of vertices in the graph, then the distance between any two points is either less than NN or else equals ∞. This means that if *dist* satisfies the following relation for all b and c:

$$dist(b, c) = \text{if } b = c$$
$$\text{then } 0$$
$$\text{else } \text{if } ndist(b, c) < NN - 1$$
$$\text{then } 1 + ndist(b, c)$$
$$\text{else } \infty$$

$$\text{where: } ndist(b, c) = \min\{dist(p, c) : p \text{ a neighbor of } b\}, \tag{5.1}$$

then $dist(b, c) = \delta(b, c)$ for all b and c.

This suggests the following algorithm for computing the distances.

```
repeat
    olddist := dist ;
    for all computers b and c
        do if b = c
            then  dist(b, c) := 0
```

$$\textbf{else} \quad ndist(b,c) := \min\{olddist(p,c) : p \text{ a neighbor of } b\}$$
$$\textbf{if } ndist(b,c) < NN - 1$$
$$\quad \textbf{then} \quad dist(b,c) := 1 + ndist(b,c)$$
$$\quad \textbf{else} \quad dist(b,c) := \infty$$
$$\textbf{fi}$$
$$\textbf{fi}$$
$$\textbf{od}$$
$$\textbf{until } dist = olddist$$

It is not hard to show that this program always terminates in at most NN iterations for any initial values of $dist$, and that it terminates with $dist(b,c) = \delta(b,c)$ for all b and c. The proof involves observing that after the kth iteration, $dist(b,c) = \delta(b,c)$ for all b and c such that $\delta(b,c) < k$.

We now transform this algorithm into a distributed one, in which each computer calculates its distance to every other computer—computer b calculating the array of values $dist(b,-)$. Each value $olddist(p,c)$ is used by every neighbor b of p in computing $dist(b,c)$. In a distributed algorithm, these neighbors need their own copies of this value. We therefore introduce a new array $dtab$ such that $dtab(b,p,c)$ represents b's copy of $olddist(p,c)$. In place of the array assignment "$olddist := dist$", we let each computer b set each neighbor p's subarray $dtab(p,b,-)$ equal to its array $dist(b,-)$. This yields the following algorithm.

$$\textbf{repeat}$$
$$\quad \textbf{for all computers } b$$
$$\quad\quad \textbf{do for all neighbors } p \text{ of } b$$
$$\quad\quad\quad \textbf{do } dtab(p,b,-) := dist(b,-) \textbf{ od}$$
$$\quad\quad \textbf{od}$$
$$\quad \textbf{for all computers } b$$
$$\quad\quad \textbf{do for all computers } c$$
$$\quad\quad\quad \textbf{do if } b = c$$
$$\quad\quad\quad\quad \textbf{then} \quad dist(b,c) := 0$$

$$\textbf{else}\quad ndist(b,c) := \min\{dtab(b,p,c) : p \text{ a neighbor of } b\}$$
$$\textbf{if } ndist(b,c) < NN - 1$$
$$\textbf{then } dist(b,c) := 1 + ndist(b,c)$$
$$\textbf{else}\quad dist(b,c) := \infty \qquad \textbf{fi}$$

$$\textbf{fi}$$

$$\textbf{od}$$

$$\textbf{od}$$

$$\textbf{until } dist(b,c) = dtab(p,b,c) \textbf{ for all } b,\, c,\, p$$

This can be regarded as a distributed algorithm, where every computer executes a separate "iteration" of each **"for all b"** statement. Moreover, computer b finishes with $dtab(b,p,-) = dist(p,-)$ for every neighbor p, so the arrays $dist$ and $dtab(b,-,-)$ contain precisely the information b needs for routing messages. Unfortunately, this is a *synchronous* algorithm—every computer must finish executing its iteration of the first **"for all b"** statement before any computer can begin its iteration of the next one, and the termination condition is a global one that an individual computer cannot evaluate by itself. Such a synchronous algorithm is not well-suited for a network of independent computers.

In this synchronous algorithm, each computer b repeatedly cycles through the following two steps:

1. For every neighbor p: put each value $dist(b,c)$ into p's array element $dtab(p,b,c)$.

2. Recompute all values $dist(b,c)$, using $dtab(b,-,-)$

To turn it into an asynchronous algorithm, we make the following changes:

- Instead of putting the value $dist(b,c)$ directly into $dtab(p,b,c)$, b will send it to computer p, and p will put it into the $dtab$ array.

- We reverse the order of the two steps. Since b repeatedly cycles through them, we can do this by simply executing the (original) first step before beginning the cycle. We then have a program in which b first sends all its values $dist(b,-)$ to each of its neighbors, then cycles through the two steps:

1. Compute the elements of $dist(b,-)$.

2. Send their values to its neighbors.

- If the value of $dist(b, c)$ is not changed by the first step of this cycle, then there is no reason to send it in the second step. Thus, b will send its neighbors only the values of $dist(b, -)$ that have changed.

- Computer b will execute this cycle whenever it receives a new value for $dtab(b, p, c)$. Since a change in the distance from p to c cannot affect the distance from b to any computer other than c, b need recompute only the single element $dist(b, c)$ when it receives this new value.

We then obtain an asynchronous algorithm in which each computer b does the following.

initialization: Send all the values $dist(b, -)$ to each of its neighbors.

loop: Whenever a new value of $dist(p, c)$ arrives from computer p:

    1. Set $dtab(b, p, c)$ to this value.

    2. Recompute $dist(b, c)$.

    3. If the value of $dist(b, c)$ has changed, then send the new value to every neighbor q.

This algorithm works even when the sending and receipt of values is completely asynchronous. However, it is not our final algorithm. Although we have assumed a fixed network topology, our real goal is an algorithm for a network in which communication lines fail and are repaired. The distance between two computers is the shortest path along *working* communication lines, which changes when the set of working lines changes. We want an algorithm that recomputes these distances when they change.

Computing the distances requires that computers be able to determine who their current neighbors are. We assume that a computer is notified when any of its communication lines fails or is repaired. How this is done will not concern us. We require only that the following conditions be satisfied:

1. Notifications of failures and repairs of any single communication line are received in the same order that the failures and repairs occur.

2. Notification of a failure is received after the receipt of any message sent over the line before it failed.

3. Notification of a repair is received before the receipt of any message sent over the line after it was repaired.

The failure of a line may result in the loss of messages that were in transit at the time of the failure, and of messages sent after the failure. Requirement 2 applies only to those messages that are not lost. A failure may cause the complete loss of a message, but we assume that it cannot garble a message. Any message that is delivered must be the same message that was sent.

We can modify our algorithm to handle failures and repairs by adding a new array $nbrs(b, -)$ to computer b, where $nbrs(b, c) = true$ if and only if b thinks that c is a neighbor. The value of $nbrs(b, p)$ can be set by b when it receives a failure or repair notification for the line joining it with p. Computer b handles the receipt of a new value of $dist(p, c)$ just as before, except using $nbrs(b, -)$ to determine who its neighbors are when recomputing $dist(b, c)$.

When b is notified that the communication line joining it with p has failed, it must set $nbrs(b, p)$ to $false$. Since the shortest path to any other node might have gone through p, computer b must recompute its entire array $dist(b, -)$, and send its neighbors any values that change.

Other than setting $nbrs(b, p)$ to $true$, it is less obvious what b should do when it learns that the line joining it with p has been repaired. When the line is repaired, both b and p have no idea what values are in the other's $dist$ array. More precisely, the entries in b's subarray $dtab(b, p, -)$ need not equal the corresponding entries in p's array $dist(p, -)$, and $vice-versa$. Therefore, the first thing that b and p should do when they learn that the line has been repaired is to send each other the values of their $dist$ array elements.

Since b does not know at this time what the entries in $dtab(b, p, -)$ should be, it should not use any of those entries. Recalling how $dtab$ is used, both for computing $dist(b, -)$ and routing messages, we see that an entry whose value is ∞ is essentially ignored. Therefore, when b is first notified of the line's repair, all the elements of $dtab(b, p, -)$ should be set to ∞, with one exception: b knows that the distance from p to itself is zero, so $dtab(b, p, p)$ should equal 0 and $dist(b, p)$ should equal 1. Putting this all together, we see that b should perform the following actions upon being notified that the line joining it with p has been repaired:

- Send all its values $dist(b, -)$ to p, except for $dist(b, b)$, which p knows to be zero.

- Set $nbrs(b, p)$ to *true*.

- Set all elements of $dtab(b, p, -)$ to ∞ except for $dtab(b, p, p)$, which is set to 0.

- Set $dist(b, p)$ to 1.

There is one last trick that we will use. Instead of setting the elements of $dtab(b, p, -)$ to ∞ when the line joining b and p is repaired, let them all, including $dtab(b, p, p)$, be set to ∞ when the line fails. When the line is repaired, $dtab(b, p, p)$ is set to 0 and the other elements are left unchanged. This means that $nbrs(b, p)$ equals *true* when $dtab(b, p, p) = 0$, and it equals *false* when $dtab(b, p, p) = \infty$. Hence, the array $nbrs$ is superfluous and can be eliminated. Moreover, since all the entries of $dtab(b, p, -)$ equal ∞ when p is not a neighbor of b, it is easy to see that the minimum of $\{dtab(b, p, c) : p$ a neighbor of $b\}$ is the same as the minimum of the entire $dtab(b, -, c)$ subarray, which simplifies the computation of $dist(b, c)$.

Finally, we eliminate the need for a special initialization step by assuming that initially all communication lines have failed and all entries of $dist$ and $dtab$ are ∞, except that $dist(b, b) = 0$ for all b. When the system is started, it must generate the appropriate repair notifications for the working communication lines.

Combining all these remarks, we obtain the following algorithm, where "recomputing" $dist(b, c)$ means setting it so it satisfies

$$
\begin{aligned}
dist(b, c) \;=\; & \text{if } b = c \text{ then } 0 \\
& \text{else } \text{if } \min\{dtab(b, -, c)\} < NN - 1 \\
& \qquad \text{then } 1 + \min\{dtab(b, -, c)\} \\
& \qquad \text{else } \infty \quad ,
\end{aligned}
\tag{5.2}
$$

and a "neighbor" of b is any computer p such that $dtab(b, p, p) = 0$.

Algorithm for Computer b

When a value for $dist(p,c)$ is received from computer p

1. Set $dtab(b,p,c)$ to this value.
2. Recompute $dist(b,c)$.
3. If the value of $dist(b,c)$ was changed, then send the new value to every neighbor of b.

When notified of the failure of the line to computer p

1. Set all elements of $dtab(b,p,-)$ to ∞.
2. Recompute all elements of $dist(b,-)$.
3. Send each value that was changed to every neighbor of b.

When notified of the repair of the line to computer p

1. Set $dtab(b,p,p)$ to 0 and $dist(b,p)$ to 1.
2. Send all elements of $dist(b,-)$ to p except for $dist(b,b)$.
3. Send $dist(b,p)$ to all neighbors of b.

This completes our informal description of the algorithm. Although differing in many details, it is basically the same as the algorithm given in [Tajibnapis 77], described with about the same degree of imprecision. There are two shortcomings of the algorithm that should be noted.

- The value of NN—or at least an upper bound for its value—must be known in advance.

- A computer b does not know when the algorithm has terminated and its distance table $dist(b,-)$ is correct. Other methods, such as the one in [Francez 80] must be used to discover this.

A rigorous, formal correctness proof would require a more precise statement of the algorithm. However, this informal description will suffice for the informal proof presented here.

A Correctness Proof

We will prove the following property of the algorithm, which is essentially the same property proved in [Tajibnapis 77]:

> If communication lines stop failing and being repaired, then the computers eventually obtain and maintain the correct values of *dist* and *dtab*.

This property has the form

$$Init \quad \supset \quad \Box\,(\,\Box A \supset \Diamond\Box B\,)$$

where A is the predicate which asserts that no failures or repairs occur, and B is the predicate which asserts that the value of *dist* and *dtab* are correct. Correctness of these value means that:

- *dist* satisfies Equation (5.1) and

- **for all** b and p:

  if there is a working communication line joining b and p
  > **then** $dtab(b, p, -) = dist(p, -)$
  > **else** $dtab(b, p, -) = \infty$

To prove this property, we prove the following two properties, where the system is said to be *stable* if there are no unprocessed failure or repair notifications and no "*dist(b, c)*" messages in transit.

C1. If the system is stable, then the values of *dist* and *dtab* are correct.

C2. In the absence of failures and repairs, the system will eventually become stable.

In terms of the predicates A and B defined above, these properties can be rewritten as

$$\mathbf{C1} \quad \equiv \quad Init \quad \supset \quad \Box\,(stable \supset B)$$
$$\mathbf{C2} \quad \equiv \quad \Box B \supset \Diamond stable$$

These two properties are proved separately.

Property **C1** is a *safety* property, of the form $Init \supset P$, mentioned in Section 2.2. Such a property is proved by finding a predicate I with the following properties:

S1. $Init \quad \supset \quad I$

S2. I is invariant.

S3. $I \supset P$.

Recall the definition of invariance given in Section 2.2.

In the proof of **C1**, P is the assertion that if the system is stable then the values of *dist* and *dtab* are correct. Recalling (5.1) and (5.2) above, it is easy to see that this is equivalent to:

> $P \equiv$ **if** the system is stable
>
>   **then** P_1: *dist* and *dtab* satisfy (5.2)   **and**
>
> P_2: **for all** b and p:
>
>   **if** there is a working communication line joining b and
>   **then** $dtab(b, p, -) = dist(p, -)$
>   **else** $dtab(b, p, -) = \infty$ (5.3)

This expression for P is convenient because the algorithm always recomputes the elements of *dist* so as to keep condition P_1 true. To satisfy condition S3—the only condition that mentions P—the invariant I must imply that P_1 and P_2 are satisfied when the system is stable.

The invariant I will be a conjunction $P_1 \wedge I_2$, where P_1 is defined in Equation (5.3), and I_2 implies that P_2 holds when the system is stable. We want I_2 to assert that *dtab* will have the correct value when all outstanding "*dist*" messages and all failure and repair notification have been processed. However, I_2 must be a predicate—a function of the current state of the system—so we have to translate the assertion "will have ... when ..." into an assertion about the current state.

In order to formulate the predicate I_2, we must state more precisely our assumptions about the order in which a computer receives messages and notifications of failure and repair. For each pair of computers b and p that are joined by a communication line, we assume that there are three queues:

$OQ(p, b)$: A queue of "*dist(p, c)*" messages in p's output buffer waiting to be sent over the line.

$TQ(p, b)$: A queue of "*dist(p, c)*" messages currently being transmitted over the line.

$IQ(p, b)$: A queue of "$dist(p, c)$" messages and failure and repair notifications for the line that b has received but not yet processed.

Note that there are two sets of unidirectional queues for the bidirectional communication line joining b and p: $OQ(p, b)$, $TQ(p, b)$ and $IQ(p, b)$ for messages from p to b; and $OQ(b, p)$, $TQ(b, p)$ and $IQ(b, p)$ for messages from b to p.

When the line is working, messages move from $OQ(p, b)$ to $TQ(p, b)$ to $IQ(p, b)$. When the line fails, a failure notification is placed at the end of $IQ(p, b)$ and the messages in $TQ(p, b)$ are thrown away. Thereafter, messages from $OQ(p, b)$ are thrown away instead of being moved into $TQ(p, b)$. When the line is repaired, a repair notification is placed at the end of $IQ(p, b)$ and normal message transmission is resumed. We let $Q(p, b)$ denote the concatenation of the queues $IQ(p, b)$, $TQ(p, b)$ and $OQ(p, b)$, so $Q(p, b)$ contains the entire queue of unprocessed messages that p has sent to b, together with b's unprocessed notifications of the failure and repair of the line joining b and p.

We now derive a predicate which expresses the assertion that $dtab$ will have the correct value when all outstanding messages and notifications have been processed. We first define a predicate $\mathcal{U}(b, p)$ which states that $dtab(b, p, p)$ will have the correct value when b has finished processing all repair and failure notifications in $IQ(p, b)$.

$\mathcal{U}(b, p) \quad \equiv$
    There are no "dist(p,p)" messages in $Q(p, b)$
               and
    if the communication line joining b and p is working
        then 1. **if** there is a failure or repair notification in $IQ(p, b)$
                then A. the last such notification is a repair notification
                else B. $dtab(b, p, p) = 0$
              fi
        else 2. **if** there is a failure or repair notification in $IQ(p, b)$
                then A. the last notification in $IQ(p, b)$ is a failure notification
                else B. $dtab(b, p, p) = \infty$
              fi
    fi

We next define a predicate $\mathcal{R}(b, p, c)$, for $c \neq b, p$, which essentially states that when

b and p have finished processing their outstanding messages and notifications, then $dtab(b,p,c)$ will wind up with the correct value—*i.e.*, with the current value of $dist(p,c)$ if the communication line joining them is working, and with ∞ if it isn't. It is defined as follows:

$\mathcal{R}(b,p,c) \quad \equiv$

    if the communication line joining b and p is working.

        then 1. **if** there is no repair notification in $IQ(b,p)$

            then if there is a "$dist(p,c)$" message in $Q(p,b)$

                then A. the last such message must follow any repair

                        or failure notifications, and must contain the

                        current value of $dist(p,c)$.

              else B. $dtab(b,p,c) = dist(p,c)$

                    and

                there are no failure or repair notifications in $IQ(p,$

      fi   **fi**

      else 2. **if** there is no failure notification in $IQ(p,b)$.

            then A. $dtab(b,p,c) = \infty$.

  fi   **fi**

The crux of the proof consists of showing that $\mathcal{U}(b,p)$ and $\mathcal{R}(b,p,c)$ remain true throughout the execution of the algorithm.

We now define I_2 to be the conjunction of the predicates $\mathcal{U}(b,p)$ and $\mathcal{R}(b,p,c)$ for all b, p and c with $b \neq p$ and $c \neq b, p$. The invariant I is $P_1 \wedge I_2$, where P_1 was defined in Equation (5.3). To prove property **C1**, we must show that I satisfies conditions S1-3.

We will refer to the various conditions in the **if** ... **then** ... **else** structure of $\mathcal{U}(b,p)$ and $\mathcal{R}(b,p,c)$ by the indicated labels. For example, condition 2A of $\mathcal{R}(b,p,c)$ states that the communication line joining b and p is not working, there is no failure notification in $IQ(p,b)$, and $dtab(b,p,c) = \infty$.

Condition S1 states that I is true initially. Recall that the initial state is one in which all communication lines are failed, there are no unprocessed messages or notifications, and all values of $dist$ and $dtab$ equal ∞, except that $dist(b,b) = 0$ for all b. To prove S1, we must show that P_1, $\mathcal{U}(b,p)$ and $\mathcal{R}(b,p,c)$ are true in this state, for all b, p and c. The reader can check that the truth of the predicates follows immediately from the initial assumptions.

We next verify condition S3, which states that I implies P. By Equation (5.3), this means we must show that if I holds and the system is stable, then P_1 and P_2 hold. Since $I = P_1 \wedge I_2$, it suffices to show that if the system is stable, then the conjunction of all the $U(b,p)$ and $R(b,p,c)$ implies P_2. Recall that P_2 essentially states that the value of each $dtab(b,p,c)$ is correct – equaling $dist(p,c)$ if the communication line joining b and p is working, and ∞ if it isn't. In a stable state, condition 1B or 2B of $U(b,p)$ holds, which handles the case when $c = p$, and condition 1A or 2A of $R(b,p,c)$ holds, taking care of the case when $c \neq p$.

Finally, we must prove condition S2—the invariance of I. This involves showing that if I is true, then any action of the system leaves I true. We have already observed that all system actions leave P_1 true, so we must show that they also leave I_2 true. We do this by showing separately that each $U(b,p)$ and $R(b,p,c)$ is invariant. From its definition, we see that the only actions which affect the truth value of any part of $U(b,p)$ are the following:

- The failure or repair of the communication line joining b and p.

- Computer b processing a failure or repair notification.

There are four actions, which are easily checked as follows.

- *Repair of the line*: This makes condition 1A true.

- *Failure of the line*: This makes condition 2A true.

- *Computer b processes a repair notification*: The only case in which this could change the truth value of $U(b,p)$ is if the line is working and this is the last notification in $IQ(p,b)$. In this case, 1A must have been true before processing the notification, which ensures that 1B will be true afterwards.

- *Computer b processes a failure notification*: This cannot change the truth value of $U(b,p)$ unless the line is not working and b is processing the last notification in $IQ(p,b)$. In this case, 2A must have been true before processing the notification, and 2B must become true afterwards.

Examining the definition of $R(b,p,c)$ shows that the following are the only actions that can affect the truth of any of its parts.

- The failure or repair of the communication line joining b and p.

- Computer b processing a "$dist(p, c)$" message or a failure notification for that line.

- Computer p processing a repair notification for the line joining it with b.

There are five of these actions, which we consider separately.

- *Failure of the communication line joining b and p*: This places a failure notification at the end of $IQ(p, b)$, making condition 2 vacuously true.

- *Repair of the communication line joining b and p*: This places a repair notification at the end of $IQ(b,p)$, making condition 1 vacuously true.

- *Computer b processes a "$dist(p, c)$" message*: This can change $R(b, p, c)$ only if 1A holds initially, there are no notifications in $IQ(p, b)$, and this is the last "$dist(p, c)$" message in $Q(p, b)$. In this case, 1A implies that the message contains the current value of $dist(p, c)$, so condition 1B will hold after b processes the message.

- *Computer b processes a failure notification from $IQ(p, b)$*: This could make $R(b, p, c)$ false only by making the if expression in condition 2 true. In this case, condition 2A will hold after b processes the notification.

- *Computer p processes a repair notification from $IQ(b, p)$*: This action can make the outer if condition true in condition 1 if it processes the last repair notification in $IQ(b, p)$. However, the action causes p to send b a "dist(p,c)" message, making condition 1A true in this case.

This completes the proof of the invariance of I, which finishes the proof of property **C1**.

Property **C2** is a *liveness* property—one which asserts that some predicate S is eventually true. In our case, S is the predicate that is true when the system is stable—i.e., when there are no unprocessed notifications or "$dist(p, c)$" messages. The traditional method of proving such a property is to find a nonnegative integer-valued function V of the system state such that if S is not true, then the value of V will eventually decrease.

Since a nonnegative integral function cannot keep decreasing forever, this implies that S must eventually become true.

Instead of choosing V to have integer values, we can let its range be any set W with a well-founded total order relation $\succ$, where an order relation is well-founded if there is no infinite decreasing chain

$$w_1 \succ w_2 \succ \ldots \quad .$$

A common choice of W is the set of all n-tuples of nonnegative integers, where $\succ$ is the lexicographical ordering defined for $n = 1$ to be the usual ordering, and defined inductively for $n > 1$ by $(a_1, \ldots, a_n) \succ (b_1, \ldots, b_n)$ if and only if $a_1 \succ b_1$, or else $a_1 = b_1$ and $(a_2, \ldots, a_n) \succ (b_2, \ldots, b_n)$.

In our proof, the function V is defined to have as its value the following $NN + 1$-tuple (recall that NN is the number of computers):

$$(e, \ m(1) + d(1), \ \ldots, \ m(NN - 1) + d(NN - 1), \ m(\infty) + d(\infty)) \,,$$

where:

$\quad e \quad$ = the total number of unprocessed repair and failure notifications

$\quad m(i)$ = the number of unprocessed "$dist$" messages reporting values equal to i

$\quad d(i) \quad$ = the number of pairs (b, c) such that $dist(b, c) = i$.

To prove **C2**, we show that in the absence of failures or repairs, if the system is not stable then the $NN + 1$-tuple V must keep decreasing.

The value of V can be affected only by the failure or repair of communication lines, and the processing of "$dist$" messages and failure or repair notifications. Since we are assuming that there are no further failures or repairs, we need only consider the latter three events. We show that each of them decreases V.

Since processing a failure or repair notification decreases the first (left-most) element of V, this obviously decreases its value. We therefore have only to consider the action of a computer b processing a "$dist(p, c)$" message, which involves the following three steps.

1. Remove the message from the input queue $IQ(p, b)$.

2. Set $dtab(b, p, c)$ equal to its value, and recompute $dist(b, c)$.

3. If the value of $dist(b, c)$ has changed, then send its new value to all the neighbors.

Let i be the value that the message gives for $dist(p, c)$, let j be the original value of $dist(b, c)$ and let j' be its new value. These three actions affect the value of V in the following ways.

1. Decreases $m(i)$ by one.

2. If $j' \neq j$, then decreases $d(j)$.

3. If $j' \neq j$, then increases $d(j')$ and $m(j')$.

We consider separately the following three cases.

$j' = j$: In this case, the only effect is to decrease $m(i)$, which decreases V.

$j' > j$: In this case, the component of V that is increased—the j'-component – lies to the right of a component that is being decreased – namely, the j-component. Hence, V is decreased.

$j' < j$: In this case, processing the message decreases the value of $dist(b, c)$. This can only happen if the value i that is received is smaller than any of the other elements in $dtab(b, -, c)$, so $j' = i + 1$. Hence, it is only the $i + 1$-component that is increased while the i-component is decreased, so V is decreased.

We thus showed that as long as there are no more failures or repairs, if there is an unprocessed failure or repair notification or "$dist$" message, then processing it will decrease the $NN + 1$-tuple V. This implies that in the absence of failures and repairs, the system must eventually reach a stable state, completing the proof of property **C2**, which completes our correctness proof.

Discussion of the Proof

Our informal proof is actually a proof for a program in which the processing of a message or notification—removing it from the input queue, recomputing $dtab$ and $dist$, and putting the appropriate "$dist(b, c)$" messages on output queues—is an indivisible atomic operation. We can write such a program in a concurrent programming language and translate our proof into a formal one. Sections 5.2 and 5.4 describe the appropriate formalism for doing this.

A real implementation is not likely to use such large atomic operations; for example, it probably could send only one message with a single operation. We are therefore left with the question of whether we have proved anything about a real implementation. One thing we could do prove the correctness of our coarse-grained program—the one with large atomic operations—and then show that a real implementation is equivalent to it. This is the easiest approach, and is therefore useful in real applications where one is content with this kind of informal reasoning. However, it is not satisfactory when very rigorous reasoning is needed, since formalizing the notion of program equivalence is very difficult.

Another approach is to write a more realistic, finer-grained program, and redo our proof for this program. Refining the program essentially requires a refinement of our invariant assertions to take account of the extra control points. Such a proof is done in [Lamport 82c].

Proving the correctness of a real program in this way will give one confidence in that program, but it tells us nothing about other programs which essentially implement the same algorithm. It would be nice to prove the correctness of the algorithm itself, rather than of some particular implementation of it. Having proved the correctness of the algorithm, the correctness of a program can be shown by proving that the program correctly implements the algorithm, which should be simpler than proving that the program satisfies **C1** and **C2**. The idea behind this approach is described in Section 5.5, but there is not time in these lectures to actually handle the Tajibnapis routing-table algorithm in this way.

5.2. Proving Safety Properties

As discussed in section 2.2, a *safety property* is one that holds for an infinite sequence of states if and only if it holds for every finite prefix of it. Such a property holds for a program if it holds for every sequence of states corresponding to an execution of that program; it will therefore be true throughout execution of the program.

Intuitively, a safety property can be thought of as stating that something "bad" doesn't happen during execution. Useful safety properties include *partial correctness*, which states that the program does not produce the wrong answer,

mutual exclusion, which states that there is never more than one process executing in a critical section,

deadlock freedom, which states that the program never reaches a state from which no transition is possible,

first-come, first-served scheduling, which states that requests are never serviced in an order different from the order in which they were made.

A safety property involves assertions about the state of a program, including the *control state* (values of "program counters"), as well as the values of program variables. For example, mutual exclusion is specified in terms of the control state. Predicates will be used to describe properties of program variables, and for program fragment π, the following will be used to describe the control state:

$at(\pi) \equiv$ "control resides at an entry point of π".

$in(\pi) \equiv$ "control resides somewhere in π, including at its entry point".

$after(\pi) \equiv$ "control resides at a point immediately following π".

When reasoning about safety properties, it will be convenient to consider what the program does when started from *any* state. We therefore do not assume a preferred starting state, allowing execution to begin in any state—even one with control in the middle of the program. If, as is usually the case, we are interested in establishing that a property P holds throughout execution of a program provided it is started with control at the beginning, then we establish the safety property $Init \supset \Box P$, where *Init* asserts that control is at the program's entry point and the program variables have their initial values.

5.2.1. Atomic Actions

When considering a safety property, it is necessary to view program execution in terms of atomic actions. This is because during execution of a program there will be times when the system is in undefined or pathological states. For example, when the contents of a bit of memory is changed, it will pass through an intermediate state in which its value is neither zero nor one. Since a safety property asserts that a predicate is always true, it is unlikely to hold if such a transient intermediate state were visible. We therefore assume the existence of atomic actions, which transform the system from one state to another without passing through any visible intermediate states. An operation whose execution is atomic will be enclosed in angle brackets.

We will place no restrictions on what can appear inside angle brackets, thereby allowing a complicated statement or sequence of statements to be atomic. This allows one to write atomic operations that need not terminate, raising the question of how a nonterminating atomic action can be executed, since, being atomic, it cannot be interrupted before completion. We answer this by requiring that an atomic operation not be executed unless it will terminate. Conditionally terminating atomic operations can then be used to represent synchronization primitives. For example, a P(s) semaphore operation can be represented by[1]

P(s): $< s := s-1$; while $s < 0$ do skip od$>$.

We do not advocate allowing a programmer to put an arbitrary program inside angle brackets; that would be impossible to implement. We simply observe that being able to put any program inside angle brackets allows reasoning about the synchronization primitives provided by concurrent programming languages, since these primitives can be represented as conditionally terminating atomic operations.

5.2.2. Invariance Properties

An *invariance property* is a safety property with the following form, for some predicates *Init* and *Etern*

IP: If the program is started in any state satisfying *Init*, then every state reached during its execution satisfies *Etern*.

Using temporal logic notation (see section . 2.2), IP is expressed formally as $Init \supset \Box Etern$.

Every safety property can be formulated as a conjunction of invariance properties [Alpern 84]. In fact, many important safety properties are formulated directly as invariance properties. For example, partial correctness for a program π with respect to a result assertion R is an invariance property where *Etern* asserts that if control reaches the exit point of the program then R holds. Stated formally, *Etern*

---

[1]This representation is consistent with the safety properties of the semaphore operation, but not its liveness properties.

is $after(\pi) \supset R$. Mutual exclusion is also an invariance property—*Etern* asserts that two or more processes are not in their critical sections.

The general method for proving IP is to find a predicate I such that:

S1. $Init \supset I$.

S2. If the program is started in any state satisfying I, then every state reached during its execution satisfies I.

S3. $I \supset Etern$.

It should be obvious that S1 — S3 imply IP. Also, note that S2 is equivalent to proving the temporal logic formula $I \supset \Box\, I$ for the program.

Properties S1 and S3 are usually easy to verify, since they are static properties of the predicates. Property S2, that I is an *invariant* of the program, is the core of the proof, since it is a property of the program's behavior. It is proved by showing that each atomic action, if started in a state satisfying I, will terminate in a state with I true. By a trivial induction argument, this implies that I is invariant. The virtue of this approach is that it considers each atomic action in isolation and thereby ignores the history of the computation.

5.2.3. Invariants and Program Annotation

Use of S1 — S3 requires finding a suitable invariant I. An invariant that is sure to work can be obtained by using a technique first proposed by Floyd [Floyd 67]: a predicate P_i is associated with each control point cp_i in the program so that:

FI: For every control point cp_i in the program, if control is at cp_i and P_i is true then if executing the next atomic action leaves control at cp_j, P_j will be true.

Then, we define I to be $\bigwedge_i (control\_at(cp_i) \supset P_i)$.

Using FI requires that we identify the control points of the program and then figure out what predicate to associate with each. Identifying the control points is straightforward if we know the atomic actions comprising the program. For each atomic action a there is a control point associated with each of its entry $(at(a))$ and exit points $(after(a))$. Selecting predicates to associate with control points is more difficult. However, since these predicates capture how the program works, this task is no more difficult than developing (or understanding) the program.

Let us consider a simple example. The program of Figure 5.2 sums the elements in a 1-dimensional array $b\,[1{:}n\,]$ and stores the result in variable s. An invariant for π_{sum} obtained along the lines outlined above is shown in Figure 5.3.

$$
\begin{aligned}
\pi_{sum}{:} \quad &<i := 0>; \\
&<s := 0>; \\
&<\text{while } i \neq n \text{ do} > \\
&\qquad <i := i+1>; \\
&\qquad <s := s + b\,[i\,]> \\
&\qquad <\text{od} >
\end{aligned}
$$

Figure 5.2: Program π_{sum}.

$I_{sum}{:}\quad at(<i := 0>) \supset (n \geq 0)$

$\quad \wedge\ after(<i := 0>) \supset (n \geq 0 \wedge i=0 \wedge at(<s := 0>))$

$\quad \wedge\ at(<s := 0>) \supset (n \geq 0 \wedge i=0)$

$\quad \wedge\ after(<s := 0>) \supset (n \geq 0 \wedge i=0 \wedge s=0 \wedge at(<\text{while } i \neq n \text{ do} >))$

$\quad \wedge\ at(<\text{while } i \neq n \text{ do} >) \supset (0 \leq i \leq n \wedge s = \sum_{j=1}^{i} b\,[j])$

$\quad \wedge\ after(<\text{while } i \neq n \text{ do} >) \supset ((0 \leq i < n \wedge s = \sum_{j=1}^{i} b\,[j] \wedge at(<i := i+1>))$

$\qquad\qquad\qquad\qquad\qquad\qquad \vee (i=n \wedge s = \sum_{j=1}^{i} b\,[j] \wedge after(\pi_{sum})))$

$\quad \wedge\ at(<i := i+1>) \supset (0 \leq i \leq n \wedge s = \sum_{j=1}^{i} b\,[j])$

$\quad \wedge\ after(<i := i+1>) \supset (0 < i \leq n \wedge s = \sum_{j=1}^{i-1} b\,[j] \wedge at(<s := s + b\,[i\,]>))$

$\quad \wedge\ at(<s := s + b\,[i\,]>) \supset (0 < i \leq n \wedge s = \sum_{j=1}^{i-1} b\,[j])$

$\quad \wedge\ after(<s := s + b\,[i\,]>) \supset (0 < i \leq n \wedge s = \sum_{j=1}^{i} b\,[j] \wedge at(<\text{while } i!{=}n \text{ do} >))$

Figure 5.3: Invariant for π_{sum}.

Writing out an invariant like I_{sum} is tiresome, to say the least. A notation that permitted the predicate associated with each control point to appear at the relevant point in the program text itself would clearly be helpful here. One way to do this is to annotate the program text by placing a predicate before and after each atomic action subject to:

PA: The predicate appearing at each control point in the annotated program text is true whenever control is at that control point.

When doing this, it is usually possible to simplify the predicate that is placed in the program text, since we know something about the value of the control state at that point. Also, by convention, predicates associated with control points in an annotated program text are enclosed within "{" and "}".[2] Thus, if we have $at(a) \supset P \land after(a) \supset Q$ in the invariant for a program then according to PA the program text is annotated by placing $\{P'\}$ immediately before a and $\{Q'\}$ immediately after a, where P' is P evaluated in control state $at(a)$ and Q' is Q evaluated in control state $after(a)$. It should be obvious from this how to write down an invariant given such an annotation. An annotation for π_{sum} based on the invariant above is shown in Figure 5.4.

$$\pi_{sum}: \quad \{n \geq 0\} \ <i := 0>; \ \{n \geq 0 \land i = 0\}$$
$$<s := 0>; \ \{n \geq 0 \land i = 0 \land s = 0\}$$
$$\{0 \leq i \leq n \land s = \sum_{j=1}^{i} b[j]\} \ <\text{while } i \neq n \text{ do}> \ \{0 \leq i < n \land s = \sum_{j=1}^{i} b[j]\}$$
$$<i := i+1>; \ \{0 < i \leq n \land s = \sum_{j=1}^{i-1} b[j]\}$$
$$<s := s + b[i]> \ \{0 \leq i \leq n \land s = \sum_{j=1}^{i} b[j]\}$$
$$<\text{od}>$$
$$\{i = n \land s = \sum_{j=1}^{i} b[j]\}$$

Figure 5.4: Annotation of π_{sum}.

[2]The fact that these delimiter symbols are used to define comments in many programming languages is not accidental. A predicate satisfying PA is a comment about the values of variables at that point in the program.

5.2.4. Verification Conditions

A program annotation is merely a piece of text—a program and some predicates. We shall say that a program annotation is *consistent* if it specifies an invariant of the program. The obvious question, then, is how to determine whether a program annotation is consistent. Experience has shown that "hand simulating" execution of the program, using knowledge about how the various statements execute, is not an effective way to do this. While machines are very good at executing programs, people are not. A better approach for checking whether an annotation is consistent is to use a *programming logic*. Such a logic is a formal system that allows the effects of program statements on the program state to be inferred in a precise and mechanical way. A programming logic suitable for our purposes was first proposed by Hoare [Hoare 69].

In Hoare's logic, a program S is viewed as a relation between two predicates: a *precondition* and a *postcondition*. The relation is expressed by the triple $\{P\} \, S \, \{Q\}$, which is *valid* if whenever S is started in a state that satisfies the precondition and S terminates, the final state will satisfy the postcondition. For example, the Assignment Axiom of the logic allows an assignment statement to be understood in terms of pre- and postconditions.

Assignment Axiom: $\{P^x_{expr}\} \quad x := expr \quad \{P\}$

Other axioms and inference rules of the logic allow valid triples to be derived for **if** statements, **while** loops, etc.

Using Hoare's logic, one can derive partial correctness properties of sequential programs from the properties of their components. Since an atomic action is such a program (enclosed in angle brackets), Hoare's logic can be used to derive partial correctness properties of atomic actions. This is exactly what we need for FI, and so we can employ the following to test whether a program annotation is consistent:

CT: Let $pre(a)$ be a predicate that precedes a in the annotation and $post(a)$ be a predicate that follows a in the annotation. If for every atomic action a in the annotation, the triple $\{pre(a)\} \, a \, \{post(a)\}$ is valid then the annotation is consistent.

CT involves *every* predicate that precedes or follows an atomic action a because it is often convenient to place two predicates between a pair of atomic actions in a program annotation. (See the predicates following $<s := 0>$ in Figure 5.4.) This is done to make it obvious to a reader why a particular triple is valid—the predicate immediately preceding and the predicate immediately following the atomic action are chosen so that they define a valid triple that can be verified by inspection. Triples involving other predicates will also be valid if whenever P and Q appear adjacent (and in that order) in the annotation, $P \supset Q$. This is because $P \supset Q$ means that whenever P is true of the program state then so is Q. Therefore, given a valid triple with Q as precondition, we can infer one with P as precondition. Similarly, given a valid triple with P as postcondition, we can infer one with Q as postcondition.

It is a simple matter to prove the consistency of our annotation of π_{sum}. We show only one step, here; the other steps are equally trivial. To check the predicates associated with control points $at(<s:=0>)$ and $after(<s:=0>)$, we first use the Assignment Axiom:

$$\{n \geq 0 \wedge i=0 \wedge 0=0\} \ <s:=0> \ \{n \geq 0 \wedge i=0 \wedge s=0\}$$
$$=\{n \geq 0 \wedge i=0\} \ <s:=0> \ \{n \geq 0 \wedge i=0 \wedge s=0\}$$

and then prove that

$$(n \geq 0 \wedge i=0 \wedge s=0) \supset (0 \leq i \leq n \wedge s = \sum_{j=1}^{i} b[j])$$

5.2.5. Non-Interference

In a concurrent program, more than one control point is active at a time, because each process has its own program counter. Checking that an annotation is consistent—making sure that FI holds—therefore requires more than CT, because execution of an atomic action in one process might invalidate the predicate associated with an active control point in another process. This happens, for example, when a shared variable is read by one process and changed by another.

To determine whether an annotation of a concurrent program is consistent, we must ensure that a predicate in one process can not be invalidated by execution of an atomic action by another. One way to do this is based on a technique proposed by Owicki and Gries [Owicki 76]:

OG: (1) Show that the annotation of each process in isolation is consistent by using CT.

(2) For each atomic action a in one process and each predicate P in the annotation of another, show that the triple

$$NI(a,P):\ \ \{P \wedge pre(a)\}\ \ a\ \ \{P\}$$

is valid.

Proving that $NI(a,P)$ is valid, is really just a proof in Hoare's logic that executing a does not invalidate P.

A simple example illustrates the technique; more substantial examples appear in section 5.3. Consider a program that consists of two processes, each of which increments a shared variable z.

cobegin $\ a1: <z := z+1> \ \|\ \ a2: <z := z+2>$ **coend**

Step (1) of OG, a consistent annotation for each of the processes in isolation, is shown in Figure 5.5. Step (2) of OG requires that the following triples be proved valid:

$NI(a1,P2):\ \{P2 \wedge P1\}\ a1\ \{P2\}$
$NI(a1,R2):\ \{R2 \wedge P1\}\ a1\ \{R2\}$
$NI(a2,P1):\ \{P1 \wedge P2\}\ a2\ \{P1\}$
$NI(a2,R1):\ \{R1 \wedge P2\}\ a2\ \{R1\}$

Unfortunately, none of these is valid, so step (2) fails. We, therefore, weaken the annotation so that execution of an atomic action does not invalidate an assertion in another process. The result is shown in Figure 5.6. In this annotation, the triples for step (2) can be shown to be valid. Thus, the annotation of the concurrent program is valid.

$$
\begin{aligned}
&\textbf{cobegin} \\
&\quad \{P1:\ z=0\} \\
&\quad a1: <z := z+1> \\
&\quad \{R1:\ z=1\} \\
&\| \\
&\quad \{P2:\ z=0\} \\
&\quad a2: <z := z+2> \\
&\quad \{R2:\ z=2\} \\
&\textbf{coend}
\end{aligned}
$$

Figure 5.5: Proposed Annotation.

cobegin

 $\{P1: z = 0 \ \lor \ z = 2\}$

 $a1: <z := z + 1>$

 $\{R1: z = 1 \ \lor \ z = 3\}$

▯

 $\{P2: z = 0 \ \lor \ z = 1\}$

 $a2: <z := z + 2>$

 $\{R2: z = 2 \ \lor \ z = 3\}$

coend

Figure 5.6: Consistent Program Annotation.

5.2.6. Generalized Hoare Logic

Generalized Hoare Logic (GHL) is a formal logical system for deriving invariance properties of programs from properties of their components. It can be used to reason about programs as well as to understand techniques for proving safety properties of programs [Lamport 80b, Lamport 84c]. We will use it to formalize method OG of section 5.2.5.

The reason GHL is well suited for concurrent programs is because invariance properties of a concurrent program can be derived from the invariance properties of its components (processes). Recall from section 2.2 that the input/output behavior of a concurrent program *cannot* be derived from the input/output behavior of its components. However, since input/output behavior of a program is a safety property (partial correctness), it can be derived from invariance properties of that program. Thus, nothing is lost by reasoning about invariance.

In GHL, a program is viewed as being made up of declarations, which we ignore, and executable *program fragments*. A program fragment may itself be composed of smaller program fragments. For example, an **if-then-else** statement is a program fragment composed of three smaller fragments: the conditional test, the **then** clause and the **else** clause. The set of atomic operations that make up program fragment π is denoted $\alpha[\pi]$. If π is composed of subfragments $\pi_1, \ \ldots, \ \pi_n$, then

$$\alpha[\pi] = \alpha[\pi_1] \cup \ldots \cup \alpha[\pi_n].$$

Note that any set of atomic operations may be regarded as a fragment.

Formulas of GHL have the form

$$I \ [\pi] \ I$$

where I is a predicate and π a program fragment. This formula means that executing any atomic action in π starting in a state in which I is true leaves I true. A simple induction argument shows that if π is the entire program, then this is equivalent to S2, so $I \ [\pi] \ I$ means that I is an invariant of π, and allows us to infer $I \supset \Box \ I$. This, then, is the connection between GHL and temporal logic.

In [Lamport 80b], GHL is described for a simple programming language. An inference rule for each language construct is given, enabling invariance properties of statements to be derived from invariance properties of their components. All these inference rules are based on the following principle:

Decomposition Principle: If $\alpha[\pi] = \alpha[\pi_1] \cup \ldots \cup \alpha[\pi_n]$ then

$$\frac{I \ [\pi_1] \ I, \ \ldots, \ I \ [\pi_n] \ I}{I \ [\pi] \ I}$$

For example, the atomic operations of $S;T$ are just the atomic operations of S together with the atomic operations of T:

$$\alpha[S;T] = \alpha[S] \cup \alpha[T],$$

so the Decomposition Principle yields the following GHL inference rule for statement concatenation:

$$\frac{I \ [S] \ I, \ \ I \ [T] \ I}{I \ [S;T] \ I}$$

We shall require some inference rules from [Lamport 80b] that apply to all programming constructs. The first rule allows invariance properties of the same program fragment to be combined. In light of the meaning of $I \ [\pi] \ I$, it is obviously valid.

Conjunction Rule:

$$\frac{I_1 \ [\pi] \ I_1, \ \ldots, \ I_n \ [\pi] \ I_n}{I_1 \wedge \ldots \wedge I_n \ [\pi] \ I_1 \wedge \ldots \wedge I_n}$$

Next, we define $P \ [\pi] \ Q$ to be an abbreviation for[3]

$$in(\pi) \supset P \wedge after(\pi) \supset Q \ \ [\pi] \ \ in(\pi) \supset P \wedge after(\pi) \supset Q.$$

If π is an atomic operation, then $P \ [\pi] \ Q$ means that executing π starting in a state

---

[3]Since $I \ [\pi] \ I$ is a special case of $P \ [\pi] \ Q$, we have seemingly defined it to have two different

in which P holds produces a state in which Q is true. (Recall that an atomic operation π cannot be executed unless it will terminate.) This is because if π is atomic, then there is only one control point inside π—the one at its entry point. When π is, in addition, a complete statement, this is the same meaning as in Hoare's programming logic.

For a program fragment π that might not be atomic, $P\ [\pi]\ Q$ means that if control is anywhere inside π and P holds, then executing the next atomic operation in π will either leave control in π with P true, or leave control at an exit point of π with Q true.

The only other GHL inference rule we need follows from the observation that it is possible to execute an atomic operation π only if $in(\pi)$ is true, and that control is at an exit point of π only if $after(\pi)$ is true.

Locality Rule:

$$\frac{in(\pi) \wedge I\ [\pi]\ after(\pi) \wedge I}{I\ [\pi]\ I}$$

Note that from the definition of $P\ [\pi]\ Q$, it follows immediately that $in(\pi) \wedge I\ [\pi]\ after(\pi) \wedge I$ means π leaves $(in(\pi) \vee after(\pi)) \supset I$ invariant.

5.2.7. Partial Correctness of Concurrent Programs

The Owicki-Gries method is a way of proving partial correctness for a concurrent program π of the form

$$\pi:\ \textbf{cobegin}\ \pi_1\ \|\ \pi_2\ \|\ ...\ \|\ \pi_n\ \textbf{coend},$$

where the processes π_k communicate only by using shared memory. Recall, partial correctness of π with respect to a precondition P and a postcondition Q is proved in two steps.

(1) It is proved for each process π_k in isolation.

(2) These proofs are combined by establishing that execution of one process does not invalidate assertions in the proof of another.

Such a proof can be formulated in GHL as follows. The partial correctness proof for each process π_k in done using S1 — S3. This means an invariant I_k is constructed such that

(i) $\qquad at(\pi_k) \wedge P \supset I_k,$

(ii) $I_k \; [\pi_k] \; I_k$,

(iii) $I_k \supset (after(\pi_k) \supset Q)$.

(These are just S1 — S3 for π_k.) Recall, I_k is constructed by associating a predicate with each control point in π_k, as specified in FI. To prove that I_k is an invariant, we must prove $I_k \; [\pi_k] \; I_k$. To do this, we use the Decomposition Principle and establish $I_k \; [a] \; I_k$ for each atomic action a in $\alpha[\pi_k]$. By applying the Locality Rule, we then reduce the problem to that of proving $in(a) \wedge I_k \; [a] \; after(a) \wedge I_k$, which is equivalent to proving $at(a) \wedge I_k \; [a] \; after(a) \wedge I_k$ because a is an atomic action. This, however, is the same as showing that the triple $\{pre(a)\} \; a \; \{post(a)\}$ is valid because $at(a) \wedge I_k$ is $pre(a)$, and $after(a) \wedge I_k$ is $post(a)$.

Having constructed an invariant for each process π_k, invariant I is the predicate $I_1 \wedge \ldots \wedge I_n$. Conditions S1 — S3 for π are

(iv) $at(\pi) \wedge P \supset I$,

(v) $I \; [\pi] \; I$,

(vi) $I \supset (after(\pi) \supset Q)$.

We assume that at the entry point of π, control is at the entry points of all the π_k; and control reaches the exit of π when it is at the exits of all the π_k[4]. This means that

$$at(\pi) \quad \equiv \quad at(\pi_1) \wedge \ldots \wedge at(\pi_n)$$

$$after(\pi) \equiv after(\pi_1) \wedge \ldots \wedge after(\pi_n).$$

From these relations, and the fact that (i) and (iii) hold for all k, we obtain (iv) and (vi) directly.

To prove (v), we apply the Decomposition Principle, reducing the problem to showing

(vii) $I \; [\pi_k] \; I$

for all k. By the Conjunction Rule, (vii) is established by proving the following for all i:

(viii) $I_k \wedge I_i \; [\pi_k] \; I_k \wedge I_i$.

---

meanings. However, the following Locality Rule implies that the meanings are equivalent.

[4] We could have introduced a more complicated control structure for the cobegin—for example, having a separate entry point at the beginning of π, before control "forks" to the beginning of the processes π_i.

For $k = i$, this is just (ii). For $k \neq i$, (viii) states that execution of π_k does not invalidate assertions in the proof of π_i. To prove (viii), we can apply the Decomposition Principle and prove $I_k \wedge I_i$ [a] $I_k \wedge I_i$ for each atomic action a in $\alpha[\pi_k]$. By using the Locality Rule, it is therefore sufficient to prove

$$in(a) \wedge I_k \wedge I_i \ [a] \ after(a) \wedge I_k \wedge I_i,$$

or equivalently,

$$at(a) \wedge I_k \wedge I_i \ [a] \ after(a) \wedge I_k \wedge I_i$$

because a is an atomic action. This is exactly the non-interference condition proved in step (2) of the Owicki-Gries method.

5.3. Proof Rules for Message Passing

Distributed programs are distinguished by their use of message passing for communication and synchronization. A variety of primitives have been proposed for this purpose. In this section, we give axioms and inference rules to augment Hoare's programming logic so that partial correctness proofs can be constructed for programs that use message passing. Recall from section 5.2 that such a logic can also be used in proving any safety property.

5.3.1. Communication with Synchronous Message-Passing

Synchronous message-passing was popularized by a programming notation proposed by Hoare, called CSP [Hoare 78]. There, an *input command*

$$inp: \ A?var$$

in a process B matches an *output command*

$$out: \ B!expr$$

in a process A if the type of *expr* and *var* are the same. Input and output commands are always executed synchronously in matching pairs, so each has the potential to delay its invoker. This is called *synchronous* message-passing (in contrast to *asynchronous* message-passing) because the sender is synchronized with the receiver. Execution of a pair of input and output commands is equivalent to the assignment *var* := *expr*. Thus, a matching pair of input and output command implements a *distributed* assignment statement.

5.3.2. Partial Correctness with Synchronous Message-Passing

A partial correctness proof of a program that uses synchronous message-passing involves three steps. First an annotation for each process in isolation is constructed. Second, assumptions made in these annotations about the effects of receiving messages are validated by performing a *satisfaction proof*. This involves constructing a collection of *satisfaction formulas* and proving them valid. Finally, *non-interference* is established, to ensure that execution of each process cannot invalidate assertions that appear in the annotation of another. Note that the first and third steps correspond to steps (1) and (2) respectively of the Owicki-Gries method, as discussed in section 5.2.5. The second step, which has no analog in the Owicki-Gries method, arises from the use of message-passing.

The axiom for an input command *inp* is

Input Command Axiom: $\{P\}$ *inp*: $A?var$ $\{R\}$,

and the axiom for an output command *out* is

Output Command Axiom: $\{Q\}$ *out*: $B!expr$ $\{U\}$.

Each allows anything to appear as its postcondition; in the parlance of [Dijkstra 76], the axioms violate the Law of the Excluded Miracle. However, this is not a problem. When executed in isolation, a communications command cannot terminate, and so the soundness of the axioms follows. The satisfaction proof imposes further restrictions on the postconditions of communications commands so that soundness is preserved even when communications commands do terminate.

In order to understand the obligations for establishing satisfaction, consider a matching pair of communications commands *inp* and *out*. According to the Input Command Axiom and the Output Command Axiom, their execution will leave the system in a state in which $R \wedge U$ is true. Since execution of the matching pair is equivalent to executing $var := expr$, it suffices for execution to be started in a state that satisfies $wp(var := expr, R \wedge U)$ to ensure that the desired postcondition will result. However, the communications axioms stipulate that $P \wedge Q$ is true of the state immediately before the assignment is made. Thus, the truth of the postconditions of a matching pair of communications commands is ensured if

$$(P \wedge Q) \supset wp(var := expr, R \wedge U)$$

or equivalently, if the satisfaction formula

$Sat_{synch}(inp, out)$: $(P \wedge Q) \supset (R \wedge U)_{expr}^{var}$

is valid.

The third and final step in proving partial correctness of a program that uses synchronous message-passing is to show non-interference. To establish non-interference, it must be shown that execution of no atomic action a parallel to I invalidates I, where an atomic action a is considered *parallel to* an assertion I if a and I appear in different processes. Thus, non-interference is established by showing that

$NI(a,I)$: $\{I \wedge pre(a)\}\ a\ \{I\}$

is valid for each assertion I and all atomic actions a that are parallel to I.

Only assignment statements and input commands can invalidate an assertion in the annotation of another process. For S an assignment statement, the Assignment Axiom is used to show that $NI(S,I)$ is valid.

For S an input command, the proof that $NI(S,I)$ is valid follows trivially from the Input Command Axiom. However, satisfaction must then be established to ensure the truth of the postcondition of $NI(S,I)$. This is done by showing that for every output command out that matches input command S and that is parallel to I, the following formula is valid.

$NI\_Sat_{synch}(S, out, I)$: $(I \wedge pre(S) \wedge pre(out)) \supset I_{expr}^{var}$

NI_Sat_{synch} is obtained from Sat_{synch} by substituting $I \wedge pre(S)$ for P, $pre(out)$ for Q, I for R, and *true* for U. Proving this formula valid corresponds to showing that executing the distributed assignment implemented by communication commands S and out does not invalidate an assertion I in a third process.

Putting this all together, we arrive at the following method for proving partial correctness of a program that uses synchronous message-passing.

Synchronous Message-Passing Proof Method:

    (1) Construct a consistent annotation for each process in isolation.

    (2) For every pair of matching communications commands inp and out, prove $Sat_{synch}(inp, out)$ valid.

    (3) For every assignment S and assertion I parallel to S, prove $NI(S,I)$ valid. For every input command S_{inp} and matching output command S_{out}, and every assertion I parallel to S_{inp} and S_{out}, prove $NI\_Sat_{synch}(S_{inp}, S_{out}, I)$ valid.

5.3.3. Example Using Synchronous Message-Passing

Consider the following producer/consumer system. A producer *prod* transfers the contents of an array $A[1:N]$ to a buffer process.

$$prod:\ \textbf{var}\ A:array\ 1..N\ of\ portion;$$
$$i:integer;$$
$$i:=1;$$
$$\textbf{while}\ i\neq N+1\ \textbf{do}$$
$$buffer!A[i];$$
$$i:=i+1$$
$$\textbf{od}$$

The consumer process *cons* obtains these values from the buffer and uses them to fill its array $B[1:N]$.

$$cons:\ \textbf{var}\ B:array\ 1..N\ of\ portion;$$
$$j:integer;$$
$$j:=1;$$
$$\textbf{while}\ j\neq N+1\ \textbf{do}$$
$$buffer?B[j];$$
$$j:=j+1$$
$$\textbf{od}$$

A single-slot buffer process helps to insulate *cons* from speed variations in the execution of *prod*.

$$buffer:\ \textbf{var}\ buff:portion;$$
$$n:integer;$$
$$n:=0;$$
$$\textbf{while}\ n\neq N+1\ \textbf{do}$$
$$prod?buff;$$
$$cons!buff;$$
$$n:=n+1$$
$$\textbf{od}$$

When *prod* and *cons* have both finished executing, we desire that the following result assertion hold:

$$(\forall k:\ 1\leq k<N+1:\ A[k]=B[k])$$

Annotations for the three processes appear in Figures 5.7 through 5.9. There, auxiliary variable *ndep*, initialized to 0, records the number of elements that have been deposited in *buff*, and *nret*, initialized to 0, contains the number of elements that have been retrieved from *buff*. The values of these variables are changed by including them in matching pairs of input and output commands.

To establish satisfaction, $Sat_{synch}(r_{buffer}, s_{prod})$ and $Sat_{synch}(r_{cons}, s_{buffer})$ are constructed and shown to be valid. First, $Sat_{synch}(r_{buffer}, s_{prod})$:

$$(n = ndep = nret \land i = ndep + 1) \supset$$
$$(buff = A[ndep] \land n + 1 = ndep = nret + 1 \land i = ndep)_{A[i], ndep + 1}^{buff, ndep}$$

$$= (n = ndep = nret \land i = ndep + 1) \supset$$
$$(A[i] = A[ndep] \land n + 1 = ndep + 1 = nret + 1 \land i = ndep)$$

This is obviously valid. Next, $Sat_{synch}(r_{cons}, s_{buffer})$:

$$(j = nret + 1 \land (\forall k : 1 \leq k < j : A[k] = B[k]) \land buff = A[ndep] \land$$

$prod$: **var** A : array $1..N$ of portion;
  i : integer;
  $i := 1;$ $\{i = 1 \land ndep = 0\}$
  while $i \neq N + 1$ **do**
    $\{i = ndep + 1\}$
    s_{prod}: buffer$!(A[i], ndep + 1)$;
    $\{i = ndep\}$.
    $i := i + 1$
  od

Figure 5.7: Annotation of *prod*.

$cons$: **var** B : array $1..N$ of portion;
  j : integer;
  $j := 1;$ $\{j = 1 \land nret = 0\}$
  while $j \neq N + 1$ **do**
    $\{j = nret + 1 \land (\forall k : 1 \leq k < j : A[k] = B[k])\}$
    r_{cons}: buffer$?(B[j], nret)$;
    $\{j = nret \land (\forall k : 1 \leq k \leq j : A[k] = B[k])\}$
    $j := j + 1$
  od
  $\{j = N + 1 \land (\forall k : 1 \leq k < j : A[k] = B[k])\}$

Figure 5.8: Annotation of *cons*.

```
buffer: var buff: portion;
            n : integer;
        n := 0;   {n=0 ∧ ndep=0 ∧ nret=0}
        while n ≠ N+1 do
            {n=ndep=nret}
        r buffer: prod?(buff, ndep);
            {buff=A [ndep] ∧ n+1=ndep=nret+1}
        s buffer: cons !(buff, nret);
            {n+1=ndep=nret}
            n := n+1
        od
```

Figure 5.9: Annotation of buffer.

$$n + 1 = ndep = nret + 1) \quad \supset$$
$$(j = nret \land (\forall k : 1 \le k \le j : A[k] = B[k]) \land n + 1 = ndep = nret)_{buff, nret+1}^{B[j], nret}$$

$$= (j = nret + 1 \land (\forall k : 1 \le k < j : A[k] = B[k]) \land buff = A[ndep] \land$$
$$n + 1 = ndep = nret + 1) \quad \supset$$
$$(j = nret + 1 \land (\forall k : 1 \le k < j : A[k] = B[k]) \land A[j] = buff \land$$
$$n + 1 = ndep = nret + 1)$$

This is also valid.

Finally, we must establish non-interference. We give an informal proof, here. No variables appear in an assertion in one process and an assignment statement in another. Therefore, $NI(S,I)$ will be valid for every assignment S and parallel assertion I. Next, note that $NI\_Sat_{synch}(r_{buffer}, s_{prod}, I)$ is valid for all I in *cons* because *cons* contains no assertions involving *ndep* or *buff*. Finally, $NI\_Sat_{synch}(r_{cons}, s_{buffer}, I)$ is valid for all I in *prod* because *prod* contains no assertion mentioning *nret* or B.

5.3.4. Communication with Virtual Circuits

Most networks provide communications services that buffer messages, ensure reliable delivery, and ensure that messages are delivered in the order sent. Such a communication channel is called a *virtual circuit* [Tanenbaum 81].

It is useful to distinguish between *sent*, *delivered*, and *received* when describing the status of a message. Execution of a **send** statement causes a message to be *sent*. A message that has been sent is subsequently *delivered* to its destination, according to the following:

VC1: All messages sent are delivered.

VC2: Messages sent on a virtual circuit between a pair of processes are delivered in the order sent.

Once delivered, a message can be *received* by executing a **receive** statement.

A virtual circuit V can be viewed as a FIFO queue. The **send** statement

$$\text{send } expr \text{ on } V$$

causes the value of *expr* to be appended to the end of the queue. Note that **send** is asynchronous—unlike a synchronous output command, the sender continues while the message is being delivered and received. Also, note that we do not prohibit a process from sending a message to itself. (This would cause the process to block forever if synchronous message-passing were used.)

A **receive** statement

$$\text{receive } m \text{ from } V$$

removes the value at the head of the queue associated with V and assigns it to m.

5.3.5. Partial Correctness with Virtual Circuits

Following the approach outlined in section 5.3.2, a partial correctness proof for a program that uses asynchronous message-passing with virtual circuits will involve three steps. However, first note that when asynchronous message-passing is used, the control state of the system includes information about messages that have been sent but not received, since this can influence execution. In order to model this aspect of the state, two auxiliary variables are associated with each virtual circuit V. The *send sequence* σ_V contains the sequence of messages sent on V; the *receive sequence* ρ_V contains the sequence of messages that have been received from V. A message can be received only if it has been sent and delivered. Therefore,

Virtual Circuit Network Axiom: $(\forall V: V \text{ a virtual circuit}: \rho_V \leq \sigma_V)$,

where $s \leq t$ means that sequence s is a prefix of sequence t.

Executing

$$\text{send } expr \text{ on } V$$

is the same as executing the assignment

$$\sigma_V := \sigma_V \cup <expr>$$

where "$\sigma_V \cup <expr>$" denotes the sequence consisting of the elements of σ_V followed by value $expr$. Using wp with respect to postcondition W, we get an axiom for the **send** statement:

Virtual Circuit Send Axiom: $\{W^{\sigma_V}_{\sigma_V \cup <expr>}\}$ **send** $expr$ **on** V $\{W\}$

When execution of a **receive** terminates, depending on the particular message received, it may be possible to make some assertion about the state of the sender. An axiom that captures this is for a **receive** r is

Virtual Circuit Receive Axiom: $\{R\}$ r: **receive** m **on** V $\{Q\}$.

In the course of establishing satisfaction, restrictions are imposed on $post(r)$, as follows. According to the operational semantics for **receive** given above, in order for execution of r to result in the receipt of a message with value $MTEXT$ (say), then (1) $\sigma_V - \rho_V \neq \Phi$, where $s - t$ is the sequence obtained by deleting prefix t from the beginning of s, and (2) $MTEXT = hd(\sigma_V - \rho_V)$, where $hd(s)$ denotes the first element of sequence s. Thus, immediately before $MTEXT$ is assigned to m, the system state can be characterized by

(i) $pre(r) \land \sigma_V - \rho_V \neq \Phi \land MTEXT = hd(\sigma_V - \rho_V)$.

Execution of r resulting in receipt of a message with value $MTEXT$ is equivalent to execution of the multiple assignment statement

$$m, \rho_V := MTEXT, \rho_V \cup <MTEXT>.$$

For this assignment to establish the postcondition of the Virtual Circuit Receive Axiom, execution must be performed in a state satisfying

$$wp(m, \rho_V := MTEXT, \rho_V \cup <MTEXT>, post(r))$$

which is $post(r)^{m, \rho_V}_{MTEXT, \rho_V \cup <MTEXT>}$. Thus, $post(r)$ will be true when r terminates provided $Sat_{asynch(r)}$

$$(pre(r) \land \sigma_V - \rho_V \neq \Phi \land MTEXT = hd(\sigma_V - \rho_V)) \supset post(r)^{m, \rho_V}_{MTEXT, \rho_V \cup <MTEXT>}$$

is valid. Note that $MTEXT$ is a free variable in $Sat_{asynch}(r)$, so it is implicitly universally quantified. This corresponds to the fact that $post(r)^{m, \rho_V}_{MTEXT, \rho_V \cup <MTEXT>}$ must be true for any message that could be received by executing r.

Non-interference is established by proving additional triples $NI(S,I)$ valid for every assertion I and every assignment, **send**, and **receive** S parallel to I. For S a **receive**, $NI(S,I)$ follows trivially from the Virtual Circuit Receive Axiom, but it is necessary to prove satisfaction. The necessary satisfaction formula $NI\_Sat_{asynch}(S,I)$ is obtained by substituting into $Sat_{asynch}(r)$ based on $NI_{asynch}(S,I)$—that is, using $I \wedge pre(S)$ for $pre(r)$ and I for $post(r)$. This results in $NI\_Sat_{asynch}(S,I)$:

$$(I \wedge pre(S) \wedge \sigma_V - \rho_V \neq \Phi \wedge MTEXT = hd(\sigma_V - \rho_V)) \supset I_{MTEXT,\rho_V \cup <MTEXT>}^{m,\rho_V}.$$

To summarize, the following method can be used to prove the partial correctness of a program that uses virtual circuits:

Virtual Circuit Proof Method:
> (1) Construct a consistent annotation for each process in isolation.
> (2) For every **receive** r, prove $Sat_{asynch}(r)$ valid.
> (3) For every assignment and **send** statement S and every assertion I parallel to S, prove $NI(S,I)$. For every **receive** r and every assertion I parallel to r, prove $NI\_Sat_{asynch}(r,I)$ valid.

5.3.6. Relationship Between Satisfaction and Non-Interference

Establishing satisfaction for **receive** r is equivalent to proving that no process invalidates $post(r)$. Therefore, one might expect this obligation to be superfluous, arguing that interference with $post(r)$ by executing an atomic action a should be detected when proving $NI(a,post(r))$ valid in the non-interference proof. Unfortunately, because messages are buffered, an atomic action a in one process can invalidate $post(r)$ even if a and r are not concurrent—that is, even if a cannot be executed immediately after r has completed. To see this, consider the following.

$$SELF: \quad x := 2;$$
$$\{x=2\}$$
$$\textbf{send } \text{'x\_js\_two' on } V;$$
$$x := 3;$$
$$\{x=3\}$$
$$\textbf{receive } m \text{ from } V;$$
$$\{m=\text{'x\_js\_two'} \wedge x=2\}$$

Here, process $SELF$ sends a message to itself and then invalidates $x=2$, the precondition of the **send**, before executing a **receive**. The sequential proof given above can be derived from our axioms and Hoare's logic. There is only one process, so non-interference is trivially established. Yet, the postcondition of the **receive** will not be true when the **receive** terminates. An attempt to establish satisfaction, however, will fail. (It is possible to construct similar pathologies for programs involving more than one process.)

This example also illustrates a common misconception about the origin of the "miraculous" postcondition of the **receive**. Earlier, we claimed that anything can appear as the postcondition of a synchronous communications command because such a statement will not terminate when executed in isolation. However, our **receive** can terminate when executed in isolation, as illustrated above. (Thus, the Virtual Circuit Receive Axiom, taken by itself, is not sound; satisfaction and non-interference proofs are required to ensure soundness.) In general, it seems that a miraculous postcondition arises from the synchronization character of a statement. If a statement can cause an arbitrary delay awaiting an event that is in no way caused by execution of that statement, then the axiom for such a statement will have a miraculous postcondition. The phenomenon is not related to message passing at all. The major complication offered by message passing is that the miracle is often an assertion about the state of another process, which cannot be directly tested and therefore does not appear in the program text of the receiver.

5.3.7. Example Using Virtual Circuits

We now return the the producer/consumer example discussed in section 5.3.3, and program it using virtual circuits. Since a virtual circuit is, itself, a buffer, there is no need to program a buffer process. The program for the producer is:

```
prod: var A : array 1 .. N of portion;
           i : integer;
      i := 1;
      while i ≠ N + 1 do
         send A [i] on V;
         i := i + 1
      od
```

And, the program for the consumer is:

```
cons:  var B : array 1 .. N of portion;
            j : integer;
        j := 1;
        while j≠N+1 do
            receive B[j] from V;
            j := j+1
        od
```

Annotations for these programs appear in Figures 5.10 and 5.11. In those annotations, the assertion I is defined to be:

I: $(\forall k : 1 \leq k \leq |\sigma_V| : \sigma_V[k] = A[k])$

where the notation $s[k]$ is used for the kth element in sequence s.

Satisfaction involves proving the validity of $Sat_{asynch}(r)$:

$(I \wedge (\forall k : 1 \leq k < j : A[k] = B[k]) \wedge |\rho_V| + 1 = j \wedge \sigma_V - \rho_V \neq \Phi \wedge$

```
prod:  var A : array 1 .. N of portion;
            i : integer;
        i := 1;   {σ_V=Φ ∧ i=1}
        while i≠N+1 do
            {I ∧ |σ_V|+1=i}
            send A[i] on V;
            {I ∧ |σ_V|+1=i+1}
            i := i+1
        od
```

Figure 5.10: Annotation of *prod*.

```
cons:  var B : array 1 .. N of portion;
            j : integer;
        j := 1;   {I ∧ j=1 ∧ ρ_V=Φ}
        while j≠N+1 do
            {I ∧ (∀k: 1≤k<j: A[k]=B[k]) ∧ |ρ_V|+1=j}
            receive B[j] from V;
            {I ∧ (∀k: 1≤k≤j: A[k]=B[k]) ∧ |ρ_v|=j}
            j := j+1
        od
```

Figure 5.11: Annotation of *cons*.

$$MTEXT = hd(\sigma_V - \rho_V)) \quad \supset$$

$$(I \wedge (\forall k: 1 \le k \le j: A[k] = B[k]) \wedge |\rho_V| = j)_{MTEXT, \rho_V \cup <MTEXT>}^{B[j], \rho_V}$$

which is valid because $I \wedge |\rho_V| + 1 = j \wedge MTEXT = hd(\sigma_V - \rho_V)$ in the antecedent implies that $MTEXT = A[j]$.

Establishing non-interference is trivial. I is the only assertion appearing in a process (*cons*) that involves variables (σ_V) changed by another process. However, I is a conjunct of every assertion of *prod*, so it is an invariant of *prod*. Thus, it will not be interfered with by execution of *prod*.

5.3.8. Communication with Rendezvous and Remote Procedures

Rendezvous is the basic mechanism for synchronization and communication in Ada [Ichbiah 79].[5] It provides a disciplined way for processes to communicate and synchronize and can be easily implemented using message passing.

A *rendezvous* results from execution of a call statement by one process and a matching accept statement by another. Execution of

$$\text{call } server.proc(in\_args \ \# \ out\_args)$$

by process *client* causes it to be delayed until a matching accept—an accept labeled *proc* in *server*—is executed.

Execution of an accept statement

$$proc: \ \text{accept}(in\_parms \ \# \ out\_parms)$$
$$body$$
$$\text{end}$$

in *server* is as follows. Process *server* is delayed until some process executes a matching call; the *in_parms* are assigned the values of the corresponding *in_args*; *body* is executed; and then the *out_args* are assigned the values of the corresponding *out_parms*. Thus, execution is equivalent to:

$$in\_parms := in\_args;$$
$$body;$$
$$out\_args := out\_parms$$

A *remote procedure* is like a procedure in a sequential programming language, except the procedure body is not necessarily executed by the caller; in particular, it

---

[5]In the following, a simplified version of the rendezvous mechanism in Ada is treated. For example, we do not consider conditional and timed entry calls, task failure and termination, or entry queues.

may be executed by another process that is synchronized with the caller so that the usual semantics of the procedure call is achieved. Parameter transmission is by value-result since the procedure body may be executed on a different processor than the one on which the caller executes. Argus (see section 7) employs a form of remote procedures.

It is simple to implement remote procedures using **call** and **accept** statements. For *client* to invoke remote procedure *server.proc*, it executes

$$\textbf{call } server.proc\,(in\_args \,\#\, out\_args\,).$$

Remote procedure *server.proc* is implemented by a process

$$
\begin{aligned}
server:\ &\textbf{while } true \textbf{ do}\\
&\quad proc:\ \textbf{accept}\,(in\_parms \,\#\, out\_parms\,)\\
&\qquad\qquad body\\
&\qquad\quad \textbf{end}\\
&\textbf{od}.
\end{aligned}
$$

Therefore, proof rules for **call** and **accept** can be used for reasoning about programs written in terms of remote procedures.

5.3.9. Partial Correctness with Rendezvous

Proof rules for **call** and **accept** can be derived from the proof obligations for an operationally equivalent program that uses synchronous message-passing.[6]

We shall employ CSP to describe our simulation of rendezvous, since CSP supports synchronous message-passing. The **call** statement

$$c:\ \textbf{call } server.proc\,(in\_args \,\#\, out\_args\,)$$

is translated into[7]

$$
\begin{aligned}
c':\ &s_{call}:\ server\,!proc\,(in\_args\,);\\
&r_{call}:\ server\,?proc\,(out\_args\,).
\end{aligned}
$$

The **accept** statement

---

[6]Thus, we are now using a different technique for deriving proof rules than was used for the proof systems for synchronous message-passing and virtual circuits.

[7]This translation works only if the meaning of the *out_args* does not change as a result of executing *proc*. For example, if $A\,[i]$ is one of the *out_args* and i is a shared variable that is changed by *proc* then the translation will be wrong.

$$proc: \textbf{accept}\,(in\_parms \;\#\; out\_parms\,)$$
$$body$$
$$\textbf{end}$$

in process *server* is translated into

$$proc': \quad \textbf{if} \;\; \underset{i}{\textstyle\|} \;\; r^i_{acpt}: client_i\,?proc\,(in\_parms\,) \;\rightarrow\; body;$$
$$s^i_{acpt}: client_i\,!proc\,(out\_parms\,)$$
$$\textbf{fi}$$

assuming $client_1$, $client_2$, ... are the processes that call *server.proc*.

Provided procedure names are distinct, the communications commands in c' will match only commands in the process corresponding to the simulation of an **accept** labeled *proc*, and communications commands in *proc'* will match only those corresponding to the simulation of a **call** naming *server.proc*.

We tentatively choose as the axiom for **call**

Call Axiom: $\{P\}$ **call** *server.proc*$(in\_args \;\#\; out\_args)$ $\{R\}$.

Based on our CSP simulation of **call**, in order to prove the Call Axiom, it is sufficient to prove

(i) $\{P\}$ s_{call}; r_{call} $\{R\}$

and establish satisfaction and non-interference.

The sequential proof of (i) follows from

(ii) $\{P\}$ *server*$!proc\,(in\_args\,)$ $\{P'\}$
(iii) $\{P'\}$ *server*$?proc\,(out\_args\,)$ $\{R\}$,

both of which are derived from the axioms for communications commands. Note that (ii) and (iii), hence (i), allow any choice of P'. This will be helpful later when deriving obligations for satisfaction.

In order to prove

$$\{Q\}$$
$$proc: \textbf{accept}\,(in\_parms \;\#\; out\_parms\,)$$
$$\{T\}$$
$$body$$
$$\{U\}$$
$$\textbf{end}$$
$$\{W\}$$

it suffices to prove

(iv) $\{Q\}$ r_{acpt}^i $\{T\}$,

(v) $\{T\}$ $body$ $\{U\}$, and

(vi) $\{U\}$ s_{acpt}^i $\{W\}$,

for all i, and establish satisfaction and non-interference. Since (iv) and (vi) follow directly from the axioms for communications commands, this suggests the following inference rule for accept.

Accept Rule:

$$\frac{\{T\}\ body\ \{U\}}{\{Q\}\ \mathbf{accept}\,(in\_parms\ \#\ out\_parms)\ body\ \mathbf{end}\ \ \{W\}}$$

To establish satisfaction for our CSP simulation, $Sat_{synch}(r_{acpt}^i, s_{call})$

(vii) $(Q \wedge P) \supset (T \wedge P')_{in\_args}^{in\_parms}$

and $Sat_{synch}(r_{call}, s_{acpt}^i)$

(viii) $(P' \wedge U) \supset (R \wedge W)_{out\_parms}^{out\_args}$

are shown to be valid for each call c in P_i and matching accept $proc$. These formulas form the basis for the satisfaction obligation for call and accept.

The appearance of P' in (vii) and (viii) is a problem in so far as P' does not appear in the original proof—it is used to characterize an intermediate state of our CSP simulation of call. Clearly, our proof rules should be in terms of assertions that are derivable from the original proof. To mitigate this problem, we stipulate that P' be chosen so that:

(ix) $P \supset P'\,_{in\_args}^{in\_parms}$

(Recall, anything can be used for P'.) This ensures that P' can be derived from assertions in the original proof. Choosing "true" for P' will always satisfy (ix). However, usually P' will be a predicate describing some aspect of the caller's state that can be asserted both before and after the call. This allows a single proof of the body of an accept to be used for all call statements.

We adopt the convention that both the precondition P of a call and the additional predicate P' used in satisfaction appear before that call in a sequential proof outline. A vertical bar will separate the two predicates, as in the following:

$$\dots$$
$$\{P \mid P'\}$$
$$c: \textbf{call} \dots$$
$$\{R\}$$
$$\dots$$

Formulas (vii), (viii) and (ix) are combined to form the satisfaction obligations for rendezvous primitives. Due to (ix), (vii) becomes

$$(Q \wedge P) \supset T_{in\_args}^{in\_parms}$$

Combining with (viii) results in the following satisfaction formula for call c and accept $proc$.

$$Sat_{rndvs}(c,proc): \quad P \supset P' {}_{in\_args}^{in\_parms} \quad \wedge \quad (Q \wedge P) \supset T_{in\_args}^{in\_parms} \quad \wedge$$
$$(P' \wedge U) \supset (R \wedge W)_{out\_parms}^{out\_args}$$

As before, showing non-interference involves proving $NI(S,I)$ for every statement S an assignment, simulation of a call, and simulation of an accept and every assertion I parallel to S.[8] The proof of $NI(S,I)$ for S a call or an accept and any assertion I follows immediately from the axioms for the communications commands that simulate S. However, satisfaction must be established for these theorems. Thus, for each matching call c and accept $proc$ $NI\_Sat_{synch}(r_{acpt}^i, s_{call}, I)$, which is $(I \wedge Q \wedge P) \supset I_{in\_args}^{in\_parms}$, and $NI\_Sat_{synch}(r_{call}, s_{acpt}^i, I)$, which is $(I \wedge P' \wedge U) \supset I_{out\_parms}^{out\_args}$, must be shown valid. Combining these, we get

$$NI\_Sat_{rndvs}(c, proc, I): \quad (I \wedge Q \wedge P) \supset I_{in\_args}^{in\_parms} \quad \wedge \quad (I \wedge P' \wedge U) \supset I_{in\_args}^{out\_args}$$

The method for proving the partial correctness of a program that uses rendezvous, is therefore:

Rendezvous Proof Method:

(1) Construct a consistent annotation for each process in isolation.

(2) For every call c and accept $proc$ that match, prove $Sat_{rndvs}(c, proc)$ valid.

(3) For every assignment statement S and assertion I parallel to S, prove $NI(S, I)$ valid. For every call S_{call} and matching accept S_{acpt} and every assertion I parallel to both S_{call} and S_{acpt}, prove $NI\_Sat_{rndvs}(S_{call}, S_{acpt}, I)$

---

[8] If "$\{P \mid P'\}$" appears in the proof of a process, then both P and P' are considered assertions that are parallel to statements in other processes.

5.3.10. Example Using Rendezvous

To illustrate rendezvous primitives we give, once again, a solution to our producer/consumer problem. The code for the producer process is:

```
prod: var A : array 1 .. N of portion;
          i : integer;
      i := 1;
      while i≠N+1 do
          p: call buffer.dep(A [i]#);
          i := i+1
      od
```

The code for the consumer process is:

```
cons: var B : array 1 .. N of portion;
          j : integer;
      j := 1;
      while j≠N+1 do
          c: call buffer.ret(# B[j]);
          j := j+1
      od
```

A buffer process smooths out speed variations between *prod* and *cons*:

```
buffer: var buff: portion;
           n : integer;
        n := 0;
        while n ≠ N+1 do
           dep: accept(val #)
                   buff := val
                   end ;
           ret: accept( # res )
                   res := buff
                   end ;
           n := n+1
        od
```

Program annotations for the processes are shown in Figures 5.12 through 5.14. There, auxiliary variable *ndep* records the number of elements that have been deposited in *buff* and *nret*, the number of elements that have been retrieved from *buff*. The auxiliary variables are initialized so that $ndep = nret = 0$.

To establish satisfaction, $Sat_{rndvs}(p, dep)$ and $Sat_{rndvs}(c, ret)$ are constructed and shown to be valid. First, $Sat_{rndvs}(p, dep)$:

prod: **var** A : *array* $1 .. N$ *of portion*;
i : *integer*;
$i := 1$; $\{i=1 \wedge ndep=0\}$
while $i \neq N+1$ **do**
  $\{i = ndep + 1 \mid true\,\}$
  p: **call** *buffer.dep*$(A[i] \#\,)$;
  $\{ndep = i\}$
  $i := i+1$
od

Figure 5.12: Annotation of *prod*.

cons: **var** B : *array* $1 .. N$ *of portion*;
j : *integer*;
$j := 1$; $\{j=1 \wedge nret=0\}$
while $j \neq N+1$ **do**
  $\{j = nret + 1 \wedge (\forall k: 1 \leq k < j: A[k]=B[k]) \wedge$
  $\mid (\forall k: 1 \leq k < j: A[k]=B[k])\}$
  c: **call** *buffer.ret*$(\# B[j])$;
  $\{j = nret \wedge (\forall k: 1 \leq k \leq j: A[k]=B[k])\}$
  $j := j+1$
od

Figure 5.13: Annotation of *cons*.

$(i=ndep+1) \supset true^{val}_{A[i]} \wedge$
$(n=ndep=nret \wedge i=ndep+1) \supset$
  $(i=ndep+1 \wedge val=A[i] \wedge n=ndep=nret)^{val}_{A[i]} \wedge$
$(true \wedge i=ndep \wedge buff=A[i] \wedge n+1=ndep=nret+1) \supset$
  $(ndep=i \wedge buff=A[ndep] \wedge n+1=ndep=nret+1)$

Clearly, this formula is valid. The proof that $Sat_{rndvs}(c, ret)$ is also valid is left to the reader.

The final step of the proof is to establish non-interference. We give an informal proof here. First, consider statements in *prod*. No statement in *prod* interferes with any assertion in *cons* because *prod* changes no variable appearing in an assertion in *cons*. To see that statements in *prod* do not interfere with assertions in *buffer*, note that i is the only variable changed by *prod* that appears in assertions in *buffer*. However, $pre(i := i+1) \supset \neg in(dep)$, and $in(dep)$ is obviously a conjunct of every assertion I in *buffer* that mentions i, since those assertions appear in the body of the **accept** labelled *dep*. Thus, $pre(NI(i := i+1,\ I)) \supset (in(dep) \wedge \neg in(dep))$, which is false, and so $NI(i := i+1,\ I)$ is a theorem for all I in *buffer*.

Similar reasoning shows that no statement in *cons* interferes with assertions in *prod* and *buffer*.

Lastly, we must show that no statement in *buffer* interferes with assertions in *prod* or *cons*. The only variables of concern here are *ndep* and *nret*: they are changed in *buffer* and appear in assertions in the other processes. However, note that $pre(ndep := ndep + 1) \supset in(dep)$. Since $\neg in(dep)$ is a conjunct of every

```
buffer: var buff: portion;
            n : integer;
        n := 0;   {n=0 ∧ ndep=0 ∧ nret=0}
        while n ≠ N+1 do
            {n = ndep = nret}
            dep: accept(val, #)
                    {i=ndep+1 ∧ val = A[i] ∧ n = ndep = nret}
                    buff := val; ndep := ndep+1
                    {i = ndep ∧ buff = A[i] ∧ n+1 = ndep = nret+1}
                 end;
            {buff = A[ndep] ∧ n+1 = ndep = nret+1}
            ret: accept(# res)
                    {j = ndep+1 ∧ buff = A[ndep] ∧ n+1 = ndep = nret+1}
                    res := buff; nret := nret+1
                    {j = nret ∧ res = buff = A[ndep] ∧ n+1 = ndep = nret}
                 end;
            {n+1 = ndep = nret}
            n := n+1
        od
```

Figure 5.14: Annotation of *buffer*.

assertion in *prod* that mentions *ndep*, by the argument given above, interference is not possible. Similarly, $pre(nret := nret + 1) \supset in(ret)$, and $\neg in(ret)$ is a conjunct of every assertion in *cons* that mentions *nret*. Therefore, interference is not possible here, either.

5.3.11. Other Proof Systems for Message-Passing

The proof rules we presented above are based on satisfaction, an approach first proposed by [Levin 81] in connection with CSP. The approach was later extended for use in programs that use asynchronous message-passing and rendezvous by Schlichting and Schneider in [Schlichting 82, Schlichting 84].

Proof rules for programs that use reliable virtual circuits were first proposed in connection with Gypsy [Good 79]. There, **send** and **receive** are characterized in terms of their effects on shared, auxiliary objects called *buffer histories*. The proof rules are then derived from the assignment axiom by translating **send** and **receive** into semantically equivalent assignments to buffer histories.

Apt *et al.* define a proof system for reasoning about CSP programs [Apt 80]. In it, each process is proved in isolation with its communications commands deleted, and then a *cooperation proof* is performed to show that these proofs can be combined. The axioms for communications commands allow anything to be asserted as the postcondition of an input or output command, and the cooperation proof establishes that assumptions made in the postcondition of a communications command will, in fact, be true whenever execution of that command completes. Performing a cooperation proof involves constructing a global invariant that characterizes pairs of syntactically matching communications commands that can actually exchange a message during some computation (called semantic matching). The global invariant is in terms of program and auxiliary variables, but auxiliary variables may not be shared (in contrast to [Levin 81]). Consequently, there is no need to construct a non-interference proof.

Proof systems based on the idea of a cooperation test have been defined for a variety of other programming notations, as well. A proof system for Distributed Processes [Brinch Hansen 78] is presented in [Gerth 82b]. In [Gerth 82a], a proof system for a subset of Ada containing rendezvous is defined and proved sound and relatively complete; in [Gerth 84] and [Barringer 82] larger subsets of the concurrency features of Ada are axiomatized.

Another approach to designing a proof system for distributed programs is based on the use of traces [Misra 81, Misra 82, Soundararajan 81, Hoare 81]. In this approach, processes and networks of processes are described in terms of their input/output histories, called *traces*. A program proof involves two steps. First, the trace of each process is characterized by using a programming logic in which input and output commands are modeled as assignments to traces. Then, proofs of processes are combined by using inference rules that relate these traces. Once the input/output history of a process or network is determined, reasoning can proceed in terms of assertions on traces, instead of assertions on program variables. This approach is particularly interesting because it allows one to reason about the result of combining a collection of components—processes or networks—without concern for their implementations.

5.4. Proving Liveness Properties

We now discuss the proof of liveness properties for concurrent programs. As we have indicated, the fundamental approach to concurrent program verification is the same for distributed programs as for nondistributed ones. In these lectures, we have time only to outline the approach. More details can be found in [Owicki 82].

5.4.1. Proof Lattices

While temporal logic provides a nice way of expressing safety properties and formally describing how they are proved, we would not need temporal logic if we were concerned only with safety properties. Temporal logic is needed for reasoning about liveness properties. We begin by introducing the style of temporal logic reasoning used for proving liveness properties.

Suppose that the following three assertions hold:

1. $P \rightsquigarrow (R1 \lor R2)$

2. $R1 \rightsquigarrow Q$

3. $R2 \rightsquigarrow Q$

We can write the meaning of each of these assertions as follows.

1. If P is true at any time i then $R1$ or $R2$ will be true at some time $j \geq i$.

2. If $R1$ is true at any time j then Q will be true at some time $k \geq j$.

3. If $R2$ is true at any time j then Q will be true at some time $k \geq j$.

We easily see from this that they imply the truth of $P \rightsquigarrow Q$.

This reasoning is conveniently described by the *proof lattice* of Figure 5.15. The two

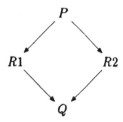

Figure 5.15: Lattice Proof Outline for $P \rightsquigarrow R$

arrows leading from P to $R1$ and $R2$ denote the assertion $P \rightsquigarrow (R1 \vee R2)$; the arrow from $R1$ to Q denotes the assertion $R1 \rightsquigarrow Q$; and the arrow from $R2$ to Q denotes the assertion $R1 \rightsquigarrow Q$.

In general, we make the following definition.

Definition: A *proof lattice* for a program is a finite directed acyclic graph in which each node is labeled with an assertion, such that:

1. There is a single *entry node* having no incoming edges.

2. There is a single *exit node* having no outgoing edges.

3. If a node labeled R has outgoing edges to nodes labeled $R_1, R_2, \ldots R_k$, then $R \rightsquigarrow (R_1 \vee R_2 \ldots \vee R_k)$ holds.

The third condition means that if R is true at some time, then one of the R_i must be true at some later time. By a generalization of the informal reasoning used for the lattice of Figure 5.15, it is easy to see that if the entry node assertion is true at some time, then the exit node assertion must be true at some later time. This is stated formally by the following theorem, whose prove may be found in [Owicki 82].

Theorem: If there is a proof lattice for a program with entry node labeled P and exit node labeled Q, then $P \leadsto Q$ is true for that program.

Proof lattices in which every node is labeled by an immediate assertion were introduced in [Lamport 77], without the use of temporal logic. What temporal logic introduces is the use of more general temporal assertions in the lattices—in particular, assertions involving the $\square$ operator.

Consider a lattice containing a node labeled R with arcs pointing to nodes labeled $R_1, \ldots, R_k$. This construction implies that if R ever becomes true during execution of the program, then one of the R_i must subsequently become true. Now suppose that R has the form $P \wedge \square Q$. Saying that R is true at some time means that P and Q are true then, and that Q will be true at all future times. In particular, Q must be true when any of the R_i subsequently become true. Hence, we could replace each of the R_i by $R_i \wedge \square Q$. More precisely, condition 3 in the definition of a proof lattice still holds if each R_i is replaced by $R_i \wedge \square Q$.

We see from this that if $\square Q$ appears as a conjunct ("and" term) of an assertion in a proof lattice, then $\square Q$ is likely to appear as a conjunct of the assertions "lower down" in the lattice. It is therefore convenient to introduce the following notation, which make the proof lattices clearer. For any assertion Q, drawing a box labeled $\square Q$ around some of the nodes in the lattice denotes that $\square Q$ is to be conjoined to the assertion attached to every node in the box. This notation is illustrated by the proof lattice of Figure 5.16, which is expanded in Figure 5.17 into the same proof lattice written without the box notation.

The lattice in Figure 5.16 also illustrates the typical structure of a proof by contradiction for $P \leadsto Q$. In the first step, the proof is split into two cases based on the temporal logic theorem

$$P \leadsto [Q \vee (P \wedge \square \neg Q)].$$

Intuitively, this theorem is true because starting from a time when P is true, either

- Q will be true at some subsequent time, or

- $\neg Q$ will be true from then on.

The former possibility is represented by the right-hand branch, the latter by the left-hand branch. Within the box labelled $\square \neg Q$ is some argument that leads to a contradiction,

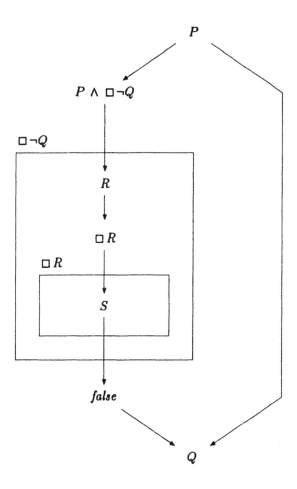

Figure 5.16: Abbreviated Lattice

which appears at the node labeled *false*. Note that *false* $\leadsto Q$ is vacuously true. Thus the general pattern of these proofs by contradiction is to assume that the desired predicate never becomes true, and then show that this assumption leads to a contradiction.

5.4.2. Program Semantics

In the preceding subsection, we have discussed a particular style of temporal logic reasoning that is used for proving liveness properties of the form $P \leadsto Q$. Temporal logic by itself is not enough to prove anything about programs. We need some way to extract temporal logic properties of the programs. Formally, this means giving a

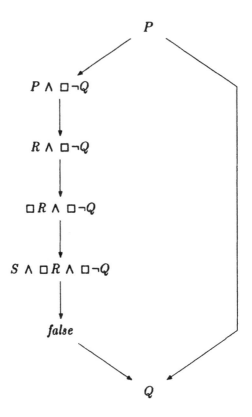

Figure 5.17: Expanded Lattice for Figure 5.16

temporal semantics for the program—i.e., a set of rules for deriving true temporal logic assertions about the program.

Section 5.2 describes how one derives safety properties of the form $Init \supset \Box P$ for a program. We now want to derive liveness properties of the form

$$Init \supset (P \leadsto Q)$$

To prove a liveness property of this form, one needs a safety property. More precisely, the proof involves the following two steps, for some predicate R:

- $Init \supset \Box R$

- $\Box R \supset (P \leadsto Q)$

We refer to Section 5.2 for the methods of proving the first assertion.

To prove any liveness property of a program, one must be able to conclude that something eventually happens. Exactly what we can assume will eventually happen depends upon the programming language. For the time being, we will ignore synchronizing primitives, and assume that all interprocess communication is by ordinary access to shared variables. More precisely, we will give a complete set of rules for reasoning about programs formed from atomic assignment statements, concatenation, **while** loops whose boolean expressions are executed as single atomic actions, and **cobegin** statements. Similar rules will hold for any programming language not containing message-passing statements or synchronization primitives. Such statements will be discussed later.

The weakest liveness assumption that one can make is that if the program has not terminated, then eventually some process will execute an atomic action. However, it is more common to make a stronger assumption that any process that has not terminated will eventually execute an atomic action. This assumption is usually called *fairness*.

Fairness is expressed formally by an axiom for each programming language construction, using the *at* and *after* notation described in Section 5.2. For example, for an assignment statement, we might have:

Atomic Assignment Axiom: For any atomic assignment statement S:

$$at(S) \rightsquigarrow after(S) \quad .$$

For **while** loops, we would use the following axiom.

While Control Flow Axiom: For the statement w: **while** $\langle\, b\, \rangle$ **do** s : S **od**

$$at(w) \rightsquigarrow (at(s) \vee after(w)).$$

One also needs some rules for reasoning about the flow of control. The following are some examples of such rules, which follow from elementary properties of temporal logic and the *at*, *in*, and *after* predicates. Note that the first two are inference rules—rules that tell us how to derive valid formulas from other valid formulas.

Concatenation Control Flow Rule: For the statement S ; T: $\models at(S) \rightsquigarrow$ $after(S)$ and $\models at(T) \rightsquigarrow after(T)$ imply $\models at(s) \rightsquigarrow after(T)$.

Cobegin Control Flow Rule: For the statement c: **cobegin** S $\square T$ **coend**: $\models at(S) \rightsquigarrow after(S)$ and $\models at(T) \rightsquigarrow after(T)$ imply $\models at(c) \rightsquigarrow after(c)$

boolean p ; **integer** x ;

   a: **cobegin**

       b: $\langle\, p := \mathit{false}\, \rangle$

     ▯

       c: **while** $\langle\, p\, \rangle$ **do** d: $\langle\, x := x+1\, \rangle$ **od**

   coend

Figure 5.18: A Terminating Concurrent Program

Exit Rule: For any statement S: $in(S)\ \supset\ (\Box\, in(S) \vee \Diamond after(S))$.

Note that the Exit Rule follows from the observation that $after(S)$ must be true immediately after control has left statement S.

The above axioms and rules refer only to the control component of the program state, and not to the values of variables. In proving liveness properties, one needs to describe the interaction between control flow and the values of program variables. For example, consider the program in Figure 5.18. It consists of two processes, one that sets the variable p false and another that loops as long as p is true. Since the first process eventually sets p false and terminates, the second process eventually terminates. Hence, the entire **cobegin** terminates. However, its termination cannot be inferred directly from the above rules, because it depends upon the interaction between the control flow in the second process and the value of the variable p set by the first process.

We now describe several rules for reasoning about the interaction between control flow and variable values. First, suppose that the safety property $\{P\}\ \langle\, S\, \rangle\ \{Q\}$ holds for the atomic assignment statement $\langle\, S\, \rangle$. This tells us that if $\langle\, S\, \rangle$ is executed when P is true, then Q will be true immediately after its execution, when control is right after $\langle\, S\, \rangle$. The Atomic Assignment Axiom tells us that if control is at $\langle\, S\, \rangle$ then $\langle\, S\, \rangle$ will eventually be executed. We can therefore deduce the following rule.

Atomic Assignment Rule: For any atomic assignment statement $\langle\, S\, \rangle$:
$\{P\}\ \langle\, S\, \rangle\ \{Q\}$ and $\models\ \Box(at(\langle\, S\, \rangle)\ \supset\ P)$ imply $\models\ at(\langle\, S\, \rangle)\ \leadsto$
$(after(\langle\, S\, \rangle) \wedge Q)$

In the application of this rule, the hypothesis $\Box(at(\langle\, S\, \rangle)\ \supset\ P$ must first be proved as a safety property, using the techniques of Section 5.2.

One might be tempted to write a rule stating that if $\{P\} \langle S \rangle \{Q\}$ holds then $(at(\langle S \rangle)) \wedge P) \rightsquigarrow (after(\langle S \rangle)) \wedge Q)$. However, this would not be valid. Even if $at(\langle S \rangle)) \wedge P$ is true at some point in an execution sequence, P may not be true when $\langle S \rangle$ is actually executed, since another process could execute a statement making P false before $\langle S \rangle$ is executed. If this happens, there is no reason why Q should be true upon completion of $\langle S \rangle$. Thus the stronger assumption in the atomic statement rule is necessary.

We next extend the Atomic Statement Rule to more general statements. Recall that the generalization of the Hoare logic assertion $\{P\} \langle S \rangle \{Q\}$ to a nonatomic statement S is the Generalized Hoare Logic assertion $P [S] Q$. If $P [S] Q$ is true for some statement S that will eventually terminate, what will guarantee that Q is true when S terminates? From the meaning of $P [S] Q$, it is clear that Q will be true upon termination of S if P is true just before the last atomic step of S is executed. This in turn will be true if P is true throughout the execution of S. This gives us the following rule.

General Statement Rule: From $P [S] Q$, $\models \Box(in(S) \supset P)$ and $in(S) \rightsquigarrow after(S)$, we can infer $in(S) \rightsquigarrow (after(S) \wedge Q)$.

The final two rules involve the atomic test in a **while** statement. Consider the statement

$$w: \textbf{while} \langle B \rangle \textbf{ do } S \textbf{ od} \quad .$$

The While Control Flow Axiom tells us that if control is at w, then it will eventually be at S or after w. We also know that control will go to S only if B is true, and will leave w only if B is false. (This is a safety property of the **while** statement.) Combining these observations, we deduce that if control is at w then eventually it will be at S with B true, or will be after S with B false, giving us the following rule.

While Test Rule: For the statement $w: \textbf{while} \langle B \rangle \textbf{ do } S \textbf{ od}$:

$$at(w) \rightsquigarrow ((at(S) \wedge B) \vee (after(w) \wedge \neg B))$$

The While Test Rule tells us that control must go one way or the other at a **while** statement test. If we know that the value of the test expression is fixed for the rest of an execution sequence, then we can predict which way the test will go. In particular, we can deduce the following:

While Exit Rule: For the statement w: **while** $\langle\, B\,\rangle$ **do** S **od**:

$$(at(w) \wedge \Box(at(w) \supset B)) \quad \leadsto \quad at(S)$$
$$(at(w) \wedge \Box(at(w) \supset \neg B)) \leadsto after(w)$$

5.4.3. A Simple Example

We now prove that the example program of Figure 5.18 terminates—that is, we prove $at(a) \leadsto after(a)$. The proof is described by the lattice of Figure 5.19. The numbers attached to the lattice refer to comments in the text below.

1. This step follows from the Atomic Assignment Rule applied to statement b, using the formula $\{true\}\ \langle\, b\,\rangle\ \{\neg p\}$. This is obviously a valid formula, since no matter what state b is started in, it ends with p having the value *false*.

2. This is a consequence of the safety property $(after(b) \wedge \neg p) \supset \Box(after(b) \wedge \neg p)$, which states that once control reaches $after(b)$ with p false, it must remain there (it has no place else to go) and p must stay false (no assignment in the program can change its value).

3. For this program, control must be either in c or after c. This step separates the two cases. Formally, it follows from the fact that the predicate $in(c) \vee after(c)$ is true in any program state. At this point we use the box abbreviation to indicate that $\Box(after(b) \wedge \neg p)$ is true at all descendants of this node.

4. This follows from the fact that $in(c)$ and $at(c) \vee at(d)$ are equivalent. Again, the branch in the lattice separates the cases.

5. This follows from the Atomic Assignment Axiom, applied to statement d, plus the fact that $after(d)$ is equivalent to $at(c)$.

6. The enclosing box tells us that $\Box \neg p$ is true at this node. Thus, we can apply the While Exit Rule to infer that control eventually leaves the **while** loop, making $after(c)$ true.

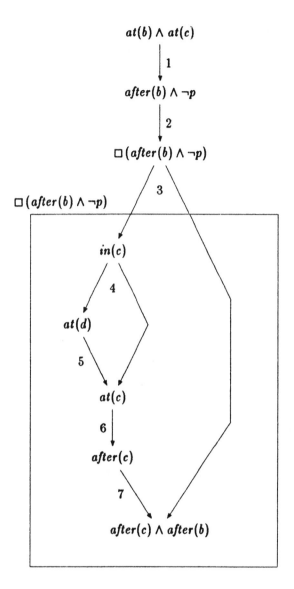

Figure 5.19: Proof Lattice for Program of Figure 5.18

boolean p ; **integer** x ;

    a: **cobegin**

        b: $\langle\, p := \textit{false}\, \rangle$

      ▯

        c: **while** $\langle\, p\, \rangle$ **do** d: $\langle\, x := x+1\, \rangle$ **od**

        e: $\langle\, p := \textit{true}\, \rangle$

    coend

Figure 5.20: Another Terminating Program

7. This is a trivial implication. The enclosing box tells us that $\Box\, \textit{after}(b)$ is true, and $\Box\, \textit{after}(b)$ implies $\textit{after}(b)$.

In this program, the termination of the **while** loop was proved by showing that $\Box\neg p$ must eventually become true. This enabled us to use the While Exit Rule to show that control must eventually leave the loop. But suppose that we wanted to verify termination for the similar program in Figure 5.20. In this program $\Box\neg p$ does not eventually hold, because after control leaves the loop, p is reset to true. How can we hope to verify such a program, since the While Exit Rule requires us to know $\Box\neg p$ in order to prove termination? The answer is given by the proof lattice in Figure 5.21. It illustrates a type of proof by contradiction that we use quite often. We start by using the Single Exit Rule to break the proof into two cases (this is the first branch in the lattice). In one of those cases, control remains forever inside the loop. In this case, we can establish that eventually $\Box\neg p$ must be true, and then our reasoning is essentially the same as before.

These proofs were quite detailed, with each application of a proof rule cited explicitly. This is the sort of proof that mechanical verifiers do well, but people find unbearably tedious. If people as well as machines are to be able to use a proof method, they must be able to omit obvious details. For example, the reasoning in step 7 of Figure 5.19 is so trivial that it does not really need to be explained—so steps 6 and 7 can be combined and the "$\textit{after}(c)$" node of Figure 5.19 eliminated. Also, steps 4-6 of the proof simply show that if control is in c and $\Box\neg p$ holds, then control must eventually be after c. This is such an obvious conclusion that it could be reached in a single step. One often

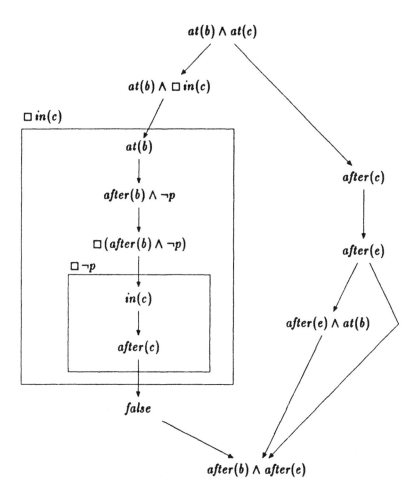

Figure 5.21: Proof Lattice for Program of Figure 5.20

combines a number of proof rules when they describe simple progress of control in a single process.

However, informal reasoning about concurrent programs often leads to errors, so we must be careful when we leave out steps in a proof. Fortunately, some kinds of informal reasoning are relatively safe. We recommend the following guidelines for constructing informal proofs.

1. Each step in the proof should combine actions from just one process.

2. To conclude that evaluating an expression E yields a value v, one must prove

$\square(E = v)$. For example, in the above proof we were able to conclude that the **while** test evaluated to "false", and the loop therefore ended, because we had proved $\square \neg p$. (The $\square$ is needed here for the same reason as in the Atomic Statement Rule.)

5.4.4. Synchronization Primitives

If interprocess communication is only through common access to shared variables, a nonterminated process can never stop. A process can wait for something to happen only by executing a "busy waiting" loop. Most languages for concurrent programming provide some synchronization primitives that let a process wait until some condition is true. Our method for proving liveness properties can be applied to programs using such synchronization primitives. We illustrate this by considering the well-known semaphore primitives. However, the method applies equally well to such other primitives as waiting for a message, or the "!" and "?" primitives of CSP.

A semaphore is a nonnegative integer variable that can be accessed by two primitive operations: P and V. A V operation increments the value of the semaphore by one, while a P operation decrements it by 1. However, since the semaphore's value must be nonnegative, a P operation can only be performed when the value is positive. This means that if a process's control is at a $P(s)$ operation when the value of the semaphore s is zero, then the process must wait until another process has performed a $V(s)$ operation before it can proceed. A $V(s)$ operation can always be performed.

In order to prove properties of programs that use the semaphore primitives, we need a precise definition of the semantics of these primitives. It is not hard to define their safety properties—see, for example, [Lamport 80b]. Specifying their liveness properties presents a more interesting problem. In fact, the liveness properties of the semaphore operations were not fully specified in their original definition, and several different versions have been implemented. The differences result from different methods of choosing which process to activate when a $V(s)$ operation is executed and several processes are waiting to execute $P(s)$ operations. There are several different ways of making that choice, each leading to different liveness properties for the semaphore operations. For our example, we assume that the choice is made "fairly".

We define the P and V operations to be atomic. The liveness axiom for the V operation is quite straightforward, simply stating that the V operation always terminates.

V Liveness Axiom: For the statement l: $\langle\, V(s)\, \rangle$:

$$at(l) \quad \leadsto \quad after(l)$$

The subtle part of the semaphore operations lies in specifying under what conditions a P operation must eventually terminate. It is obviously not enough that the semaphore be positive when control reaches the P operation, because it could be decremented by another process before that operation is executed. The following axiom states that a process trying to perform a P operation will not have to wait forever while other processes keep executing P operations on that semaphore.

P Liveness Axiom: For the statement l: $\langle\, P(s)\, \rangle$:

$$(at(l) \wedge \Box\Diamond s > 0) \quad \leadsto \quad after(l)$$

This axiom states that a P operation will be executed if the semaphore repeatedly assumes a positive value. (The formula $\Box\Diamond s > 0$ states that s is positive infinitely often.)

The Single Exit and General Statement Rules apply to the P and V statements. Since a $V(s)$ statement is really just an assignment statement $(\, s := s+1\,)$, the Atomic Assignment Rule holds for it. (It can be derived from the V Liveness Axiom and the General Statement Rule.)

We illustrate the use of these semaphore axioms with the simple mutual exclusion algorithm of Figure 5.22. We illustrate the use of these semaphore axioms with the simple mutual exclusion algorithm of Figure 5.22. Mutual exclusion is proved by showing that $Init \supset \Box I$, where I is defined by

$$I \equiv 0 \le s \le 1 \wedge 1 - s = \text{number of processes } i \text{ such that } near(CS_i) \text{ is true}$$

where $near(CS_i) \equiv in(CS_i) \vee after(CS_i)$.

Our Liveness Axiom for the P operation guarantees that any process that wants to enter its critical section will eventually do so, unless the other process remains forever inside its critical section. Thus, we have the following liveness property for Process 1:

$$(at(a_0) \wedge \Box\Diamond\neg in(CS_2)) \supset (at(a_1) \leadsto in(CS_1)) \ . \tag{5.4}$$

A similar liveness property holds for Process 2.

semaphore s ;

$a_0 : \langle\, s := 1 \,\rangle$;

    cobegin

      w_1 : **while** $\langle\, true \,\rangle$

            do NC_1: *noncritical section* 1 ;

                a_1: $\langle\, P(s) \,\rangle$;

                CS_1: *critical section* 1 ;

                d_1: $\langle\, V(s) \,\rangle$

            od

        ◻

      w_2 : **while** $\langle\, true \,\rangle$

            do NC_2: *noncritical section* 2 ;

                a_2: $\langle\, P(s) \,\rangle$;

                CS_2: *critical section* 2 ;

                d_2: $\langle\, V(s) \,\rangle$

            od

    coend

Figure 5.22: Mutual Exclusion Algorithm Using Semaphores

To prove (5.4), we first prove the following formula, which states that the semaphore repeatedly assumes a positive value unless some process stays inside its critical section forever:

$$Init \ \supset \ [(\Box I \wedge \Box\Diamond\neg near(CS_1) \wedge \Box\Diamond\neg near(CS_2)) \ \supset \ (s = 0 \rightsquigarrow s = 1)] \quad (5.5)$$

(I and *near* are as defined above.) Its proof is given by the lattice of Figure 5.23, with the steps explained below.

1. The predicate attached to the box is just the hypothesis of the implication we are trying to prove.

2. The invariant I implies that when the semaphore has the value 0, one of the processes is near its critical section.

3. The assumption that a process does not remain in its critical section, together

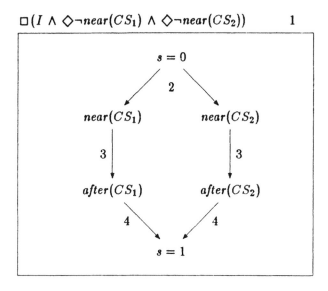

$$\Box(I \land \Diamond\neg near(CS_1) \land \Diamond\neg near(CS_2)) \qquad 1$$

Figure 5.23: Proof Lattice for (5.5)

with the Single Exit Rule, guarantees that if a process is near its critical section then it is eventually after it.

4. The Liveness Axiom for the V operation implies that if control is after CS_i, then the subsequent V operation will terminate. We can then apply the General Statement Rule to conclude that s will equal 1 when the $V(s)$ operation terminates. This is based on the truth of $\{s \geq 0\}\ V(s)\ \{s\ )0\}$, and the fact that the invariant implies that s is always 0 or 1.

Using (5.5), we now prove (5.4) with the lattice of Figure 5.24, whose steps are explained below.

1. As before, we put a box around the whole lattice labeled with the hypothesis.

2. This is an application of the Single Exit Rule, noting that $at(a_1) = in(a_1)$ since a_1 is atomic.

3. Since $at(a_1)$ implies $\neg near(CS_1)$, we can conclude from (5.5) that $s = 0 \rightsquigarrow s = 1$. Since s is always nonnegative, this implies $\Box\Diamond s > 0$.

4. The Liveness Axiom for the $P(s)$ operation implies that if control is at a_1 and $\Box\Diamond s > 0$ is true, then eventually the $P(s)$ operation will be executed and

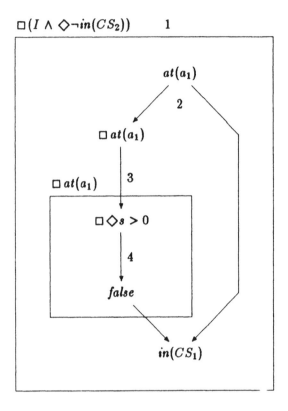

Figure 5.24: Proof Lattice for Semaphore Program

control will be after a_1, contradicting the assumption of the inner box that control is forever at a_1.

This completes the proof of (5.4), the liveness property for Process 1. The corresponding property for Process 2 is proved in exactly the same way.

The above proof may may have seemed rather long for the simple program of Figure 5.22, whose correctness seems obvious. However, liveness properties for programs using semaphores tend to be rather subtle, and there are quite reasonable ways of defining the semaphore operations for which the algorithm would not guarantee the liveness property (5.4).

5.5. Specification

Thus far in this section, we have discussed how to reason about programs written in an executable programming language. Understanding how to reason about concurrent programs is an essential prerequisite to understanding their formal specification.

The specification of a program module may be viewed as a contract between the user of the module and its implementer. It must contain all the information needed to:

1. Enable the user to design a program that uses the module, and verify its correctness, without knowing anything about how the module is implemented.

2. Enable the implementer to design the module, and verify its correctness, without knowing anything about the program that uses the module.

The whole issue of formal specification revolves around the issue of verifying correctness—correctness of the program using the module and correctness of the module's implementation. We know that we have a truly rigorous, formal specification method if these verifications can be carried out formally.

The word "specification" is often used to denote what we would call a high-level design. A specification of a program describes what the program should do; a high-level design describes how it should do it. This distinction is not a formal one, since even a machine language program can be made into a specification by prefacing it with: "Any program that computes the same result as ... ". This "specification" does not say how the results are to be computed, but it would certainly bias an implementer toward a particular method. Any specification will probably have some bias toward a certain type of implementation, so there is no sharp dividing line between specifications and high-level designs. However, we propose that with any true specification method, it should be easy to specify programs that cannot be implemented, since describing what should be done need not imply that it can be done. For example, specifying a program to decide if a finite state machine will halt and specifying a program to decide if a Turing machine will halt should be equally easy – even though one of the programs can be written and the other cannot.

The formal specification method described here is based upon temporal logic; it was introduced in [Lamport 83a]. We have found this method to be quite successful for specifying a variety of small problems, and have been quite pleased with its utility. In this method, one chooses a complete set of state functions containing all the information needed to describe the instantaneous state of the system. Safety properties are specified by axioms that prescribe how these state functions are allowed to change, and liveness properties are specified by writing temporal logic formulas. Other specification methods based upon temporal logic, such as the method described in [Schwartz 83], differ mainly in replacing many of the state functions by temporal assertions.

In these lectures, we introduce a variation of our method in which a new class of formulas are introduced. These formulas can be thought of as "backwards-looking" temporal assertions, but they are actually just state functions. In addition to introducing this new class of formulas, we have also developed a more systematic methodology for writing specifications. A difficulty with axiomatic specification methods has been figuring out how to find the appropriate axioms. While previous axiomatic specifications may appear quite plausible, they have been presented in their final form, with no indication of how one goes about constructing them. Here, we describe a well-defined sequence of steps one goes through in writing a specification.

The specification method described here is called the *transition axiom* method—"transition" to indicate the important role played by the transitions that change state functions, and "axiom" to emphasize that, despite the resemblance to more traditional state machine methods, ours are axiomatic specifications.

5.5.1. The Formalism

As we saw in Section 2.2, a system execution consists of a set Σ of sequences of the form

$$s_0 \xrightarrow{\alpha_1} s_1 \xrightarrow{\alpha_2} s_2 \cdots$$

where the s_i are elements in a set of *states* $\mathbf{S}$, and the α_i are elements in a set of *actions* $\mathbf{A}$. The sequences in Σ represent all possible executions in an "operational" or "behavioral" model. The sets $\mathbf{S}$ and $\mathbf{A}$ are determined by the model of computation one chooses, which in turn depends upon the level at which one views the system. Three possible choices are:

- A "Pascal" model in which an action represents the execution of an atomic program statement in a Pascal-like language.

- A "machine" model in which an action represents the execution of a single computer instruction.

- A "hardware" model, in which an action represents an operation in the register-transfer description of the computer.

In any of these models, concurrent activity is represented by the interleaving of atomic actions.

The choice of model does not concern us, since the specifications we write are independent of the underlying model; the specification is the same, regardless of whether it is implemented in Pascal or silicon. For example, we might consider a machine model of a multiprocess computer, in which a state consists of the values of all memory locations and registers, including the program counters, index registers, interrupt registers, etc. An action is a particular program instruction—for example, a *load accumulator* instruction at memory location 27264. A sequence in Σ represents a possible execution of the program.

In verifying concurrent programs, the set of sequences Σ is defined by the program, and we must prove properties of it. In writing specifications, we take the inverse approach. We write a set of temporal logic axioms that Σ must satisfy. In other words, our specification is a set of formulas A_i, and a program satisfies this specification if the set of behaviors Σ of that program satisfy $\forall i : \Sigma \models A_i$.

In the interest of simplicity, we will ignore the actions and consider a behavior to be a sequence

$$s_0 \rightarrow s_1 \rightarrow s_2 \rightarrow \cdots$$

of states. For convenience, we also assume all sequences to be infinite; a finite computation ending in a state s_n being represented by the infinite sequence ending with

$$s_0 \rightarrow \cdots s_n \rightarrow s_n \rightarrow s_n \rightarrow \cdots .$$

Finite sequences simply add some irrelevant details to the formalism; the role of actions can be found in [Lamport 83a].

We will not use the temporal logic of Section 2.2 to write the specifications. Our specifications can be translated into a collection of standard temporal logic formulas, using the method indicated in the appendix of [Lamport 83a]. However, it is convenient to describe our specifications in terms of a slightly different formalism. You should keep in mind, though, that because everything can be translated into the formalism of Section 2.2, all of our specifications are invariant under "stuttering", so we are not implicitly using the next-time operator $\bigcirc$.

In Section 2.2, we defined the meaning of $\sigma \models F$ for any temporal logic formula F

and any sequence $\sigma \in \Sigma$. We now define

$$\sigma, i \models F \quad equiv \quad \sigma^{+i} \models F$$

In other words, $\sigma, i \models F$ asserts that F is true at time i during the execution σ.

A *transition specification* is a boolean relation on states—in other words, a boolean-valued function on $S \times S$. We think of a transition as a pair of states—an old (starting) state and a new (final) state, so a transition specification is a relation between an old and a new state. If τ is a transition specification, then a transition (s, t) for which $\tau(s, t)$ is true is said to be a τ *transition*. For a transition specification τ, and a sequence

$$\sigma \quad = \quad s_0 \rightarrow s_1 \rightarrow \cdots$$

we define

$$\sigma, i \models \tau \quad \equiv \quad \tau(s_{i-1}, s_i)$$

where s_{-1} is defined to equal s_0. A transition specification is a relation between two states; it is true at time i if the relation holds between the state just before the ith transition and the state just after it. We define a special transition 0 that is true only on the starting transition—*i.e.*,

$$\sigma, i \models 0 \quad \equiv \quad i = 0 .$$

We now introduce a notation for writing transition specifications. As an example of the notation, if x and y are integer-valued state functions, then $y_o < x_n$ is the transition specification that is true if the value of y in the old state is less than the value of x in the new state. Thus $y_o < x_n$ is the relation that is true on the pair of states (s, t) if and only if the value of y_o in state s is less than the value of x_n in state t. In general, given any boolean-valued expression composed of state functions, we form a transition specification by subscripting each state function with either o (for *old*) or n (for *new*). The value of this transition specification on the pair of states (s, t) is the value obtained by evaluating each state function subscripted o on s and each state function subscripted n on t.

Note that since transition specifications are boolean-valued functions, we can form new transitions by taking logical combinations of them. Thus, if τ and μ are transition specifications, then $\tau \wedge \mu$ and $\neg \tau$ are also transition specifications. A transition is a $\tau \wedge \mu$

transition if and only if it is both a τ transition and a μ transition; it is a $(\neg\tau)$ transition if and only if it is not a τ transition. We can also form the *composition* $\tau \circ \mu$ defined by

$$\tau \circ \mu(s,t) \equiv \exists u : \tau(s,u) \wedge \mu(u,t) ,$$

so a $\tau \circ \mu$ transition is one that could have been the result of first performing a τ transition and then performing a μ transition.

Finally, given transition specifications τ and μ, we define the *backward temporal assertion* $\left[\tau \xleftarrow{\neg\mu}\right]$ by

$$\sigma, i \models \left[\tau \xleftarrow{\neg\mu}\right] \equiv \exists j \leq i : (\sigma, j \models \tau \wedge \forall k : j \leq k \leq i \supset \sigma, k \models \neg\mu)$$

Intuitively, $\left[\tau \xleftarrow{\neg\mu}\right]$ is true at time i if, looking backwards in time, one reaches a τ transition before reaching a μ transition. In other words, $\left[\tau \xleftarrow{\neg\mu}\right]$ is initially false; it is made true by a τ transition and made false by a μ transition. (A transition that is both a τ and a μ transition makes it false.) Note that $\left[\tau \xleftarrow{\neg\mu}\right]$ is false at time i if the ith transition is both a τ and a μ transition. To make sure that you understand these backwards temporal assertions, you should convince yourself that the following is a tautology:

$$\neg\left[\tau \xleftarrow{\neg\mu}\right] \equiv \left[\mu \vee 0 \xleftarrow{\neg\tau}\right] .$$

Another useful pair of equivalences is the following:

$$\left[\tau_1 \vee \tau_2 \xleftarrow{\neg\mu}\right] \equiv \left[\tau_1 \xleftarrow{\neg\mu}\right] \vee \left[\tau_2 \xleftarrow{\neg\mu}\right]$$
$$\left[\tau \xleftarrow{\neg(\mu_1 \vee \mu_2)}\right] \equiv \left[\tau \xleftarrow{\neg\mu_1}\right] \wedge \left[\tau \xleftarrow{\neg\mu_2}\right] \tag{5.6}$$

We permit a backward temporal assertion to appear anywhere that a state predicate is allowed, so we may write temporal logic formulas like

$$\square(x > 0) \supset \square\lozenge\left[\tau \xleftarrow{\neg\mu}\right] .$$

In particular, we may use backward temporal formulas to construct transition specifications, which in turn can be used to form backward temporal formulas. Thus, given transitions specifications α, β, γ and δ, we may construct the following backward temporal formula F:

$$\left[\left[\alpha \xleftarrow{\neg\beta}\right]_n \wedge \gamma \xleftarrow{\neg\delta}\right] .$$

To interpret the formula F, we first observe that the transition specification $\left[\alpha \xleftarrow{\neg\beta}\right]_n \wedge \gamma$ is satisfied by a transition if and only if it is a γ transition for which $\left[\alpha \xleftarrow{\neg\beta}\right]$ is true of the new (final) state. Thus, F is made true by such a γ transition, and is made false by a δ transition.

Intuitively, you can think of a backwards temporal formula $\left[\tau \xleftarrow{\neg\mu}\right]$ as a statement about the past. As we shall see later, it will turn out to be a state predicate. In order for this to happen, we shall restrict the type of transition specifications τ and μ that can appear.

5.5.2. How to Write a Specification

By a *module*, we mean some logical component of a system. The modules we consider here are collections of subroutines, but our method applies to other kinds of modules too—for example, a functional unit on a VLSI chip. To specify a module, one first chooses a collection of state functions and a set of transition specifications, called the *allowed transitions*, that describe how those state functions may change. For each state function, one gives the range of values it may assume, its possible initial values, and the allowed transitions that may change its value.

For each allowed transition, one specifies if it represents an action of the module or of its environment. In specifying one module of a system, one must include constraints on what other parts of the system are allowed to do. For example, a subroutine in a concurrent program cannot function properly if a concurrently executed process can arbitrarily change that subroutine's local variables. When writing a program, such assumptions are tacitly made by the programming language semantics. However, since our specification is independent of any underlying language—indeed, the other part of the system might be circuitry that is connected to the circuit implementing the module— such assumptions must be made explicit.

We illustrate our method by specifying a module for implementing a queue. This module has two subroutines: *put* and *get* that are used to put an element in the queue and remove an element from the queue, respectively. We allow two different processes to perform concurrent *put* and *get* operations, but assume that concurrent calls of either one are prohibited. Other than state functions involved in calling and returning from a subroutine, such as the state function specifying the argument of a call to *put*, our specification explicitly mentions only one state function: *queue*, which is a finite sequence of *elements*. We need not specify what an "element" is.

There are six allowed transitions:

call.put(v): A call of the *put* subroutine with argument v.

ret.put: A return from the *put* subroutine.

call.get: A call of the *get* subroutine.

ret.get(v): A return from the *get* subroutine with argument v.

enq(v):   The action of adding element v to *queue*.

deq(v):   The action of removing element v from *queue*.

Note that an allowed transition like *call.put(v)* is actually a set of separate allowed transitions, one for each possible value of v. We let *call.put(·)* denote any one of those allowed transitions. More precisely, *call.put(·)* denotes the transition specification $\exists v : call.put(v)$. The transitions *call.put(v)* and *call.get* are external (represent actions of the environment); the others are internal to the module.

The state function *queue* has the initial value λ (the empty sequence). The value of *queue* may be changed only by the *enq* and *deq* transitions. This means that in any successive states s_i, s_{i+1} in any execution σ, if the value of *queue* in state s_{i+1} is different from its value in state s_i, then the transition (s_i, s_{i+1}) must be an *enq* or a *deq* transition.

These transitions represent atomic actions in the implementation, so the operations of adding and removing an element from *queue* must be atomic. However, this does not mean that the implementation must manipulate an entire queue element with a single atomic operation. For example, in a machine language implementation, the state function *queue* may be a complex function of memory location values and register values. It can be defined in such a way that it changes atomically, even though the program may actually move elements in and out of the queue one bit at a time. An example of how such a state function can be defined is given in [Lamport 83a].

After stating what the allowed transitions are, we must write their specifications. It is convenient to separate the transition specifications into two parts: an *effect* and an *enabling* transition. The transition specification is the conjunction ($\wedge$) of these two parts. The effect specifies *what* the transition does to the state functions, while the enabling transition specifies *when* the transition may occur. This separation is for convenience only, and has no formal standing.

The effect specification for the subroutine calls and returns specifies the module's interface, and will not be discussed here. The effects of the *enq* and *deq* transitions are as follows, where * denotes concatenation.

$enq(v)$: $queue_n = queue_o * v$

$deq(v)$: $queue_o = v * queue_n$

Observe that we have specified a FIFO queue—elements are added to one end and removed from the other. To specify a LIFO queue or stack, we could just reverse the order of concatenation in either one of the formulas. To specify an undisciplined queue— *i.e.*, a collection elements in which items can be removed in any order, we change *queue* from a sequence to a bag (a set with repeated elements) and replace concatenation by bag union. To specify a sorted queue, in which the *get* returns the largest element in the queue, we then add the requirement that v be $\geq$ every element of $queue_n$. In this manner, it is easy to express any desired form of queueing discipline.

We now describe the enabling conditions for the allowed transitions. An enabling condition is a transition specification, so it is a relation between an old and a new state. However, enabling conditions are almost always functions only of the old state. When this is the case, we omit the subscripts on the component state functions, letting the subscript o be implicit. We use the notation that $|queue|$ denotes the length of the sequence *queue*.

$call.put(v)$: ...

> The enabling condition for calling *put* is part of the interface specification. It must ensure that no process can call *put* if another process is currently executing that subroutine.

$ret.put$: $\left[enq(\cdot) \xleftarrow{\neg ret.put} \right]$

> The *put* subroutine can return only if an *enq* has been performed since the last time it returned—*i.e.*, only if an *enq* has been performed during the current call

to *put*. Note that this condition is added to (more precisely, conjoined with) the interface specification for the transition.

call.get: ...

As with *call.put(v)*, this is part of the interface specification.

$ret.get(v)$: $\left[deq(v) \xleftarrow{\neg ret.get(\cdot)} \right]$

The *get* subroutine can return the value v only if an $enq(v)$ has occurred during the current call.

$enq(v)$: $\left[call.put(v) \xleftarrow{\neg enq(v)} \right] \wedge |queue| < maxsize$

The first condition states that the value v can be enqueued only if a call of *put* occurred with argument v, and no $enq(v)$ transition has occurred since then. The second condition states that the element can be enqueued only if the current (old) length of the queue is less than *maxsize*. Hence, we are specifying a bounded queue of maximum size *maxsize*. (To specify an unbounded queue, we would just eliminate this condition.)

$deq(v)$: $\left[call.get \xleftarrow{\neg deq(\cdot)} \right] \wedge |queue| > 0$

The first condition states that an element can be dequeued only if a *get* has been called and no other *deq* transition has occurred since then. (The effect part of the specification constrains the value of v to be the element now at the head of the queue.) Note that had we written $deq(v)$ instead of $deq(\cdot)$ in the backwards temporal assertion, the transition specification would not have ruled out the possibility of dequeueing of two or more different elements on the same call to *get*.

The second condition requires that the queue must be nonempty in order to dequeue an element. This is actually redundant, since the effect specification implies that $queue_o$ must be nonempty, but we have included it to maintain the symmetry of the *enq* and *deq* transitions specifications.

This completes the specification of the safety properties of the queue module. Note that no temporal assertions are used, except for the backwards temporal assertions that will turn out to be state functions. This is not surprising, since temporal logic is needed only for liveness properties. Safety properties can be expressed and verified using only a generalized concept of invariance, which is embodied in our allowed transition specifications, without introducing the full power of temporal logic.

The enabling conditions for the allowed transitions assert when a transition *may* occur. To specify liveness properties, we need conditions that assert when a transition *must* occur. We would like to write such a condition for transition τ as $C \rightsquigarrow \tau$ for some temporal logic assertion C. However, we cannot do this because a transition specification may not appear in a temporal logic formula. Instead, we must write the condition in one of the following two forms:

$$C \rightsquigarrow \left[\tau \xleftarrow{\neg\mu} \right]$$

$$C \rightsquigarrow \neg[\mu \xleftarrow{\neg\tau}]$$

The formulas to the right of the "$\rightsquigarrow$" are both made true by a τ transition (except that the first is made false if it is also a μ transition). The choice of which form to use depends upon the desired condition, but the second seems to be more common. A particularly common form is the condition

$$true \rightsquigarrow \neg[\mu \xleftarrow{\neg\tau}]$$

which asserts that whenever a μ transition occurs, if it is not also a τ transition then a τ transition must occur some time in the future. This condition is abbreviated as $\mu \rightsquigarrow \tau$.

We now describe the liveness conditions for each of the allowed transitions.

call.put(v): none

ret.put: $enq(\cdot) \rightsquigarrow ret.put$

The *put* subroutine must return after it has enqueued an element.

call.get: none

ret.get(v): $deq(v) \rightsquigarrow ret.get(v)$

The *get* subroutine must return after it has dequeued an element.

$enq(v)$: $|queue| < minsize \rightsquigarrow \neg\left[call.put(v) \xleftarrow{\neg enq(v)} \right]$

Note that this assertion is true at any time when $\left[call.put(v) \xleftarrow{\neg enq(v)} \right]$ is false—in other words, it is automatically true unless a call of *put* has occurred

state functions

    queue: **range** = sequence of *element*

           initial value: λ

           changed by $enq(\cdot)$, $deq(\cdot)$

allowed external transitions

    call.put(v): safety: ...

              liveness: none.

    call.get: safety: ...

              liveness: none.

allowed internal transitions

    ret.put: safety: $\left[enq(\cdot) \xleftarrow{\neg ret.put} \right] \rightarrow \ldots$

              liveness: $enq(\cdot) \rightsquigarrow ret.put$

    ret.get(v): safety: $\left[deq(v) \xleftarrow{\neg ret.get(\cdot)} \right] \rightarrow \ldots$

              liveness: $deq(v) \rightsquigarrow ret.get(v)$

    enq(v):   safety: $\left[call.put(v) \xleftarrow{\neg enq(v)} \right] \wedge |queue| < maxsize \ \rightarrow$

                         $queue_n = queue_o * v$

              liveness: $|queue| < minsize \rightsquigarrow \neg \left[call.put(v) \xleftarrow{\neg enq(v)} \right]$

    deq(v):   safety: $\left[call.get \xleftarrow{\neg deq(\cdot)} \right] \wedge |queue| > 0 \ \rightarrow queue_o = v * queue_n$

              $|queue| > 0 \rightsquigarrow \neg \left[call.get \xleftarrow{\neg deq(\cdot)} \right]$

Figure 5.25: Specification of the Queue Module

that has not yet been followed by the corresponding *enq*. The condition asserts that if this is the case, and if the length of the queue is less than *minsize*, then the *enq* must eventually occur. We are thus specifying a queue that has room for at least *minsize* elements. (To specify a queue with an unbounded capacity, this hypothesis is removed, so the condition becomes $call.put(v) \rightsquigarrow enq(v)$.) Note how the requirement of a minimum capacity is a liveness property, while the requirement of a maximum capacity is a safety property.

$$deq(v): \; |queue| > 0 \; \rightsquigarrow \; \neg\left[call.get \xleftarrow{\neg deq(\cdot)}\right]$$

This is analogous to the liveness specification for the *enq* transition: a call of *get* must lead to a *deq* if the queue is nonempty. Note the use of $deq(\cdot)$ rather than $deq(v)$ in this specification. We needn't specify what element will be dequeued, since that is determined by the transition specification. However, we could also write the equivalent specification

$$head(queue) = v \; \rightsquigarrow \; \neg\left[call.get \xleftarrow{\neg deq(v)}\right]$$

The complete specification is given in Figure 5.25, except that parts of the specification representing the interface specification are omitted, the omissions indicated by "...". The transition specifications are written in the form

$$enabling \; condition \; \rightarrow \; effect$$

instead of

$$enabling \; condition_o \; \wedge \; effect \; .$$

5.5.3. Backwards Temporal Assertions as State Functions

Thus far, everything we have done is essentially the same as the method in [Lamport 83a], with a slightly different syntax, except for the backwards temporal assertions. We now show how to convert these assertions into state functions, thus reducing our method to the formalism of [Lamport 83a]. To illustrate the general idea, we consider the assertion $\left[deq(v) \xleftarrow{\neg ret.get(\cdot)}\right]$ that appears in the transition specification for *ret.put*. By formula (5.6) of Section 5, recalling that

$$ret.get(\cdot) \; \equiv \; \exists\,u : ret.get(u) \; ,$$

we see that

$$\left[deq(v) \xleftarrow{\neg ret.get(\cdot)}\right] \; \equiv \; \exists\,u : \left[deq(v) \xleftarrow{\neg ret.get(u)}\right] \; .$$

Thus, we need only specify $\left[deq(v) \xleftarrow{\neg ret.get(u)}\right]$ as a state function. This is done by adding the following to the *state functions* part of the specification of Figure 5.25.

$$\left[deq(v) \xleftarrow{\neg ret.get(u)}\right] : \; \textbf{range} = boolean$$

$$\textbf{initial value:} \; false$$

changed by $deq(v)$, $ret.get(u)$

Remembering that $\left[deq(v) \xleftarrow{\neg ret.get(u)}\right]$ is made true by a $deq(v)$ transition and is made false by a $ret.get(u)$ transition, we must add the condition $\left[deq(v) \xleftarrow{\neg ret.get(u)}\right]_n =$ $true$ to the effect part of the $deq(v)$ transition specification, and add the condition $\left[deq(v) \xleftarrow{\neg ret.get(u)}\right]_n = false$ to the effect part of the $ret.get(u)$ transition. However, this eliminates the possibility that a single transition can be both a $deq(v)$ and a $ret.get(u)$ transition. If we want to allow that possibility, then the condition we add to the $deq(v)$ specification is:

$$\left[deq(v) \xleftarrow{\neg ret.get(u)}\right]_n = true \ \vee \ ret.get(u) \ .$$

By these changes to the specification, we have turned the backwards temporal logic assertion $\left[deq(v) \xleftarrow{\neg ret.get(\cdot)}\right]$ into an ordinary state function.

To generalize this method of converting $\left[\tau \xleftarrow{\neg\mu}\right]$ into a state function, we must place some restrictions on τ and μ. We require that they both be disjunctions of transition specifications of the form $\alpha \wedge \rho$, where α is one of the allowed transitions and ρ is any transition specification. Since we can use formulas 5.6 to reduce $\left[\tau \xleftarrow{\neg\mu}\right]$ if τ and μ are disjunctions, we need consider only the backwards temporal formula $\left[\alpha \wedge \rho \xleftarrow{\neg(\beta \wedge \kappa)}\right]$, where α and ρ are allowed transitions. To specify this formula as a state function, we let its initial value be $false$ and α and β be the transitions that may change it. We add

$$\kappa \supset \left[\alpha \wedge \rho \xleftarrow{\neg(\beta \wedge \kappa)}\right]_n = false$$

to the transition specification of β and

$$(\beta \wedge \kappa) \ \vee \ \left(\rho \supset \left[\alpha \wedge \rho \xleftarrow{\neg(\beta \wedge \kappa)}\right]_n = true\right) \ .$$

5.5.4. Using Specifications

The true test of a specification method is how easy the specifications are to use. With formal specifications, this means asking how easy it is to reason formally about the specifications. Recall that there are two uses to which we wish to put the specification of a module:

1. To verify the correctness of a program that uses it.

2. To verify the correctness of a program that implements it.

Our specification method was chosen explicitly with these verification tasks in mind. Verification of a program that uses the module is done by the same methods as before. The state functions of the specification are used very much like ordinary program variables in the proof, and the transitions play the part of atomic program actions. One constructs predicates with program variables and the module's state functions. Invariance is proved by showing that each atomic action of the program and each transition of the specification leave the predicate true. Liveness properties are proved from the usual liveness rules for program statements plus the liveness axioms of the module's specification.

To verify the correctness of a program that implements the specification, one must define the module's state functions as functions of the program's state. Internal state functions can be defined in a completely arbitrary manner. However, interface state functions must be constrained in some manner to insure that the program really interacts with its environment in the proper way. The question of verifying the interface is an important one that is neglected in most work on formal specification. However, it is of vital importance in practice. In our method, verifying the interface involves checking how the interface state functions are defined in terms of the implementing program's state.

Defining the specification's state functions in terms of the implementation's state is the hard part of verifying the implementation. Once it is done, verification is straightforward. Safety properties of the specification are verified by showing that every atomic program action either leaves all the state functions unchanged, or else performs one of the specified transitions—i.e., one must show that the values of the state functions in the old and new states satisfy a transition specification. Liveness properties are proved by the methods indicated in Section 5.4.

In both kinds of verification—of a program that uses the module and of a program that implements the module—the program need not be written in an executable programming language. Instead, the program could be specified using our method. In this case, rather than having a program and a specification, we have two different levels in a hierarchy of specifications. Everything we have just said applies in this case as well, we just have to replace "program" by "specification", "atomic action" by "transition" and "program state" by "state functions". Thus, we can use our specification method in a hierarchical fashion.

Unfortunately, time does not permit an example here of this kind of verification. Such examples may be found in [Lamport 83a]. A discussion of hierarchical specification may also be found in [Lamport 83b].

Chapter 6

Language Constructs for Distributed Programs

There are several reasons for discussing language constructs in the context of specification. Given a formal specification of an algorithm in any notation, we have to design a correct program executable on a specific machine. The aim is to verify the correctness of the program with respect to its formal specification. This can be done analytically using prove rules as shown e.g. in [Gries 81] or by construction using semantics–preserving transformation rules as advocated by [Bauer 82]. In both cases we have to argue about the target notation consisting of high–level language constructs. So it is impossible to talk about formal specification without profound knowledge of language constructs.

A second reason is that designers of modern programming languages tend to integrate language constructs which allow to denote aspects, classically attributed not to the programming level but to the design level. One example for this is the step from Pascal to Modula [Wirth 77a, Wirth 77b, Wirth 77c] integrating the aspect of modularity.

Of course we will discuss in the paper only language concepts important for the construction of distributed programs as modularity, concurrency, communication, exception handling, real–time and configuration description. We will show those concepts using the notation of different recent programming languages. Even if there are no compilers available for some of those languages they are useful to guide the program design process by high level thinking patterns defining adequate levels of abstraction and to facilitate correctness proofs.

We may even see such programs as formal operational specifications of lower level programs (e.g. assembler). We can construct lower level programs then applying semantics–preserving transformation rules again. Naturally such an implementation based on an operational specification will presumably be close related to the high level algorithmic solution (but not necessarily has to be!) as is typically the problem with implementations derived from operational specifications.

6.1. Modularity Concepts

6.1.1. The Notion of Modularity

Our limited ability to understand and construct complex systems forces us to reduce their complexity by *decomposition* and *abstraction*. Designing the architecture of large software systems two decomposition methods can be applied.

The first method is to construct a *hierarchy* of abstract machines [Goos 73]. Each abstract machine defines an abstract language which can be used to construct a more problem–oriented abstract machine on top of it. In this way the whole software system is decomposed into a (fairly small) number of hierarchical layers of abstract machines (Figure 6.1). This method was successfully used in structuring an operating system and first described by [Dijkstra 68a].

The second method is to decompose the software system into *modules*. By modules we understand components of a software system forming logical units from some point of view. The operation of the whole software system is achieved by combining those modules. We can think of one abstract machine to be composed of several modules. There is no general agreement, however, in which way hierarchical and modular structure are related. Some people also think of a module to be structured hierarchically in contrast to our model (Figure 6.1).

One important property of a module is its ability to *hide* information from its outside user thus abstracting from implementation details and controlling the *visibility* of algorithms and data structures. Using a module it

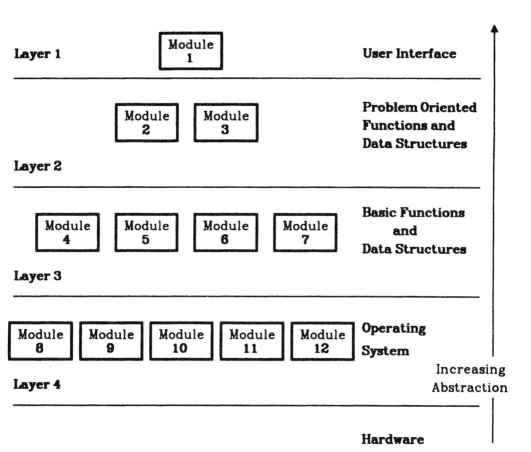

Figure 6.1: Hierarchical and modular structure of a software system

is sufficient to know its *interface* to the outside world. Another equal important property is that different people can work independently on different modules, only loosely tied together by the contract the interface they agreed upon is representing.

Collaboration of several people implementing a large software system is only feasible in a reasonable way if they can compile their part independently. Due to their properties it is reasonable to choose one or more modules as compilation units. We often distinguish *independent* versus *separate compilation.* Many FORTRAN compilers allow independent compilation of subroutines. That means that the compiler has no information on number and type of parameters when translating a subroutine call.

Separate compilation in modern programming languages means that the compiler must have full information about all interfaces of modules compiled previously to enable e.g. full type checking.

In the context of distributed programming a further aspect of modularity is that modules are units that can be *distributed* onto different computers. That does not imply, of course, that one computer hosts precisely one module.

We know only from one programming language to offer different concepts for the description of hierarchical and modular structures [Bayer 81]. In most modern programming languages modularity is defined recursively so that by nesting of modules we can achieve the same visibility structure (Figure 6.2).

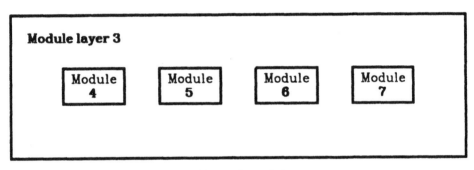

Figure 6.2: Nested module structure

Designing the hierarchical and modular structure of a software system from a given problem specification is a difficult task that requires much experience. It is beyond the scope of this paper to present criteria to be used in decomposing systems into modules [Parnas 72]. But it is useful to give a classification of modules we may find during the decomposition process and look how they can be mapped into different modularity concepts in programming languages.

The most simple module classes either contain only a collection of data (*data module*) or collection of functions (*function module*). Examples for those module classes are a pool of common used constants (pi, e,...) respectively a pool of common used mathematical functions (sin, cos, ...).

The *abstract data structure module* contains data structures and operations to manipulate those data structures. The data structures are invisible from outside the module ("abstract"). Some (or all) of the operations are exported so that the manipulation of the data structure from outside is only possible using these operations. Classical examples are stacks and queues. The important difference between this module class and the function module is, that function modules do not remember previous calls of their exported functions whereas the local data structure in an abstract data structure module can be regarded as a memory of the module. Calls to exported functions (e.g. pop element from stack) thus give different results depending on the calling history.

The **abstract data type module** is similar to the abstract data structure module. Instead of local data structures it contains definitions of data types and operations to manipulate objects of that data types. In this way only the construction principle for data structures of the same type is defined. Exporting the data type but hiding its fine structure allows the outside user to declare any number of objects of that type and manipulate those objects using the exported operations.

Generic abstract data type modules allow to define only templates that can be used to instantiate related abstract data type modules. If we want to handle e.g. stacks of integer objects and stacks of real objects we can generate two abstract data type modules by *instantiation* from one generic module. Those modules are related in this sense that we can implement stacks of both types using the same composition mechanism (e.g. arrays) and that assignation of individual objects of both types is syntactically denotable in the same way (e.g. :=). The same denotation for operators, functions and procedures manipulating objects of different type (even user-defined types) is thus necessary to exploit the full power of generic mechanisms. The possibility to use the same name for different routines is often called *overloading*. Different concepts can be applied to identify overloaded routines unambiguously as for example taking into account number and type of parameters and additionally the result type (for functions and operators).

Modules with implicit and explicit synchronization properties define restrictions on how exported and hidden operations of modules are synchronized in non-sequential programs. The best known example for an abstract data type module with implicit synchronization properties is the *monitor* [Brinch Hansen 73a, Hoare 74]. Monitor operations are defined such that they are executable only in mutual exclusion. An explicit specification of synchronization constraints allowing more flexible concurrency control can be achieved using *path expressions* [Campbell 74, Campbell 79].

Atomic abstract data type modules [Liskov 84a] are another class of modules that show additional properties to regular abstract data type modules. Operations defined in the module can be taylored such that they show *atomicity* [Lampson 81a]. That means that an operation either succeeds or, if it fails, does not change the state of the whole (distributed) system. Moreover, the execution of such an operation does not interfere with concurrent operations so that we can think it to be executed indivisibly. Atomic abstract data types are valuable for constructing fault-tolerant programs.

Thinking of systems to be composed of abstract data types has proved to be one of the most valuable abstractions in designing large programs. Additional properties such as concurrency control, synchronization and fault-tolerance seem to fit nicely into the general concept.

Modularity concepts in programming languages differ in the extent of support for the above mentioned module classes and the way how visibility control or information hiding is realized. The first language to support modularity was SIMULA 67 [Dahl 70] introducing the class concept. After the paper on programming with abstract data types [Liskov 74] several languages like SLAN [Hommel 76] (now ELAN [Hommel 78]), Alphard [Shaw 77], CLU [Liskov 77], Mesa [Geschke 77a], and Modula [Wirth 77a, Wirth 77b, Wirth 77c] were designed to support abstraction by different modularity concepts. We will show the use of modularity concepts in Modula-2 [Wirth 83] and Ada [Ada 83].

6.1.2. Modularity in Modula-2 and Ada

The first example (Figure 6.3) shows the implementation of a queue in Modula-2 as an abstract data structure.

```
DEFINITION MODULE Queue;
   FROM SomeModule IMPORT SOMETYPE;
```

```
    EXPORT QUALIFIED enqueue, dequeue, nonempty, nonfull;
    VAR nonempty, nonfull: BOOLEAN;
    PROCEDURE enqueue (elem: SOMETYPE);
    PROCEDURE dequeue (VAR elem: SOMETYPE);
END Queue.

IMPLEMENTATION MODULE Queue;
    FROM SomeModule IMPORT SOMETYPE;
    CONST MaxLength = 100;
    VAR head, tail: [0..MaxLength-1];
    length   : [0..MaxLength];
    queue    : ARRAY [0..MaxLength-1] OF SOMETYPE;

    PROCEDURE enqueue (elem: SOMETYPE);
    BEGIN
      IF length < MaxLength THEN
        queue [tail]:= elem;
        tail:= (tail + 1) MOD MaxLength;
        INC (length);
        nonfull:= length < MaxLength;
        nonempty:= TRUE
      END
    END enqueue;

    PROCEDURE dequeue (VAR elem: SOMETYPE);
    BEGIN
      IF length > 0 THEN
        elem:= queue [head];
        head:= (head + 1) MOD MaxLength;
        DEC (length);
        nonempty:= length > 0;
        nonfull:= TRUE
      END
    END dequeue;
```

```
BEGIN (* Initialization of Module Queue *)
    length:= 0; head:= 0; tail:= 0;
    nonempty:= FALSE; nonfull:= TRUE
END Queue.
```

Figure 6.3: Modula–2 implementation of an abstract data structure

Hiding of information is supported by textual separation of the module interface (*definition module*) and the implementation details (*implementation module*). As both parts are compiled separately, the user of the module only needs to know the definition module. The definition module contains lists of the imported and exported objects and the declarations of the exported objects representing a concise interface description. QUALIFIED export allows different modules designed by different programmers to export objects with the same name. In this case the identification of the wanted objects is performed by prefixing its identifier with the module's name (e.g. Queue.nonfull). Denoting the import like in our example with the FROM clause and a module identifier unqualifies the imported identifiers so that we can use them without qualifier like in our example. Alternatively we could have specified import by

IMPORT SomeModule;

thus importing all objects of the module SomeModule. In this case qualification had to be used:

PROCEDURE enqueue (elem: SomeModule.SOMETYPE);

The implementation modul contains the local data structure which can be manipulated using the two procedures enqueue and dequeue. The body of a module is executed when a procedure of the module is called the first time thus elaborating the statement sequence for initialization exactly once.

The Ada implementation of the same module is shown in the following Figure 6.4.

```
with SOMEMODULE; use SOMEMODULE;
package QUEUE_HANDLING is
    NONEMPTY, NONFULL : BOOLEAN;
    procedure ENQUEUE (ELEM: in SOMETYPE);
```

```
  procedure DEQUEUE (ELEM: out SOMETYPE);
private
  NONEMPTY : BOOLEAN := FALSE;
  NONFULL : BOOLEAN := TRUE;
end QUEUE_HANDLING;

package body QUEUE_HANDLING is
  MAXLENGTH : constant NATURAL := 100;
  type QUEUE is
    record
      HEAD : INTEGER range 0..MAXLENGTH - 1 := 0;
      TAIL : INTEGER range 0..MAXLENGTH-1 := 0;
      LENGTH : INTEGER range 0..MAXLENGTH := 0;
      Q : array (0.. MAXLENGTH) of SOMETYPE;
    end record;
  LOCAL_QUEUE: QUEUE;
  procedure ENQUEUE (ELEM: in SOMETYPE ) is
    begin
      if LOCAL_QUEUE.LENGTH < MAXLENGTH then
        LOCAL_QUEUE.Q(LOCAL_QUEUE.TAIL) := ELEM;
        LOCAL_QUEUE.TAIL := (LOCAL_QUEUE.TAIL + 1) mod MAXLENGTH;
        LOCAL_QUEUE.LENGTH := LOCAL_QUEUE.LENGTH + 1;
        NONFULL := LOCAL_QUEUE.LENGTH < MAXLENGTH;
        NONEMPTY := TRUE;
      end if;
    end ENQUEUE;

  procedure DEQUEUE (ELEM: out SOMETYPE) is
    begin
      if LOCAL_QUEUE.LENGTH > 0 then
        ELEM:= LOCAL_QUEUE.Q (LOCAL_QUEUE.HEAD);
        LOCAL_QUEUE.HEAD:=(LOCAL_QUEUE.HEAD+1) mod MAXLENGTH;
        LOCAL_QUEUE.LENGTH:=LOCAL_QUEUE.LENGTH-1;
        NONEMPTY:=LOCAL_QUEUE.LENGTH>0;
        NONFULL:= TRUE
```

```
      end if;
    end DEQUEUE;
  end QUEUE_HANDLING;


with QUEUE_HANDLING;

...

begin

...

  if QUEUE_HANDLING.NONFULL then
    QUEUE_HANDLING.ENQUEUE (ONE_ELEMENT);
  end if;
```

Figure 6.4: Ada implementation of an abstract data structure

Similar to Modula-2, in Ada modules are textually separated in a *package specification* and a *package body*. The specification part contains in its visible part all exported objects. There is no import specification inside the package specification. Objects exported from other modules that are to be used are made visible by a *context specification*. Using the *with clause* all the objects exported from the specified module are made visible. The *use clause* allows the unqualified use of all imported identifiers. Without the use clause we had to change our program e.g. to:

procedure ENQUEUE (ELEM: **in** SOMEMODULE.SOMETYPE);

The private part contains in our first example only initializations hidden to the user. In the package body we made a slight change compared to the Modula example. The explicit type definition with initializations in the record definition allows us to get rid of the whole initialization part we had to program in Modula.

Our next example (Figure 6.5) gives an implementation for an abstract data type module in Modula-2 .

```
DEFINITION MODULE QueueHandler;
  FROM SomeModule IMPORT SOMETYPE;
  EXPORT QUALIFIED genqueue, enqueue, dequeue, nonempty, nonfull,
            Queue;
```

```
TYPE Queue; (* hidden *)
PROCEDURE genqueue (VAR Q: Queue);
PROCEDURE enqueue  (Q: Queue; elem: SOMETYPE);
PROCEDURE dequeue  (Q: Queue; VAR elem: SOMETYPE);
PROCEDURE nonempty (Q: Queue): BOOLEAN;
PROCEDURE nonfull  (Q: Queue): BOOLEAN;
END QueueHandler.


IMPLEMENTATION MODULE QueueHandler;
 FROM SomeModule IMPORT SOMETYPE;
 FROM Storage   IMPORT ALLOCATE;
 CONST MaxLength = 100;
 TYPE Queue = POINTER TO Qtype;
 Qtype = RECORD
           head, tail: [0..MaxLength-1];
           length    : [0..MaxLength];
           queue     : ARRAY [0..MaxLength-1] OF SOMETYPE;
         END;

 PROCEDURE genqueue (VAR Q: Queue);
 BEGIN
   ALLOCATE (Q,TSIZE(Qtype));
   WITH Q^ DO
     length:= 0; head:= 0; tail:= 0;
   END
 END genqueue;

 PROCEDURE enqueue (Q: Queue; elem: SOMETYPE);
 BEGIN
   WITH Q^ DO
     IF length < MaxLength THEN
       queue [tail]:= elem;
       tail:= (tail + 1) MOD MaxLength;
       INC (length);
```

```
      END
    END
  END enqueue;

  PROCEDURE dequeue (Q: Queue; VAR elem: SOMETYPE);
  BEGIN
    WITH Q^ DO
      IF length > 0 THEN
        elem:= queue [head];
        head:= (head + 1) MOD MaxLength;
        DEC (length);
      END
    END
  END dequeue;

  PROCEDURE nonempty (Q: Queue): BOOLEAN;
  BEGIN
    RETURN Q^.length > 0
  END nonempty;

  PROCEDURE nonfull (Q: Queue): BOOLEAN;
  BEGIN
    RETURN Q^.length < MaxLength
  END nonfull;

END QueueHandler.
```

Figure 6.5: Implementation of an abstract data type module in Modula-2

The definition modul now contains additionally the declaration of the type Queue. If we had given the realization of the type at this point the export would have been *transparent*. That means that an outside user would have access to the fine structure of the type. As we wanted to hide the fine structure we choose the export to be *opaque*. Now the realization of the type is only visible in the implementation module. As we are going to handle different queues we have to parametrize enqueue and dequeue with an additional parameter. For the same reason the former variables nonempty and nonfull turn to parametrized functions. The procedure genqueue is necessary to initialize an outside declared object of type Queue because Modula-2 does not allow initializations in declarations.

The realization of the type Queue and of the genqueue procedure is not quite obvious. Opaque export in Modula-2 is restricted to pointers (and subranges of standard types). That is the reason for defining the exported type Queue to be a pointer to Qtype. The consequence is that we have to use the standard procedure allocate in genqueue to generate objects on the heap. ALLOCATE and TSIZE, yielding the actual length of some object of a given type, have to be imported from the predefined modules. Our implementation does not provide for freeing the storage which is no longer used. The implementation of such a procedure is not difficult, however.

The problem with this solution is that the user can not be forced to call the procedure genqueue prior to any other procedure of the module. The declaration alone is not sufficient. A more secure solution had to check the existence of the queue each time one of the procedures is called. The deficiencies of Modula-2 shown in this example are the restriction of opaque export to pointers and the missing initialization in declarations. Other deficiencies are missing overloading facilities and the lack of operator definitions. This experience was gained when we tried to implement abstract data types predefined in the robot programming language AL [Mujtaba 79].

We do not give the identical solution in Ada but show how to implement a generic abstract data type for queues in Ada in the following Figure 6.6.

```
generic
  type SOMETYPE is private;
package QUEUE_HANDLING is
  type QUEUE (MAXLENGTH : NATURAL) is private;
  procedure ENQUEUE (SOMEQ : in out QUEUE; ELEM : in SOMETYPE);
  procedure DEQUEUE (SOMEQ : in out QUEUE; ELEM : out SOMETYPE);
  function NONEMPTY(SOMEQ : in QUEUE) return BOOLEAN;
  function NONFULL (SOMEQ : in QUEUE) return BOOLEAN;
private
```

```
subtype INDEX is CARDINAL range 0..CARDINAL'LAST;
type QUEUE (MAXLENGTH : NATURAL) is
  record
    HEAD : INDEX := 0;
    TAIL : INDEX := 0;
    LENGTH : INDEX := 0;
    Q : array (0..MAXLENGTH - 1) of SOMETYPE;
  end record;
end QUEUE_HANDLING;

package body QUEUE_HANDLING is
  procedure ENQUEUE (SOMEQ : in out QUEUE; ELEM : in SOMETYPE) is
  begin
   if SOMEQ.LENGTH < MAXLENGTH then
     SomeQ.Q(SOMEQ.TAIL) := ELEM;
     SOMEQ.TAIL := (SOMEQ.TAIL + 1) mod MAXLENGTH;
     SOMEQ.LENGTH := SOMEQ.LENGTH + 1;
    end if;
  end ENQUEUE;

  procedure DEQUEUE (SOMEQ : in out QUEUE; ELEM : out SOMETYPE) is
  begin ...
  end DEQUEUE;

  function NONEMPTY (SOMEQ : in QUEUE) return BOOLEAN is
  begin
    return SOMEQ.LENGTH < MAXLENGTH;
  end NONEMPTY;

  function NONFULL (SOMEQ : in QUEUE) return BOOLEAN is
  begin ...
  end NONFULL;

end QUEUE_HANDLING;
```

Figure 6.6: Ada implementation of a generic abstract data type for queues

...

```
declare
  package INT_QUEUE is new QUEUE_HANDLING (INTEGER);
  use INT_QUEUE;
  LONGQUEUE: QUEUE (200);
  SHORTQUEUE: QUEUE (10);
    begin
      ...
      if NONFULL (SHORTQUEUE) then
        ENQUEUE (SHORTQUEUE, 13);
      end if;
      ...
    end;
```

Figure 6.7: Instantiation, declaration, and use of a generic data type in Ada

In contrast to our first Ada example (Figure 6.4) we now define the type of our queue elements to be generic in the *generic part* of the package specification. This so-called *generic parameter* is visible in the package specification and in the package body. We might have choosen the constant MAXLENGTH to be a generic parameter as well but we decided to declare queues of different size by using the possibility to define a *dynamic array* in the type definition for QUEUE. This solution is superior to defining an additional generic parameter because we have to instantiate e.g. only one module for queues of type integer. The length of the queue is actually defined in the declaration as can be seen in Figure 6.7.

Hiding the realization of the type QUEUE is achieved by deferring the definition of its fine structure to the *private part* of the package specification. In the visible part this is indicated by the word **private**. In Ada it is possible to graduate the visibility of exported types. For private types assignment and comparisons for equality or inequality are available without explicit export specification. Designating types additionally to be **limited private** makes those operations invisible.

As initializations are possible in the type definition we do not need to export a procedure for this purpose. The declaration of a data object is sufficient for the outside user to guarantee its immediate usability (in contrast to Modula-2).

Aspects of modularity not covered in our examples are e.g. nesting of modules. Modula-2 takes a very reasonable approach to that problem defining local modules to be of a simpler syntactic structure. Local modules are not separately compilable and are in the responsibility of the programmer of the surrounding module. Local modules thus have not to be separated textually into a definition module and an implementation module. In this limited context export of objects from the local module is not opaque but transparent. This enables access to components of structured types using their component identifiers. Usually modules are intended to fence in data objects, data types and procedures; the declaration of modules within procedures is possible but not encouraged.

In Ada modules are equally treated as the two other program units, subprograms and tasks. This fully orthogonal design can be abused to define arbitrary nesting structures leading to obscure programs.

Both languages, Ada and Modula-2, allow to export variables. For security reasons access to those variables outside the exporting module should be restricted to read-only. The export of two variables (nonempty, nonfull) in our first Modula example (Figure 6.3) is not good programming practice (but efficient) and should be avoided by exporting procedures, yielding the value of those variables as shown in our consecutive examples.

Our last remark on modularity concerns efficiency considerations. Programming with abstract data types shows that a lot of operations as functions, procedures or operators have only few lines of code. A possibility to enforce in-line code generation for selected operations seems highly desirable for efficiency reasons.

Separate compilation, especially of small pieces of code, may cause efficiency problems because global optimization techniques cannot be applied across module boundaries. Further research is needed in this area.

6.2. Concurrency Concepts

In programming languages for distributed processing concurrency concepts are essential as several processors are available for concurrent execution of parallel processes. Even in monoprocessor systems concurrency concepts are important if a problem solution can be adequately expressed in this way. This is always the case with commutative operations thus avoiding overspecification of an algorithm by arbitrary serialization of the operations.

Another important case is problem inherent concurrency as for example in process control applications. In a technical process many sensors and actuators have to be controlled in parallel. The mapping of such a concurrent environment into a program for its control naturally results in a concurrent program. On a monoprocessor those programs can be executed only quasi-parallel; the processor has to be multiplexed by the processes.

In a real distributed system there will always be some mixture of processes being executed quasi-parallel in one node of the system and true parallel processes on different computers.

Essentially two concepts are used in recent programming languages to specify concurrent execution: *parallel blocks* and *process declarations*. Other concurrency concepts like the *fork and join* mechanism or the *coroutine* are not discussed here. Fork and join are dangerous control elements comparable to the goto statement supporting neither structured programming nor program proving. The coroutine concept allows to implement concurrent programs on a monoprocessor system, explicitly specifying processor switching from one coroutine to another. This makes it to be an adequate concept for a system programming language in a single processor environment and is contained e.g. in Modula-2. True parallelism, however, is not supported as only one coroutine can be executed at a time.

6.2.1. Concurrency in CSP

Parallel blocks denoted as **parbegin** by [Dijkstra 68b], have been first included in ALGOL 68 [van Wijngaarden 75]. We will show the notation used in

Communicating Sequential Processes (CSP) [Hoare 78]; a different form in Argus is shown in [Liskov 84a]. Although CSP was not intended to be a complete programming language, it contains important concepts integrated into more recent languages. It is worth to be studied because also many theoretical papers on program proving are based on CSP concepts.

In CSP parallel blocks are called *parallel commands*. In the most simple case we can denote the parallel execution of two assignment commands by:

$[x := a + 1 \parallel y := b + 1]$

The two parallel processes, each consisting of an assignment command, are started simultaneously and are terminated only after the last process (whichever this may be) has terminated successfully. In this example the processes are anonymous. In a parallel command access to global variables from different processes is allowed to be read–only.

Processes may be named and it is possible to define arrays of processes:

$[room :: ROOM \parallel fork (i : 0..4) :: FORK \parallel phil (i : 0..4) :: PHIL]$

This parallel command defines eleven parallel processes. The first process is named room. The capitalized word ROOM denotes a sequence of commands defined elsewhere. The five processes for fork are identified by fork(0), fork(1), ... fork(4). FORK defines one sequence of commands in which the bound variable i indicates the identity of the respective fork process. The names of the processes defined in a parallel command are visible throughout the whole command, that means in particular they are accessible in the elsewhere defined sequence of commands for e.g. FORK. In general it is possible to nest parallel commands as any command in a process may be a parallel command itself.

In contrast to fork and join, parallel blocks help in structured programming, defining a control structure with one entry and one exit. The number of parallel processes is determined statically from the program text. This facilitates the understandability of a program but may be too restrictive in some applications.

6.2.2. Concurrency in PEARL

Process declarations are probably the most often used way to describe concurrency in programming languages. In PEARL [DIN 66 253] a process is called task. Tasks in PEARL are close related to parameterless procedures. They are declared in a module and are allowed to communicate via global objects. In former versions of PEARL subtasking, that is nesting of tasks, was allowed but some years of industrial applications showed that this feature was never used due to its expensive implementation. As a consequence this feature was discarded. As PEARL is a language for process control applications it allows the specification of priorities for tasks. Priorities are to indicate the relative degree of urgency of a task and should not be used for synchronization purposes. Specifying priorities fairness can no longer be guaranteed. The declaration of a process in PEARL is shown in Figure 6.8.

```
MODULE (TEMP);
  PROBLEM;
    declaration of global objects;
    TEMPCONTROL : TASK PRIORITY 5;
    declaration of local variables and procedures;
    BEGIN
      statements;
    END;
  END;
  ...
MODEND;
```

Figure 6.8: Task declaration in PEARL

The activation of a task is performed explicitly similar to a procedure call; a priority specification is optional:

ACTIVATE TEMPCONTROL PRIORITY I + 1;

Besides ACTIVATE there are several tasking statements to change the state of a task, e.g.:

```
TERMINATE T;        /* terminate task T */
SUSPEND T;          /* task T is suspended and can only be */
CONTINUE T;         /* continued using the continue statement */
```

In PEARL only one incarnation of a task can be active at a time. The activation of an already active task is buffered and only executed when the first incarnation of the task has been terminated.

6.2.3. Concurrency in DP

A quite different approach is taken by Distributed Processes (DP) [Brinch Hansen78], a language which has influenced subsequent languages like Ada and Argus. A process declaration has the form:

process name
    declaration of local own variables
    declaration of common procedures
    initialization

A DP process may be interpreted as an abstract data structure with operations that are not passive procedures like usual but active processes. In the process only the local own variables (own in the sense of ALGOL 60) and common procedures declared in the same or in another process are visible; access to global variables is not allowed.

A DP program consists of a fixed number of processes that are activated simultaneously and never terminate. A process is executed by first executing its initialization. Either the initialization terminates (not terminating the process!) or is suspended waiting for a condition to become true. At that point one of the "procedures" can be activated due to an *external request* from some other process. Granting external requests and executing the initialization part is interleaved such that only one activity is possible at a time. This implicit synchronization is similar to the monitor concept [Brinch Hansen 73a, Hoare 74] with the already mentioned difference that the passive monitor procedures are replaced by active processes. As an example we show the implementation of a semaphore [Dijkstra 68b] as an abstract data structure in Figure 6.9.

```
process semaphore;
  sema : int; {local own variable}
  proc wait
    when sema > 0: sema := sema − 1 end;
  proc signal
    sema := sema + 1;
  sema := 1 {initialization}
```

Figure 6.9: Semaphore implementation in DP

The activation of this process is started with the initialization sema := 1 which terminates after the assignment. As the process continues to exist it is now able to grant external requests like

call semaphore.wait   and   **call** semaphore. signal

A similar process concept like in PEARL can be achieved in DP by simply not declaring common procedures so that only the initialization part is left. Basic concurrency concepts in Argus are similar to those in DP but it contains additional elements discussed by [Liskov 84a].

6.2.4. Concurrency in Ada

Process declarations in Ada are more related to processes in DP than in PEARL. Syntactically a process in Ada is called *task* and is similar to a package. That means that tasks are one of the three forms of program units that may be compiled separately and may as well be defined to be generic. Like a package, a task is generally provided in two parts: a *task specification* and a *task body*. The task specification may be seen as the interface to the outside user where the exported operations are specified. An exported operation is called an *entry*. The task body defines the execution of the task. The syntactical form is essentially:

```
task type name is
  entry declarations;
end name;
```

```
task body name is
  local declarations;
begin
  sequence of statements;
end name;
```

Similar to DP we can construct either classical tasks in the sense of PEARL, defining no entries, or we can see tasks to implement abstract data types. Generally a task specification in Ada defines a *task type* if the reserved word **type** is present. An object of type task is defined then by declaration. If the word **type** is omitted in the task specification this is shorthand and declares a single object of type task. In this case the introduced name is the name of the task and not the name of a task type. Integrating tasks into the type mechanism of Ada makes them a very powerful construct as most language elements applicable to objects of some type are available for tasks too.

Here is an example:

```
task type KEYBOARD_DRIVER is
  entry READ (C: out CHARACTER);
  entry WRITE (C: in CHARACTER);
end KEYBOARD_DRIVER;

...

TELETYPE : KEYBOARD_DRIVER;
type KEYBOARD is access KEYBOARD_DRIVER;
POOL : array (1..10) of KEYBOARD;

...

begin
  for I in 1..10 loop
    POOL(I) := new KEYBOARD_DRIVER;
  end loop;
```

First we specify a task type KEYBOARD_DRIVER with two entries. The task body is omitted in our example. As tasks are activated implicitly when their declaration is elaborated, the following declaration of a task TELETYPE immediately effects its activation. The next line shows the declaration of an *access type*. Access types in Ada are pointers which are only allowed to point to objects of a distinct type. In the example objects of type KEYBOARD like POOL are only allowed to point to objects of type KEYBOARD_DRIVER. The declaration of POOL creates access values but no task objects. This is accomplished by means of the *allocator* **new**. Executing **new** KEYBOARD_DRIVER in the loop dynamically creates task objects being activated immediately as mentioned above.

Although most applications get along without a dynamically changing number of tasks, there are some areas where this could be very usefull. Imagine for example a telephone exchange systems where the varying number of parallel active calls could nicely be modelled by dynamic task creation and termination.

A task is terminated normally when its execution reaches the end of its task body. There is another possibility to terminate a task which we will discuss later in the context of communication.

We did not show an example of a task body and how the entries declared in the task specification are reflected there. The following example (Figure 6.10) is rather simple-minded and avoids the use of language constructs we want to discuss later in the section on communication concepts.

```
task ALTERNATION is
  entry DEPOSIT (I: in INTEGER);
  entry REMOVE (I: out INTEGER);
end ALTERNATION;

task body ALTERNATION is
  ELEM : INTEGER; -- local depot
begin
  loop
    accept DEPOSIT (I: in INTEGER) do
      ELEM := I;
    end DEPOSIT;
    accept REMOVE (I: out INTEGER) do
      I:= ELEM;
```

end REMOVE;
end loop;
end ALTERNATION;

Figure 6.10: Task specification and task body in Ada

The specification of the task contains the declaration of two entries, DEPOSIT and REMOVE. The "procedure body" of an entry is defined in the task body in a corresponding accept statement. In our example we find two accept statements, the first to grant entry calls of DEPOSIT, the second for REMOVE. As accept statements are normal statements in an arbitrary statement sequence, the task body in our example allows only a strict alternation of one DEPOSIT and one REMOVE due to the loop statement. If the same entry is called subsequently before the calls can be granted by the corresponding accept statements the calls are queued. An individual queue is associated with each entry and each execution of an accept statement removes one call from the queue in FIFO order.

Ada's accept statements do not define autonomous processes as the common procedures of DP do. Allowing accept statements in the normal statement sequence guarantees that only one of them can be executed at a time. It is obvious that the language elements of Ada discussed till now are not sufficient for practical applications. Imagine a slightly extended example where we want items to be deposited in and removed from a buffer in deliberate order (in consideration of the constraints empty and full). Language elements to describe such non-determinism will be considered in the section on communication concepts.

Similar to PEARL, Ada allows to define the priority of a task as a *pragma* in the task specification.

pragma PRIORITY (5);

Dynamic priorities are not allowed, however.

6.3. Communication Concepts

Communication is one of the major problems in distributed systems. In monoprocessor systems or in multiprocessor systems, sharing common memory, communication between processors and memory is supported by hardware guaranteeing highly reliable data transfer. Due to the properties of transmission channels communication in distributed systems is unreliable unless specific precautions are taken.

Communication between concurrent processes is necessary if they have to cooperate in some way. It is useful to distinguish two aspects of communication. The first is that processes simply have to arrange which of both will be allowed to use a resource (e.g. data or devices) exclusive for some time. This problem is known as *synchronization* by *mutual exclusion*. Mutual exclusion allows that a sequence of statements, the so called *critical section*, in one process is executed as an indivisible operation.

The second aspect of communication is that processes depend on each other in that way that one process cannot continue unless other processes have installed a well-defined state of the system. That may be e.g. that a process has to wait for another process to produce a data object which is required by it for further execution (the classical producer-consumer relationship [Dijkstra 68a]). This problem is known as *logical synchronization* or *condition synchronization*.

Those two types of communication can be implemented efficiently in computer systems with common memory e.g. using semaphores [Dijkstra 68b]. Other synchronization primitives based on shared variables are reviewed by [Andrews 83].

In distributed systems the only way to implement communication is *message passing*. That means that processes communicate by *sending* and *receiving* messages instead of reading and writing global objects residing in a common memory. Synchronization primitives that behave like semaphors ("netglobal semaphores") cannot be implemented without an underlying message system that has to ensure the consistency of local copies of a netglobal object.

Various patterns of communication structures are useful. To establish a *one-to-one* communication we could send a message from process1 to process2 by:

send message **to** process2;

and could receive this message in process2 by:

receive message **from** process1;

Specifying the name of the receiving and the sending process respectively in the communication statements establishes a static *communication channel* by *direct naming*.

Often a one-to-one communication structure is not sufficient. Especially if processes cooperate in a *client/server* (sometimes called *master/slave*) *relationship* it is typical that several clients share one server e.g. if there is one device driver for a single device which has to be used by different processes (*many-to-one*). Another case is that there are several identical devices and the client does not care which one will be the destination of its request (*one-to-many*) or even that there are many clients and some servers (*many-to-many*). A one–to–many relationship is also called *broadcast* if we want the message of one process to be received by many processes.

As direct naming is not well suited for communication structures other than one–to–one, other concepts have been provided. Definition of *global names*, often called *mailboxes*, allow a many–to–many communication structure. Any process who wants to send a message may send it to the global available mailbox. In the same way any process may receive a message from that mailbox. This concept may cause heavy traffic on communication lines because the arrival of a message in the mailbox has to be broadcasted to all processes receiving from that mailbox. The same occurs after a message has been consumed from the mailbox as to indicate that the message is no longer available.

A much more efficient solution for the many–to–one communication structure is possible using *ports* [Balzer 71]. We can think of ports to be simplified mailboxes. If any process can send messages to a port and there is only one process which is allowed to receive from that port the whole notification of other processes is saved.

In some languages establishing communication structures statically or even dynamically is treated as a separate concern. We will discuss this in the chapter on configuration description.

Communication structures are one aspect to classify message passing concepts. Another equal important aspect for classification is the semantics of message passing statements showing different synchronization properties [Liskov 79b]. Let us first have a look at the various properties of message sending.

The execution of a send statement does not delay the sending process, it continues execution immediately. This may be achieved by buffering the message between sending and receiving. We call this a *non-blocking send, no-wait send*, or *asychronous message passing*.

If there is no buffer where the sender can deposit its message the sender is delayed until the message has been received. This is called *blocking send, synchronization send*, or *synchronous message passing*. One step further a sender could not only wait until its message has been received but even until an answer has been received by the sender. We call this a *remote invocation send* which is of course blocking and synchronous message passing as well.

Message receipt may be either *explicit* using a receive statement which may be either blocking or non-blocking or *implicit* invoking some piece of code similar to an interrupt triggering an interrupt handler.

The combination of remote invocation send and implicit receive is often called *remote procedure call* as it behaves much the same like an ordinary procedure call [Nelson 81]. Combining remote invocation send and explicit receive statements is referred to as *rendezvous concept* [Ada 83].

We could discuss only some of the manifold possibilities to define message passing. All variants show advantages for certain applications and deficiencies for others. To overcome deficiencies other language concepts can be used. We will discuss this showing some examples in different programming languages.

6.3.1. Communication in CSP

In CSP [Hoare 78] message passing is based on direct static naming of communication channels and synchronization send. Send and receive is realized using output and input commands, denoted in a very concise but somewhat cryptic notation:

destination process ! expression   {send expression to destination process}

source process ? target variable   {receive message from source process and assign it to the target variable}

Input and output commands are said to *correspond* if the communication channel between two issuing processes is established and if the type of the expression matches the type of the target variable. The effect of two corresponding commands is to assign the value of the expression to the target variable.

There are many problems where we do not know in advance which of several processes will try to communicate with a distinct process first. What we want to do is to serve that process first that tries to communicate with this process first. As the receive in CSP is blocking this communication pattern can not be realized directly. Synchronous message passing takes away much of the concurrency of parallel processes. On the other hand using non-blocking receive, synchronization could only be realized by busy waiting. Concurrency lost with blocking receive is gained back in CSP using *nondeterministic constructs* which are derived from Dijkstra's *guarded commands* [Dijkstra 75]. The major difference is that guards can contain input commands.

First we show a nondeterministic *alternative command* to compute the maximum of two variables x and y:

[x ≥ y   -> max := x

] y ≥ x   -> max := y

]

In this example the guards are simple boolean expressions. The statement following guard -> can be executed only if the guard does not fail, i.e. the boolean expression yields true. If more than one guard does not fail, a nondeterministic choice between the following statements is taken (in our example in the case of $x = y$).

The following example shows a *repetitive command* with guards containing input commands:

•[(i: 1..10) continue(i); console(i) ? c -> X ! (i,c); console(i)! ack();

$$\text{continue(i)} := (c \text{ ● sign off})$$

]

The statements in square brackets preceded by ● are repeated until all guards fail. This notation with the bounded variable i is equivalent to a notation where i is consistently replaced by numbers one to ten. That means that this statement contains ten guarded commands. Continue is a boolean array. Guards are evaluated from left to right and the first boolean expression yielding false terminates the evaluation resulting in a failure of the guardian. Thus the input command console(i) ? c can only be executed if continue(i) is true. A second condition for executing an input command is that the corresponding output command can be executed. If several true guard lists end in an input command and no corresponding output command is executed the command has to be delayed until one of the output commands is executed. That may result in deadlock if this never happens.

In our example we obviously try to input a character c from any of ten consoles as long as continuation is possible (continue(i) = true). Having read from a console i character c, this character together with the identification i of the sending console is output to the process X. Then an acknowledge signal ack() is sent back to the console. If the last character sent from the console was a sign off character the console is prevented from sending by setting continue(i) false.

Our next example in Figure 6.11 will show how to realize queue handling if a producer process issues enqueue operations and a consumer process dequeue operations which have to be synchronized.

```
QUEUE::
queue: (0..99) sometype;
head, tail, length : integer;
head := 0; tail := 0; length := 0;
•[ length < 100; producer ? queue(tail);  {enqueue}
          ->tail := (tail + 1) mod 100;
            length := length + 1
[] length > 0; consumer ? more();  {dequeue}
```

```
        -> consumer ! queue(head);
      head := (head + 1) mod 100;
      length := length - 1
```

]

Figure 6.11: Queue handling in CSP

As only input commands are allowed in guards our solution is not symmetrical with respect to the guarded commands. So we first have to receive the signal more() from the consumer process before we can send the first element of the queue. Allowing output commands in guards as well would have simplified the second guarded command to:

```
[] length > 0; consumer ! queue(head);
          -> head := (head + 1) mod 100;
        length := length - 1
```

Integration of input and output commands into guards is very tempting but has serious drawbacks on efficiency. The problem is to decide which processes should communicate if several are nondeterministically able to do so. One solution of this problem is discussed in [Silberschatz 79].

6.3.2. Communication in DP

In DP [Brinch Hansen 78] communication is based on remote procedure call. In the semaphore example of the previous chapter we have already seen how remote procedures are called and how remote procedures are declared in a process without mentioning the name of this communication concept. We already mentioned that only one activity is possible at a time so that the initialization part and the procedures are executed interleaved. This interleaving is only possible if, like in CSP, additional concurrency is introduced. Processes can switch from one activity to another either when an operation terminates or waits for a condition within a *guarded region* which is a variant of *conditional critical regions* [Hoare 72b, Brinch Hansen 72, Brinch Hansen 73b].

There are two forms of guarded regions: the *when statement* and the *cycle statement.*

when guard 1 : statement 1
 | guard 2 : statement 2
 | ...
end

The meaning is that the process will be blocked until one of the guards yields true and then executes the corresponding statement. If several guards are successful a non−deterministic choice among the statements is made. After the execution of one of the statements the when statement terminates. The cycle statement endlessly repeats a when statement. The syntax is:

cycle guard 1 : statement 1
 | guard 2 : statement 2
 | ...
end

A second form of non−determinism is introduced in DP by guarded commands [Dijkstra75]. As DP uses remote procedure call no explicit receive and send operations are available and thus guards are, as usual, only boolean expressions not blocking execution. Despite from that, their semantics is like the semantics of alternative respectively repetitive commands in CSP. The syntax is slightly different:

if guard 1 : statement 1
 | guard 2 : statement 2
 | ...
end

and

do guard 1 : statement 1
 | guard 2 : statement 2
 |...
end

Now we can fully understand the previous semaphore example (Figure 6.9) where we already made use of the when statement. At that point all processes issuing a call of the remote procedure *wait* are blocked if the first has succeeded and no call of the remote procedure *signal* has been executed.

Our next example in Figure 6.12 shows an implementation of the queue process in DP.

```
process queue;
  queue : array [100] sometype;
  head, tail, length : int;
  proc enqueue (elem : sometype);
    when length < 100 :
      tail := (tail mod 100) + 1;
      length := length + 1;
      queue [tail] := elem
    end;

  proc dequeue (#elem : sometype);
      when length > 0 :
      head := (head mod 100) + 1;
      length := length − 1;
      elem := queue [head]
    end;
  head := 0; tail := 0; length := 0
```

Figure 6.12: Queue handling in DP

Note that the remote procedures enqueue and dequeue are totally symmetrical. The guarded regions have only one guard each. This example also shows how message passing is realized with remote procedure calls. The formal parameter of enqueue *elem* is an input parameter. This means that the calling process has to evaluate the actual parameter expression. The value of this expression is sent to the queue process. The formal parameter of dequeue is an output parameter. That means that the value assigned to this parameter has to be sent back to the calling process where it is assigned to the actual parameter in the call. Input and output parameters can be simultaneously in each remote procedure, of course.

6.3.3. Communication in Ada

In Ada [Ada 83] communication is based on the rendezvous concept. Having enlightened message passing concepts we can take a second look at our ALTERNATION example (Figure 6.10) of the previous chapter. We can see that the accept statement takes the role of an explicit receive. The essential difference between an accept statement and a remote procedure like in DP is that there may be only one procedure declaration but several accepts for the same entry, causing different statement sequences to be executed. The parameter mode of an entry (**in, out**) determines the direction of a message like in DP. The remote invocation send in Ada looks exactly like a procedure call, e.g. ALTERNATION.DEPOSIT (5); the name of an entry in the call is prefixed by the task name, in which the remote procedure is located.

As with all synchronous message passing concepts additional concurrency is required to allow waiting for different entry calls.

The *selective wait* statement in Ada introduces nondeterminism close related to CSP's alternative command. The syntax is:

select
  guard 1 => select alternative 1
or
  guard 2 => select alternative 2
or ...
else statements
end select;

The guards in the alternatives are optional. If a guard is true or missing the alternative is said to be open. Select alternatives can either start with an accept or delay statement followed by an arbitrary statement sequence. Using the else part avoids blocking receive if no other alternative can be selected immediately.

Blocking of the calling process can be overcome in a similar way issuing *conditional entry calls*:

```
select
  entry call; statements
else
  statements
end select;
```

The entry call is selected only if an immediate rendezvous is possible; otherwise the statements of the else part are executed. In this case no message is transmitted, of course, so that asynchronous message passing cannot be achieved in this way.

Let us conclude communication concepts of Ada with our queue handling example in Figure 6.13.

```
task QUEUE_HANDLING is
  entry ENQUEUE (ELEM : in SOMETYPE);
  entry DEQUEUE (ELEM : out SOMETYPE);
end QUEUE_HANDLING;

task body QUEUE_HANDLING is
  MAXLENGTH ; constant NATURAL := 100;
  HEAD, TAIL : INTEGER range 0.. MAXLENGTH − 1 := 0;
  LENGTH : INTEGER range 0.. MAXLENGTH := 0;
  Q : array (0.. MAXLENGTH − 1) of SOMETYPE;
begin
  loop
    select
      when LENGTH < MAXLENGTH =>
        accept ENQUEUE (ELEM : in SOMETYPE) do
          Q (TAIL) := ELEM;
        end;
      TAIL := (TAIL + 1) mod MAXLENGTH;
      LENGTH := LENGTH + 1;
    or
      when LENGTH > 0 =>
        accept DEQUEUE (ELEM : out SOMETYPE) do
```

```
        ELEM := Q (HEAD);
      end;
      HEAD := (HEAD + 1) mod MAXLENGTH;
      LENGTH := LENGTH − 1;
    or
      terminate;
    end select;
  end loop;
end QUEUE_HANDLING;
```

Figure 6.13: Queue handling in Ada

This solution is symmetric in ENQUEUE and DEQUEUE like in DP. The administration of the queue (HEAD, TAIL, LENGTH) is executed not within the rendezvous thus allowing the communicating tasks to continue concurrently as soon as possible. This is not possible e.g. in DP as the administration is included in the remote procedures.

Two other aspects are worth mentioning. In Ada tasks can communicate accessing global variables what is not allowed in CSP or DP. This is a dangerous feature as it is in the responsibility of the user to ensure that several tasks will not modify the same global object simultaneously. Global objects will usually prevent accessing tasks to be distributed to various nodes of a distributed system. Ada does not give any hints or language elements to master the problem of distribution of program units.

The second aspect is the description of communication structures. Ada and DP nicely manage the problem to provide library units any other program unit can communicate with via entry call or remote procedure call. The direct naming solution is not acceptable from a software engineering point of view as library units should be usable by anybody without knowledge of their details. In his paper on CSP Hoare mentions as an alternative to direct naming the concept of ports which has been included in recent languages [Kramer 83, Magee 83].

In which way fault tolerance considerations influence communication concepts is discussed in [Liskov 84a].

6.4 Exception Handling

The execution of a program may infrequently result in a state of the system where continuation of the execution in the predefined way is not sensible or even impossible. Such a situation is called an *exception*. Typical exceptions are e.g. division by zero or reading an end of file marker. In many applications it is no problem to terminate the execution of the program if an exception has been raised. This is the only reasonable action to take if a language does not provide for explicit exception handling mechanisms ("panic mode").

In process control applications the termination of a control program could have disastrous effects; exception handling is inevitable in this field. Of course exceptions like division by zero could be avoided with the usual control structures: before each division we could test the denominator in an if clause. The result is a clumsy and inefficient program.

If an exception is raised the predefined flow of control is not continued. As a reaction to an exception a special piece of code, the exception handler is executed.

Exception handling mechanisms differ especially in the philosophy what should be done after the exception was handled. The *first concept* is to resume execution at the point where the exception was raised. In this case handling an exception is like calling a procedure.

The *second concept* is that after the execution of the exception handler the execution of the program unit to which the exception handler belongs to is terminated. The second concept is based on the experience that reasonable error treatment is often not possible in a local context. This is especially true if a routine is provided in a module, implemented by another programmer who did not and should not know anything about the use of his module.

Think for example of a recursive descent compiler scanning a sequence of characters in a string constant. If the program is erroneous such that the end-of-string delimiter is missing, the scanning routine will sooner or later detect an end-of-file delimiter. At that level the exception handler could close the file and print the rather unspecific error message "end-of-file detected". The scanning routine cannot do any more for the programmer because it has no information about the identity of its caller.

In this situation the scanning routine would better close the file and leave the printing of an error message to the calling routine. The calling routine must of course be informed that an exception has been raised. An elegant way to do this is simply to raise the exception again, so that it can be handled in the surrounding context. Raising an exception again is called *propagation*. Propagation of the end–of–file exception in our example to the routine building a string constant allows an exception handler in this routine to issue a more specific error message "end–of–string delimiter missing".

Exception handling is more and more used in conventional programming. It is in accordance with our definition of an exception to regard the finding of a distinct element in a searching algorithm as an exception. We do not advocate this programming style but would rather think of an exception if that element is expected to be found but does not show up. But, of course, there are no precise rules where to program with exception handling mechanisms and where not.

Different exception handling concepts were discussed in [Horning 74, Randell 75a, Goodenough 75, Parnas 76, Geschke 77b, Levin 77, Liskov 79b]. We will show an example of exception handling in PEARL and Ada representing the two different concepts mentioned above. Exception handling in Argus is discussed in [Liskov 84a].

6.4.1. Exception Handling in PEARL

Exception handling in PL/I using on–conditions is very baroque and follows the first concept described above [Noble 68]. Part of it is implemented in PEARL (Figure 6.14) using similar syntax:

```
READLOG : TASK
DCL some local declarations;
...
OPEN LOGFILE;
ON EOF:
  BEGIN
```

```
      CLOSE LOGFILE;
      TERMINATE READLOG;
    END;

   ...

   READ DATA FROM LOGFILE;

   ...

  END;
```

Figure 6.14: Exception handling in PEARL

The exception handler is visible in the task READLOG after the execution of the on–statement. If in the subsequent READ the exception EOF is raised, the block after the on–statement is executed, closing LOGFILE and terminating the task. This termination prevents the execution to be resumed at the point where the exception was raised. The deficiency of this concept is that communication e.g. with other tasks is only possible via global objects and that all exceptions are predefined in the system. A user cannot define his own exceptions.

6.4.2. Exception Handling in Ada

Exception handling in Ada follows the second concept described above. In our example of a generic abstract data type (Figure 6.6) for queues we defined two functions NONEMPTY and NONFULL. The user of the module cannot be forced to call those functions ensuring himself that ENQUEUE respectively DEQUEUE operations make sense. In this case raising an exception in the QUEUE_HANDLING package (Figure 6.15) is the best solution to force the user to take care of an error.

```
generic
  type SOMETYPE is private;
package QUEUE_HANDLING is
  type QUEUE (MAXLENGTH : NATURAL) is private;
  procedure ENQUEUE (SOMEQ : in out QUEUE; ELEM : in SOMETYPE);
  procedure DEQUEUE (SOMEQ : in out QUEUE; ELEM : out SOMETYPE);
  FULLQUEUE, EMPTYQUEUE : exception;
```

```
private
  subtype INDEX is CARDINAL range 0..CARDINAL'LAST;
  type QUEUE (MAXLENGTH : NATURAL) is
    record
      HEAD : INDEX := 0;
      TAIL : INDEX :=0;
      LENGTH : INDEX := 0;
      Q : array (0..MAXLENGTH - 1) of SOMETYPE;
    end record;
end QUEUE_HANDLING;

package body QUEUE_HANDLING is
  procedure ENQUEUE (SOMEQ : in out QUEUE; ELEM : in SOMETYPE) is
  begin
    if SOMEQ.LENGTH < MAXLENGTH then
      SomeQ.Q(SOMEQ.TAIL) := ELEM;
      SOMEQ.TAIL := (SOMEQ.TAIL + 1) mod MAXLENGTH;
      SOMEQ.LENGTH := SOMEQ.LENGTH + 1;
    else raise FULLQUEUE;
    end if;
  end ENQUEUE;

  procedure DEQUEUE (SOMEQ : in out QUEUE; ELEM : out SOMETYPE) is
  begin
    ...
  end DEQUEUE;

end QUEUE_HANDLING;
```

Figure 6.15: Ada implementation of a generic data type with exceptions

Suppose this package is used in a procedure P (Figure 6.16) then an exception handler could be specified in P as follows:

```
with QUEUE_HANDLING; use QUEUE_HANDLING;
procedure P is
```

```
...
begin
  ...
  ENQUEUE (SHORTQUEUE, ELEM);
  ...
exception
  when FULLQUEUE =>
    PUT ("QUEUE IS FULL");
    DEQUEUE (SHORTQUEUE, TRASH);
    ENQUEUE (SHORTQUEUE, ELEM);
    PUT ("YOUR OLDEST ENTRY WAS REPLACED");
  when EMPTYQUEUE => ... ;
  when NUMERIC_ERROR | STORAGE_ERROR =>
    PUT ("NO REPAIR POSSIBLE");
    raise SEVERE_ERROR;
  when others =>
    PUT ("FATAL ERROR");
    raise PANIC;
end;
```

Figure 6.16: Exception handling in Ada

This example shows how exceptions are propagated using the raise statement and how exception handlers are attached to a subprogram. Exceptions could as well be attached to other frames like blocks, tasks and packages.

If an exception is raised in a frame where no handler is defined the execution is abandoned and the exception is propagated. Exceptions are not propagated, however, if the frame is a task body. In this case the task is simply terminated.

The previous paragraph does not apply if the exception is raised in a statement sequence contained in an accept statement, i.e. during a rendezvous. If there is no handler for this exception in the frame of the accept statement the exception is propagated to two points: first to the point immediately following the accept statement in the called task; second to the point of the entry call in the calling task.

A task issuing an entry call, however, does not affect the called task even if it is terminated abnormally in the midst of an rendezvous.

6.5. Real-Time Concepts

Programming real-time applications does not imply using real-time concepts embedded in higher programming languages. Most applications are programmed either still in assembler or in languages that do not provide for real-time concepts. Even languages often apostrophized as real-time languages like CORAL 66 or RTL/2 allow only for assembler code insertions or for calls of operating system routines.

6.5.1. Real-Time Elements in PEARL

PEARL claims that real-time programming is not a task only for system programmers but as well for application engineers. Thus the approach of PEARL was to integrate as many real-time concepts as possible. The approach in Ada was to integrate as many real-time concepts as necessary to allow experienced programmers to build a real-time environment appropriate for a specific application.

There are two predefined real-time specific abstract data types in PEARL: DURATION and CLOCK. DURATION objects denote intervals in time; CLOCK objects denote points in time. A declaration might look like:

DECLARE
DURATION SCANNINGRATE INIT (1 MIN 4.3 SEC);
CLOCK START INIT (22 : 5 : 55.7);

All meaningful operations (+, −, *, /, <, >, =,...) are defined on objects of those both data types e.g. 4 HRS/1 SEC yielding the floating point value 14400.0.

As already mentioned in chapter 6.2 tasking statements are used in PEARL to explicitly change the state of a task. Those changes can depend on external events (objects of type INTERRUPT), on a successful p operation (called REQUEST) on a semaphore, or on time schedules. Here are some examples:

WHEN ALARM ACTIVATE T;   /* the interrupt ALARM activates T*/

ACTIVATE T USING SEMA;   /* if any task issues a REQUEST SEMA, task T
                             is activated; at termination of T, SEMA is
                             implicitly released*/

AFTER 2 HRS ALL 5 MIN DURING 12 HRS ACTIVATE T; /* time schedule
                             based on durations*/

AT 12 : 0 : 0 EVERY 1 MIN UNTIL 18 : 0 : 0 ACTIVATE T; /* time schedule
                             based on system time*/

PREVENT T;   /* prevents T to be activated, cancels all
                             schedules */

It is possible to almost arbitraryly combine those schedule elements so that all relevant timing patterns can easily be specified. We can imagine, however, that writing efficient real–time operating systems for the requirements of PEARL is not too simple.

6.5.2. Real-Time Elements in Ada

In Ada there is a predefined type DURATION representing intervals of time in seconds. A type TIME and appropriate operations are provided in the predefined library package CALENDAR. The only statement in Ada changing the state of a task is the delay statement:

delay expression of type duration;

The effect is that the task is suspended for the specified duration. This statement can be used together with some arithmetics on durations and times to achieve similar time schedules for a task as it is possible in PEARL. But note that the cyclic activation of a task at equidistant time intervalls is not expressible in a straightforward way.

In chapter 6.3 we discussed communication concepts in Ada. Especially in real-time systems it is important to control that neither an entry call nor an accept statement can deliberately delay further execution of the communicating tasks. Such a delay might e.g. be caused by interrupted communication lines or by hardware faults. Ada allows to specify timeout conditions in the calling and in the called task.

We have already treated one special case of timeout conditions in entry calls. In a conditional entry call the else part is executed if no immediate rendezvous is possible (timeout = 0 sec). In a *timed entry call* the else part is replaced by a *delay alternative*:

```
select
    entry call; statements
or
    delay statement; statements
end select;
```

The effect of a timed entry call is that after the time specified in the delay statement, the entry call is cancelled unless the rendezvous could be started within that interval. If the entry call had to be cancelled, the statement sequence following the delay statement is executed.

Note that the rendezvous has only to be started within the specified time but that the specified time does not guarantee a distinct reaction time of the called task. If the rendezvous was started the calling task has no more chance to cancel the entry call. In the best case an erroneous situation occuring in the called task during the rendezvous will raise an exception that is propagated also to the calling task. An interrupted communication line, however, could easily prevent this.

Timeout conditions in the called task are specified in a select statement using a delay statement in select alternatives:

```
select
    accept DRIVER_AWAKE_SIGNAL;
or
    delay 30.0;
```

STOP_THE_TRAIN;

end select;

This example does not show that the *delay alternative* may be guarded exactly like normal accept alternatives. Open delay alternatives are only selected if no other alternative can be selected within the specified time. If a delay alternative is selected, the optional statement sequence following the delay statement is executed. Specifying an open delay alternative with delay 0.0 is equivalent to an else part in a selective wait statement.

6.6. Configuration Description

Discussing the aspect of configuration description we must distinguish three separate concerns. The *logical structure* describes software components and their logical interconnections. The *physical structure* describes hardware components and their physical interconnections. The third concern is how the logical structure is *mapped* into the physical structure.

There has been much discussion whether configuration description should be included in the program or whether there should be a separate language describing this aspect. Most language designers decided to integrate the description of the logical structure into the language and not to cope with the physical structure. This is the case for CSP, DP, and Ada.

One of the first to advocate a separate module interconnection language (MIL 75) to describe the logical structure of a software system was [De Remer 76]. This approach is also taken in some more recent languages for distributed programming as e.g. PRONET [Maccabe 82, Le Blanc 82] and CONIC [Kramer 83, Magee 83]. CONIC allows in the current version also to specify the mapping of the logical into the physical structure; we will have a closer look at CONIC in chapter 6.7.

Another approach is taken in a variant of PEARL, enhanced for distributed programming [Steusloff 81]. In standard PEARL the physical structure can be described in a connection specification limited to devices. An enhancement of this feature allows to specify properties of distributed systems. Thus the configuration description is part of a PEARL program.

6.6.1. Configuration Description in PEARL

Let us first have a look at configuration descriptions in PEARL. Figure 6.17 shows a small example of the physical structure in a process control application. This can be described in a connection specification in the system part of a PEARL program as shown in Figure 6.18

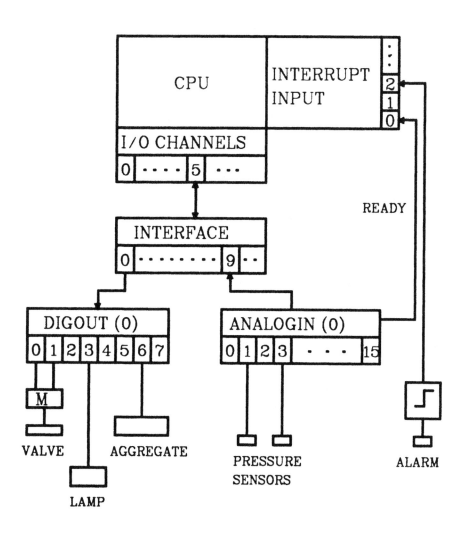

Figure 6.17:   Physical structure of a process control application

```
MODULE (PIPELINECONTROL);
  SYSTEM;
    INTERFACE <-> CPU*5;  /* channel 5*/
    DIGOUT (0) <- INTERFACE *0;
    ANALOGIN (0) -> INTERFACE *9;
    VALVE : <- DIGOUT (0) * 0,2;  /*channel 0, 2 bits */
    LAMP : <- DIGOUT (0) * 3,1;    /*channel 3, 1 bit */
    AGGREGATE : <- DIGOUT (0) * 6,1;
    PRESSURE SENSOR1 : -> ANALOGIN (0) * 1;
    PRESSURE SENSOR2 : -> ANALOGIN (0) * 3;
    READY: -> INTERRUPTINPUT * 0;
    ALARM : INTERRUPTINPUT * 2;
```

Figure 6.18: Connection specification in PEARL

Each PEARL program for a distributed system can be enhanced by a
LOAD–division and by additional specifications in the SYSTEM–division as
shown in Figure 6.19 [Steusloff 81]. A STATIONS–division specifies hardware
capabilities, error condition codes and operating system capabilities for each
node in the system.

```
MODULE (TEMPCONTROL);
LOAD;
  TO STATION1 LDPRIO 5 INITIAL START NO 1
  TO STATION3 LDPRIO 5 ON (STA1PR AND NOT STA3PR) RES;
SYSTEM;
  /* some connection specifications*/
  TEMP :  -> ANALOGIN 560 * 8/*$
            -> ANALOGIN 571 * 5;
               CORR : TEMP := TEMP/3 - 16
            -> ANALOGIN 572* 5,
               CORR : ADJUST.(TEMP, 2)
            -> REP : TEMP := 1300,
            PLAUS : (HI = 1600, LO = 100, DELTA = 10) */;

  ...
```

PROBLEM;
    /* algorithmic part */
MODEND;

Figure 6.19 : Configuration description in PEARL

The LOAD–division describes the mapping of the module into the physical structure. This specification contains also the description of *dynamic reconfiguration* in the case of failures and a *graceful degradation* strategy. The first line specifies that initially this module has to be down–line loaded to a node with identifier STATION1. The startnumber 1 specifies that during start–up this module has to be installed first. The RES (IDENT) attribute specifies that the module has to be loaded during start–up in a redundant node.

The second line describes dynamic reconfiguration which has to be carried out if the condition following ON becomes true as the result of a failure. Graceful degradation can be managed by specifying a load priority LDPRIO for a module in a specific node. This is a relative degree of importance of a module compared to others in one node and allows a system to maintain only the most important tasks if some nodes collapse.

In the system part we can find alternative *data path descriptions*, *replacement values*, and *plausibility specifications*. As not to invalidate standard PEARL compilers those specifications are included in comment brackets. The dollar sign is a compiler pragma for enhanced PEARL compilers. Normally the first data path is used for reading a value from a temperature sensor. If this value is out of the range 100..1600 or if it differs from the previous read value by more than 10 (specified in PLAUS) the next data path is used. In the case of a defect ADC (analogue digital converter) this may be successful because the sensor is also connected to another ADC (ANALOGIN 571). As this ADC may have different range and gain, correction algorithms can be specified (CORR). It is important that even in the case that all alternative data paths fail some value is yielded as not to stop the technical process. This can be achieved by specifying a replacement value (REP).

The whole design is guided by concentrating all hardware–dependend properties in the SYSTEM–division. The algorithmic part in the PROBLEM–division is thus highly portable. In this case it would only contain a read statement of the form:

READ TEMPERATURE FROM TEMP;

Redundancy and availability considerations are such considered to be a separate concern.

6.6.2. Configuration Description in PRONET

PRONET [Maccabe 82, Le Blanc 82] allows to specify the logical structure of a system using two completely separate languages: NETSLA for the specification of the network and ALSTEN for the description of parallel processes. The physical structure is not specified by the user of PRONET; the network operating system has a global view of the state of the system and decides how to map the dynamically changing logical structure into the physical structure.

ALSTEN is an algorithmic, Pascal based language which allows to define templates of parallel processes called **process scripts**. Communication between processes is performed by send and receive statements. The receive statement may wait in a non–deterministic way for different messages presenting a restricted form of the Ada select statement. Messages are sent to or received from typed and directed (**in, out**) ports.

Those ports are visible to network specifications written in NETSLA where the message exchange proper is handled. Sending a message is thus one of the possible connections between ALSTEN and NETSLA. The execution of a send operation causes a transmission event to be announced implicitly in the network specification.

Besides this connection there is a more flexible connection between ALSTEN and NETSLA. In ALSTEN it is possible to declare an **event** which may be **announced** to the network specification. Implicit and explicit announcements may give rise to dynamic reconfigurations described in NETSLA.

An example for a process template in ALSTEN is given in Figure 6.20.

```
process script mailbox
  port input in letter;
  port output out letter;
  port deliver_mail in signal;
  event mailbox_empty;
  var
    next_response : user_response;
    done : boolean;
  begin
    repeat
      receive from deliver_mail;
      next_response.kind := mail_item;
      done := false;
      repeat
      when
        receive next_response.let from input do
          send next_response to output;
        otherwise
          done := true
      end (* when *)
      until done
      next_response.kind := empty;
      send next_response to output;
      announce mailbox_empty
    until false
end (*mailbox script*)
```

Figure 6.20: A process template in ALSTEN

NETSLA is in effect an algorithmic language, as well, which allows to dynamically initialize, create, and terminate processes, to connect and to disconnect ports and to handle events announced by the ALSTEN program. Given a process script in ALSTEN as described in the example of Figure 6.21 we can create for example a simple static net shown in the graphical representation of Figure 6.22 by the NETSLA specification of Figure 6.23.

process script simple_process
  port input **in** letter;
  port output **out** letter;
  local declarations
begin
  body
end (*simple_process*)

Figure 6.21: Template for process simple_process in ALSTEN

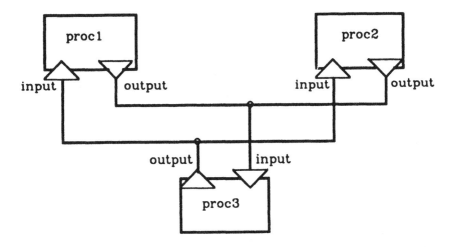

Figure 6.22:   Graphical representation of logical process structure

network static_net
  process class simple_process
    port input **in** letter;
    port output **out** letter;
  end simple_process;

  initial
    create proc1: simpleprocess;
    create proc2: simpleprocess;

```
    create proc3: simpleprocess;
    connect proc1.output to proc3.input;
    connect proc2.output to proc3.input;
    connect proc3.output to proc1.input;
    connect proc3.output to proc2.input;
end static_net
```

Figure 6.23: NETSLA specification of a simple static net

The aspect of dynamic reconfiguration can best be explained using our mailbox example (Figure 6.20). As soon as there are no more letters in the mailbox to be transmitted to the output we announce the event mailbox_empty to the network specification. In this case we want the network specification to change the logical structure in disconnecting the output port of the corresponding mailbox. This can be done using the NETSLA specification of Figure 6.24.

```
network simple_mail
    ...
    when mailbox_empty announced by
      box: mailbox (*identification of announcing process*)
      do disconnect box.output
    end when
end simple_mail
```

Figure 6.24: NETSLA specification with dynamic reconfiguration

6.7. Case Study for a Real-Time Distributed System

After the discussion of various language concepts for distributed programming we want to discuss in the following case study how real-time constraints influence the design of a programming language. The CONIC system [Kramer 83, Magee 83] is a well suited object for a case study because it reveals all aspects of language constructs considered so far and is one of the few languages in the field of real-time systems. The examples to illustrate the language concepts are taken from [Kramer 83].

Experience with large real—time systems shows that there is not only a need for systematic but also for unpredictable changes. Changes may affect software or hardware. They are due to progressive automation, better analysis and knowledge of the technical process, progress in sensor and actuator technique, or simply to failures of hardware components. As changes mostly affect only a part of a distributed system one of the most important requirements is that the system can be reconfigured dynamically without stopping the whole production process.

A major objective in CONIC is to enable dynamic reconfiguration. Configuration description and reconfiguration management thus are central parts of CONIC. A system in CONIC consists of module instances, the interconnection of which is specified by the configuration description. Thus compilation units are templates of modules that may be parametrized. As parameters are not allowed to be types, this mechanism is not as powerful as the generic mechanism in Ada.

Communication between modules is performed by sending and receiving messages. Direct naming is avoided by defining *exitports* and *entryports* that form the interface of a module. Modules in CONIC are with respect to this more similar to Ada types than to Ada modules.

As exitports and entryports are typed, only messages of one type can be sent to or received from a specific port. In the configuration description the connection of the ports, defined in different modules, is specified. The types of the ports are defined in a global accessible file so that any module can import the types it needs for communication.

Let us have a closer look to configuration descriptions in CONIC. Suppose we have compiled three module templates named pumpcontroller, operatormod, and environmentmod. First we have to load those modul types into particular nodes, say station1, station2, and station3:

LOAD pumpcontroller AT station1;
LOAD operatormod AT station2;
LOAD environmentmod AT station3;

Then we have to instantiate modules at the nodes:

CREATE pump: pumpcontroller (#177562) AT station1;
CREATE surface : operatormod AT station2;
CREATE env: environmentmod AT station3;

In the example the module instance pump is initialized with an octal device address. After the creation, modules are linked together by connecting entryports and exitports:

LINK surface.out TO pump.cmd;
LINK pump.environrequest TO env.environrequest;
LINK env.alarm TO pump.alarm, surface.alarm;

The last statement above shows how to specify a one–to–many communication structure. After that the system can be started:

START pump, surface, env;

Reconfiguration of the system can be performed using additionally STOP, UNLINK, and DELETE statements.

In contrast to PEARL and CONIC it is possible to reconfigure the system any time by changing the configuration description. As this is not part of a program available at runtime, no automatic reconfiguration triggered by some event can be specified. PEARL and CONIC allow for such an automatic reconfiguration but reconfiguration in a not previously predicted way requires the program to be changed and recompiled. Maybe a combination of both concepts could be useful for many applications.

As already discussed, communication between modules is performed by message passing. CONIC offers a variety of message passing patterns that are commonly used in real–time applications.

The first variant is the asynchronous no–wait send which is often used for sending alarm or status information. This no–wait send does not block the sending task and is therefore especially useful in time–critical processes. Theoretically this send operation requires dynamic buffer management as many send operations may be executed before one receive operation occurs. As this is time–consuming, too, it is reasonable in a real–time environment to compromise. CONIC allows to define a fixed dimensionable queue of buffers to be attached to each entryport, e.g.:

ENTRYPORT in : status QUEUE 80;

If the queue is full, the latest entry is overwritten. If no queue length is specified the default length is one.

If the following exitports are declared:

EXITPORT out : status;
ENTRYPORT in: status;
the corresponding message passing statements could be:

SEND statusbit TO out;   and   RECEIVE statusbit FROM in;

The receive statement in CONIC is a blocking receive.

The second variant is a remote invocation send which may be combined with a timeout specification and an exception handling part for treating unlinked exitports:

SEND start TO pump
  WAIT response => -- actions after successful response
  TIMEOUT period => -- actions in case of timeout
  FAIL => -- actions if exitport is not linked
END

This looks very similar to a timed entry call in Ada but reveals more appropriate semantics for real-time applications. The message passing statement aborts if after the specified timeout no response is available. The problems with the timed entry call in Ada have been discussed in chapter 6.5.2.

The corresponding RECEIVE ... REPLY statement can be used in connection with a select statement close related to the selective wait statement in Ada. Timeout conditions are specified in an else part:

SELECT
  WHEN guard1 RECEIVE msg1 FROM port1
    => ...
      REPLY response TO port1;

```
   ...
OR
  WHEN guard2 ...
OR
  RECEIVE ...  -- no guard specified
ELSE TIMEOUT period
  => ...  -- actions in case of timeout
END;
```

What remains to be discussed are some more real-time concepts. Scheduling of processes can be implemented like in Ada using the function *time* yielding the current time and a *delay* procedure. A procedure *waitio(x)* suspends a calling process until an interrupt specified by x occurs. Priorities *low*, *medium*, *high*, and *system* can be attributed to processes; a process with priority *system* is not interruptable.

The development of the CONIC system is still in progress but it seems that a good compromise between expensive but theoretically desirable concepts and real-time constraints will be effected.

Chapter 7

The Argus Language and System

Technological advances have made it cost-effective to construct large systems from collections of computers connected via networks. To support such systems, there is a growing need for effective ways to organize and maintain *distributed programs*: programs in which modules reside and execute at communicating, but geographically distinct, locations. In these lectures we present an overview of an integrated programming language and system, called Argus, that was designed for this purpose.

Distributed programs run on *nodes* connected (only) via a communications network. A node consists of one or more processors, one or more levels of memory, and any number of external devices. Different nodes may contain different kinds of processors and devices. The network may be longhaul or shorthaul, or any combination, connected by gateways. Neither the network nor any nodes need be reliable. However, we do assume that all failures can be detected as explained in [Lampson 79]. We also assume that message delay is long relative to the time needed to access local memory, and therefore access to non-local data is significantly more expensive than access to local data.

The applications that can make effective use of a distributed organization differ in their requirements. We have concentrated on a class of applications concerned with the manipulation and preservation of long-lived, on-line data. Examples of such applications are banking systems, airline reservation systems, office automation systems, data base systems, and various components of operating systems. In these systems, real-time constraints are not severe, but reliable, available, distributed data is of primary importance. The systems may serve a geographically distributed organization. Our language is intended to support the implementation of such systems.

The application domain, together with our hardware assumptions, imposes a number of requirements:

Service. A major concern is to provide continuous service of the system as a whole in the face of node and network failures. Failures should be localized so that a program can perform its task as long as the particular nodes it needs to communicate with are functioning and reachable. Adherence to this principle permits an application program to use replication of data and processing to increase availability.

Reconfiguration. An important reason for wanting a distributed implementation is to make it easy to add and reconfigure hardware to increase processing power, decrease response time, or increase the availability of data. It also must be possible to implement logical systems that can be reconfigured. To maintain continuous service, it must be possible to make both logical and physical changes *dynamically*, while the system continues to operate.

Autonomy. We assume that nodes are owned by individuals or organizations that want to control how the node is used. For example, the owner may want to control what runs at the node, or to control the availability of services provided at the node. Further, a node might contain data that must remain resident at that node; for example, a multi-national organization must abide by laws governing information flow among countries. The important point here is that the need for distribution arises not only from performance considerations, but from political and sociological considerations as well.

Distribution. The distribution of data and processing can have a major impact on overall efficiency, in terms of both responsiveness and cost-effective use of hardware. Distribution also affects availability. To create efficient, available systems while retaining autonomy, the programmer needs explicit control over the placement of modules in the system. However, to support a reasonable degree of modularity, changes in location of modules should have limited, localized effects on the actual code.

Concurrency. Another major reason for choosing a distributed implementation is to take advantage of the potential concurrency in an application, thereby increasing efficiency and decreasing response time.

Consistency. In almost any system where on-line data is being read and modified by on-going activities, there are consistency constraints that must be maintained. Such constraints apply not only to individual pieces of data, but to distributed sets of data as well. For example, when funds are transferred from one account to another in a banking system, the net gain over the two accounts must be zero. Also, data that is replicated to increase availability must be kept consistent.

Of the above requirements, we found consistency the most difficult to meet. The main issues here are the coordination of concurrent activities (permitting concurrency but avoiding interference), and the masking of hardware failures. To support consistency we had to devise methods for building a reliable system on unreliable hardware. Reliability is an area that has been almost completely ignored in programming languages (with the exception of [Lomet 77, Randell 75, Shrivastava 78]). Yet our study of applications convinced us that consistency is a crucial requirement: an adequate language must provide a modular, reasonably automatic method for achieving consistency.

Argus is described in the following sections. First we discuss the principal concepts that underlie the design of Argus. Then we decribe most of the linguistic mechanisms in Argus, and illustrate their use in an example. After that we discuss the form of programs in Argus, and how to configure and reconfigure distributed programs. Next we describe part of the Argus implementation. Then we discuss a new kind of data abstraction that is useful in building highly concurrent and available systems. We conclude with a brief evaluation of Argus.

7.1. Concepts and Issues

In this section, we discuss the two main concepts, guardians and actions, that Argus provides to support the construction of fault-tolerant distributed systems.

7.1.1. Guardians

In Argus, a distributed program is composed of a group of *guardians*. A guardian encapsulates and controls access to one or more resources, e.g., databases or devices. A guardian makes these resources available to its users by providing a set of operations called *handlers*, which can be called by other guardians to make use of the resources. The guardian executes the handlers, synchronizing them and performing access control as needed.

Internally, a guardian contains data objects and processes. The processes execute handler calls (a separate process is spawned for each call) and perform background tasks. Some of the data objects, e.g., the actual resources, make up the *state* of the guardian; these objects are shared by the processes. Other objects are local to the individual processes.

Guardians allow a programmer to decompose a problem into units of tightly coupled processing and data. Within a guardian, processes can share objects directly. However, direct sharing of objects between guardians is not permitted. Instead, guardians must communicate by calling handlers. Handler calls are performed using a message-based communication mechanism. The language implementation takes care of all details of constructing and sending messages (see [Herlihy 82]).

The arguments of handler calls are passed by value: it is impossible to pass a reference to an object in a handler call. This rule ensures that objects local to a guardian remain local, and thus ensures that a guardian retains control of its own objects. It also provides the programmer with a concept of what is expensive: local objects, which can be accessed directly, are close by and inexpensive to use, while non-local objects are more expensive to use and can be accessed only by making handler calls.

A guardian runs at a single node, but can survive crashes of this node with high probability. A guardian's state consists of *stable* and *volatile* objects. The stable objects are written periodically to stable storage devices; such devices can survive failures with arbitrarily high probability [Lampson 79]. When a guardian's node crashes, the volatile data, and the processes that were running at the time of the crash, are lost, but the stable data survives. Since the probability of loss of volatile objects is relatively high, these objects must contain only redundant information if the system as a whole is to avoid loss of information. Such redundant information is useful for improving efficiency, e.g., an index into a data base for fast access.

After a crash and subsequent recovery of the guardian's node, the Argus support system re-creates the guardian with the stable objects as they were when last written to stable storage. A recovery process is started in the guardian to restore the volatile objects. Once the volatile objects have been restored, the guardian can resume background tasks, and can respond to new handler calls.

Crash recovery is illustrated in Fig. 7-1. Fig. 7-1a shows a snapshot of a guardian that provides three handlers, H1, H2 and H3. At the moment the snapshot was taken, there were three processes running inside the guardian. Process B is running a background activity that is independent of any handler call. Processes P1 and P2 are running handler calls; these might be calls of different handlers (e.g., H1 and H2) or they might be two distinct calls of the same handler. The three processes all share a piece of stable data; this is the data item labelled X. They also share a piece of volatile data, Y. In addition, each process has local data; only one such item, Z, is shown.

Now suppose that a crash occurs. After the crash the Argus system brings the guardian up in the state shown in Fig. 7-1b. Only the stable data, X, has survived the crash; all the volatile data and the processes that were running at the time of the crash have been lost. The system has started the recovery process, R; R has access to the stable data X.

The job of the recovery process is to reconstruct the shared volatile data, Y, in a state that is consistent with the state of X. The situation just after completion of R is shown in Fig. 7-1c. Now both the stable and volatile data exist. In addition, a process, B, has been created to run the background activity. B is the only process running at this moment, but the guardian is ready to accept new handler calls, and more processes will be started when these calls arrive.

Guardians are created dynamically. The programmer specifies the node at which a

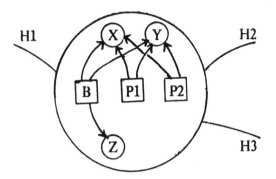

a. A guardian snapshot.

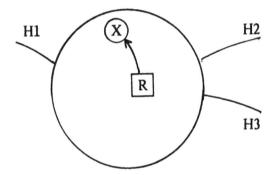

b. After a crash.

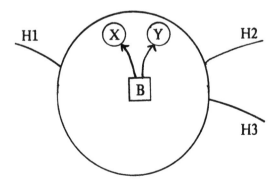

c. After recovery.

Figure 7-1: Crash Recovery

guardian is to be created; in this way individual guardians can be placed at the most advantageous locations within the network. The (name of the) guardian and (the names of) its handlers can be communicated in handler calls. Once (the name of) a guardian or one of its handlers has been received, handler calls can be performed on that guardian. Handler calls are location independent, however, so one guardian can use another without knowing its location. In fact, handler calls will continue to work even if the called guardian has changed its location, allowing for ease of system reconfiguration.

Guardians and handlers are an abstraction of the underlying hardware of a distributed system. A guardian is a logical node of the system, and inter-guardian communication via handlers is an abstraction of the physical network. The most important difference between the logical system and the physical system is reliability: the stable state of a guardian is never lost (to a very high probability), and the semantics of handler calls ensures that the calls either succeed completely or have no effect.

7.1.2. Atomic Actions

Although a distributed program might consist of a single guardian, more typically it will be composed of several guardians, and these guardians will reside at different nodes. For example, Fig. 7-2 shows a distributed program composed of five guardians residing at five nodes.

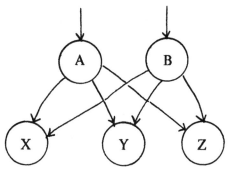

Figure 7-2: A Distributed System

The guardians A and B represent the "front ends" of the system: any client (i.e., any other guardian that uses the service provided by this distributed system) will make handler calls on the handlers of either A or B. To carry out such a call, A (or B) in turn makes calls on X, Y and Z. A system like this one might implement a distributed database, where A and B are query processors, and the actual data of the system, replicated to increase availability, resides at X, Y and Z.

In a system composed of many guardians, the state of the system is distributed: it resides at the different guardians. This distributed state must be kept consistent in the presence of concurrency, and in spite of the fact that the hardware components on which the system runs can fail independently. To provide consistency of distributed data, Argus supports a second fundamental concept, *atomicity*.

An activity in Argus can be thought of as a process that attempts to examine and transform some objects in the distributed state from their current (initial) states to new (final) states, with any number of intermediate state changes. Two properties distinguish an activity as being atomic: indivisibility and recoverability. *Indivisibility* means that the execution of one activity never appears to overlap (or contain) the execution of any other activity. If the objects being modified by one activity are observed over time by another activity, the latter activity will either always observe the initial states or always observe the final states of those objects. *Recoverability* means that the overall effect of the activity is all-or-nothing: either all of the objects remain in their initial state, or all change to their final state. If a failure occurs while an activity is running, it must be possible either to complete the activity, or to restore all objects to their initial states.

We call an atomic activity an *action*. (In the database literature, atomic activities are referred to as transactions.) An action may complete either by *committing* or *aborting*. When an action aborts, the effect is as if the action had never begun: all modified objects are restored to their previous states. When an action commits, all modified objects take on their new states.

One simple way to implement the indivisibility property is to force actions to run sequentially. However, one of our goals is to provide a high degree of concurrency, so instead we guarantee *serializability* [Eswaren 76], namely, actions are scheduled in such a way that their overall effect is as if they had been run sequentially in some order. To prevent one action from observing or interfering with the intermediate states of another action, we need to synchronize access to shared objects. In addition, to implement the recoverability property, we need to be able to undo the changes made to objects by aborted actions.

Since synchronization and recovery are likely to be somewhat expensive to implement, we do not provide these properties for all objects. For example, objects that are purely local to a single action do not require these properties. The objects that do provide these properties are called *atomic objects*, and we restrict our notion of atomicity to cover only access to atomic objects. That is, atomicity is guaranteed only when the objects shared by actions are atomic objects.

Atomic objects are encapsulated within *atomic abstract data types*. An abstract data type consists of a set of objects and a set of primitive operations; the primitive operations are the only means of accessing and manipulating the objects [Liskov 74]. Atomic types have operations just like normal data types, except the operations provide indivisibility and recoverability for the calling actions. Some atomic types are built-in while others are user-defined. Argus provides, as built-in types, atomic arrays, records, and variants, with operations nearly identical to the normal arrays, records, and variants provided in CLU [Liskov 77, Liskov 81b]. In addition, objects of built-in scalar types, such as characters and integers, are atomic, as are structured objects of built-in immutable types, such as strings, whose components cannot change over time.

Our implementation of (mutable) built-in atomic objects is based on a fairly simple locking model. There are two kinds of locks: read locks and write locks. Before an action uses an object, it must acquire a lock in the appropriate mode. The usual locking rules apply: multiple readers are allowed, but readers exclude writers and a writer excludes readers and other writers. When a write lock is obtained, a *version* of the object is made, and the action operates on this version. If, ultimately, the action commits, this version will be retained, and the old version discarded. If the action aborts, this version will be discarded, and the old version retained. For example, atomic records have the usual component selection and update operations, but selection operations obtain a read lock on the record (not the component), and update operations obtain a write lock and create a version of the record the first time the action modifies the record.

All locks acquired by an action are held until the completion of that action, a simplification of standard two-phase locking [Eswaren 76]. This rule avoids the problem of *cascading aborts* [Wood 80]: if a lock on an object were released early, and the action later aborted, any action that had observed the new state of that object would also have to be aborted.

Within the framework of actions, there is a straightforward way to deal with hardware failures at a node: they simply force the node to crash, which in turn forces actions to abort. As was mentioned above, the stable state of guardians is stored on stable storage devices. However, we do not actually copy information to stable storage until actions commit. Instead, versions made for a running action and information about locks are kept in volatile memory. This volatile information will be lost if the node crashes. If this happens the action must be forced to abort.

To ensure that an action either commits everywhere or aborts everywhere, we carry out a distributed commitment protocol. A standard two-phase commit protocol [Gray 78] is used. In the first phase, an attempt is made to verify that all locks are still held, and to record the new version of each modified object on stable storage. If the first phase is successful, then in the second phase the locks are released, the recorded states become the current states, and the previous states are forgotten. If the first phase fails, the recorded states are forgotten and the action is forced to abort, restoring the objects to their previous states. Our commitment protocol is discussed in more detail in Section 7.5.3.

Turning hardware failures into aborts has the merit of freeing the programmer from low-level hardware considerations. It also reduces the probability that actions will commit. However, this is a problem only when the time to complete an action approaches the mean time between failures of the nodes. We believe that most actions will be quite short compared to realistic mean time between failures for hardware available today.

It has been argued that indivisibility is too strong a property for certain applications because it limits the amount of potential concurrency (see, e.g. [Birrell 82]). We believe that indivisibility is the desired property for most applications, *if* it is required only at the appropriate levels of abstraction. Argus provides a mechanism for *user-defined* atomic data types. These types present an external interface that supports indivisibility, but can offer a great deal of concurrency as well. We will present our mechanism for user-defined atomic types in Section 7.6

Nested Actions

So far we have presented actions as monolithic entities. In fact, it is useful to break down such entities into pieces; to this end we provide hierarchically structured, *nested* actions. Nested actions, or *subactions*, are a mechanism for coping with failures, as well as for introducing concurrency within an action. An action may contain any number of subactions, some of which may be performed sequentially, some concurrently. This structure cannot be observed from outside; i.e., the overall action still satisfies the atomicity properties. Subactions appear as atomic activities with respect to other subactions of the same parent. Subactions can commit and abort independently, and a subaction can abort without forcing its parent action to abort. However, the commit of a subaction is conditional: even if a subaction commits, aborting its parent action will undo its effects. Further, object versions are written to stable storage only when top-level actions commit.

Nested actions aid in composing (and decomposing) activities in a modular fashion. They allow a collection of existing actions to be combined into a single, higher-level action, and to be run concurrently within that action with no need for additional synchronization. For example, consider a database replicated at multiple nodes. If only a majority of the nodes need to be read or written for the overall action to succeed, this is accomplished by performing the reads or writes as concurrent subactions, and committing the overall action as soon as a majority of the subactions commit, even though some of the other subactions are forced to abort.

Nested actions have been proposed by others [Davies 78, Reed 78]; our model is similar to that presented in [Moss 81]. The locking and version management rules for nested actions are shown in Fig. 7-3. To keep the locking rules simple, we do not allow a parent action to run concurrently with its children. The rule for read locks is extended so that an action may obtain a read lock on an object provided every action holding a write lock on that object is an ancestor. An action may obtain a write lock on an object provided every action holding a (read or write) lock on that object is an ancestor. When a subaction commits, its locks and versions are inherited by its parent; when a subaction aborts, its locks and versions are discarded.

Note that the locking rules permit multiple writers, which implies that multiple versions of objects are needed. However, since writers must form a linear chain when

Acquiring a read lock:
> All holders of write locks on X must be ancestors of S.

Acquiring a write lock:
> All holders of read and write locks on X must be ancestors of S.
> If this is the first time S has acquired a write lock on X,
>> push a copy of S's parent's version on top of the version stack.

Commit:
> S's parent acquires S's lock on X.
> If S holds a write lock on X, then S's version (which is on the top of the
> version stack for X) becomes S's parent's version.

Abort:
> S's lock and version (if any) are discarded.

Figure 7-3: Locking and Version Management Rules for a Subaction, S, on Object X.

ordered by ancestry, and actions cannot execute concurrently with their subactions, only one writer can ever actually be executing at one time. Hence, it suffices to use a stack of versions (rather than a tree) for each atomic object. All reading and writing uses the version on top of the stack. A new version is pushed on the stack whenever a subaction acquires a write lock for the first time. On commit, the top version on the stack becomes the new version for the parent; on abort the top version is simply discarded. Since versions become permanent only when top-level actions commit, the two-phase commit protocol is used only for top-level actions. A detailed description of locking and version management in a system supporting nested actions is presented in [Moss 81].

In addition to nesting subactions inside other actions, it is sometimes useful to start a new top-level action inside another action. Such a "nested" top action, unlike a subaction, has no special privileges relative to its parent; for example, it is not able to read an atomic object modified by its parent. Furthermore, the commit of a nested top action is not relative to its parent; its versions are written to stable storage, and its locks are released, just as for normal top actions. Nested top actions are useful for benevolent side effects. For example, in a naming system a name look-up may cause information to be copied from one location to another, to speed up subsequent look-ups of that name.

Copying the data within a nested top action ensures that the changes remain in effect even if the parent action aborts. An example of a nested top action is given in Section 7.3.

7.1.3. Communication

Perhaps the single most important application of nested actions is in masking communication failures. Although communication among guardians in Argus requires messages to be sent over the network, the form of communication available at the language level is the *handler call*. Handler calls are remote procedure calls. The caller supplies the name of the called handler and some arguments. When the handler returns, the caller receives the results and can then continue processing. The arguments and results are passed by value.

The Argus system constructs and sends the call and reply messages needed to implement a handler call. Furthermore, we guarantee that handler calls have *at-most-once* semantics, namely, that (effectively) either the call message is delivered and acted on exactly once at the called guardian, with exactly one reply received, or the message is never delivered and the caller is so informed. The rationale for the high-level, at-most-once semantics of handler call is presented in [Liskov 81a] (also see [Spector 82]). Briefly, we believe the system should mask low-level issues, such as packetization and retransmission, from the user and should make a reasonable attempt to deliver messages. However, we believe the possibility of long delays and of ultimate failure in sending a message cannot and should not be masked. In such a case, the handler call would fail. (For example, the system would cause the call to fail if it were unable to contact the called guardian after trying for some period of time. We believe the system, and not the programmer, should take on this kind of responsibility, because the programmer would find it difficult to define reasonable timeouts.) The caller can then cope with the failure according to the demands of the particular application. However, coping with the failure is much simpler if it is guaranteed that in this case the handler call had no effect.

The all-or-nothing nature of a handler call is similar to the recoverability property of actions, and the ability to cope with communication failures is similar to the ability of an action to cope with the failures of subactions. Therefore, it seems natural to implement a handler call as a subaction: communication failures will force the subaction to abort, and the caller has the ability to abort the subaction on demand. However, as mentioned above, aborting the subaction does not force the parent action to abort. The caller is free to find some other means of accomplishing its task, such as making a handler call to some other guardian.

7.1.4. Remarks

In our model, there are two kinds of actions: subactions and top-level actions. We believe these correspond in a natural way to activities in the application system. Top-level actions correspond to activities that interact with the external environment, or, in the case of nested top actions, to activities that should not be undone if the parent aborts. For example, in an airline reservation system, a top-level action might correspond to an interaction with a clerk who is entering a related sequence of reservations. Subactions, on the other hand, correspond to internal activities that are intended to be carried out as part of an external interaction; a reservation on a single flight is an example.

Not all effects of an action can be undone by aborting that action, since a change to the external environment, e.g., printing a check, cannot be undone by program control alone. But as long as all effects can be undone, the user of Argus need not write any code to undo or compensate for the effects of aborted actions.

Before doing something like printing a check, the application program should make sure that printing the check is the right thing to do. One technique for ensuring this is to break an activity into two separate, sequential top-level actions. All changes to the external environment are deferred to the second action, to be executed only if the first action is successful. Such a technique will greatly decrease the likelihood of actions having undesired effects that cannot be undone.

The commit of a top-level action is irrevocable. If that action is later found to be in error, actions that compensate for the effects of the erroneous action (and all later actions that read its results) must be defined and executed by the user. Compensation must also be performed for effects of aborted actions that cannot be undone. Note that in general there is no way that such compensation could be done automatically by the system, since extra-system activity is needed (e.g., cancelling already issued checks).

Given our use of a locking scheme to implement atomic objects, it is possible for two (or more) actions to *deadlock*, each attempting to acquire a lock held by the other. Although in many cases deadlock can be avoided with careful programming, certain deadlock situations arc unavoidable. Rather than having the system prevent, or detect and break, deadlocks, we rely on the user to time out and abort top-level actions. These timeouts generally will be very long, or will be controlled by someone sitting at a terminal. Note that such timeouts are needed even without deadlocks, since there are other reasons why a top action may be too slow (e.g., contention).

A user can retry a top action that aborted because of a timeout or crash, but Argus provides no guarantee that progress will be made. Argus will be extended if needed, e.g., by raising the priority of a top action each time it is repeated [Rosenkrantz 78] or by using checkpoints [Gray 78, Gray 81].

7.2. Argus Features

This section contains an overview of the syntax and semantics of the Argus language. The most novel features are the constructs for implementing guardians and actions. To avoid rethinking issues that arise in sequential languages, we have based Argus on an existing sequential language. CLU [Liskov 77, Liskov 81b] was chosen because it supports the construction of well-structured programs through abstraction mechanisms, and because it is an object-oriented language, in which programs are naturally thought of as operating on potentially long-lived objects. A detailed description of Argus is contained in [Liskov 83b].

The syntax of a guardian definition is shown in Fig. 7-4. In the syntax, optional clauses are enclosed with [ ], zero or more repetitions are indicated with { }, and alternatives are separated by |.

A guardian definition implements a special kind of abstract data type whose operations are handlers. The name of this type, and the names of the handlers, are listed in the guardian header. In addition, the type provides one or more creation operations, called *creators*, that can be invoked to create new guardians of the type; the names of the creators are also listed in the header. Guardians can be *parameterized*, providing the ability to define a class of related abstractions by means of a single module. Parameterized types are discussed in [Liskov 77, Liskov 81b].

$name =$ **guardian** $\big[$ *parameter-decls* $\big]$ **is** *creator-names*
$\qquad\qquad \big[$ **handles** *handler-names* $\big]$

$\big\{$ *abbreviations* $\big\}$

$\big\{$ $\big[$ **stable** $\big]$ *variable-decls-and-inits* $\big\}$

$\big[$ **recover** *body* **end** $\big]$

$\big[$ **background** *body* **end** $\big]$

$\big\{$ *creator-handler-and-local-routine-definitions* $\big\}$

end *name*

Figure 7-4: Guardian Structure

The first internal part of a guardian is a list of abbreviations for types and constants. Next is a list of variable declarations, with optional initializations, defining the guardian state. Some of these variables can be declared as **stable** variables; the others are volatile variables.

The stable state of a guardian consists of all objects *reachable* from the stable variables; these objects, called stable objects, have their new versions written to stable storage by the system when top-level actions commit. Argus, like CLU, has an object-oriented semantics. Variables name (or refer to) objects residing in a heap storage area. Objects themselves may refer to other objects, permitting recursive and cyclic data structures without the use of explicit pointers. The set of objects reachable from a variable consists of the object that variable refers to, any objects referred to by that object, and so on.[1] Guardian instances are created dynamically by calling creators of the guardian type. For example, suppose a guardian type named *spooler* has a creator with a header of the form:

create = **creator** (dev: printer) **returns** (spooler)

---

[1] In languages that are not object-oriented, the concept of reachability would still be needed to accommodate the use of explicit pointers.

When a process executes the expression

    spooler$create(pdev)

a guardian object is created at the same physical node where the process is executing and (the name of) the guardian is returned as the result of the call. (As in CLU, the notation $t\$op$ is used to name the *op* operation of type t.) Guardians can also be created at other nodes. Given a variable *home* naming some node,

    spooler$create(pdev) @ home

creates a spooler guardian at the specified node.

When a creator is called, a new guardian instance is created, and any initializations attached to the variable declarations of the guardian state are executed. The body of the creator is then executed; typically, this code will finish initializing the guardian state and then return the guardian object. (Within the guardian, the expression self refers to the guardian object.)

Aside from creating a new guardian instance and executing state variable initializations, a creator has essentially the same semantics as a handler, as described in the next section. In particular, a creator call is performed within a new subaction of the caller. The newly-created guardian will be destroyed if this subaction or one of its ancestor actions aborts. The guardian becomes *permanent* (i.e., survives node crashes) only when the action in which it was created commits to the top level. A guardian cannot be destroyed from outside the guardian (except by aborting the creating action). Once a guardian becomes permanent, it can be destroyed only by itself, by means of a destroy primitive.

After a crash, the Argus system re-creates the guardian and restores its stable objects from stable storage. Since updates to stable storage are made only when top-level actions commit, the stable state has the value it had at the last commit of a top-level action that used the guardian before the crash. The effects of actions that had executed at the guardian prior to the crash, but had not yet committed to the top level, are lost and the actions are aborted.

After the stable objects have been restored, the system starts a recovery process in the guardian. This process executes any initializations attached to declarations of volatile variables of the guardian state and then executes the **recover** section (if any). The recovery process runs as a top-level action. Recovery succeeds if this action commits; otherwise the guardian crashes and recovery is retried later.

After the successful completion of a creator, or of recovery after a crash, two things happen inside the guardian: a process is created to run the **background** section, and handler calls may be executed. The **background** section provides a means of performing periodic (or continuous) tasks within the guardian; an example is given in Section 7.3. The **background** section is not run as an action, although generally it creates top-level actions to execute tasks, using constructs explained below.[2]

7.2.1. Handlers

Handlers (and creators), like procedures in CLU, are based on the termination model of exception handling [Liskov 79]. A handler can terminate in one of a number of conditions: one of these is considered to be the "normal" condition, while others are "exceptional," and are given system or user-defined names. Results can be returned both in the normal and exceptional cases; the number and types of results can differ among conditions. The header of a handler definition lists the names of all exceptional conditions and defines the number and types of results in all cases. For example,

$$\text{files\_ahead\_of} = \textbf{handler} \text{ (entry\_id: int) } \textbf{returns} \text{ (int)}$$
$$\textbf{signals} \text{ (printed(date))}$$

might be the header of a spooler handler used to determine how many requests are in front of a given queue entry. Calls of this handler either terminate normally, returning an integer result, or exceptionally in condition *printed* with a date result. In addition to the named conditions, any handler call can terminate in the *failure* or *unavailable* conditions, returning a string result; such termination may be caused explicitly by the user code, or implicitly by the system when something unusual happens, as explained further below.

---

[2] A process that is not running as an action is severely restricted in what it can do. For example, it cannot call operations on atomic objects or call handlers without first creating a top-level action.

A handler call executes as a subaction. As such, in addition to returning or signalling, it must either commit or abort. We expect committing to be the most common case, and therefore execution of a **return** or **signal** statement within the body of a handler indicates commitment. To cause an abort, the **return** or **signal** is prefixed with **abort**.

Given a variable x naming a guardian object, a handler h of the guardian may be referred to as $x.h$. Handlers are invoked using the same syntax as for procedure invocation, e.g.,

    x.h("read", 3, false)

As with an ordinary procedure call, the caller of a handler is suspended until the call completes. However, whereas procedure calls are always executed locally within the current action, and always have their arguments and results passed *by sharing*,[3] handler calls are always executed as new subactions, usually in a different guardian, and always have their arguments and results passed by value.

Let us examine a step-by-step description of what the system does when a handler is called:

1. A new subaction of the calling action is created. We will refer to this new subaction as the *call action*. The following steps all take place within the call action.

2. A message containing the arguments is constructed. Since part of building this message involves executing user-defined code (see [Herlihy 82]), message construction may fail. If so, the call action aborts and the call terminates with a *failure* exception.

3. The system determines the node at which the called guardian resides and sends the message to that node. If the guardian no longer exists, the call action aborts and the call terminates with a *failure* exception.

---

[3] Somewhat similar to passing by reference. See [Liskov 81b].

4. The system makes a reasonable attempt to deliver the message, but success is not guaranteed. The reason is that it may not be sensible to guarantee success under certain conditions, such as a crash of the target node. In such cases, the call action aborts and the call terminates with the *unavailable* exception. The meaning of unavailable is that there is a very low probability of the call succeeding if it is repeated immediately; in contrast, the meaning of failure is that there is no chance of the call succeeding if it is repeated.

5. When the call message is received at the called guardian, the system creates a process and another subaction, the *handler action*, at the receiving guardian to execute the handler. The handler action is a subaction of the call action. (Two actions are needed so that the call can be aborted, as in Step 4, even if handler action commits.) The system then attempts to decompose the message. As in message construction, decomposition involves executing user code and may fail. If so, the handler action aborts and the handler terminates in the failure exception.

6. If no problems were encountered in steps 2-5, the handler code is executed. Note that multiple instances of the same handler may execute simultaneously. The system takes care of locks and versions of atomic objects used by the handler in the proper manner, according to whether the handler action commits or aborts.

7. When the handler terminates, a message containing the results is constructed, the handler process is destroyed, and the message is sent. If the message cannot be constructed (as in step 2 above) the handler action aborts; if it cannot be decomposed (as in step 5), the call action aborts; in either case, the call terminates with a *failure* exception.

8. When the reply message is received at the calling guardian, the calling process continues execution. Its control flow is affected by the termination condition as explained in [Liskov 79]. For example,

```
count: int := spool.files_ahead_of(ent)          % normal return
    except when printed (at: date): ...            % exceptional returns
           when failure (why: string): ...
           when unavailable (why: string): ...
           end
```

As in CLU, the **except** statement can be placed on any statement containing the calls whose exceptions it handles.

Since a new process is created to perform an incoming handler call, guardians have the ability to execute many requests concurrently. (Synchronization of these processes occurs through their use of atomic objects.) Such an ability helps to avoid having a guardian become a bottleneck. Of course, if the guardian is running on a single-processor node, then only one process will be running at a time. However, a common case is that in executing a handler call another handler call to some other guardian is made. It would be unacceptable if the guardian could do no other work while this call was outstanding.

The scheduling of incoming handler calls is performed by the system. Therefore, the programmer need not be concerned with explicit scheduling, but instead merely provides the handler definitions to be executed in response to the incoming calls. An alternative structure for a guardian would be a single process that multiplexes itself and explicitly schedules execution of incoming calls. We think our structure is more elegant, and no less efficient since our processes are cheap: creating a new process is only slightly more expensive than calling a procedure (see [Liskov 83a] for a discussion of this point).

As was mentioned above, the system does not guarantee message delivery; it merely guarantees that if message delivery fails there is a very low probability of the call succeeding if it is repeated immediately. Hence, there is no reason for user code to retry handler calls. If a handler call does not succeed, a user program can try an alternative method, e.g., making a call to another guardian. Ultimately, as mentioned earlier, user programs make progress by retrying top-level actions. User code must be prepared to retry top-level actions in any case, since they may fail because of node crashes even if all handler calls succeed.

7.2.2. Inline Actions

Top-level actions are created by means of the statement:

enter topaction *body* **end**

This causes the *body* to execute as a new top-level action. It is also possible to have an inline subaction:

enter action *body* **end**

This causes the *body* to run as a subaction of the action that executes the **enter**.

When the body of an inline action completes, it must indicate whether it is committing or aborting. Since committing is assumed to be most common, it is the default; the qualifier **abort** can be prefixed to any termination statement to override this default. For example, an inline action can execute

leave

to commit and cause execution to continue with the statement following the **enter** statement; to abort and have the same effect on control, it executes

abort leave

Falling off the end of the *body* causes the action to commit.

7.2.3. Concurrency

The language as defined so far allows concurrency only between top actions originating in different guardians. The following statement form provides more concurrency:

coenter **{** *coarm* **}** **end**

where

> *coarm* ::= *armtag* **[** **foreach** *decl-list* **in** *iter-invocation* **]**
>   *body*

armtag ::= **action** | **topaction**

The process executing the **coenter**, and the action on whose behalf it is executing, are suspended; they resume execution after the **coenter** is finished.

A **foreach** clause indicates that multiple instances of the coarm will be activated, one for each item (a collection of objects) yielded by the given iterator invocation.[4] Each such coarm will have local instances of the variables declared in the *decl-list*, and the objects constituting the yielded item will be assigned to them. Execution of the **coenter** starts by running each of the iterators to completion, sequentially, in textual order. Then all coarms are started simultaneously as concurrent siblings. Each coarm instance runs in a separate process, and each process executes within a new top-level action or subaction, as specified by the *armtag*.

A simple example making use of **foreach** is in performing a write operation concurrently at all copies of a replicated database:

```
coenter
    action foreach db: db_copy in all_copies(...)
        db.write(...)
    end
```

This statement creates separate processes for the guardian objects yielded by *all_copies*, each process having a local variable *db* bound to a particular guardian. Each process runs in a newly created subaction and makes a handler call.

A coarm may terminate without terminating the entire **coenter** either by falling off the end of its *body* (as in the above example) or by executing a **leave** statement. As before, **leave** may be prefixed by **abort** to cause the completing action to abort; otherwise, the action commits.

A coarm also may terminate by transferring control outside the **coenter** statement. Before such a transfer can occur, all coarms of the **coenter** must be terminated. To accomplish this, the system forces all other coarms that are not yet completed to abort.

---

[4] An iterator is a limited kind of coroutine that provides results to its caller one at a time [Liskov 77, Liskov 81b].

A simple example where such early termination is useful is in performing a read operation concurrently at all copies of a replicated database, where a response from any single copy will suffice:

```
coenter
    action foreach db: db_copy in all_copies(...)
        result := db.read(...)
        exit done
    end except when done: ... end
```

Once a read has completed successfully, the **exit** will commit it and abort all remaining reads. The aborts take place immediately; in particular, it is not necessary for the handler calls to finish before the subactions can be aborted. (Such aborts can result in *orphan* handler processes that continue to run at the called guardians and elsewhere. We have developed algorithms for dealing with orphans; orphans are discussed further in Section 7.5.5.

There is another form of **coenter** for use outside of actions, as in the **background** section of a guardian. In this form the *armtag* can be **process** or **topaction**. The semantics is as above, except that no action is created in the **process** case.

7.3. Example

In this section we present a simple mail system, designed somewhat along the lines of Grapevine [Birrell 82]. This is a pedagogical example: we have chosen inefficient or inadequate implementations for some features, and have omitted many necessary and desirable features of a real mail system. However, we hope it gives some idea of how a real system could be implemented in Argus.

The interface to the mail system is quite simple. Every user has a unique name (*user_id*) and a mailbox. However, mailbox locations are hidden from the user. Mail can be sent to a user by presenting the mail system with the user's user_id and a *message*; the message will be appended to the user's mailbox. Mail can be read by presenting the mail system with a user's user_id; all messages are removed from the user's mailbox and are returned to the caller. For simplicity, there is no protection on this operation: any user may read another user's mail. Finally, there is an operation for adding new users to the system, and operations for dynamically extending the mail system.

All operations are performed within the action system. For example, a message is not really added to a mailbox unless the sending action commits, messages are not really deleted unless the reading action commits, and a user is not really added unless the requesting action commits.

The mail system is implemented out of three kinds of guardians: mailers, maildrops, and registries. *Mailers* act as the front end of the mail system: all use of the system occurs through calls of mailer handlers. To achieve high availability, many mailers are used, e.g., one at each physical node. A *maildrop* contains the mailboxes for some subset of users. Individual mailboxes are not replicated, but multiple, distributed maildrops are used to reduce contention and to increase availability, in that the crash of one physical node will not make all mailboxes unavailable. The mapping from user_id to maildrop is provided by the *registries*. Replicated registries are used to increase availability; at most one registry need be accessible to send or read mail. Each registry contains the complete mapping for all users. In addition, registries keep track of all other registries.

Two built-in atomic types are used in implementing the mail system: *atomic_array* and *struct*. Atomic arrays are one-dimensional, and can grow and shrink dynamically. Of the array operations used in the mail system, *new* creates an empty array, *addh* adds an element to the high end, *trim* removes elements, *elements* iterates over the elements from low to high, and *copy* makes a complete copy of an array. A read lock on the entire array is obtained by *new*, *elements*, and *copy*, and a write lock is obtained by *addh* and *trim*. Structs are immutable (hence atomic) records: new components cannot be stored in a struct object once it has been created. However, the fact that a struct is immutable does not prevent its component objects from being modified if they are mutable.

The mailer guardian is presented in Fig. 7-5. The mailer keeps track of two registries; *some*, which is the mailer's stable reference to the entire mail system, and a volatile reference, *best*, representing the "best" access path into the system. The *background* code periodically polls all registries; the first to respond is used as the new *best* registry.

The *create* operation receives a registry as an argument, and uses this registry to

```
mailer = guardian is create
                handles send_mail, read_mail, add_user,
                        add_maildrop, add_registry, add_mailer


    reg_list = atomic_array[registry]
    msg_list = atomic_array[message]


    stable some: registry      % stable reference to some registry
    best: registry             % volatile reference to some registry


    recover
        best := some           % initialize after a crash
        end


    background
        while true do
            enter topaction   % find a new best registry
                regs: reg_list := best.all_registries( )   % get a list of all registries
                coenter
                    action foreach reg: registry in reg_list$elements(regs)
                        reg.ping( )    % see if it responds
                        best := reg    % make it best
                        exit done      % abort all others
                    end except when done: end
                end except when failure, unavailable (*): end
            sleep(...)    % some amount of time
            end           % while
        end               % background


create = creator (reg: registry) returns (mailer)
    some := reg        % initialize stable and volatile state
    best := reg
    return (self)      % return new mailer guardian to caller
    end create


send_mail = handler (user: user_id, msg: message)
        signals (no_such_user, unavailable)
    drop: maildrop := best.lookup(user)      % find user's maildrop
        resignal no_such_user, unavailable
    drop.send_mail(user, msg) resignal unavailable      % and deposit mail there
    end send_mail
```

```
read_mail = handler (user: user_id) returns (msg_list)
          signals (no_such_user, unavailable)
      drop: maildrop := best.lookup(user)      % find user's maildrop
          resignal no_such_user, unavailable
      return (drop.read_mail(user)) resignal unavailable      % retrieve user's mail
      end read_mail


add_user = handler (user: user_id, home: node)
          signals (user_exists, unavailable)
      begin
          drop: maildrop := best.select(home)      % get a maildrop for user
          regs: reg_list := best.all_registries( )
          coenter
              action
                  drop.add_user(user)      % add user to maildrop
              action foreach reg: registry in reg_list$elements(regs)
                  reg.add_user(user, drop)      % register <user, drop> at all registries
              end      % coenter
          end resignal user_exists, unavailable
      end add_user


add_maildrop = handler (home: node) signals (unavailable)
      begin
          drop: maildrop := maildrop$create( ) @ home
          regs: reg_list := best.all_registries( )
          coenter
              action foreach reg: registry in reg_list$elements(regs)
                  reg.add_maildrop(drop)   % register new maildrop at all registries
              end      % coenter
          end resignal unavailable
      end add_maildrop


add_registry = handler (home: node) signals (unavailable)
      best.new_registry (home) resignal unavailable
      end add_registry


add_mailer = handler (home: node) returns (mailer) signals (unavailable)
      m: mailer := mailer$create(best) @ home resignal unavailable
      return (m)
      end add_mailer


end mailer
```

Figure 7-5: Mailer Guardian

initialize both *some* and *best*. It then returns its own guardian, which it refers to by the reserved word **self**. Create does not bother to select a "best" registry since the background code will do so shortly.

A mailer performs a request to send or read mail by using the best registry to look up the maildrop for the specified user, and then forwarding the request to that maildrop. A mailer adds a new user by first calling the registry *select* handler to make sure the user is not already present and to choose a maildrop; then concurrently the new user/maildrop pair is added to each registry and the new user is added to the chosen maildrop. A maildrop is added by creating the maildrop and then concurrently adding it to all registries. A new mailer is created with the current best registry for its stable reference.

As was mentioned earlier, any handler or creator call can terminate with the unavailable exception. This exception can be raised either by the system, as was discussed in Section 7.2.1, or explicitly by the called handler or creator. All of the mailer's handlers signal unavailable explicitly; in this way they reflect the unavailability of registries and maildrops back to the caller. We require that unavailable be listed in the header of any handler or creator that signals it explicitly. Unavailable need not appear in the header of a handler or creator that does not signal it explicitly. This is why unavailable is listed in the headers of the mailer's handlers and also the registry handler, new_registry, but nowhere else.

Figure 7-6 shows the registry guardian. The state of a registry consists of an atomic array of registries together with a *steering list* associating an array of users with each maildrop. When a registry is created, it is given the current steering list, and an array of all other registries, to which it adds itself. The *lookup* handler uses linear search to find the given user's maildrop. The *select* handler uses linear search to check if a user already exists, and then chooses some existing maildrop. The *add_user* handler uses linear search to find the specified maildrop, and then appends the user to the associated user list. The *add_user* and *add_maildrop* handlers perform no error-checking because correctness is guaranteed by the mailer guardian.

The maildrop guardian is given in Fig. 7-7. The state of a maildrop consists of an atomic array of mailboxes; a mailbox is represented by a struct containing a user_id and an atomic array of messages. A maildrop is created with no mailboxes. The *add_user*

```
registry = guardian is create
                    handles lookup, select, all_registries, ping,
                              add_user, add_maildrop, new_registry, add_registry

    reg_list = atomic_array[registry]
    steer_list = atomic_array[steering]
    steering = struct[users: user_list,         % users with mailboxes
                        drop: maildrop]          % at this maildrop
    user_list = atomic_array[user_id]

    stable regs: reg_list          % all registries
    stable steers: steer_list      % all users and maildrops

create = creator (rlist: reg_list, slist: steer_list) returns (registry)
    reg_list$addh(rlist, self)     % add this registry to list
    regs := rlist                  % initialize stable state
    steers := slist
    return (self)                  % return new registry
    end create

lookup = handler (user: user_id) returns (maildrop) signals (no_such_user)
    for steer: steering in steer_list$elements(steers) do
        for usr: user_id in user_list$elements(steer.users) do
            if usr = user then return (steer.drop) end
            end
        end
    signal no_such_user
    end lookup

select = handler (home: node) returns (maildrop) signals (user_exists)
    for steer: steering in steer_list$elements(steers) do
        for usr: user_id in user_list$elements(steer.users) do
            if usr = user then signal user_exists end
            end
        end
    return(...) % choose, e.g., maildrop with few users that is close to this user
    end select

all_registries = handler ( ) returns (reg_list)
    return (regs)
    end all_registries
```

```
ping = handler ( )
    end ping        % just return immediately

add_user = handler (user: user_id, drop: maildrop)
    for steer: steering in steer_list$elements(steers) do
        if steer.drop = drop
            then user_list$addh(steer.users, user)        % append user
                return
            end
        end
    end add_user

add_maildrop = handler (drop: maildrop)
    steer: steering := steering${users: user_list$new( ),
                                  drop:  drop}
    steer_list$addh(steers, steer)
    end add_maildrop

new_registry = handler (home: node) signals (unavailable)
    begin
        new: registry := registry$create(regs, steers) @ home
        coenter
            action foreach reg: registry in reg_list$elements(regs)
                reg.add_registry(new)
            end
        end resignal unavailable
    end new_registry

add_registry = handler (reg: registry)
    reg_list$addh(regs, reg)
    end add_registry

end registry
```

Figure 7-6: Registry Guardian.

```
maildrop = guardian is create
                    handles send_mail, read_mail, add_user

    box_list = atomic_array[mailbox]
    mailbox = struct[mail: msg_list,          % messages for
                     user: user_id]           % this user
    msg_list = atomic_array[message]

    stable boxes: box_list := box_list$new( )

create = creator ( ) returns (maildrop)
    return (self)
    end create

send_mail = handler (user: user_id, msg: message)
    for box: mailbox in box_list$elements(boxes) do
        if box.user = user              % find user's message list
            then msg_list$addh(box.mail, msg)       % append message
                return
            end
        end
    end send_mail

read_mail = handler (user: user_id) returns (msg_list)
    for box: mailbox in box_list$elements(boxes) do
        if box.user = user              % find user's message list
            then mail: msg_list := msg_list$copy(box.mail)
                msg_list$trim(box.mail, 1, 0)       % delete messages
                return (mail)       % return all messages
            end
        end
    end read_mail

add_user = handler (user: user_id)
    box: mailbox := mailbox${mail: msg_list$new( ),
                 user: user}
    box_list$addh(boxes, box)         % append user's info
    end add_user

end maildrop
```

Figure 7-7: Maildrop Guardian

handler is used to add a mailbox. Note that this handler does not check to see if the user already exists since the mailer performs this check. The *send_mail* and *read_mail* handlers use linear search to find the correct mailbox. When the mailbox is found, *send_mail* appends a message to the end of the message array; *read_mail* first copies the array, then deletes all messages, and finally returns the copy. Both handlers assume the user exists; again, the mailer guarantees this.

Now that we have all the pieces of the mail system, we can show how the initial configuration of the mail system is created:

> reg: registry := registry$create(reg_list$new( ), steer_list$new( )) @ home1
> m: mailer := mailer$create(reg) @ home2

where *reg_list* and *steer_list* are defined as in the registry. The resulting mailer can then be used to add maildrops and users, as well as more registries and mailers.

Now we can show a use of the mail system, namely, sending a message to a group of users, with the constraint that the message be delivered either to all of the users or to none of them:

> **enter action**
>   **coenter**
>   **action foreach** user: user_id **in** user_group("net")
>   m.send_mail(user, msg)
>   **end except when** no_such_user, failure (*), unavailable (*):
>   **abort leave end**
>   **end**

The message is sent to all users simultaneously. A non-existent user or a failure to send a message transfers control outside the **coenter**, forcing termination of all active coarms; the outer action is then aborted, guaranteeing that none of the messages are actually delivered. (The notation failure (*) means that the argument of the exception is being ignored.)

7.3.1. Remarks

One obvious problem with the mailers as implemented is that if the best registry for a mailer goes down, the mailer effectively goes down as well, since every task the mailer performs (including choosing a new *best* registry) requires communication with that registry. A better implementation might be for each mailer to have stable and volatile references to multiple registries, and for mailer handlers to try several registries (sequentially) before giving up. For example, the following implementation of *send_mail* uses the *some* registry as a backup if the *best* registry is unavailable:

```
send_mail = handler (user: user_id, msg: message)
        signals (no_such_user, unavailable)
    drop : maildrop
    drop := best.lookup (user)
        except when unavailable(*): drop := some.lookup (user)
                end resignal unavailable, no_such_user
    drop.send_mail (user, msg) resignal unavailable
    end send_mail
```

If the handler call to the *best* registry signals unavailable, we try the *some* registry; only when that registry is also unavailable, or if the user's maildrop is unavailable, does *send_mail* signal unavailable.

One striking fact about the code of the mailer is how much of it is concerned with reflecting the unavailable exception up to the caller. It is inevitable that a guardian, like the mailer, that provides the user-interface to a system, will be concerned with coping with the unavailable exceptions arising from the calls of lower-level guardians that implement its system. In general, we may expect more interesting behavior than simply reflecting this signal as is done in the mailer; the user-interface guardian to a highly available system will attempt to mask rather than reflect this exception. A simple example of such masking was shown above.

Close examination of the mail system will reveal places where the particular choice of data representation leads to less concurrency than might be expected. For example, in the maildrop guardian, since both *send_mail* and *read_mail* modify the message array in a mailbox, either operation will lock out all other operations on the same mailbox until the executing action commits to the top level. Even worse, since *add_user* modifies the user list array, it will lock out all operations on all mailboxes at that maildrop. It will not be possible to send or read mail from that maildrop, or even to *lookup* users with mailboxes at the given maildrop. In addition, an *add_maildrop* operation will lock out all *lookup* operations.

In a traditional mail system this lack of concurrency might be tolerable, since the probability of conflict is small. But there are other, similar systems where it would not be acceptable. What is needed are data types that allow more concurrency than atomic arrays. For example, an associative memory that allowed concurrent insertions and lookups could replace the mailbox array in maildrops and the steering list in registries; a queue with a "first-commit first-out" semantics, rather than a "first-in first-out" semantics, could replace the message arrays in maildrops. Such types can be built as user-defined atomic types, which are discussed in Section 7.6.

The concurrency that *is* built in to the mail system can lead to a number of deadlock situations. When several calls are made in parallel in a **coenter**, the order in which these calls occur is not determined. So, for example, if two *add_registry* (or *add_maildrop*) requests are running concurrently, one might modify registry R first and registry S later while the other modifies registry S first and registry R later. Neither request will be able to proceed in such a case since each needs to obtain locks held by the other. Some of these deadlocks can be eliminated simply by reducing concurrency. To avoid deadlocks between *add_registry* requests, all *new_registry* calls could be made to a distinguished registry, and *new_registry* could obtain a write lock on the registry list before creating the new registry. Other deadlocks would disappear if data representations allowing more concurrency were used. For example, the use of a highly concurrent associative memory for the steering list would allow all *add_maildrop* requests to run concurrently.

It may be argued that the strict serialization of actions enforced by the particular implementation we have shown is not important in a real mail system. This does not mean that actions are inappropriate in a mail system, just that the particular granularity of actions we have chosen may not be the best. For example, if an action discovers that a user does (or does not) exist, it may not be important that the user continues to exist (or not to exist) for the remainder of the overall action. It is possible to build such "loopholes" through appropriately defined abstract types. As another example, it might not be important for all registries to have the most up-to-date information, provided they receive all updates eventually. In particular, when adding a user, it may suffice to guarantee that all registries eventually will be informed of that user. This could be accomplished by keeping appropriate information in the stable state of one of the registries, and using a background process in that registry to (eventually) inform all other registries.

7.4. Subsystems

In this section we discuss Argus programs or *subsystems*: what they are, how they are created, how they are made available to users, and how they are configured and reconfigured.

7.4.1. Program Development

Argus, like CLU, provides separate compilation of modules with complete type checking at compile time (see [Liskov 81b]). Separate compilation is performed in the context of a program library, consisting of *description units* (DUs). Each DU contains information about a single abstraction. There are four kinds of abstractions: data, procedural and iteration abstractions (see [Liskov 77]) and guardian abstractions. Each Argus module implements a single abstraction, and there is a different kind of module for each kind of abstraction. For example a guardian definition implements a guardian abstraction, while a *cluster* implements a data abstraction (see [Liskov 77]).

A DU contains all information about an abstraction. One piece of information is the *interface description*; this is defined when the DU is created and is never allowed to change. The interface description describes the interface that must be supported by any implementation of the abstraction. For example, for each guardian abstraction the library maintains information about the names of all its creators and handlers, and the types of all arguments and results for each creator and handler.

In addition, a DU contains zero or more implementations. When a module implementing the DU's abstraction is compiled, the compiler checks that it supports the interface. In addition, the compiler checks that all abstractions used by the module being compiled are used in accordance with their interfaces. If any interface errors are discovered, compilation fails; otherwise, the resulting object code is stored in the DU together with information identifying all the abstractions used by the compiled code.

The result of compilation is object code that is bound to abstractions, not to implementations of abstractions. To actually run the code it is necessary to select an implementation for each used abstraction. This linking is done on a per-guardian basis; the result is called a *code image*. To build a code image of a guardian definition, it is necessary to select implementations for the data, procedural, and iteration abstractions that are used, but not for other guardian abstractions.

Notice that each guardian is linked and loaded separately. In fact, each guardian is independent of the implementation of all other guardians, including those belonging to its own guardian abstraction, because the code images are distinct and because our method of communicating data values between guardians is implementation-independent (see [Herlihy 82]). In addition, new abstractions can be added to the library, and new implementations can be added for both old and new abstractions, without affecting any running guardian.

Before creating a guardian at a node, it is first necessary to load a code image of that guardian at that node. Then any number of guardians of that type can be created at that node. It is also possible to replace the code image of some guardian type at some node with a different code image. Such a replacement does not affect any existing guardians at that node, but guardians created later will run the new code image.

Guardians are constrained to communicate with other guardians only via handlers whose types were known when the guardian was compiled. Communication via handlers of unknown type is not sensible; the situation is exactly analogous to calling a procedure of unknown type. Of course, a guardian or handler argument of known type can be very useful. We *do* provide this: guardians and handlers can be used as arguments in local procedure calls and in handler calls. For example, a registry guardian was an argument to the mailer creator.

Compile-time type-checking does *not* rule out dynamic reconfiguration. By receiving guardians and handlers dynamically in handler calls, a guardian can communicate with new guardians as they are created or become available. In addition, the Argus system contains a distributed *catalog* that registers guardians and handlers according to their type. For example, all mailers in the mail system would be registered in the catalog. Then some other guardian could call a catalog operation to obtain a mailer to use in sending or receiving mail.

7.4.2. Subsystems and their Specifications

A *susbsystem* is an active entity that exists to provide a service to clients. To the clients, a subsystem looks like a guardian: it is an object that can be observed and manipulated by making handler calls. Typically a subsystem will be implemented by many different guardians, belonging to several different guardian types, and residing at different nodes in the network. The mail system described in the preceding section is such a subsystem. A subsystem may also be implemented by a single guardian, or by several guardians of the same type at different nodes.

A subsystem is an abstract object whose behavior should be described by means of a specification. In this specification, the internal structure of the subsystem's implementation is hidden. Instead, the subsystem is described by defining the behavior of each of its handlers; such a description is similar to the specification of a data abstraction (see [Guttag 78]). Methods of formally specifying subsystems are under study (e.g. [Stark 84]). In this section, we provide an intuitive discussion of the information in specifications and the issues that must be addressed.

Unlike traditional data abstractions, there is substantial concurrency in subsystems, both at the level of use, and at the level of implementation. However, this concurrency can be ignored in the specification. The reason is that all interactions with a subsystem in Argus occur by means of handler calls, and handler calls run as actions. Therefore, their effect is the same as if they were run sequentially in the serialization order. For example, the actual order of calls of *send_mail* and *read_mail* is not significant; the mail returned by *read_mail* is determined by the order in which the actions that made the calls are serialized. The specification need only define this sequential behavior. Similarly, we can ignore failures in the specification. Since handler calls made on behalf of actions that abort later have no effect, we can simply ignore them in the specification, and only define the effects of committed actions.

A subsystem is an abstract object that has a particular state. It is important to realize that even though the state of a subsystem is distributed in the subsystem's implementation, it is *logically centralized*: from the point of view of the user, it is simply an object that can be observed and manipulated via handler calls. For example, the abstract state of the mail system is a mapping from user-ids to sets of messages; messages and users can be added and removed from this mapping by making handler calls. The fact that mail is actually stored in mailboxes that are distributed in various locations in the network is not of interest to a user who merely wants to send and receive mail. (Distribution is of interest to someone who is controlling system configuration; configuration is discussed below.)

An important part of specifying a subsystem is describing its abstract state and how it is modified and observed by handler calls. For example, we require in the mail system that the mail delivered by *read_mail* is precisely the mail sent by committed *send_mail* handlers minus mail already delivered by committed *read_mail* handlers. This is a very strong requirement; weaker requirements are also possible. For example, we could require merely that *read_mail* return some portion of the existing messages. Note that such a specification is non-deterministic: it does not state exactly what portion of the existing messages need be returned. If we made this weaker requirement, we would also want to require that mail delivery be "timely", i.e., if a call of *read_mail* is made in the near future, then the messages not returned by the previous call will now be delivered. It is not at all clear how to specify timeliness; notice that the situation is complicated by the fact that any individual call on *read_mail* may not complete because a registry or maildrop guardian has crashed or is isolated by a network partition.

Notice how we are taking actions for granted. We view the state of a subsystem as being modified when actions commit; actions that abort have no effect on the state, and the effects of running actions are invisible until they commit. Actions greatly simplify the specification, since we can discuss the effects of the handlers as if they were executed sequentially. In the absence of actions, we would have to discuss interleavings of calls.

Although concurrency can be ignored in writing a specification, it is very important to define a subsystem in such a way that implementations with lots of concurrency are permitted. The desire to permit highly concurrent implementations is an important factor in deciding how a subsystem should behave. Depending on this behavior, more or less concurrency will be possible. One way to permit more concurrency is by having the subsystem behave non-deterministically. For example, a non-deterministic mailer in which the *read_mail* handler returns some subset of the user's mail permits an implementation in which *read_mail* and *send_mail* can run concurrently even for the same user.

To sum up the above discussion, a subsystem is simply an abstract object that can be observed and manipulated by handler calls. These calls can be specified sequentially; the order in which they are thought of as occurring is the serialization order of the calling actions. Finally, considerable concurrency and improved performance can be made possible by making the specifications of some of the operations non-deterministic.

In addition to specifying the behavior of a subsystem, it is also necessary to specify its performance. Some performance issues have been mentioned above, e.g., timeliness. Similar issues are deadlock and starvation: the user of a subsystem needs to know whether deadlock and starvation are possible, and if so, under what conditions. In addition, we are interested in the reliability and availability of the subsystem. It is not understood at present how to specify such properties; this is an area in which research is needed.

7.4.3. Configuration and Reconfiguration

In the preceding section we argued that the internal structure of a subsystem was not of interest to its users and should not be described in its specification. This statement is true for the subsystem's *clients*, who are interested only in the service that the subsystem provides. However, a subsystem in Argus will usually have more handlers than those of interest to clients. These additional handlers are intended to be used in controlling how the subsystem is configured.

For example, clients of the mail system are primarily interested in the *read_mail* and *send_mail* handlers. They may, in addition, be interested in the *add_user* handler, although we may expect use of this handler to be limited to a system administrator who decides what users can use the mail system. However, clients are not interested in the other mailer handlers, *add_registry*, *add_maildrop*, and *add_mailer*, nor are they interested in the mailer creator. These handlers and creators are used to control configuration.

Handlers and creators that provide configuration control tend to expose information about the implementation of the subsystem. This is certainly true of *add_registry* and *add_maildrop*, which identify lower-level guardian abstractions used in implementing the mail system. Such operations should be specified separately from the handlers used by clients. Furthermore, their use should be protected, so that only someone authorized to do configuration can use them.

The mailer shown in Fig. 7-5 does not provide sufficient handlers to support all the kinds of reconfiguration that may be wanted. For example, we may want to remove a maildrop or registry. Additional handlers are needed for this purpose, for example, *remove_registry, remove_maildrop* in mailer, *terminate* and *remove_maildrop* in registry, and *terminate* in maildrop. To show how these might work, we present in Fig. 7-8 an implementation of the three operations involved in destroying a maildrop.

```
remove_maildrop = handler (n: node) signals (unavailable, last_one)
    best.remove_maildrop(n) resignal unavailable, last_one
    end remove_maildrop
```

a. New handler in mailer.

```
remove_maildrop = handler (n: node) signals (unavailable, last_one)
    if steer_list$size(steers) <= 1        % don't destroy last maildrop
        then signal last_one
        end
    d: drop := ...        % find maildrop at node n
    b: boxlist := d.terminate( ) resignal unavailable
    % distribute mailboxes in b among remaining mail drops
    % and remove d from steers of all registries
    end remove_maildrop
```

b. New handler in registry.

```
terminate = handler ( ) returns (box_list)
    destroy return (boxes)        % return all mailboxes
    end terminate
```

c. New handler in maildrop.

Figure 7-8: Handlers for Removing Registries and Maildrops.

Notice that the *terminate* handler of maildrop makes use of a feature of Argus that has not yet been illustrated, namely, the **destroy** primitive. The **return** statement of this handler is prefixed with the keyword **destroy**. Execution of this statement will commit the handler action and then crash the guardian. (This crash will cause any active actions that had run handlers at the guardian to abort.) Later, if the top action that caused the call of the *terminate* handler to be made commits, the guardian will really be destroyed. On the other hand, if the top action aborts, the guardian will simply recover from the crash.

Destruction of a maildrop proceeds as follows. The argument of the call to the mailer handler *remove_maildrop* is the node at which the maildrop guardian to be destroyed resides (we assume only one mail drop per node), and the mailer handler simply passes this information on to the registry handler, which does the real work. The registry handler refuses to destroy the last maildrop, and it conveys its refusal to its caller via an exception. Otherwise the registry finds the appropriate maildrop to destroy, and asks it to destroy itself by calling its terminate handler. The maildrop destroys itself, but it returns its mailboxes and their contents to its caller. The registry then distributes this information among the other maildrops, and deletes references to the destroyed maildrop at all registries.

Notice how important it is that the above activity occur as an atomic action. Either the maildrop will be destroyed, and its information distributed among the other maildrops, or, if the action aborts, the maildrop will simply recover from the crash, and the distributed information will disappear from the other maildrops.

Another reconfiguration possibility is that we may want to add a new maildrop and off-load some of the messages from existing maildrops that are overloaded, or we may wish to balance the load among existing maildrops. Additional operations are required here; the work that needs to be done is similar to what is done in *remove_maildrop*. Notice that if a person is to make decisions about load balancing, additional operations are needed to allow the user to determine what the current loads are.

In the above discussion, configuration of subsystems is done by privileged users. The subsystem provides for configuration control by providing handlers for these users to call, but it does not do any configuration management itself. Such a method seems a bit primitive. Can we hope to do better? For example, perhaps the mail system could decide itself when new maildrops were needed or maildrops could be destroyed. However, it is not clear how it would decide where to place the new maildrops, or what maildrop to destroy. Perhaps it would be possible for it to make use of a "topology" subsystem that presents it with a model of the network; it could use this model to decide about placement. What such a model should be, and how to make decisions based on it, is not at all clear. Research is needed in this area. (Of course, the topology subsystem itself would have handlers that would be used to inform it of changes in topology, so it appears that we have merely succeeded in pushing the problem down one level. However, perhaps the topology subsystem would be the only subsystem requiring a configuration interface.)

Another reconfiguration problem is to add registries (or maildrops) because the network has grown and they are needed for availability. Perhaps the mail subsystem could sample the current topology periodically, and add additional components based on the new information. Removal of registries and maildrops because of deletion of nodes could be accomodated by some additional built-in mechanism that informed a guardian of its impending demise.

Not all kinds of reconfiguration can be done by means of handler calls or predefined mechanisms. For example, it may be that the mail system has become so large that it is no longer practical to store all registration information at each registry. Instead, we need to partition the registration data among the registries in some way. Unlike the previous kinds of reconfiguration, this change constitutes a change in the way the subsystem as a whole is implemented. Such changes are discussed in the next section.

7.4.4. Dynamic Replacement

Argus supports the execution of long-lived subsystems. We must expect that changes in the implementation of such systems will be needed over time. However, clients entrust important information to subsystems, and this information must not be lost. Therefore, it is necessary to find ways to replace a subsystem's implementation without loss of information in the subsystem's state, and without loss of the clients' access to that information.

There are three reasons why implementation changes are needed. First, the new implementation may have better performance than the old; for example, it may run faster or be more available or require less space. Reconfiguration of the mail system to partition the registries falls into this category. Second, the new subsystem may be an *enhancement* of the old one: it provides all the old behavior, and in addition some new handlers. Third, reimplementation may be needed to correct bugs. This third kind of change should have the same goals as the first two, but it will probably not be possible to achieve those goals completely.

The following summarizes the work of Bloom on dynamic replacement [Bloom 83]. The basic replacement method is the following:

1. We start up a top action to carry out replacement. By doing replacement within an action, we can guarantee that either the replacement happens entirely, or it has no effect.

2. We destroy all the guardians that make up the subsystem. Recall that this causes them to crash, but they will not be really destroyed unless the replacement action commits. If the replacement action aborts, they will recover from the crash.

3. We create the new guardians that will make up the new subsystem, but we do not run creators in them; their stable and volatile variables are declared but not initialized.

4. The state of a subsystem is really its stable state. We collect the stable state of some or all of the crashed old guardians. For example, in replacing the mail system, we would collect together the stable states of all the maildrops but only one of the registries, since the other registries just contain copies of this information. We then transform this state appropriately, and install it as the stable state of the new guardians. Not only do we initialize the stable variables of the new guardians, but we record the state in stable storage.

5. We run the recovery process in each new guardian to initialize the volatile variables.

6. Handlers that are accessible to external users of the subsystem (e.g., the clients) are bound to handlers of the new guardians; after replacement a call to an old

handler will be sent to the new handler to which it is bound. Type checking is done here; an old handler can be bound to a new handler only if both agree about the types of arguments and results.

7. We commit the replacement action.

The effect of this method on the clients is that the service becomes unavailable while replacement is going on, possibly causing some actions to abort, but once replacement is done clients can continue to interact with the subsystem as in the past.

An important issue in doing replacement is to determine what constitutes a valid replacement. This question is interesting at both the abstraction and implementation levels. At the implementation level, the way to view replacement is the following. At the time replacement takes place, the subsystem is in a particular state, and this state represents (via the *abstraction function* [Hoare 72]) a particular abstract state. It is this abstract state that is visible to users. Replacement transforms the current system state into a system state of the new implementation. Replacement is correct if the new state represents the same abstract state as before, where now the abstraction function of the new implementation is being used. Furthermore, of course, the new implementation must be correct.[5] An abstraction can be extended only if its behavior with respect to any current clients is unchanged. All existing handlers must continue to exist and have the same argument and result types. Furthermore, the new handlers cannot have any effect on the behavior of the old handlers, as that behavior is defined by the specification. For example, suppose the specification of the mail subsystem permitted us to deduce that once a user has been added to the system, that user remains forever. Then it would not be possible to extend the mail subsystem with a *remove_user* handler. On the other hand, such a handler could be added if the mail subsystem were specified in a way that ruled out the deduction.

In the previous section, we discussed the fact that if configuration were performed via handler and creator calls, it is necessary to distinguish the interface provided by the

---

[5]It is not always possible to replace one implementation with another, even when both are correct implementations of the abstraction. This problem only arises when there is non-determinism in the specification. See Bloom's thesis for details [Bloom 83].

subsystem to its clients from that used for configuration control. Notice that it may be desirable to do a replacement that preserves or extends the client interface but changes the configuration interface. This implies that it may be important to recognize that there are *multiple views* of an abstraction, with each view having its own specification, and being independently changeable. How to fit multiple views into a type system remains a matter for research.

7.4.5. Structure of Subsystems

Above we stated that a subsystem interface was like a guardian interface in the sense that all users of the subsystem communicated with it by making handler calls. In fact, it is possible to have subsystems that appear to their users more like ordinary data objects than like guardians. Below we discuss the various forms of subsystems.

The mailer subsystem is an example of a subsystem that looks like a guardian to its users. We refer to such subsystems as *guardian-based* subsystems. Guardian-based subsystems are independent of any of their users in the sense that none of the code and data of the subsystem resides in the users' guardians. This situation is shown in Fig. 7-9a. Here the user guardians U1, U2 and U3 know only the names of some of the handlers provided by the subsystem; this knowledge is represented by the lines linking the user guardians to the subsystem.

An alternative kind of subsystem looks like a data object to its users. In this case, the users call the operations of the subsystem's type to interact with the subsystem. We refer to this kind of subsystem as a *cluster-based* subsystem, because the top level of such a subsystem would be implemented by a cluster [Liskov 77, Liskov 81b] in Argus. In contrast to the guardian-based subsystem, some of the code and data of a cluster-based subsystem resides at user guardians, as is shown in Fig. 7-9b.

For example, suppose the mail system were defined as a cluster-based subsystem. This could be accomplished by having a mailer cluster instead of a mailer guardian. This cluster implements mailer objects; each guardian that uses the mail subsystem must store one of these objects in its stable or volatile state. There is one operation of the mailer cluster for each handler of the mailer guardian. These operations have the same names as their associated handler, and behave similarly. In addition, the cluster provides one more operation, the *create* operation. This operation is analogous to the creator of the

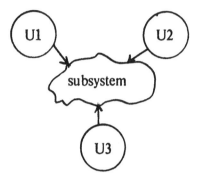

a. Guardian-based subsystem.

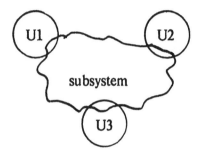

b. Cluster-based subsystem.

Figure 7-9: Subsystem Structures.

mailer guardian.

A portion of the mailer cluster is shown in Fig. 7-10. The representation of a mailer object is shown on the line

    rep = registry

This line means that each mailer object simply consists of the name of a registry guardian that can be called to carry out the user's requests. Implementations are shown for the *create* and *send_mail* operations. These implementations are similar to the associated mailer = **cluster is** create, send_mail, ...

    rep = registry   *% all requests are sent to this registry*

    create = **proc** (r: registry) **returns (cvt)**
       return (r)
       end create

    send_mail = **proc** (m: **cvt**, user: user_id, msg: message)
            signals (no_such_user, unavailable)
       drop: maildrop := m.lookup (user) **resignal** no_such_user, unavailable
       drop.send_mail (user, msg) **resignal** unavailable
       end send_mail

    ...

end mailer

Figure 7-10: The Mailer for a Cluster-Based Subsystem.

creator and handler in the mailer guardian.[6] The **rep** of this cluster stores information similar to what was kept in the mailer guardian's volatile state. Since there is no background code in a cluster, it is not possible to update this information periodically independent of operation calls. However, we can imagine the following analogous situation; on every *nth* call, the called operation selects a new best registry. In this case the **rep** would be a record containing as components both a *best* and a *some* registry.

Treating the mail system as a cluster-based subsystem is attractive because it may be more efficient. To make the mail subsystem as available as the registries and maildrops needed to carry out a user's request, it is necessary to place a mailer guardian at every node. All these extra guardians may be expensive, and the cluster-based subsystem avoids them.

However, a cluster-based subsystem has a serious defect with respect to

---

The use of the reserved word cvt in the header of the create operation means that the representation of the mailer object is being sealed so that it can only be used by calling the clusters operations. Cvt in the header of the *send_mail* operation means that *send_mail* can unseal the mailer object to use the registry that represents it. See [Liskov 77, Liskov 81b] for more information.

reconfiguration and replacement. The difficulty is that some kinds of changes require finding all the user's guardians and modifying the part of the subsystem that resides there. For example, to remove a registry, we must make sure to update *some* and *best* at each mailer guardian. In the cluster-based subsystem, this information resides at the user's guardians in the **reps** of the mailer objects. Because of the difficulty of reconfiguration and replacement, we believe it is better to limit subsystems to be guardian-based.

There are several forms that guardian-based subsystems can take. One is the form illustrated by the mailer. In this form, all communication with the subsystem goes to guardians of a single type, e.g., the mailer type. However, other forms can be imagined. For example, perhaps each user of the mail subsystem is given his maildrop guardian, and can communicate with it directly from then on. Direct communication with this maildrop guardian might be regarded simply as a fast path to the mail; if the maildrop guardian were destroyed, the user would call a handler of the mailer to be connected with his new maildrop. In such a case, the handlers of the subsystem correspond to handlers provided by various types of guardians that implement the subsystem. We are investigating the properties of such alternative structures; they appear satisfactory as far as reconfiguration and replacement are concerned.

7.5. Implementation

The Argus implementation includes an operating system kernel that supports execution and scheduling of guardians and their processes, and also some form of message communication. In addition, it contains a distributed transaction system, and a recovery system.

A distributed computation in Argus consists of a top action and all of its subactions. Each individual action runs at a single guardian; we will refer to this guardian as the *action's guardian*. An action can affect other guardians by means of handler calls. A distributed computation starts as a top action at some guardian and spreads to other guardians by means of handler calls, which are performed as subactions of the calling action. A handler call subaction may make further handler calls to other guardians; it may also make use of the objects at its own guardian and thus acquire locks on them and also (if it modifies the objects) cause new volatile versions to be created. Since these versions are in volatile storage, they will be lost if their containing guardian crashes before the top action commits. Therefore, when a top action commits, a distributed commitment procedure must be carried out to guarantee that the new versions of objects modified by descendants of that action are copied to stable storage.

In this section, we describe how the distributed transaction system is implemented. We begin by describing a model of actions that can be used both to discuss how actions execute, and what happens when actions complete. We use this model to describe the information that is collected at guardians as the action and its subactions run and how this information is used during distributed commitment. Finally, we discuss lock propagation and orphan detection.

7.5.1. Action Trees

A top action and its descendants can be modelled by means of a tree structure called an *action tree*. The root of the tree is labelled by the top action; the interior nodes are labelled by descendant subactions. Only subactions appear below the root of the tree; a nested top action will be represented by its own tree. Each node of the tree contains information about the state of its action (active, committed or aborted) and the guardian at which the action is running or ran. Fig. 7-11 shows a tree that might exist just before the top action, A, commits.

A subaction is said to have *committed to the top* if it committed, and so have all its ancestors up to, but not including, the top action. For example, A.2.1 committed to the top, but A.1.1 and A.1.2 did not. When a top action commits, it is necessary to communicate with the guardians of all actions that committed to the top. The guardians are called the *participants*. We need not communicate with guardians of actions that did not commit to the top (for example, guardian G4 in the figure), which is fortunate since such communication may be impossible. For example, the reason A.1 aborted may have been because a network partition made it impossible to receive the results from G4.

If a top action's tree were known at the top action's guardian when the top action is about to commit, the information in it could be used to control distributed commitment. The participants can be computed from the tree, and if, in addition, the tree were sent to all participants, then they could determine which of the subactions that ran locally

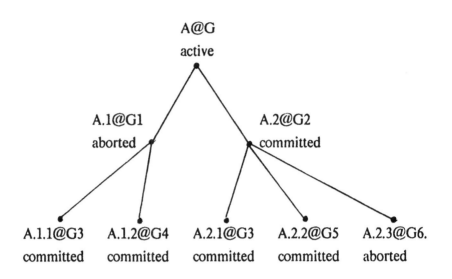

Figure 7-11: An Action Tree Just Before Committing of Top Action A.

should have volatile versions written to stable storage, and which should have their volatile versions discarded. For example, at G3 it would be known that A.2.1's volatile versions should be written to stable storage, but A.1.1's versions should be discarded. However, the tree may be large, so we have chosen a different approach. Rather than building the tree at the top action's guardian as the top action and its descendants run, we keep parts of the tree at the descendants' guardians. Some information must still be collected at the top action's guardian, but the amount of information is reduced.

Before discussing the stored information, it is necessary to say a few words about action identifiers (*aids*). The action identifier of a subaction, e.g., A.2.2, contains within it the guardian identifier (*gid*) of the guardian at which the subaction ran, e.g., G5, and also the aids of all the ancestors of the subaction, e.g., A.2 and A. Furthermore, given two aids, it is possible to tell whether one is an ancestor of the other. Thus some of the information in the action tree is stored in the aids.

Fig. 7-12 shows the information kept at the guardians where descendants ran for the action tree shown in Fig. 7-11. These guardians remember, in a local, volatile data structure called *committed*, those handler subactions that ran at the guardian and then committed. In addition, for each of these subactions, the guardian remembers all the atomic objects on which the subaction holds locks. This information is used to determine what needs to be written to stable storage during two-phase commit and to

@G1   No information

@G2   A.2 committed

@G3   A.1.1 committed
       A.2.1 committed

@G4   A.1.2 committed

@G5   A.2.2 committed

@G6   No information

Figure 7-12: Information Stored at Subactions' Guardians.

release locks. Handler subactions that ran at the guardian and then aborted are forgotten; these subactions hold no locks (the locks were released at the time of the abort) and no information need be written to stable storage for them.

At the top action's guardian, we remember (in volatile storage) the parts of the tree that are not stored at the subactions' guardians. First there is a data structure called the *plist* that lists the participants. Second, there is the *aborts_list*, which lists those subactions that aborted but that might have committed descendants at other guardians. For the action tree in Fig. 7-11, we have

plist = {G2, G3, G5}
aborts_list = { A.1 }

Notice that the *aborts_list* need not contain aborted subactions that have no remote descendants (e.g., A.2.3), because this information is (effectively) stored at the aborted subaction's guardian. Notice also that the *aborts_list* need not contain two subactions where one is an ancestor of the other; in such a case only the older of the two subactions need be remembered.

7.5.2. Constructing the Action Tree

While an action is running, the implementation maintains the following volatile information for it at its guardian:

plist
: The list of guardians visited by committed descendants of this action, where all ancestors of the descendant up to this action have committed (i.e., the descendant committed to this action).

aborts_list
: The list of aborted descendants of this action that may have committed descendants at other guardians

olist
: The list of local atomic objects used by this action and its local committed descendants

These lists are empty when an action starts. Whenever an action uses an atomic object, this information is added to its *olist*. The other data are modified as descendants of the action commit or abort. If a local subaction commits, its *olist, plist* and *aborts_list* are merged with those of its parent. Also its locks and versions are propagated to its parent. If the local subaction aborts, its locks and versions are discarded (using the information in the *olist*). Since the action is aborting, it is contributing no participants to its parent, and therefore its *plist* is discarded. Finally, the aborting subaction's aid is added to its parent's *aborts_list* if it may have committed descendants at other guardians. This will be true if either its *plist* or its *aborts_list* is non-empty, or if it is waiting on a handler call when it aborts.

When a handler call is made, a call message is constructed and sent to the handler's guardian. Later a reply message is sent from the handler's guardian to the caller's guardian. This reply message contains a *plist* and an *aborts_list*, which are merged with those of the caller. The *olist* is not sent back in the reply; information about used objects is kept locally at the guardian that contains the objects.

When the call message is received at the handler's guardian, a subaction is created for it, with its associated *plist, aborts_list* and *olist*, all empty. As the handler action runs, these data are modified as described above. Now let us consider what happens when the handler action completes. First, suppose it commits. In this case its aid and *olist* are stored in *committed* at its guardian. Its gid is added to its *plist* and then its *plist* and *aborts_list* are sent back to the calling guardian as part of the reply message. If the handler call aborts, its locks are released. The *plist* in the reply message is empty. If the aborting subaction made no remote calls that may have committed at other guardians (i.e., its *plist* and *aborts_list* are empty), the *aborts_list* in the reply message is empty; otherwise it contains the aid of the aborting handler action.

For example, when A.2 in Fig. 7-11 commits, its *plist* with its gid added is {G2, G3, G5} and its *aborts_list* is empty; this information is sent to G in the reply message. When A.1 aborts, its *plist* is non-empty, so the reply message contains *aborts_list* {A.1}. When this information is merged at G we end up with the *plist* and *aborts_list* discussed earlier.

In the above discussion, we assumed that when the reply message arrived at the calling guardian, the caller was waiting for the reply. However, this is not necessarily so. The calling guardian may have crashed before the reply arrived, the calling action may have aborted because of the termination of a coenter, or the call may have been timed out by the system because of a network partition. In all these cases the reply message is discarded. Furthermore, we can be certain that either the top action of the call has aborted (this would happen, for example, if the top action ran at the crashed guardian), or that some ancestor of the handler call will contain an appropriate aid, i.e., an ancestor of the call, in its *aborts_list*.

For example, consider the case of the system aborting the call. Recall that in executing a handler call, the system actually creates two subactions, one, the *call action*, at the calling guardian and another, the *handler action*, at the called guardian. The call action is a child of the action making the call, and the handler action is a child of the call action. Two actions are needed so that the call can be aborted independently at the calling guardian even if the handler action committed at the called guardian. This detail was suppressed in the action tree shown in Fig. 7-11. When the system aborts the call action at the calling guardian, it inserts the aid of this subaction in the *aborts_list* of its parent. Thus, the *aborts_list* of an ancestor of the handler action contains an appropriate aid.

7.5.3. Two-phase Commit

Distributed commitment in Argus is carried out by a two-phase commit protocol. In this protocol, the guardian of the commiting top action acts as the *coordinator*. The other guardians, namely those in the *plist*, act as the *participants*.

The Coordinator

The coordinator carries out the following protocol when it commits top action A:

Phase 1:

1. The coordinator sends a "prepare (A, plist, aborts_list)" message to all participants. The arguments of the message are the aid, plist and aborts_list of the committing action.

2. The coordinator acts as a local participant, writing information to stable storage as discussed below.

3. The coordinator waits for responses from the participants. If any participant refuses to prepare (by sending a "refuse (A)" message), or does not respond, then the coordinator aborts the transaction. It writes an "abort A" record to stable storage and sends "abort (A)" messages to the participants; at this point the commitment protocol is complete. If all participants indicate that they have prepared (by sending "prepared (A)" messages to the coordinator), then the coordinator writes a "committed A plist" record to stable storage. At this point the action is really committed, and the coordinator enters phase 2.

Phase 2:

1. The coordinator sends "commit (A)" messages to the participants.

2. The coordinator acts as a local participant as discussed below.

3. The coordinator waits for acknowlegement messages from all participants. If any participant does not respond, the coordinator sends it another commit

message. When all participants have acknowledged, the coordinator writes a "done A" record to stable storage. Now two-phase commit is complete.

The Participant

Each participant guardian carries out the following protocol when it receives a 'prepare (A, plist, aborts_list)" message from the coordinator:

Phase 1:

1. If there are no descendants of A in *committed*, a "refuse (A)" message is sent back to the coordinator. This situation can happen only if the participant has crashed since some descendant of A ran there.

2. Otherwise, every descendant, D, of A in committed is compared with the actions listed in the aborts_list. If D is not a descendant of some action in the aborts_list, then it is known to have committed to A. In this case, its *olist* is used to cause all new versions created for it to be written to stable storage. If D is a descendant of some action in the aborts_list, its effects are undone: its *olist* is used to cause its locks to be released and its versions discarded.

3. The participant writes a "prepare A plist olist" record to stable storage, and then sends a "prepared (A)" message to the coordinator. It now enters its phase 2.

Phase 2:

During phase 2, the participant is pledged to either commit or abort the action, depending on what the coordinator tells it. It waits for a message from the coordinator. If the message is an abort, it writes an "abort A" record to stable storage; if the message is a commit, it writes a "commit A" record to stable storage. In either case, it releases A's locks (using the olist). Finally, in the case of commit it sends an acknowledgement message to the coordinator.

If the participant does not hear from the coordinator, it can send a query message to the coordinator, asking about the result; the aid, A, can be used to determine which guardian is the coordinator. If the coordinator is in phase 2, it will respond "commit

(A)" to this query. If the coordinator is still in phase 1, it can discard the query message, since the appropriate response will be sent later. If the coordinator has forgotten about A, it will respond "abort (A)"; this situation can occur only if A has aborted.

Discussion

The protocol described above is resilient to node crashes and network partitions. If either a participant or the coordinator crashes before entering phase 2 (before writing the prepare or committed records to stable storage, respectively) commitment will fail. If the coordinator crashes in phase 2, then after recovery the information in the committed record in stable storage is sufficient to enable phase 2 to be carried out again. Similarly, if a participant crashes in phase 2, the information in the prepare record enables it to pick up phase 2 after recovery.

One problem with the protocol is that there is a "window of vulnerability" for each participant between the time it sends the prepared message to the coordinator and the time it receives the commit or abort message from the coordinator. If the coordinator crashes during this window, the participant may be unable to proceed until the coordinator recovers. The participant does know all the other participants, so it can send query messages to them, asking them about the outcome. If any participant knows the outcome (because the coordinator sent a commit or abort message to it before the crash), then this information can be forwarded to the querying participant. If any participant has not received the prepare message, or knows nothing about any descendants of the top action, then the action can be aborted. However, if all participants are prepared but none knows the outcome, it is not possible to either abort or commit, since any decision reached by the participants may disagree with the decision made by the coordinator. Thus, such measures reduce the window of vulnerability, but do not eliminate it. The window can be further reduced, but at substantial cost; it can never be eliminated entirely [Fischer 82].

Several optimizations of the above protocols are possible, of which the most significant is the following. In phase 1, the participant can release any read locks held by the committing action. If, after releasing these locks, the committing action holds no locks at the participant, the participant can inform the coordinator of this fact in its prepared message. Such a participant need not be included in phase 2. (However, if such a participant knows nothing about the action, that fact cannot be used to resolve the outcome as discussed in the preceding paragraph.)

Processing of actions in Argus has been designed to satisfy two constraints: limited information flow and limited delay, both while actions are running and during two-phase commit. Information flow has been limited by not sending the entire action tree in reply and prepare messages. Instead we send the *aborts_list* and the *plist*. We believe that the *aborts_list* will be small because network partitions happen infrequently and it is unlikely that an action aborts when it may have committed descendants elsewhere. However, the *plist* will be large for an action that visits many guardians. It is possible to maintain the *plist* incrementally: each guardian remembers only the guardians where it made handler calls. However, that strategy introduces more delay during two-phase commit, since the coordinator can send prepare messages only to those participants it knows, and they in turn must send prepare messages to further participants. For example, for the action tree in Fig. 7-11, the coordinator would communicate with G2, and it, in turn, would communicate with G3 and G5. We decided to send the entire list of participants to the coordinator to reduce delay: Prepare messages can be sent to all participants in parallel in phase 1, which would not be possible if the participants were not known at the coordinators' guardian. We also send the list of participants in the prepare messages to reduce the window of vulnerability, as discussed above.

A further way in which we reduce delay is by doing *early prepare* at the participants. We write the new versions of modified objects to stable storage as convenient, for example, whenever the participant is not busy. Then, when the prepare message arrives, the only thing left to do may be to write the prepare record to stable storage. If the handler subactions do not commit to the top, we will have written unnecessary information to stable storage, but this will happen rarely if aborts are rare, and the work was done during idle time anyway.

The protocol described above is not quite correct. If a guardian crashes after running some handler calls that are subactions of top action A, and then runs more handler calls that are subactions of A after it recovers, only the latter calls will be listed in *committed*. If a handler call that ran before the crash committed to the top, it versions should be written to stable storage. Since the versions were lost in the crash, the guardian should refuse to prepare. However, given the information discussed so far, there is no way that it could know this. For example, consider the action tree of Fig. 7-11, and suppose that A.2.1 committed at G3, then G3 crashed, and after G3 recovered A.1.1 ran and committed there. Since there is a descendant of A in *committed*, the algorithm discussed above will (erroneously) prepare. Such a situation is not a problem for us because of orphan detection, which is described in section 7.5.5.

7.5.4. Lock Propagation

Our lock propagation rule specifies that when a subaction commits, its locks and versions are propagated to its parent; when it aborts, its locks and versions are discarded. Propagation of an object's locks and versions is always performed at the object's guardian. In addition, we carry out this propagation immediately only for local actions. For example, when a handler action commits, we do not propagate its locks and versions to its parent, nor do we communicate with the guardians of its non-local descendants to cause the appropriate propagation of locks for their local objects. In this way we avoid the delays that such communication would cause; only when top actions commit is this communication necessary.

Since communication only happens when top actions commit, certain problems can arise. For example, consider the action tree in Fig. 7-11. How does guardian G4 discover that the locks held by A.1.2 should be released? A related problem may occur at G3. Suppose that A.1.1 and A.2.1 modify the same object, X. Suppose further that A.1 and A.2 are actually running concurrently, so that it is possible that either A.1.1 or A.2.1 may get to G3 first. If A.1.1 modified X first, then before A.2.1 can use X, we must discard A.1.1's lock and version of X. To do this, we must learn at G3 about the abort of A.1. Alternatively, if A.2.1 modified X first, then before A.1.1 can use it we must learn about the commit of A.2, and propagate the lock and version of X to A. Only then can A.1.1 use X.

We solve problems like these by means of *lock propagation queries*. As mentioned earlier, when a handler call commits, we continue to keep all its used objects locked on its behalf. If later some other action wants to use the locked object, the object's guardian will send a query to determine the fate of the handler action that holds the lock. Such a query will be sent to a guardian at which an ancestor of the handler action ran. Recall that the aid of a subaction can be used to determine the aids of the ancestors of the subaction and thus the guardians of the ancestors.

In the following, we discuss two actions, H and R. H is a committed handler action that holds a lock on some object. R is an active action that wants to acquire a lock on that object. H and R's guardian will send a query to some other guardian. That other guardian will respond with a *query response* telling what it knows, and H and R's quardian will then act on that information.

There are two situations to consider, depending on whether H is related to R or not. If H and R are not related, then H's lock can be broken only if H did not commit to the top or H's top action, T, aborted. A good place to send the query is to T's guardian, GT. There are the following possibilties at GT:

1. T is not known at GT, and the query response so indicates. There are two possibilities here: T aborted, or T committed but two-phase commit is finished. In the latter case, if H committed to the top, its guardian will have already discarded its locks and made its versions the current versions, and the query response will be ignored. If H still holds locks when the query response is received. its locks will be released and its versions discarded.

2. T is in the second phase of two phase commit. Again, there are two possibilities: either H's guardian is not a participant, or it is. If H's guardian is a participant, it will either be in phase 2 or finished with two phase commit for T when the query reponse arrives, and will ignore the response; otherwise, it will discard H's locks and versions.

3. If T is active or in phase 1, but H is a descendant of some action in T's *aborts_list*, then the query response can indicate that some ancestor of H aborted. In this case H's locks and versions can be discarded.

4. If T is in phase 1, but H is not a descendant of some action in the *aborts_list*, then we can discard the query, since H's guardian is about to receive appropriate information anyway as part of two-phase commit.

5. If T is active and H is not a descendant of some action in the *aborts_list*, then the query cannot be resolved yet. In this case, H's guardian cannot release H's locks;

it can query to GT again later, or it could query to guardians of other ancestors
of H to try to discover if some ancestor of H aborted. This additional querying is
useful only if an ancestor of H is active at some other guardian; such information
can be included in the query response.

For example, suppose that A.1.1 of Fig. 7-11 is the holder, and the requestor, R, is a
non-relative. The query would be sent to G. If G knows nothing about A, or is in phase
two for A, or A is active or in phase 1 but A.1 appears in the *aborts_list*, then G3 can be
told to release A.1.1's lock. (In fact, all of A.1.1's locks will be released and its versions
discarded at this point.) The only other possibility for this action tree is that A.1 is still
active; in this case G3 might try a query to G1.

The second situation is when H and R are related. In this case we are interested in
an ancestor of H and R called the *least common ancestor* (the LCA). The LCA is the
action that is an ancestor of both H and R, and that is younger than all other ancestors of
H and R. For example, for the action tree of Fig. 7-11, A.2 is the LCA of A.2.1 and
A.2.2, while A is the LCA of A.1.2 and A.2.2. To satisfy R's request for the object, we
must learn whether or not H committed to the LCA. If H did commit to the LCA, its
locks and versions can be propagated to the LCA and then R can obtain its needed lock.
Notice that in this case R will observe any modifications made by H. The other cases are
described below.

So, when H and R are related, a query is sent to the LCA's guardian. There are the
following possibilities:

1. If the LCA is active and H is a descendant of some action in its *aborts_list*, then
   the query response can indicate that some ancestor of H aborted. In this case,
   H's locks and versions can be discarded, and then R can obtain its needed lock.

2. If the LCA is active, H is not a descendant of an action in the *aborts_list*, and the
   handler call that gave rise to H has completed, then the query response can
   indicate that H did commit to the LCA. In this case, H's locks and versions can
   be propagated to the LCA and then R can acquire the needed lock.

3. If the LCA is active and the handler call that gave rise to H is still active, then
   the query cannot be resolved at the LCA's guardian. In this case H's guardian

may query to other guardians where ancestors of H are running.

4. Otherwise, the LCA is no longer active at its guardian. In this case, the fate of H is not known at the LCA's guardian, but R is an orphan. We will discuss orphans in the next section. When H's guardian receives this response, it will leave H's locks and versions intact, but destroy R as discussed below.

It is worth noting that queries are the glue that holds the system together. For example, when a handler action aborts, we may choose to notify guardians where descendants committed about the abort, but this is strictly an optimization to avoid queries later. We do not need to communicate before the reply message for the aborting handler is sent to its caller, so we incur no delay in the processing of actions. Instead we can communicate when it is convenient, for example when the handler's guardian is not doing anything. Furthermore, we need not try very hard to communicate, since if a message is lost, the information can always be obtained by a query.

7.5.5. Orphans

An *orphan* is any active action whose results are no longer wanted (see also [Nelson 81]). Orphans arise from two different sources: explicit aborts and crashes. Let us consider the case of explicit aborts first. One way aborts happen is when the system determines that a handler call cannot be completed right now. As mentioned above, a handler call causes two subactions to be created, and the call action will commit only after it has received the handler's reply and extracted the results from that reply message. This can occur only if the handler action has actually finished and either committed or aborted. On the other hand, the call action can abort without receiving a reply from the handler, and in this case the handler action (or some descendant of it) may still be running as an orphan.

Aborts also happen when an arm of a coenter exits the coenter and causes other arms to abort. The local subactions that correspond to these other arms will be terminated when this occurs, but if any of those arms is waiting for a handler call to complete, we abort the call action immediately and may leave an orphan at some other guardian.

The second way orphans arise is due to crashes. For example, the guardian making a call may crash, leaving the handler action as an orphan. Another possibility is the following: Suppose subaction S running at guardian GS made a call to guardian GC. Suppose this call committed, but subsequently GC crashed. In this case S must ultimately abort, because it depends on information at GC that has now been lost. Therefore, S is an orphan.

Since S is an orphan, it cannot commit and therefore none of its changes will become visible to other actions. Nevertheless, orphans are bad for two reasons. Since their results are not wanted, they are wasting resources. For example, some other action may be delayed because an orphan holds a needed lock. In addition, because they depend on locks that have been broken (for example, S depends on locks acquired by the handler call to GC), there is a danger that they may observe inconsistent data. Such inconsistent data can cause a program that behaves reasonably when the data is consistent to behave bizarrely; for example, a program that would ordinarily terminate may loop forever. In addition, if the program is interacting with a user, it may display inconsistent data to the user.

To illustrate this problem of inconsistent data, consider the following example. Suppose guardian Y replicates the data stored at another guardian X. The consistency constraint between each object x at X and its replica y at Y is that $x = y$. Now consider the scenario shown in Fig. 7-13: First suppose that top action S makes a call, S.1, to S.1 reads x, thus obtaining a read lock on x, displays the value of x to a user at a console, and then commits. Next X crashes and subsequently recovers; however, S.1's lock on x has been lost. Then another top action T makes a call to X; this call, T.1, changes the value of x to $x + 1$ and commits. Next T makes a call T.2 to Y, which changes y to $y + 1$ (thus preserving the invariant) and commits. Finally T commits, so the locks on x and y held by its descendants are released, and x and y take on their new values. Now S makes a call S.2 to Y, which reads the new value of y and displays this value to the user at the console. The new value of y is different from the value of x displayed previously, so the user has seen inconsistent data.

In Argus, we guarantee to eliminate orphans quickly enough that an orphan can never observe data in a state that could not be observed by a non-orphan. As a result of this guarantee, it is not necessary to worry about orphans when writing Argus programs. For example, the programmer need not be concerned that a program might expose

S @ G$_S$:   T @ G$_T$:

   S.1 @ X:
      display x to user
      commit

X crashes and recovers -

                            T.1 @ X:
                               $x := x + 1$
                               commit

                            T.2 @ Y:
                               $y := y + 1$
                               commit

                            T commits

   S.2 @ Y:
      display y to a user

Figure 7-13: An Orphan Scenario.

inconsistencies of the sort discussed above to the user.

In the remainder of this section, we sketch the orphan detection algorithm. Our method of detecting orphans is to send extra information in some of the messages that guardians use to communicate, namely, call and reply messages, prepare messages, and queries and query responses. We also keep extra information at each guardian. First each guardian has a *crash count*; this is a stable counter that is incremented after each crash. In addition, the guardian maintains two stable data structures: *done* and *map*. *Done* lists all actions known to this guardian that may have orphans somewhere. Like the *aborts_list*, it is not necessary to keep two actions in *done* where one is an ancestor of the other; instead only the older of the two actions need be kept. *Map* lists all guardians known to this guardian and their latest known crash counts.

In each message we include *done* and *map* of the sending guardian, and, in addition, the *dlist*, which lists the guardians *depended on* by the action on whose behalf the message is being sent. Intuitively, an action depends on a guardian if a crash of that guardian would cause it to become an orphan. The guardians an action depends on can be computed from information in plists: An action depends on all the guardians in its plist, but it also depends on all guardians listed in plists of all its ancestors at the time it was created. The *dlist* is maintained for each running action (along with the *plist*, etc.).

The information in a message is used at the receiving guardian to detect and destroy any local orphans and possibly to reject the incoming message; it is also merged with local information to bring that information more up to date. For example, a call message, C, is processed as follows:

1. We check for any action running at the receiving guardian that is a descendant of an action in C's *done*, or that depends on a guardian whose crash count in C's *map* is higher than what is known locally. Such an action is an orphan. These orphans are destroyed before the call message is acted upon.

2. We check that the call itself is not being performed on behalf of an orphan. The call is an orphan if its aid is a descendant of some action in the local *done*, or if any guardian in C's *dlist* has a lower crash count in C's *map* than in the local *map*. If the call action is an orphan, we send back a special reply rejecting the call.

3. Otherwise, we merge C's *map* and *done* with the local *map* and *done* and then run the handler action. In merging the maps, if the two maps disagree about the crash count of a guardian, the higher crash count is retained.

Orphan detection will prevent the problem illustrated by the scenario in Fig. 7-13. When subaction T.1 of T runs at X, X has a higher crash count than it did when subaction S.1 ran there. This information is propagated to GT in the reply message of T.1, and then to Y in the call of T.2. The new information about X's crash count will then be recorded in Y's *map*. Later, when the call of S.2 arrives at Y, it will be rejected because the *map* sent in this call will contain the old crash count for X.

Notice that the information in the map is just what is needed to correct the problem in two-phase commit mentioned earlier. For example, consider the situation discussed earlier, in which A.2.1 committed, then G3 crashed and recovered, and later A.1.1 arrived. There are two possibilities. If A.1 and A.2 are sequential (in which case A.2

actually ran before A.1), then A.1 depends on G3; the *map* in the call message for A.1.1 will list G3's old crash count, so the call will be rejected by G3 as an orphan. Another possibility is that A.1 and A.2 are concurrent. In this case, whichever one commits to A first indicates one crash count for G3, while the second one to commit to A indicates a different crash count for G3. In either case, when the second one commits to A, A will be recognized as an orphan and aborted; two-phase commit will not be carried out.

The practicality of orphan detection depends primarily on the amount of information that need be sent in messages. Both *map* and *done* are potentially very large, but it is nevertheless possible to limit the information that need be sent. Different techniques are applicable to the two cases. The size of *done* can be constrained by removing actions from it quickly. An action can be removed from *done* if we are certain it has no orphans anywhere. We are currently studying a number of methods for removing actions from *done*. We intend to avoid entirely sending the *map* in messages by associating a timestamp with each unique map, and sending these timestamps in messages instead of their maps. Each guardian still maintains its local map, and in addition that map's timestamp. When a guardian receives a message, it compares the incoming timestamp with its own. If the incoming timestamp is greater, this means that some information in the guardian's *map* is out of date. The guardian then communicates with a highly available map subsystem to obtain the missing information.

In the above, we discussed how orphans are detected, but simply assumed that, once detected, it was a simple matter to destroy an orphan. In fact, orphan destruction is not too difficult in Argus. Any process within a guardian can be destroyed without impact on the guardian's data provided that it is not in a critical section. Since the action of the process aborts, this ensures that any modifications to atomic objects are undone. (Note that we do rely on actions sharing only atomic objects; as discussed in Section 7.1, this restriction is needed if the actions are to be atomic.)

Argus processes enter critical sections in two ways: explicity, by gaining possession of special built-in objects called *mutex* objects, which are similar to semaphores, and implicitly, by executing some system code that runs in a critical section. For example, the operations on the built-in atomic objects run in a critical section while examining the current status of the object (whether it is locked on behalf of some action). We keep track for each process of whether or not it is in a critical section. If it is not, we can destroy it immediately and abort its action. If it is, we let it run until it exits its critical sections. If it does not exit its critical sections, we can always crash the guardian as a last resort.

7.6. User-defined Atomic Data Types

In Argus, atomicity is enforced by the objects shared among actions, rather than by the individual actions. Types whose objects ensure atomicity of the actions sharing them are called *atomic types*; their objects are called *atomic objects*. An atomic data type, like a regular abstract data type [Liskov 74], provides a set of objects and a set of operations. As with regular abstract types, the operations provided by an atomic type are the only way to access or manipulate the objects of the type. Unlike regular types, however, an atomic type provides serializability and recoverability for actions that use objects of the type. For example, relations in most relational databases provide operations to add and delete tuples, and to test for the existence of tuples; these operations are synchronized (for example, using two-phase locking [Eswaren 76]) and recovered (for example, using logs [Gray 78, Gray 81]) to ensure the atomicity of actions using the relations. In addition, an atomic type must be *resilient*: the type must be implemented so that objects of the type can be saved on stable storage. This ensures that when a top action commits the effects of all subactions that committed to the top-level will survive crashes.

Argus provides a number of built-in atomic types and, in addition, facilities for users to implement their own atomic types. In this section, we discuss why users need to implement their own atomic types. Then we define what it means for a type to be atomic, and finally we describe the mechanisms provided by Argus to support the implementation of user-defined atomic types. A more detailed discussion of these topics can be found in [Weihl 84].

Why do users need to define their own atomic types? The reason is that the built-in atomic types in Argus are somewhat limited in their provision of concurrency. Users may very well invent new atomic types that permit a great deal of concurrency. If users were constrained to implementing new atomic types only in terms of the built-in atomic types, the desired concurrency could not be achieved.

For example, consider the *semi-queue* data type. Semi-queues are similar to queues except that dequeuing does not happen in strict FIFO order. They have three operations: *create*, which creates a new, empty semi-queue; *enq*, which adds an element to a semi-queue, and *deq*, which removes and returns an arbitrary element *e* that was enqueued previously (by a committed action) and has not yet been dequeued (by a committed action). Notice that the behavior of semi-queues is non-deterministic; if there are several elements that can be dequeued, we do not specify which one should be dequeued. This non-determinism is the source of potential concurrency.

Semi-queues have very weak constraints on concurrency. Two *enq* operations can run concurrently as can an *enq* and a *deq* operation or two *deq* operations as long as they involve different elements. Thus many different actions can *enq* concurrently, or *deq* concurrently. Furthermore one action can *enq* while another *deq's* provided only that the latter not return the newly *enq'd* element. We do require that *deq* eventually remove any element *e* that is eligible for dequeuing. This constraint on the element returned by *deq* is enough for a printer subsystem to guarantee that each file queued by an action that later commits will eventually be printed.[7] The semi-queue data type could be implemented using an atomic array as a representation, e.g.,

rep = atomic_array[elem]

In this case, the implementation of *enq* would simply be to *addh* the new element to the atomic array. Since atomic arrays are implemented using read/write locks and *addh* is a writer, an *enq* operation performed on behalf of some action A would exclude *enq* and *deq* operations from being performed on behalf of other actions until A completed. As observed above, the specification of the semi-queue permits much more concurrency than this. Note that the potential loss of concurrency is substantial since actions can last a long time. For example, an action that performed an *enq* may do a lot of other things (to other objects at other guardians) before committing.

To avoid loss of concurrency, it is necessary to provide a way for users to implement new atomic types directly from non-atomic types. Before describing the mechanisms

---

[7] This is not quite true when we consider failures: the action that dequeues a file to print it could abort every time, preventing any progress from being made. As long as failures do not occur sufficiently often to cause this situation, every file will be printed eventually. An interesting open question is how to state service requirements for systems that can fail.

provided by Argus for this purpose, however, we first discuss atomicity and how much concurrency a given atomic type permits.

7.6.1. Understanding Atomicity

An atomic type is an abstraction, and hence is described by a specification. The specification describes the behavior of objects of the type as observed (via calls on the operations of the type) by the users of those objects. An important question about the specification of an atomic data type is whether the use of the word "atomic" is justified: Are the type's objects defined to behave in a way that ensures the atomicity of actions using the objects? This question has received intense study for a few types (like files and relations) [Papadimitriou 79]. Experience with implementing these types has shown that the problem is difficult and subtle [Eswaren 76, Gray 76]. If programmers are to implement new, user-defined atomic types, it is especially important to understand in general what behavior is acceptable for an atomic type.

In writing specifications for atomic types, we have found it helpful to pin down the behavior of the operations by assuming no concurrency and no failures, and then dealing with concurrency and failures later. In other words, we imagine that the objects will exist in an environment in which all actions are executed sequentially, and in which actions never abort. Although a sequential specification of this sort does not say anything explicit about permissible concurrency, it does impose limits on how much concurrency can be provided. Implementations can differ in how much concurrency is provided, but no implementation can exceed these limits. Some implementations, like that for the built-in type atomic_array, may allow less concurrency than is permitted by their sequential specifications.

This section provides a precise definition of permissible concurrency for an atomic type. Our definition is based on three facts about Argus and the way it supports implementations of atomic type. First, once an action has committed in Argus, it is not possible for it to be aborted later. (This restriction prevents the problem of cascading aborts.) Therefore, it is not necessary for an implementation of an atomic type to hide the changes made by committed actions, but it must prevent one action from observing the modifications of other actions that are still active. Second, the only method available to an atomic type for controlling the activities of actions is to delay actions while they are executing operations of the type. An atomic type cannot prevent an action from calling an operation, nor can it prevent an action that previously finished a call of an operation from completing either by committing or aborting. Third, Argus serializes actions dynamically, in their commit order.

Based on the above facts, we impose two concurrency constraints. First, we require that an action can observe the effects of other actions only if those actions committed. Recall that the notion of commitment is relative in Argus. When a subaction commits, its changes become visible to its parent, which inherits the subaction's locks and versions. Since the parent is still active, only the parent (and its descendants) can see those changes; other actions cannot. When a top action commits, its changes, including those inherited from its descendants, become visible to all other actions. This requirement constrains the results that can be returned by operations executed by an action. For example, for an atomic array a, if one action completes the call *store*(a, 3, 7), a second, unrelated action can receive the answer "7" from a call of *fetch*(a, 3) only if the first action committed. If the first action is still active, the second action must be delayed until the first action commits or aborts.

This first constraint supports recoverability since it ensures that effects of aborted actions cannot be observed by other actions. It also supports serializability, since it prevents concurrent actions from observing one another's changes. However, more is needed for serializability. Thus, we have our second constraint: operations executed by one action cannot invalidate the results of operations executed by a concurrent action. For example, suppose an action A executes the *size* operation on an atomic array object, receiving n as the result. Now suppose another action B is permitted to execute *addh*. The *addh* operation will increase the size of the array to $n + 1$, invalidating the results of the *size* operation executed by A. Since A observed the state of the array before B executed *addh*, A must precede B in any sequential execution of the actions (since sequential executions must be consistent with the sequential specifications of the objects). Now suppose that B commits. By assumption, A cannot be prevented from seeing the effects of B. If A observes any effect of B, it will have to follow B in any sequential execution. Since A cannot both precede and follow B in a sequential execution, serializability would be violated. Thus, once A executes *size*, an action that calls *addh* must be delayed until A completes.

To state our requirements more precisely, let us begin by considering a simple situation involving two concurrent actions each executing a single operation on a shared atomic object O. (The actions may be executing operations on other shared objects also: we are defining a local atomicity property, so we focus on the operations involving a single object.) A fairly simple condition that guarantees serializability is the following. Suppose O is an object of type T. O has a current state determined by the operations performed by previously committed actions. Suppose O1 and O2 are two executions of operations on O in its current state. (O1 and O2 might be executions of the same operation or different operations.) If O1 has been executed by an action A and A has not yet committed or aborted, O2 can be performed by a concurrent action B only if O1 and O2 commute: given the current state of O, the effect (as described by the sequential specification of T) of performing O1 on O followed by O2 is the same as performing O2 on O followed by O1. It is important to realize that when we say "effect" we include both both the results returned and any modifications to the state of O.

The intuitive explanation of why the above condition works is as follows. Suppose O1 and O2 are performed by concurrent actions A1 and A2 at O. If O1 and O2 commute, then the order in which A1 and A2 are serialized does not matter at O. If A1 is serialized before A2 then the local effect at O is as if O1 were performed before O2, while if A2 is serialized before A1, the local effect is as if O2 were performed before O1. But these two effects are the same since O1 and O2 commute.

Notice that the common method of dividing operations into readers and writers and using read/write locking works because it allows operations to be executed by concurrent actions only when the operations commute. Our condition permits more concurrency than readers/writers because the meaning of the individual operations and the arguments of the calls can be considered. For example, calls of the atomic array operation *addh* always commute with calls of *addl*, yet both these operations are writers. As another example, store(O, i, e1) and store(O, j, e2) commute if i ≠ j.

Note that we require that O1 and O2 commute only when they are executed starting in the current state. For example, consider a bank account object, with operations to deposit a sum of money, to withdraw a sum of money (with the possible result that it signals *insufficient funds* if the current balance is less than the sum requested), and to examine the current balance. Two withdraw operations, say for amounts m and n, do not commute when the current balance is the maximum of m and n: either operation when executed in this state will succeed in withdrawing the requested sum, but the other operation must signal *insufficient funds* if executed in the resulting state. They do commute whenever the current balance is at least the sum of m and n. Thus if one action has executed a withdraw operation, our condition allows a second action to execute another withdraw operation while the first action is still active as long as there are sufficient funds to satisfy both withdrawal requests.

Our condition is similar to the commutativity condition identified in [Bernstein 81]. The condition in [Bernstein 81], however, appears to require that O1 and O2 commute in all possible states if they are to be executed by concurrent actions. This condition is more restrictive than ours, and does not permit two actions to execute withdraw operations concurrently. The greater generality of our condition may be important for achieving reasonable performance.

Our condition must be extended to cover two additional cases. First, there may be more than two concurrent actions at a time. Suppose A1,...,An are concurrent actions, each performing a single operation execution O1,...,On, respectively, on O. (As before, the concurrent actions may be sharing other objects as well.) Since A1,...,An are permitted to be concurrent at O, there is no local control over the order in which they may appear to occur. Therefore, all possible orders must have the same effect at O. This is true provided that all permutations of O1,...,On have the same effect when executed in the current state, where effect includes both results obtained and modifications to O.

The second extension acknowledges that actions can perform sequences of operation executions. For example, suppose action A executed *addh* followed by *remh* on an array. This sequence of operations has no net effect on the array. It is then permissible to allow a concurrent action B to execute *size* on the same array, provided the answer returned is the size of the array before A executed *addh* or after it executed *remh*. To extend the definition, consider concurrent actions A1,...,An each performing a sequence S1,...,Sn, respectively, of operation executions. This is permissible if all sequences Si1,Si2,...,Sin, obtained by concatenating the sequences S1,...,Sn in some order, produce the same effect.

Note that in requiring certain sequences of operations to have the same effect, we are considering the effect of the operations as described by the specification of the type.

Thus we are concerned with the abstract state of O, and not with the concrete state of its storage representation. Therefore, we may allow two operations (or sequences of operations) that do commute in terms of their effect on the abstract state of O to be performed by concurrent actions, even though they do not commute in terms of their effect on the representation of O. This distinction between an abstraction and its implementation is crucial in achieving reasonable performance, and is the basis for the example implementation to be presented below.

It is important to realize that the constraints that are imposed by atomicity based on the sequential specification of a type are only an upper bound on the concurrency that an implementation may provide. A specification may contain additional constraints that further constrain implementations; these constraints may be essential for showing that actions using the type do not deadlock, or for showing other kinds of termination properties. For example, the specification of the built-in atomic types explicitly describes the locking rules used by their implementations; users of these types are guaranteed that the built-in atomic types will not permit more concurrency than allowed by these rules (for instance, actions writing different components of an array, or different fields of a record, cannot do so concurrently).

7.6.2. Implementing Atomic Types in Argus

In this section we describe how user-defined atomic types can be implemented in Argus.

To some extent, the issues involved in implementing an atomic type are similar to those that arise in implementing other abstract types. The implementation must define a representation for the atomic objects, and an implementation for each operation of the type in terms of that representation. However, the implementation of an atomic type must solve some problems that do not occur for ordinary types, namely: inter-action synchronization, making visible to other actions the effects of committed actions and hiding the effects of aborted actions, and providing for resilience.

A way of thinking about the above set of problems is in terms of events that are of interest to an implementation of an atomic type. Like implementations of regular types, these implementations are concerned with the events corresponding to operation calls and returns; here, as usual, control passes to and from the type's implementation. In addition, however, events corresponding to termination (commit and abort) of actions that had performed operations on an object of the type are also of interest to the type's implementation.

Linguistic mechanisms to support implementation of atomic types can be divided into two categories based on how information about termination events is conveyed to a type's implementation. In the *explicit approach*, an implementation would find out about these events explicitly, e.g., by providing special commit and abort operations that are called by the runtime system when actions commit and abort. Alternatively, in the *implicit approach* an implementation is not informed about action termination, but rather must find out about it after the fact.

Argus provides an implicit mechanism in which programs find out about commit and abort events after the fact through the use of objects of built-in atomic types. The representation of a user-defined atomic type is a combination of atomic and non-atomic objects, with the non-atomic objects used to hold information that can be accessed by concurrent actions, and the atomic objects containing information that allows the non-atomic data to be interpreted properly. The built-in atomic objects can be used to ask the following question: Did the action that caused a particular change to the representation commit (so the new information is now available to other actions), or abort (so the change should be forgotten), or is it still active (so the information cannot be released yet)? The operations available on built-in atomic objects have been extended to support this type of use, as will be illustrated below.

The use of atomic objects permits operation implementations to discover what happened to previous actions and to synchronize concurrent actions. However, the implementations also need to synchronize concurrent operation executions. Here we are concerned with *process concurrency* (as opposed to action concurrency), i.e., two or more processes are executing operations on the same object at the same time.

We provide process synchronization by means of a new data type called *mutex*. Mutex objects provide mutual exclusion, as implied by their name. A mutex object is essentially a container for another object. This other object can be of any type, and mutex is parameterized by this type. An example is

```
mutex[array[int]]
```

where the mutex object contains an array of integers. Mutex objects are created by calling operation

create = **proc** (x: T) **returns** (mutex [T])

which constructs a new mutex object containing *x* as its value. The contained object can be retrieved later via operation

get_value = **proc** (m: mutex [T]) **returns** (T)

This operation delivers the value of the mutex object, namely (a pointer to) the contained T object, which can then be used via T operations. *Get_value* can be called via the syntactic sugar *m. value* where *m* is a mutex object.

The **seize** statement is used to gain possession of a mutex object:

seize *expr* **do** *body* **end**

Here *expr* must evaluate to a mutex object. If that object is not now in the possession of a process, this process *gains possession*. The process then executes the *body*. Possession is *released* when control leaves the *body*. If some process has possession, this process waits until possession is released.[8] If several processes are waiting, one is selected fairly as the next one to gain possession.

The **seize** statement as explained above is semaphore-like: it could be translated to

P(m.sem)
body
V(m.sem)

where *m* is the mutex object obtained by evaluating *expr* and we imagine this object has a semaphore as a component. However, the **seize** statement is more powerful than this because inside its *body* it is possible to release possession temporarily. This is done by executing the **pause** statement:

---

[8] A runtime check is made to see if possession is held by this process. In this case, the process is permitted to continue.

pause

Execution of this statement releases possession of the mutex object that was obtained in the smallest statically containing **seize** statement. The process then waits for a system determined amount of time, after which it attempts to regain possession; any competition at this point is resolved fairly. Finally, once it gains possession it starts executing in the *body* at the statement following the **pause**.

The combination of **seize** with **pause** gives a structure that is similar to monitor condition variables [Hoare 74]. However, **pause** is simply a delay; there is no guarantee that when the waiting process regains possession, the condition it is waiting for will be true.[9] The reason why we do not provide an analog of a monitor's condition variables is the following: Often the conditions these processes are waiting for concern commit and abort events. These are not events over which other user processes have any control. Therefore, it would not make sense to expect user processes to signal such information to each other.

Implementation of Semi-queues

In this section we present an example implementation of the semi-queue data type described earlier. We use this example to illustrate how objects of built-in atomic type can be used to find out about the completion of actions, and how mutex can be used to synchronize user processes.

The implementation appears in Fig. 7-14. The implementation is simply a cluster [Liskov 77, Liskov 81b]. For simplicity we are assuming the elements in the semi-queue are integers. The plan of this implementation is to keep the enqueued integers in a regular (non-atomic) array. This array can be used by concurrent actions, but it is enclosed in a mutex object to ensure proper process synchronization. All modification and reading of the array occurs inside a **seize** statement on this mutex object.

To determine the status of each integer in the array, we associate with each integer an atomic object that tells the status of actions that inserted or deleted that item. For this purpose we use the built-in atomic type, *atomic_variant*. Atomic variant objects are

---

[9] In Mesa [Lampson 80] there is similarly no guarantee when a waiting process awakens.

```
semiqueue = cluster is create, enq, deq

    qitem = atomic_variant[enqueued: int, dequeued: null]
    buffer = array[qitem]
    rep = mutex[buffer]

    create = proc ( ) returns (cvt)
        return(rep$create(buffer$new( )))
        end create

    enq = proc (q: cvt, i: int)
        item: qitem := qitem$make_dequeued(nil) % deq'd if action aborts
        qitem$change_enqueued(item, i)         % enqueued if action commits
        seize q do
            buffer$addh(q.value, item)              % add new item to buffer
            end
        rep$changed(q)          % notify system of modification to buffer
                                % (explained later)

        end enq

    deq = proc (q: cvt) returns (int)
        cleanup(q)
        seize q do
            while true do
                for item: qitem in buffer$elements(q.value) do
                    % look at all items in the buffer
                        tagtest item        % see if item can be deq'd by this action
                        wtag enqueued (i: int): qitem$change_dequeued(item,nil)
                                                    return(i)
                    end % tagtest
                end % for
            pause
            end % while
        end % seize
    end deq
```

```
cleanup = proc (q: rep)
    enter topaction        % start an independent action
        seize q do
            b: buffer := q.value
            for item: qitem in buffer$elements(b) do
                tagtest item        % remove only qitems in the dequeued state
                    tag dequeued:  buffer$reml(b)
                    others: return
                    end % tagtest
                end % for
            end % seize
        end % enter -- commit cleanup action here
    end cleanup

end semiqueue
```

Figure 7-14: Implementation of the Semiqueue Type

similar to variant records. An atomic variant object can be in one of a number of states; each state is identified by a tag and has an associated value. Atomic variant operation *make_t* creates a new variant object in the *t* state; this state is the object's "base" state, and the object will continue to exist in this state even if the creating action (or one of its ancestors) aborts. Operation *change_t* changes the state (the tag and value) of the object; this change will be undone if the calling action (or one of its ancestors) aborts. There are also operations to decompose atomic variant objects, although these are usually called implicitly via special statements. Atomic variant operations are classified as readers and writers; for example, *change_t* is a writer, while *make_t* and the decomposition operations are readers.

In this paper, atomic variant objects will be decomposed using the **tagtest** statement.

```
tagtest expr
    { tagarm }
    [ others : body ]
    end
```

where

$$tagarm ::= tagtype \; idn \left[(decl) \right] : body$$
$$tagtype ::= \textbf{tag} \mid \textbf{wtag}$$

The *expr* must evaluate to an atomic variant object. Each *tagarm* lists one of the possible tags; a tag can appear on at most one arm. An arm will be selected if the atomic variant object has the listed tag, and the executing action can obtain the object in the desired mode: read mode for **tag** and write mode for **wtag**. If an arm can be selected, the object is obtained in the desired mode. Then, if the optional declaration is present, the current value of the atomic variant object is assigned to the new variable. Finally, the associated *body* is executed. If no arm can be selected and the optional **others** arm is present, the *body* of the **others** arm is executed; if the **others** arm is not present, control falls through to the next statement.[10]   The semi-queue operations are implemented as follows. The *create* operation simply creates a new empty array and places it inside of a new mutex object. The *enq* operation associates a new atomic variant object with the incoming integer; this variant object will have tag "enqueued" if the calling action commits (to the top) later, and tag "dequeued" otherwise. Then *enq* seizes the mutex and adds the new item to the contained array.

The *deq* operation seizes the mutex and then searches the array for an item it can dequeue. If an item is enqueued and the action that called *deq* can obtain it in write mode, that item is selected and returned after changing its status to "dequeued". Otherwise the search is continued. If no suitable item is found, **pause** is executed and later the search is done again.

Proper synchronization of actions using a semi-queue is achieved by using the *qitems* in the buffer. An *enq* operation need not wait for any other action to complete. It simply creates a new *qitem* and adds it to the array. Of course, it may have to wait for another operation to release the mutex object before adding the *qitem* to the array, but this delay should be relatively short. A *deq* operation must wait until some *enq* operation has committed; thus it searches for a *qitem* with tag "enqueued" that it can write.

The *qitems* are also used to achieve proper recovery for actions using a semi-queue.

---

[10]The **tagtest** statement can be used to discover information about concurrent actions, and thus violate atomicity (although we don't do this in the example). There is another decomposition statement, **tagwait**, that cannot be used to violate atomicity.

Since the array in the mutex is not atomic, changes to the array made by actions that abort later are not undone. This means that a *deq* operation cannot simply remove a *qitem* from the array, since this change could not be undone if the calling action aborted later. Instead, a *deq* operation changes the state of a *qitem*; the atomicity of *qitems* ensures proper recovery for this modification. If the calling action commits to the top, the *qitem* will have tag *dequeued* permanently. Such *qitems*, which are also generated by *enq* operations called by actions that abort, have no effect on the abstract state of the semi-queue. Leaving them in the array wastes storage, so the internal procedure *cleanup*, called by *deq*, removes them from the low end of the array. (A more realistic implementation would call *cleanup* only occasionally.) It seems characteristic of the general approach used here that reps need to be garbage collected in this fashion periodically.

Cleanup cannot run in the calling action because then its view of what the semi-queue contained would not be accurate. For example, if the calling action had previously executed a *deq* operation, that *deq* appears to have really happened to a later operation execution by this action. But of course the *deq* really has not happened, because the calling action has not yet committed to the top level.

To get a true view of the state of the semi-queue, *cleanup* runs as an independent top action. This action has its own view of the semi-queue, and since it has not done anything to the semi-queue previously, it cannot obtain false information. The independent action is started by the **enter** statement:

enter topaction *body* **end**

It commits when execution of the *body* is finished.

An independent action like the *cleanup* action commits while its calling action is still active. Later the calling action may abort. Therefore, the independent action must not make any modifications that could reveal intermediate states of the calling action to later actions. The *cleanup* action satisfies this condition because it performs a *benevolent side effect*: a modification to the semi-queue object that cannot be observed by its users.

Resilience

Both built-in and user-defined atomic objects must be copied to stable storage when the actions that modified them commit. This requirement raises the question of how the user controls what is written to stable storage. If we were using an explicit approach, the user might provide an operation that the system could call to cause writing to stable storage. However, in our implicit approach we must make do without such an operation. Our solution is to extend the meaning of mutex.

So far, mutex has been used only for synchronization of user processes. Now it will be used for three additional functions: notifying the system when information needs to be written to stable storage, defining what information is written to stable storage, and ensuring that information is written to stable storage in a consistent state.

The system knows when a built-in atomic object has changed: this can happen only if the committing action holds a write lock on the object or created the object. New mutex objects are also written to stable storage when the creating action commits. In addition, we provide mutex operation

$$\text{changed} = \text{proc (m: mutex[T])}$$

for notifying the system that an existing mutex object should be written to stable storage. Calling this operation will cause m to be written to stable storage by the time the action that executed the *changed* operation commits to the top. Note that *changed* is not really needed; the system could keep track of all mutex objects used by an action (via the *get_value* operation) and write these to stable storage. But we are concerned that writing to stable storage is expensive and therefore should be avoided if possible. The *changed* operation allows the user to avoid copying of mutex objects that need not be copied (e.g., were only read).

Copying a mutex object involves copying the contained object. By choosing the proper granularity of mutex objects the user can control how much is written to stable storage. For example, a large data base can be broken into partitions that are written to stable storage independently by partitioning it among several mutex objects. The *changed* operation can be used to limit writing to stable storage to just those partitions actually modified by a committing action.

Finally, mutex objects can be used to ensure that information is in a consistent state when it is written to stable storage. The system will gain possession of a mutex object before writing it to stable storage. By making all modifications to these objects inside seize statements, the user's code can prevent the system from copying the object when it is in an inconsistent state.

In the semi-queue example in the previous section, the addition of a new *qitem* to the array by an *enq* operation certainly needs to be stably recorded if the calling action commits to the top level; otherwise no permanent record of the *enq* operation would exist. Thus the *enq* operation uses the *changed* operation to notify the system of this fact. Then, when the enqueuing action commits to the top level, the system writes the array, including the value of the new *qitem*, to stable storage. A *deq* operation modifies an existing *qitem*; this change will be stably recorded since *qitems* are atomic. The effect of a *deq* operation on the array, however, does not need to be stably recorded. A *deq* operation only modifies the array in an invocation of *cleanup*. If these changes are forgotten in a failure that restores an earlier state of the array, the presence of the extra *qitems* in the array will not affect later operations, and *cleanup* will remove them again the next time it is executed. Thus the modification made by *cleanup* need not be recorded stably (though it will be when the next action that executes *enq* commits to the top level).

The above discussion of copying to stable storage has ignored two issues that must now be discussed. The first concerns the recoverability of copying mutex objects to stable storage. Clearly, the copying of each individual mutex object must be all-or-nothing. But, can the copying of several mutex objects be all-or-nothing? Our answer is to provide recoverability on a per guardian basis, but not for the system as a whole. Our condition guarantees consistency within each guardian, but not between guardians.

The second issue concerns mutex and built-in atomic objects that refer to one another. Suppose the system is copying a mutex object that contains as a component a mutex or built-in atomic object. Should that contained object be copied to stable storage too? And, if so, in what order are the two objects copied, and, if they are both mutex objects, does the system gain possession of both before copying either?

The method we use for copying data to stable storage has the following properties.

1. It minimizes writing: only those objects actually modified by the committing action are copied.

2. It is incremental: each built-in atomic object and each mutex object is written to stable storage in a separate, atomic step. In copying each such object, the system copies all portions of the object except contained mutex and atomic objects. These are copied separately if they were modified, or if they have no copy on stable storage.

3. It is order-independent: the atomic and mutex objects are written to stable storage in an arbitrary order (chosen to increase the efficiency of the system).

Thus, when the action that executed an *enq* operation commits to the top level, the system gains possession of the mutex object, waiting if necessary, and then copies the names (but not the values) of the contained *qitems* to stable storage.[11] In addition, those *qitems* that were modified by the committing action, or that are new (e.g., the newly enqueued *qitem*), are also written to stable storage, but this is done independently of the copying of the array state. In particular, the system does not have possession of the mutex object while copying the *qitems* to stable storage. Furthermore, the order in which these various objects are written to stable storage is undefined; the system might copy the array state first and later a contained modified *qitem*, or vice versa.

Copying to stable storage is incremental for the following reason. The alternative would be to write all modified objects together. To do so the system would have to gain possession of all changed mutex objects before writing any of them. Such a requirement would be likely to delay the system substantially (especially when you consider that the objects are distributed), leading to an unacceptable delay in the execution of the first phase of two-phase commit. In fact it might be impossible for the system ever to obtain all locks. We chose the incremental scheme to avoid such problems.

The incremental scheme has the following impact on programs. The true state of an object usually includes the states of all contained objects, and a predicate expressing a consistency condition on an object state would normally constrain the states of contained

---

[11]This copying is done at the latest during the prepare phase of 2-phase commit.

objects (this predicate is usually referred to as the *representation invariant* [Guttag 78]). For example, suppose we had an atomic type *double-queue* that (for some reason) kept two copies of the semi-queue and was represented by

rep = **record** [first, second: semiqueue]

where the representation invariant required that the states of the two semi-queues be the same. Now suppose the system is handling the commit of some action A that modified both semi-queues contained in the double-queue, and while this is happening a second action B is modifying those semi-queues. Then it is possible that when the *first* semi-queue is written to stable storage it contains B's changes, but when the *second* semi-queue is written to stable storage it does not contain B's changes. Therefore, the information in stable storage appears not to satisfy the representation invariant of the double-queue.

However, the representation invariant of the double-queue really is satisfied, for the following reason. First note that the information in stable storage is only of interest after a crash. So suppose there is a crash. Now there are two possibilities:

1. Before that crash, B also committed. In this case the data read back from stable storage is, in fact, consistent, since it reflects B's changes to both the *first* and *second* semi-queues.

2. B aborted or had not yet committed before the crash. In either case, B aborts. Therefore, the changes made to the *first* semi-queue by B will be hidden by the semi-queue implementation: at the abstract level, the two semi-queues *do* have the same state.

The point of the above example is that if the objects being written to stable storage are atomic, then the fact that they are written incrementally causes no problems.

On the other hand, when an atomic type is implemented with a representation consisting of several mutex objects, the programmer must be aware that these objects are written to stable storage incrementally, and care must be taken to ensure that the representation invariant is still preserved and that information is not lost in spite of incremental writing. We have explored several atomic type implementations that use more than one mutex. Often incremental writing is not a problem; for example, this is the case when a database is simply implemented as a number of partitions. Sometimes the implementations are more complex because of incremental writing. We have developed a general method that seems to work well in managing this complexity. To ensure that various mutexes are written to stable storage in the proper order, separate actions must be used. For example, for a write ahead log, the implementation might make changes to the log in one action A, and change the database by a separate action B that runs only after A has committed. This technique is discussed in [Weihl 82].

7.7. Discussion

Argus provides two main mechanisms: guardians and actions. Below we discuss these mechanisms and how they support the requirements of distributed programs.

Guardians permit a programmer to identify tightly coupled data and processing as a unit. The data and processing are placed together at a single node so that access to the data is inexpensive. In this sense, guardians are similar to modules provided in other languages for distributed programs (e.g., Ada [Ada 82], CSP [Hoare 78], SR [Andrews 81], and DP [Brinch Hansen]). However, guardians differ from these other modules in two significant ways. First, guardians support a varying number of processes that share the data directly. Second, guardians address the problem of node crashes.

We are convinced that having a dynamically varying number of processes in a guardian is better than limiting processes to just one or a statically determined number. This point is discussed in detail in [Liskov 83a]; a brief summary of the arguments is presented here. Since any individual handler action may be delayed either because a needed resource (e.g., an atomic object) is not available or because it is waiting for a reply from a remote call, it is necessary to provide a method to multiplex a guardian. Dynamic concurrency as in Argus is one such method. An alternative method is to provide a monitor-like structure to solve the first problem, and to decouple sending of a call message and receiving of the reply message to solve the second problem. Although such a method can work, it is considerably more complicated for the programmer, who must now get involved in scheduling the guardian. For example, if the sending process can continue after making a call, the programmer must now explicitly turn the attention of this process to some other task. Another problem with such a method is that if an algorithm has natural concurrency in it, such concurrency cannot be expressed in a straightforward manner. Finally, if the language does not provide for a dynamic number of processes and in addition does not permit sends and replies to be decoupled, there is a substantial loss of expressive power. Ada suffers from this problem, as is discussed in [Liskov 84].

Any realistic language for distributed programs must provide some solution to the problems stemming from unreliable hardware. Guardians address node crashes by having stable state that is written to stable storage when top actions commit. It is by no means clear that this is the best method of addressing node crashes. The major problem is the following: The state of Argus guardians is replicated on the physical devices that implement stable storage. In this way guardians provide a solution to the reliability problem, but not the availability problem. If a subsystem is to provide availability, this must be accomplished by replicating guardians. But, if guardians are replicated, then perhaps it is not necessary for the state of each guardian to also be replicated. It is not clear at this point whether a mechanism that combines a solution to reliability and availability is better than an Argus-like method that separates them. More research is needed in this area.

The other major linguistic mechanism in Argus is atomic actions. Atomic actions enable the program to identify computations that must be performed indivisibly and recoverably. We think that atomicity is a fundamental concept that is needed to support implementations of many applications, including non-distributed implementations. We also think that nested atomic actions are needed. However, many questions remain about how to support atomic actions.

Most other work on atomic actions has occurred outside of programming languages. The alternative is to provide a language-independent transaction management system coupled with either a file system (e.g., [Sturgis 80]) or a database system (e.g., [Lindsay 84]). It is worth pointing out that the language approach provides several advantages, of which the most important are the following. First, the language provides a much more flexible notion of data object than is supported by a file system or a database system. Using the objects in Argus, the programmer can tailor a representation to the needs of the application, and achieve whatever level of concurrency is required. Files and databases each provide a single method of representing data, but experience in programming indicates that flexible user control over representation is needed. This need can be addressed directly in a language like Argus.

Second, the language can provide a simple interface, in which certain errors that can arise in the other approaches are ruled out. For example, action identifiers are never accessible to Argus programs. As a result, it is possible to identify each action with a single guardian, and to ensure that an action cannot commit in one place and abort in another.

Third, and most important, only a language supports the notion of a computation; a file or database system merely provides a subsystem to be used by a computation. Therefore a language can provide the ability to make a computation atomic, rather than just providing atomicity in the interaction of the computation with the file or database system. Identifying computations with actions is the source of the simple interface mentioned above. It also simplifies the computations as a whole. For example, in Argus if a remote call fails, there is no need to be concerned about the state of the called guardian, since the call is an atomic action. Also, there is no need to be concerned about any orphans at that guardian.

Many question remain concerning how atomic actions should be supported in a programming language. For example, in Argus atomicity of actions is provided by the shared atomic objects. Probably this approach is right; all existing action systems work this way (actions are synchronized and recovered through the shared files or databases). What is not so clear is how synchronization and recovery should be accomplished. Argus built-in atomic objects use two-phase locking. There are several other viable techniques. For example, timestamps [Reed 78] allow read only actions to run without interfering with other actions.

There are also questions about what mechanisms to provide for users to build their own atomic objects. This area is relatively unexplored; for existing work, see [Weihl 84] and [Allchin 83]. It is worth noting that any mechanism for user-defined types is affected by the way that the built-in objects work. For example, if timestamps were the synchronization method, user-defined objects would make use of timestamps also. An even more striking example concerns optimistic techniques [Kung 81]. These are techniques in which actions are not synchronized while they run, but instead when an action commits a check is made to see if it conflicted with another action. If it did, it is forced to abort. With this approach, the user-defined objects would not delay operation executions, but instead would need to check for conflicts at action commit or later. Much more study is needed of mechanisms for user-defined types and their interaction with the different synchronization techniques.

In designing Argus, an important goal was to make the programmer's job as easy as possible. We might hope that, given suitable linguistic constructs, it would be as simple to implement a distributed program as a sequential program. To a certain extent, this hope has been realized in Argus. For example, handler calls are very much like regular procedure calls in a sequential language; in particular, the uncertainties introduced by potential failures of the network and the target node need not concern the programmer. As a second example, handler actions are synchronized by their use of shared atomic objects; as a result, coding of handlers is similar to the coding of ordinary procedures.

However, distributed programs are more difficult to implement than sequential programs, even given the help that Argus provides. The basis of the difficulty lies in the problem domain, which is inherently complex. Distributed programs must cope with a number of problems, e.g., concurrency, availability and reliability, that simply do not arise in sequential programs.

Argus provides some help for these problems because it supports a programming methodology that allows for separation of concerns. Implementers of user-defined atomic types are the only ones who need to be concerned with synchronization of concurrent processes. In addition, they must be concerned with reliability in the sense that they need to control how abstract objects are written to stable storage. Finally, they must worry about deadlock and starvation. The reasoning involved in sorting out these issues can be quite complex, but at least it is limited to the implementation of a single data abstraction, so only local reasoning is needed.

Availability and reliability are tackled when implementing subsystems. Reliability is fairly simple. It is only necessary to decide what constitutes the stable state of a guardian; copying of that information will be taken care of automatically. Availability is more difficult; it is necessary to decide where to replicate data and how to partition it. On the other hand, synchronization is not much of an issue, since the atomic objects take care of that. In fact, sequential reasoning can usually be used to understand the code in guardians. However, potential deadlocks must be recognized, and an explicit decision made about whether to avoid them or not.

To really evaluate Argus, it must first be implemented. We are working on a preliminary implementation at present; we hope to have something usable running by September of 1984. Once the Argus implementation exists, the next step is to implement various applications in Argus. Argus can then be evaluated with respect to the ease with which the applications were implemented, and with respect to the performance of the applications.

We have already begun working on some applications; for example, the implementation of the catalog mentioned in Section 7.4 is underway. Our preliminary experience with Argus is favorable; it appears to be relatively easy to implement applications in it. Further evaluation must wait until the Argus implementation exists.

Chapter 8

Paradigms for
Distributed Programs

Reinventing the wheel is never an effective way to spend one's time. Nor is describing a wheel an effective way to communicate the idea, when the term "wheel" is known to all. For these reasons, programmers have identified paradigms they have found to be helpful in the design of programs. Examples of paradigms include divide-and-conquer, dynamic programming, as well as use of queues, stacks and other data structures. In some cases, these paradigms are programming problems that arise in a variety of contexts; for example, divide-and-conquer. In others, the paradigms are abstractions that underly a variety of programming problems. A queue is an example of this latter type of paradigm.

A good programmer attempts to formulate a programming problem in terms of known paradigms whenever possible. This saves the programmer from reinventing the wheel, because once a paradigm has been identified, an existing body of information can be consulted for implementation techniques and analysis. The use of paradigms is also an aid in documentation and discussions with other programmers—it saves the programmer from having to "describe the wheel." In this regard, paradigms can be viewed as a method of specification.

In this section some paradigms associated with programming distributed systems are described. Since we are only just starting to identify paradigms for distributed programs, the collection is small. As experience accumulates, other important and recurring problems will be identified, and practical solutions to them will be developed. In the meantime, it behooves the designer of distributed programs to understand the paradigms that have been identified, so that energy need not be spent solving solved problems.

8.1. A, B, C's of Agreement and Commitment

The first paradigm we will explore is that of establishing agreement in a distributed system. The problem is to devise a protocol whereby all processors agree on a value. This value may be some input data, like the value of a digital altimeter on an airplane, or the value may be the outcome of a decision, such as whether or not to install the effects of a transaction.

The agreement problem is trivial if processors don't fail. The possibility of failures complicates matters because a faulty processor might neglect to relay messages or might relay conflicting messages to other processors. Below, we discuss two solutions to the problem and then describe an important application of agreement commit protocols. Our solutions assume a collection of interconnected processors satisfying

Reliable Communications Property:

RCP1: Each non-faulty processor can send messages to every other non-faulty processor.

RCP2: Messages between every pair of non-faulty processors are delivered uncorrupted and in the order sent.

Clearly, to achieve this property in the presence of k or fewer faults there must be at least $k + 1$ independent paths between any two processors. These paths may be direct or may involve relaying messages through other processors. Although this is likely to be expensive, it is necessary since it is impossible to distribute a message to a processor if there is no way to communicate with it.

Formally, the *agreement problem* is to devise a protocol in which a value known to a designated processor, called the *transmitter*, is disseminated to the other processors such that

Interactive Consistency:

IC1: All non-faulty processors agree on some value.

IC2: If the transmitter is non-faulty then all non-faulty processors use its value as the one they agree on.

A number of variants of the problem exist, depending on whether processor failures can be detected, whether the relative speeds of processors are bounded, and whether messages can be authenticated [Fischer 83]. The two variations discussed below are instances of the problem that arise in practice.

8.1.1. Agreement Among Fail-Stop Processors

A *fail-stop processor* [Schneider 83, 84a]

(1) halts in response to any failure, instead of performing an erroneous state transformation that might be visible to other processors, and

(2) can detect whenever another fail-stop processor has halted due to a failure.

Thus, fail-stop processors never "lie" and we can assume the existence of a predicate *failed(p)* that can be tested by every processor and is true if and only if processor p has failed. Fail-stop processors are useful abstractions; they have been approximated by a number of the manufacturers of highly reliable systems.

To establish interactive consistency in a a distributed system consisting of fail-stop processors, it is sufficient to establish:

Fault-tolerant Broadcast:

If any functioning processor has a copy of m then every functioning processor has a copy of m.

This is because a faulty processor halts and therefore never relays an erroneous value.

We now outline a protocol for performing Fault-tolerant Broadcasts in systems of fail-stop processors. A complete derivation and proof of the protocol is given in [Schneider 84b].

Broadcast Strategies

A *broadcast strategy* describes how a message being broadcast is to be disseminated to the processors in the network. We represent a broadcast strategy by a rooted, ordered tree in which the root corresponds to the transmitter. Other nodes correspond to the other processors, and there is an edge from p to q if processor p should forward to processor q the message being broadcast.[1] When a node has more than one successor in the tree, the message is forwarded to each of the successors in a predefined order, also specified by the broadcast strategy.

Given a broadcast strategy represented by a graph (V, E), we define

$$SUCC(Q) \equiv \{p \mid q \in Q \land pq \in E\}.$$

---

[1]Restriction to trees is not a limitation when considering broadcast strategies that ensure minimum time to completion. A broadcast strategy that cannot be represented as a tree must include a processor that receives the same message more than once.

$SUCC^+$ and $SUCC^*$ denote the conventional transitive and reflexive transitive clo sures of $SUCC$.

Generally speaking, the successors of a node in the broadcast strategy will be neighbors of the node in the network, but this is not necessary. The broadcast stra tegy defines how a message is to be broadcast; it is the duty of a lower-level protoco to ensure delivery of messages to their destinations, as postulated in the Reliable Communications Property. Also note that a broadcast strategy describes a *pre ferred* method of broadcasting: as long as no processors fail, messages are dissem inated as prescribed by the broadcast strategy. Processor failure may require devia tion from the strategy. Clearly, the broadcast strategy to employ in a given situa tion depends on what is to be optimized. However, use of broadcast strategies that can be represented by a subgraph of the processor interconnection graph seems rea sonable, since it minimizes message relaying.

Two common broadcast strategies are the "bush" of Figure 8.1a and the "chain" of Figure 8.1b. In some sense, these are the limiting cases of the continuum of broadcast strategies. A more complex broadcast strategy is shown in Figure 8.1c.

Fault-tolerant Broadcast Protocol

We now present a Fault-tolerant Broadcast protocol for any broadcast strategy represented by an ordered tree with root b. A copy of the protocol runs at each processor; the copy for processor b is slightly different because broadcasts are ini tiated there. Throughout, m denotes the value of the message currently being broadcast by b.

Let m_p be a local variable at processor p that contains the last message delivered to it. A fault-tolerant broadcast protocol establishes the truth of $FTB(m)$, where

$$FTB(m) \equiv (\exists p: p \in SUCC^*(\{b\}): \neg failed(p) \land m = m_p) \supset B(b,m)$$

and

$$B(j,m) \equiv (\forall p: p \in SUCC^*(\{j\}): failed(p) \lor m = m_p)$$

$FTB(m)$ is just a formal statement of the Fault-tolerant Broadcast property.

Restarting a failed processor can falsify $FTB(m)$. To avoid this problem, we postulate that once a processor has failed, it remains failed. A *restart protocol* can be defined that allows a processor to be reintegrated into the system. Such a proto col is described in [Schneider 84b].

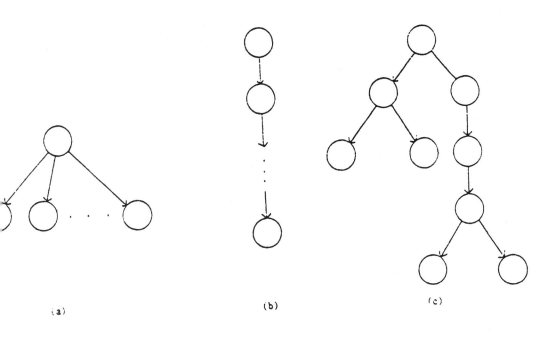

Figure 8.1: Some Broadcast Strategies.

Assuming the Transmitter does not Fail. We begin by assuming that the transmitter b does not fail, but other processors may. Thus, at least one functioning processor—b—has received m, so in order to make $FTB(m)$ true, $B(b,m)$ must be established. To do this, we employ a divide-and-conquer strategy. When a processor i receives m and stores it in its local variable m_i, its duty is to establish $B(i,m)$—to make sure that all functioning members of its subtree receive m—and then to acknowledge it. Upon receipt of m, i relays it to every processor p in $SUCC(\{i\})$. Each of these establishes $B(p,m)$ and then returns an acknowledgement to i. When (and if) all these acknowledgements are received by i, $B(i,m)$ has been established and an acknowledgement can be sent.

When a processor p from which i is expecting an acknowledgement for m fails, there is no guarantee that processors in p's subtree have received m. Therefore, upon detecting that p has failed, i sends m to all processors in $SUCC(\{p\})$, which is always possible due to the Reliable Communications Property, and waits for acknowledgements from these processors instead of from p.

Assuming the Transmitter may Fail. We now investigate the complications that arise when b may fail. If b fails and no other functioning processor has received m, $FTB(m)$ is true (the antecedent is false), so the broadcast is completed. Otherwise, some functioning processor that received m must establish $B(b,m)$. Since no harm is done if $B(b,m)$ is established by more than one processor, we allow more than one to establish it. However, this means that i may receive more than one copy of m, each corresponding to a request for i to establish $B(i,m)$, and must respond to each with an acknowledgement. In order to return these acknowledgements, processor i maintains a variable containing the set of processors to which acknowledgements must be sent. Thus, three set-valued variables are used by each processor:

$sendto$ $\equiv$ the set of processors to which m_i must be sent;

$ackfrom$ $\equiv$ the set of processors from which acknowledgements for m_i are awaited;

$ackto$ $\equiv$ the set of processors that sent m_i to i for which acknowledgements must be returned.

After receiving m, process i monitors b until it recognizes that $failed(b)$ or that $FTB(m)$ is true. Therefore, some means must be found to notify processes that $FTB(m)$ is true. Unfortunately, performing this notification is equivalent to performing a fault-tolerant broadcast! The way out of this dilemma is to use a sequence number in each message and require that b does not initiate a broadcast until its previous broadcast has been completed.[2] Now, receipt by process i of a message m' with a higher sequence number than that of the last message it received originated by the transmitter means that the broadcast of the last message has completed. Thus, b can notify processes of completion of a broadcast simply by initiating the next one. Unfortunately, this means that there is always some uncertainty

---

[2]This is not really a restriction. A processor can have several identities and can concurrently run a separate instance of the protocol for each identity. This allows that processor to concurrently perform multiple broadcasts.

about the completion of the last broadcast.

As it now stands, each processor monitors b. This is not necessary. If b fails before $B(b,m)$ is established, then some functioning processor must have received the message from a processor that subsequently failed. This allows each processor to monitor the one from which it received m instead of monitoring b. However, now more than one processor may attempt to establish $B(b,m)$, even if b does not fail.

To summarize the protocol:

Fault-tolerant Broadcast Protocol:

Upon receipt of a message m from processor p, processor i establishes $B(i,m)$ and acknowledges m. Thereafter, i monitors p and, if p fails, i attempts to establish $B(b,m)$.

A Detailed Implementation

An implementation of the protocol outlined above appears in Figure 8.2. There, processors communicate by exchanging *messages* and *acknowledgements*. Each message m contains the following information:

$m.sender$ the name of the processor that sent m.

$m.info$ the information being broadcast.

$m.seqno$ a sequence number assigned to the message by the processor b that initiates the broadcast.

Let m be a message. Execution of the asynchronous send

$$\textbf{send } msg(m) \textbf{ to } q$$

by processor p sends a message m' to q with $m'.sender = p$, $m'.info = m.info$ and $m'.seqno = m.seqno$. Execution does not delay p.

Execution of

$$??msg(m)$$

by a processor delays that processor until a message is delivered; then that message is stored in variable m.

Acknowledgements are sent and received using the same primitives, except $ack(m)$ is used in place of $msg(m)$.

$m := (sender: b,\ info:nil,\ seqno: 0);$
$ackto,\ sendto,\ ackfrom := \Phi,\ \Phi,\ \Phi;$
$r := i;$
$\textbf{do }\ sendto \neq \Phi \ \rightarrow\ dest := choose(sendto);$
$\qquad\qquad\qquad sendto := sendto - \{dest\};$
$\qquad\qquad\qquad \textbf{if } dest = i \ \rightarrow\ skip$
$\qquad\qquad\qquad [\!]\ dest \neq i \ \rightarrow\ ackfrom := ackfrom \cup \{dest\};$
$\qquad\qquad\qquad\qquad\qquad\qquad dest\,!!msg(m)$
$\qquad\qquad\qquad \textbf{fi}$
$[\!]\ ackfrom \cap FAILED \neq \Phi \ \rightarrow\ t := ackfrom \cap FAILED;$
$\qquad\qquad\qquad\qquad\qquad\qquad sendto := sendto \cup SUCC(t);$
$\qquad\qquad\qquad\qquad\qquad\qquad ackfrom := ackfrom - t;$
$[\!]\ ??ack(a) \ \rightarrow\ \textbf{if } a.seqno = m.seqno \ \rightarrow\ ackfrom := ackfrom - \{a.sender\}$
$\qquad\qquad\qquad\qquad [\!]\ a.seqno < m.seqno \ \rightarrow\ skip$
$\qquad\qquad\qquad \textbf{fi}$
$[\!]\ m.sender \in FAILED \ \wedge\ r \neq b \ \wedge\ ackfrom = \Phi \wedge\ sendto = \Phi \ \rightarrow$
$\qquad\qquad\qquad\qquad\qquad\qquad\qquad\qquad r,\ sendto := b,\ SUCC(\{b\});$
$[\!]\ ??msg(new) \ \rightarrow\ \textbf{if } new.seqno = m.seqno \ \rightarrow\ ackto := ackto \cup \{new.sender\}$
$\qquad\qquad\qquad\qquad [\!]\ new.seqno < m.seqno \ \rightarrow\ new.sender\,!!ack(new)$
$\qquad\qquad\qquad\qquad [\!]\ new.seqno > m.seqno \ \rightarrow\ \textbf{forall } p \in ackto:$
$\qquad\qquad\qquad\qquad\qquad\qquad\qquad\qquad \textbf{send } ack(m) \textbf{ to } p$
$\qquad\qquad\qquad\qquad\qquad\qquad\qquad m,\ r := new,\ i;$
$\qquad\qquad\qquad\qquad\qquad\qquad\qquad ackto := \{m.sender\};$
$\qquad\qquad\qquad\qquad\qquad\qquad\qquad sendto := SUCC(\{i\});$
$\qquad\qquad\qquad\qquad\qquad\qquad\qquad ackfrom := \Phi$
$\qquad\qquad\qquad \textbf{fi}$
$[\!]\ ackto \neq \Phi \ \wedge\ (r = b \vee (sendto = \Phi \wedge ackfrom = \Phi)) \ \rightarrow\ \textbf{forall } p \in ackto:$
$\qquad\qquad\qquad\qquad\qquad\qquad\qquad\qquad\qquad\qquad \textbf{send } ack(m) \textbf{ to } p;$
$\qquad\qquad\qquad\qquad\qquad\qquad\qquad\qquad\qquad\qquad ackto := \Phi$
$\textbf{od}$

For processor b, the guarded command beginning with $m.sender \in FAILED$ is replaced by
the following guarded command:

$ackfrom = \Phi \ \wedge\ sendto = \Phi \rightarrow$ Delay until a new message m is ready to be broadcast;
$\qquad\qquad\qquad\qquad\qquad \text{Increment } seqno;$
$\qquad\qquad\qquad\qquad\qquad sendto := SUCC(\{b\})$

Figure 8.2: Fault-tolerant Broadcast Protocol for Processor i.

This notation is inspired by the input and output commands of CSP [Hoare 78]. As in CSP, we allow receive commands (??) to appear in the guards of guarded commands. Such a guard is never false; it is true only if execution of the receive would not cause a delay. In our notation, two queries (??) are used, instead of one, to indicate that messages are buffered by the communications network and therefore a sender is never delayed. Also, in contrast to CSP, the sender names the receiver but the receiver does not name the sender.

Finally, we use *FAILED* to record the set of processes p for which *failed(p)* is true. It should be clear from the way *FAILED* is used in the program that the entire set does not have to be computed and maintained at each site—our use of the set variable merely simplifies the presentation.

8.1.2. Byzantine Agreement

We now consider the problem of establishing agreement when no assertion can be made about the behavior of faulty processors. To simplify the problem a bit, let us assume that clocks on non-faulty processors are approximately synchronized, message delivery time is bounded, and that every message is "signed" by its sender with an unforgeable signature that is a function of the contents of the message and the identity of the sender. The assumption about clocks is reasonable since fault-tolerant clock synchronization algorithms exist [Lamport 84b, Halpern 84] and a processor with a clock that runs too quickly or too slowly can be considered faulty. The message delivery time assumption is also reasonable: one simply must ensure that the network has sufficient capacity to handle the load. Finally, the assumption that messages are "signed" can be approximated by using digital signatures [Rivest 78].

The fact that a faulty processor can exhibit arbitrary behavior considerably complicates the design of an agreement protocol. Recall that in the Fault-tolerant Broadcast protocol, each message contained the same value. The problem was to arrange for all processors to receive a copy of the message despite the fact that a faulty processor would not continue relaying the message. Now, a processor that has failed might send different values to different processors. Therefore, care must be taken that all non-faulty processors agree on the same value.

Synchronous Protocol Using Signed Messages

To ensure IC1, it is sufficient that when the protocol terminates the set of values received by each non-faulty processor is the same, because then each processor can compute some deterministic function on the contents of this set and obtain a value on which all will agree. However, the details of this and ensuring that IC2 also holds are subtle.

For one thing, faulty processors might selectively fail to relay values. Then, a processor might be forever delayed awaiting a value. To handle this difficulty, the assumptions made above about clock speeds and message delivery delays are exploited. Approximately synchronized clocks and bounded message delivery delays allow a processor to determine when it can expect no further messages from non-faulty processors. Thus, no (faulty) processor can cause another to be delayed indefinitely awaiting a message that will never arrive.

A second problem is that a faulty processor might relay different values to different processors. However, use of signed messages prevents a (faulty) processor p from forging a message. If p receives a message m from q, then an attempt by p to change the contents of m before relaying the message will not succeed: q will have signed the message and so p's tampering with its contents will invalidate q's signature, which would be detectable by any recipient of the message. Thus, by using signatures we can ensure that the values received by a processor are a subset of the values originally sent by the transmitter.

The remaining problem is to ensure that not only are the values received by each non-faulty processor a subset of the values sent by the transmitter, but that all non-faulty processors agree on the contents of this set. This is solved by having processors sign and relay the messages they receive. It turns out that if at most t processors can be faulty, then $t+1$ rounds of message relay suffice. The reasons for this are shown in the proof below.

Putting all this together, we get the following protocol for Byzantine Agreement, assuming there are no more than t faulty processors in the system.

Byzantine Agreement:

The transmitter signs and sends a copy of its value to every processor.

Every other processor p performs $t+1$ rounds, as follows.[3] Whenever p

---

[3]Since the clocks on non-faulty processors are approximately synchronized and message delivery time is bounded, each processor can independently determine when each round starts and finishes.

receives a message with a signature that indicates the message has not been modified, it adds the value in that message to V_p the set of values it has received, appends its signature to the message, and relays the signed message to all processors that have not already signed it.

At the end of the $t + 1^{st}$ round, to select the agreed upon value, each processor computes the same given deterministic function on its set V_p.

We now give an informal proof that the protocol satisfies IC1 and IC2. First, we show that the protocol establishes IC1. If all non-faulty processors p have the same set of values V_p at the end of the protocol then they will agree on the same value because each applies the same deterministic function to V_p to compute that value.

Consider a value placed in V_p by p in round r of the protocol, where $r \leq t$. Thus, a correctly signed message m that is signed by processors $p_1, p_2, ..., p_k$ must have been received by p at the beginning of round r. Clearly, $p_1, p_2, ..., p_k$ have received m, so m has been stored in the set of values associated with each of those processors. Since p is non-faulty, it will sign and relay m to all other processors. Thus, by round $r + 1$, all processors will have received a copy of m.

Now consider a value placed in V_p in round $t + 1$ as a result of receiving a message m in round $t + 1$. Such a message must already contain $t + 1$ signatures. By hypothesis, at most t processors are faulty, so at least one non-faulty processor received the message in an earlier round. According to the protocol, this non-faulty processor will relay the message to all others. Thus, by round $t + 1$ all non-faulty processors will receive a copy of the message.

We now show that the protocol establishes IC2. If the transmitter is non-faulty, then it will send the same value to every processor. Thus, this value will be included in the set of values received by each non-faulty processor. Since a processor cannot undetectably modify the contents of a message it has received prior to forwarding it, no processor p will put any value other than this one in its set of values V_p.

Other Excursions Into Byzantium

Protocols have been devised for Byzantine Agreement in a variety of environments. A survey of these appears in [Strong 83]. Interactive consistency was first identified in designing a fault-tolerant computing system for fly-by-wire aircraft

[Pease 80]. The name Byzantine Agreement has its origins in a metaphor describe in [Lamport 82b] involving generals of the Byzantine Army who are trying to coordinate an attack, despite traitors in their ranks.

To date, a number of fundamental constraints have been identified for achieving Byzantine Agreement. [Pease 80] proves that without signed messages, no protocol exists that will work in the presence of one third or more faulty processors. The startling (and disturbing) consequence of this result is that majority logic and triple-modular redundancy (tmr) won't always work when failures can result in arbitrary behavior, unless signed messages are used. This is because tmr implicitly assumes that all units process the same input, and it is not possible for only three processors to achieve Byzantine Agreement on their input without using signed messages.

Whether or not authentication is available, a Byzantine Agreement protocol must perform at least $t + 1$ rounds of information exchange [Dolev 82a, 82b]. However, it is possible to reach agreement in fewer than $t + 1$ rounds if fewer than t processors are faulty, assuming processors need not all decide on their value in the same round [Dolev 82c].

8.1.3. Commitment

It is not unusual in a distributed system to coordinate a collection of actions at different processors so that all actions occur or none do. For example, when a file is replicated at several processors, update information must be propagated in such a way that all copies or no copy of the file is updated, thereby ensuring the copies remain identical. Or, in an Argus program, the result of executing a collection of nested actions must be visible at all sites or at no site. In both these examples, the fundamental problem is agreement on whether or not to perform an action. The new complication is that the transmitter does not know *a priori* what value will be agreed upon. In the replicated file example, one of the processors may be unable to update the file for one reason or another; in an Argus program, an action may have already aborted and so other actions must not be allowed to install their effects.

Commit Protocol Sampler

A *commit protocol* is an agreement protocol in which the value agreed upon is computed by applying a *decision function* to the values the participants. Thus, a commit protocol establishes:

Commit Requirements:

    CP1: All non-faulty processors agree on some value (as per IC1).

    CP2: The value agreed upon is the result of applying a decision function to the values of all participants.

Contrast this with the agreement protocols described above, where the value agreed upon is determined by the transmitter alone. Nevertheless, given an agreement protocol and a decision function, it is a simple matter to construct a commit protocol.

The following is a simple Commit Protocol. Notice that there is a special process called the coordinator that serves only to get things started.

Decentralized Commit:

    1. The coordinator uses an agreement protocol to disseminate its value to all other processors.

    2. Upon receipt of this, each processor uses an agreement protocol to disseminate its value to all other processors.

    3. Each processor then uses the decision function on the values proposed by other processors to decide upon a value.

To see that Decentralized Commit satisfies CP1 and CP2, note the following. According to step 3, each non-faulty processor will arrive at the same decision if each has received the same proposed values. Therefore, CP2 will hold. The agreement protocol in step 2 ensures that all non-faulty processors agree on the proposed value of every processor that executes step 2. Thus, CP1 will hold provided all non-faulty processors agree on whether or not to execute step 2. Step 1 ensures that all non-faulty processors will agree on whether to execute step 2, since all will agree on receiving a value from the coordinator.

Note that the Decentralized Commit protocol can be used with either fail-stop processors or processors that can exhibit arbitrary behavior as a result of a failure. In the fail-stop case, the Fault-tolerant Broadcast Protocol of section 8.1.1 is used as the agreement protocol; in the other case, the Byzantine Agreement protocol of section 8.1.2 is used.

By making assumptions about the reliability of some of the processors, it is possible to implement a commit protocol that avoids much of the work of Decentralized Commit. By assuming that the coordinator does not fail during execution of the entire protocol, the agreement protocols in step 1 and 2 can be replaced: it suffices for the coordinator to send a message to each processor and receive its reply. In addition, we can depend on a reliable coordinator to decide on a value and dissem inate it, instead of having each processor independently make that decision. Th result is the classic two-phase commit protocol [Gray 79].

Two-Phase Commit:

1. The coordinator sends to each processor a request for its proposed value.

2. Upon receipt of this, each processor replys to the coordinator with a proposed value.

3. The coordinator uses the decision function on the values proposed by processors to decide upon a value. It then sends to all other processors the action it decided upon.

Related Work

Commit protocols have received considerable study by researchers studying database systems. The Two-Phase commit protocol was first described in writing by Lampson [Lampson 76]. It is also discussed in [Gray 79]. Skeen [Skeen 82] generalized this work and proposed a family of protocols that are resilient to more general types of failures. Practical protocols based on Byzantine Agreement are described in [Dolev 82d, Mohan 83].

8.2. The State Machine Approach

One of the reasons it is difficult to design distributed programs is because message passing, the only way processes can communicate in a distributed system involves substantial delivery delays relative to process execution speeds. Thus receipt of a message reveals information about a past state of the sender and not necessarily the sender's current state. Consequently, the state of the system can be known to no process.

In this section, we describe a way convert a program that solves a problem in the absence of failures into a version that is fault-tolerant and runs on a distributed system. The approach is based on replication and has proven particularly useful for implementing synchronization in distributed systems.

8.2.1. State Machines

A *state machine* cyclically reads its input, performs some computation based on its current state and that input, and generates some output. Any sequential program can be structured as a state machine. For example, a process control program structured in this way is shown in Figure 8.3. Here, sensors are the *source* of the input to the state machine, and actuators are the *destination* of the output.

Any concurrent program can be structured as a collection of concurrent processes that interact by making requests and awaiting replies from a state machine. Processes are the *source* of input to the state machine as well as the *destination* for its output. A shared memory is a primitive example of such a state machine, a communications network another example, and the transaction manager of a distributed database system is a third example.

When a concurrent program is viewed in terms of a state machine, a process makes a request of the state machine whenever

(1) it needs to be delayed until the system state is conducive to continued execution,

(2) it has changed the system state, and consequently there might be delayed processes that can continue executing, or

(3) it needs information about the state of the system to determine how to proceed.

Uses (1) and (2) allow the state machine to synchronize processes. Use (3) allows the state machine to control what processes do.

$$
\begin{aligned}
proc\_cntl: \ &\textbf{do } true \rightarrow \ \text{read from sensors ;} \\
&\qquad\qquad\qquad \text{compute output ;} \\
&\qquad\qquad\qquad \text{write output to actuators} \\
&\textbf{od}
\end{aligned}
$$

Figure 8.3: State Machine for Process Control.

An example of a state machine that controls a collection of concurrent processes is shown in Figure 8.4. It allows the set of *client* processes *SYS* to decide on whether to install or discard an update.[4] For simplicity, we have assumed that all processes already know about the update and that only one update is considered at a time. Thus, the state machine merely ensures that an update is installed if and only if all processes consent.

To use *commit*, a client registers whether or not it can install the update by making a request of the appropriate type:

install   if the requester can install the update, and

discard   if the requester cannot install the update.

After making a request, the client waits for a reply from the state machine and proceeds accordingly.

Note that the *commit* state machine is designed to tolerate invalid requests by processes. Thus, in some sense, it is fault-tolerant. However, if some process in

```
commit:  var vote_install, vote_discard : set of process,
             outcome : (install, discard);
         vote_install := Φ;  vote_discard := Φ;
         do  true → receive(request);
             if request.type =install → vote_install := vote_install ∪ request.sender
             ▯ request.type =discard → vote_discard := vote_discard ∪ request.se
             ▯ else → skip
             fi;
             if (vote_install ∪ vote_discard)=SYS →
                         outcome := decision_function(vote_install, vote_disca
                         forall p ∈ SYS:
                            send outcome to p
                         vote_install := Φ;  vote_discard := Φ
             ▯ else → skip
             fi
         od
```

Figure 8.4: State Machine for Commit.

---

[4]Recall from section 8.1.3 that this is exactly the task performed by a commit protocol.

SYS makes no request, no decision will ever be made by *commit*, and all processes will remain delayed. This can be avoided by adding a *timeout transition* to the machine. Such a transition, which would be triggered by a real-time clock instead of an explicit request from a client, can be thought of as a request made by the state machine to itself. In this case, the prudent course would be for the timeout transition to cause the update to be discarded.

8.2.2. Fault-tolerance: Replicating the State Machine

There are problems with using a single state machine when fault-tolerance is desired, because the processor executing the state machine could fail. A state machine executing on a faulty processor might generate incorrect output or no output at all. To avoid this, we will replicate the state machine and run a copy of it on several processors in the system. Provided each instance executed on a non-faulty processor starts in the same state and reads the same input, each instance will independently generate the same output. However, unless fail-stop processors are used, instances of the state machine running on faulty processors may generate different (incorrect) outputs. One way for a destination to choose among the different outputs is to take the majority value. This means that "correct" output will be chosen by a destination provided a majority of the processors running instances of the state machine are non-faulty.

Notice that we have devised a simple way for constructing a distributed computing system that performs the same computation as a single state machine, but can tolerate a bounded number of failures. In particular, a system with $2f+1$ processors can tolerate as many as f faulty processors.

It is easy to ensure that each instance of a state machine starts in the same state by use of initialization code. Each instance will receive the same input values and process them in the same order if the following hold:

Input Dissemination:

All input to the state machine is disseminated to all instances being executed by non-faulty processors.

Input Order:

Input values are processed in the same order by all instances of the state machine being executed by non-faulty processors.

The Input Dissemination Property will hold if a protocol that establishes Interactive Consistency (section 8.1) is employed by each source in disseminating input to instances of the state machine. Since sensors and other input devices do not implement such protocols directly, in the following we will assume that all input sources are processes. Sensor input is obtained by the state machine from a process that reads that sensor and then executes an appropriate agreement protocol.

Two ways to satisfy the Input Dissemination and Input Order properties are discussed below. One is based on logical clocks and makes no assumptions about message delivery delays or relative speeds of processes, but assumes fail-stop processors. The other involves assumptions about delivery delays and execution speeds, but makes no assumption about the behavior of faulty processors.

Coordinating Replicated State Machines on Fail-stop Processors

In a system of fail-stop processors, the Fault-tolerant Broadcast protocol of section 8.1.1 can be used to satisfy the Input Dissemination Property. In order to satisfy the Input Order property, logical clocks can be used. A *logical clock* [Lamport 78a] is a mapping from events to the integers. $C(E)$, the "time" assigned to an event E by logical clock C is such that for any distinct events E and F, either $C(E) < C(F)$ or $C(F) < C(E)$, and if E might be responsible for causing F then $C(E) < C(F)$.

It is a simple matter to implement logical clocks in a distributed system. Associated with each process p is a counter $c(p)$. A *timestamp* is included in each message sent by p. This timestamp is the value of $c(p)$ when the message is sent. In addition, $c(p)$ is changed according to:

CU1: $c(p)$ is incremented after each event at p.

CU2: Upon receipt of a message with timestamp r, process p resets $c(p)$:
$$c(p) := \max(c(p), r) + 1.$$

The value of $C(E)$ is the value of $c(s)$ when the event occurs, followed by a fixed-length bit string that uniquely identifies s, where s is the processor on which the event occurred.

Notice that timestamps on messages define a fixed order on the input values contained in those messages. Unfortunately, the Input Order property is not satisfied if each instance of the state machine takes the input values it has received and processes them in ascending order by timestamp. This is because these values could be delivered to different state machine instances in different orders. After receiving an input value some input value with smaller timestamp might be delivered to that instance. Therefore, we must devise a way to delay a state machine instance from processing an input value if the possibility exists that one with lower timestamp might still be delivered to that instance.

We shall say that an input value is *stable at p* once no input value with lower timestamp can be delivered to the state machine instance running on processor p. If we make the following Delivery Order Assumption, then a simple test for stability exists.

Delivery Order Assumption:

Messages originated by a given input source are received by each instance of the state machine in the order sent.

The test for stability is:

Logical Clock Input Stability Test:

An input value is stable at p if an input value with larger timestamp has been received by p from every input source.

The proof that this test ensures request stability follows directly from the Delivery Order Assumption and the definition of logical clocks. A message sent by a source must have a greater timestamp than any previous message sent by that source because the "times" assigned to events according to a logical clock are consistent with potential causality. According to the Delivery Order Assumption, messages from a given source will be received in the order sent. Thus, once a message is received by an instance of the state machine from a source s, no message from s with smaller timestamp can be received.

One last problem remains with our Logical Clock Input Stability Test. For an input to be processed, it must eventually satisfy the stability test. Unfortunately, if a processor fails, processes running on it will not send messages, since a fail-stop processor halts in response to a failure. If one of these processes is a source then requests made by no source will be able to pass the Logical Clock Input Stability Test, since the required higher-timestamped input values will not be forthcoming. Thus, no instance of the state machine will be able to make progress.

To deal with this problem, we modify the stability test. Recall that failure of a fail-stop processor is detectable by other processors. In addition, it is reasonable to make the following Failure Detection Assumption due to the Delivery Order

Assumption and the fact that failure detection is typically implemented by using timeouts on the communications channel between p and q.

Failure Detection Assumption:

A processor p will detect failure of another processor q only after p has received the last message sent to p by q.

Since no input value can be forthcoming from a source running on a faulty (stopped) processor, faulty fail-stop processors are not capable of activity that could violate stability. Thus, an instance of the state machine need not wait for higher timestamped messages from sources running on failed processors, and the Logical Clock Input Stability Test can be weakened to the following, which allows progress to be made even if there are failures.

Logical Clock Input Stability Test With Failures:

An input value is stable at p if an input value with larger timestamp has been received by p from every source running on a processor not known to have failed.

This test can be formalized as a predicate $STBL(m,p)$ that is true if and only if the input value in message m is stable at p. In $STBL(m,p)$, ALL is the set of processors on which source processes execute, $FAILED(p)$ is the set of processors that p has found to be faulty, $m.sender$ is the processor running the process that sent message m, and $t(m)$ is the timestamp on message m.

$$STBL(p,m): \quad (\forall q: q \in (ALL-FAILED(p)):$$
$$(\exists m': m' \text{ received by } p \ \wedge \ m'.sender = q: t(m') \geq t(m)))$$

Provided $STBL(p,m)$ holds for any input value m that is processed by a state machine instance and input values are processed in ascending order by timestamp, the desired Input Order Property will hold. A proof of this can be found in [Schneider 82].

Coordinating Replicated State Machines on Malevolent Processors

We now turn to the problem of satisfying the Input Dissemination and Input Order Properties in systems where faulty processors can exhibit arbitrary behavior.

In most distributed systems, it is reasonable to assume both that a bound exists on the length of time it takes a message sent by one processor to be received by another and that execution speeds of processes executed on non-faulty processes are relatively close. These assumptions make it possible to keep the clocks on non faulty processors approximately synchronized, as shown in [Lamport 84b, Halpern 84]. The assumptions also allow construction of an agreement protocol that establishes

Real-Time Interactive Consistency:

If a transmitter p initiates the broadcast of a value at time τ on its clock then:

RT-IC1: Each non-faulty processor agrees on some value by time $\tau + \Delta$ on its clock.

RT-IC2: If the transmitter is non-faulty then all non-faulty processors use its value as the one they agree on.

Parameter Δ is determined by the end-to-end delivery delay δ and ϵ the upper bound on the time difference of two (synchronized) clocks on non-faulty processors.

An agreement protocol that establishes RT-IC1 and RT-IC2 can be implemented along the same lines as the Byzantine Agreement protocol in section 8.1.2. As before, a process will "sign" every message it sends to another process, which allows the receiver to reject any message that has been tampered with. In addition, for Real-Time Interactive Consistency, a process will include in every message a timestamp τ with the time that message was sent (according to the sender's clock), and the receiver will reject a message received at time T on its clock, if $\tau < T - \delta - \epsilon$. Thus, we are treating the late arrival of a message as a failure of the sender, and can do so because processor clocks are synchronized within ϵ and message delivery delay is known to be bounded by δ when no failures occur.

We can use an agreement protocol that establishes Real-Time Interactive Consistency to satisfy the Input Dissemination Property, since RT-IC1 and RT-IC2 imply the Input Dissemination Property.

To satisfy the Input Order property, each source uses the (real-time) clock on its processor to obtain a timestamp for each input value it provides to the state machine. Assuming that these clocks have sufficient resolution to ensure that two input values from the same source are assigned different timestamps, the timestamps will define a fixed order on input values. (Two input values with the same timestamp must come from different sources. Such inputs are ordered according to the names of their sources, as was done with logical clocks.) However, as before, it is not sufficient for state machine instances to receive input values and process them in ascending order by timestamp. We must be sure that if an instance of the state machine processes an input value, no input with smaller timestamp will be received—we must ensure that an input value is processed only after it becomes stable.

Testing for stability of an input value is accomplished by exploiting the real time bound Δ in RT-IC2. If input values are disseminated using an agreement protocol that satisfies RT-IC2 in a system where clocks are (approximately) synchronized, then once the clock on a processor p reads time T, p cannot subsequently receive an input value with timestamp less than $T - \Delta$. Therefore, a stability test for use with processors that can exhibit arbitrary behavior when they fail is:

Input Stability Test with Malevolent Failures:

An input value is stable at p if the timestamp on the input value is τ and the clock at p has a value greater than $\tau + \Delta$.

Provided the Input Stability Test with Malevolent Failures holds for any input value that is processed by a state machine instance and input values are processed in ascending order by timestamp, the desired Input Order Property will hold. A proof of this can be found in [Lamport 84a].

Reconfiguration and Restart

When the state machine approach is used, the mean time between system failures can be increased by removing faulty processors from the system and reintegrating repaired processors. Correct output will be produced by a majority of the state machines instances when each instance runs on a separate processor, provided a majority of those processors are non-faulty. If faulty processors are removed from the system, then it is possible for a majority of the processors in the system to be non-faulty long after a majority of the processors in the original system have failed. Of course, one cannot remove faulty processors from a finite system indefinitely. Therefore, it is desirable to be able to reintegrate repaired processors into the system. This also increases the resilience of the system to concurrent failures, since a system consisting of $2f + 1$ processors can tolerate as many as f concurrent failures.

The cost of satisfying the Input Dissemination property provides a second reason it is efficacious to remove faulty processors from a system. The cost of executing an agreement protocol is a function of the number of processors that must agree. Since in satisfying the Request Dissemination property we don't care whether a state machine instance being executed by a faulty processor agrees on the input value, removing such processors from the system allows reduction in the cost of the agreement protocol.

Reconfiguration of a state machine—adding or deleting a state machine instance, a source process, or a destination—is quite simple. Each state machine instance stores the name and location of every state machine instance, source process, and destination comprising the state machine. Reconfiguration of a state machine is accomplished by making a request to the state machine. The state machine then informs all sources and destinations of the change in configuration before actually putting it into effect. Sources are informed so that they can include the correct state machine instances in the agreement protocol used to disseminate an input value; destinations are informed so that they know from which state machine instances output can be expected, and how many instances define a majority for the new configuration.

In order to reintegrate a repaired processor into the system, instances of state machines must be started at that processor. A state machine is *self-stablizing* [Dijkstra 74] if its current state is completely defined by the previous k inputs it has processed, for some fixed k. An instance of a state machine that is self-stablizing will generate the same output as the other instances of that state machine after processing k inputs, provided the instance receives the same input values and processes them in the same order as the other instances. Thus, after handling k inputs, a state machine instance that is self-stablizing is completely integrated into the system. Unfortunately, the design of self-stablizing state machines is very difficult.

The following scheme can be used to restart a state machine that is not self-stablizing. Let Q_t be the state of the state machine in question at time t. Then, to start an instance of a state machine at time t', it is sufficient that the instance be started in state Q_t and that it receive every input value with timestamps t through t'. State Q_t can be obtained from another instance of the state machine; the messages containing values with timestamps t through t' will be received if the relevant change to the configuration has been made. Details for this scheme are described in [Schneider 82] for systems for fail-stop processors and [Lamport 84a] for processors that can exhibit arbitrary behavior as a result of a failure.

8.2.3. Discussion

The state machine approach has was first described in [Lamport 78a] for environments in which failures could not occur. That work was extended in [Schneider 82] for systems of fail-stop processors and in [Lamport 78b] for systems in which arbitrary behavior could result from a failure. The state machine approach has been applied to the design of a fault-tolerant process control applications [Wensley 78], and more recently, it has been used in the design of a fail-stop processor approximations in terms of processors that can exhibit arbitrary behavior in response to a failure [Schlichting 83, Schneider 84a].

Most synchronization protocols for distributed systems can be derived by using the state machine approach and then applying application dependent optimizations For example, the Decentralized Commit protocol of section 8.1.3 is based on the state machine of Figure 8.4. Distributed read/write locks and distributed semaphores have been constructed using the state machine approach, and are described in [Schneider 80]; a decentralized implementation of input/output guards for CSP and conditional Ada SELECT statements is described in [Schneider 82].

8.3. Computing Global States

8.3.1. Introduction

In Section 2.2, we saw that there are two different ways to describe a distributed system: the space-time view and the interleaving view. The interleaving view is based upon a total ordering of system events, and uses the concept of a global system state. The space-time view is more natural in the sense that it more accurately describes physical reality. In the space-time view, one has a set of events which are partially ordered by causality connections—for example, the requirement that a message be sent before it is received. The total ordering of the interleaving view, with its resulting global states, is a mathematical fiction that is not directly observable.

While the global states of the interleaving view are a fiction, they are a very useful fiction. For a distributed banking system, it is convenient to be able to say that the total assets of the bank is x dollars, meaning that the sum of all account balances equals x *in the current state*. While the current global state is a mathematical fiction, it is intuitively clear that the statement that there are x dollars in the bank is meaningful. We now investigate its meaning by describing the connection between the interleaving and space-time views. As a result of this investigation, we will derive an algorithm for computing the global state of a distributed system and give some applications. A more complete discussion of the algorithm can be found in [Chandy 84]

8.3.2. The Two Views

We consider a specific model of a distributed system consisting of a network of processes connected by unidirectional channels over which messages can be sent. An example of a network containing three processes p, q and r and four channels C_{pq}, C_{qp}, C_{qr} and C_{rq} is given in Figure 8.5. We assume that the channels are lossless and that

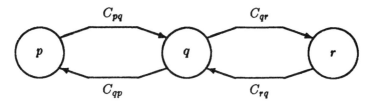

Figure 8.5: An example of a network

messages are delivered in the order they are sent.

There are three kinds of events in the system:

- The sending of a message.

- The receipt of a message.

- A "spontaneous" event within a process.

The third class includes everything that happens other than the sending and receiving of system messages. Such an event may be generated by an interaction with the outside world—for example, by a user typing a command on his terminal—or it may be a purely internal—for example, generated by a timeout.

Each event occurs in a process. Since a process is localized, we can, in principle, observe its entire state at one time. Therefore, we assume that a process has a state, which is changed only by events in that process. Formally, an event consists of the following:

- The type of event and the process in which it occurs.

- A pair of states—the initial and final states.

- For a send event, the message and the channel over which it is sent.

- For a receive event, the message and the channel over which it is received.

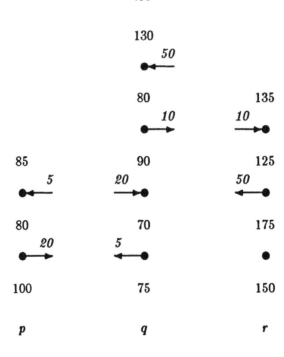

Figure 8.6: A set of processes and events.

Since a process is localized, we can also observe the order in which events at the process occur. Therefore, for each process, we assume a starting state and a sequencing of the events $e_1, e_2, \ldots$ in that process such that the starting state of e_i is the ending state of e_{i-1}, or the initial state if $i = 1$.

An example of such a set of events and processes is a distributed banking system based upon the network of Figure 8.5. Each process is a branch of the bank, and the state of the process indicates the total amount of money on deposit in the bank. A message represents the transfer of funds from one branch to another. The set of events is shown in Figure 8.6. The dots represent events, the sequence of events within a process being read from bottom to top. The numbers written between events represent the process states. Thus, process q begins in an initial state with $75 on deposit. Its first event is the sending of $5 to process p on channel C_{qp}, which reduces the amount on deposit to $70. The second event in process q is the receipt of $20 from process p over channel C_{pq}, and its third event is the sending of $10 to process r over channel C_{qr}. The only internal event in this picture is the first event of process r, which adds $25 to its assets—presumably the result of a deposit by a customer.

Not every such set of events describes the execution of a system. For example,

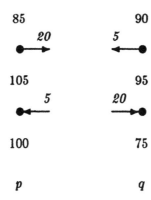

Figure 8.7: An impossible set of events

consider the two processes and four events described in Figure 8.7. A little thought will reveal that there is no way such a set of events could have occurred.

Given such a set of process states and events, what conditions must it satisfy to represent a possible system execution? Our two different views of distributed systems provide two apparently different answers to this question. To construct the space-time view of the system, we require a 1-1 correspondence η that associates the event of sending a message with the event of receiving that message. Formally, we add a mapping η from the set of message-send events to the set of message-receive events satisfying the following properties.

1. η is a 1-1 correspondence.

2. If e is an event that sends message m over a channel c, then $\eta(e)$ is an event that receives message m from channel c.

3. If e and f are two events in a process p that send messages over the same channel c to a process q such that e precedes f (in the sequencing of the events of p), then $\eta(e)$ precedes $\eta(f)$ (in the sequencing of the events of q).

The last condition is the formal statement of the assumption that messages over a single channel are received in the same order in which they are sent.

The existence of the mapping η does not guarantee that a set of process events is a possible system history. For example, such a mapping is easily defined for the example of Figure 8.7. However, given η, we can define a relation $\rightarrow$ on the set of events to be the smallest transitively closed relation such that:

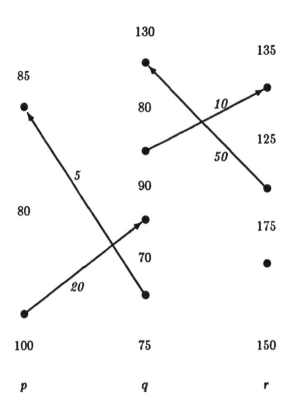

Figure 8.8: A space-time picture of the events of Figure 8.6.

- If e and f are distinct events in the same process and e precedes f in the sequencing of the events in that process, then $e \rightarrow f$.

- For any message-sending event e: $e \rightarrow \eta(e)$.

A necessary and sufficient condition for the set of events to be a possible system history is that the relation $\rightarrow$ be an irreflexive partial ordering. (Since $\rightarrow$ is, by definition, transitively closed, this is equivalent to the assumption that there are no cycles.)

For the set of events in Figure 8.6, we can define η as shown in Figure 8.8, where we have drawn an arrow from a message-sending event e to the corresponding receive event $\eta(e)$. Note that the set of events in Figure 8.7 does not satisfy this condition, since the relation $\rightarrow$ is the complete relation in which $e \rightarrow f$ for every pair of events e and f.

The interleaving view begins with the same set of processes and events. However, instead of simply assuming the correspondence η between the sending and receipt of messages, this view takes a different approach. Since there does exist a notion of global time, the events in the system "really do" take place in some definite order. For example, we can order the events by their starting times. Without infinitely precise clocks, we can never be sure what this total ordering is. However, since it must exist, we can postulate its existence.

Therefore, in the interleaving view, one assumes a *total* ordering $\Rightarrow$ on the set of events which satisfies two conditions. The first condition is that $\Rightarrow$ is consistent with the sequencing of events within the individual processes. More precisely, if e and f are distinct events in the same process and e precedes f in the sequencing of the events in that process, then $e \Rightarrow f$.

If we assume a notion of global time, we can talk about the global state of the system at a particular time, where the state consists of the state of each process and the sequences of messages in transit over each communication line. Even though this global state is not directly observable, we know that it must exist and can reason about it. Actually, to talk about global states, we don't need a concept of global time; all we need is a total ordering of the events. Given such an ordering, we can define the concept of the global state between events. The second condition that we place upon $\Rightarrow$ is that this total ordering defines a reasonable sequence of states and events.

To state this condition precisely, we need some definitions. A *global state* of the system is defined to consist of a state for each process and a sequence of messages in transit on each communication link. The global initial state consists of the initial state of each process and the empty sequence on each link. Let s_0 be the global initial state and let $e_1, e_2, \ldots$ be the set of events, ordered so that $e_1 \Rightarrow e_2 \Rightarrow \cdots$. We inductively define the global state s_i after the execution of e_i to be the same as s_{i-1} except for the following:

- If e_i is an event in process p, then the local state of p is changed to be the final state of event e_i.

- If e_i sends message m on channel c, then m is appended to the tail of the sequence of messages in that channel.

- If e_i receives a message from channel c, then the message at the head of the sequence of messages in that channel is deleted (if there is one).

What must be true for this sequence of states and events to be reasonable—that is, for it to define a global state-machine description of the system? First of all, recall that an event e_i in process p is already defined to have a starting and ending state, which are (local) states of p. In the interleaving view, we are viewing e_i to be an event that transforms the global state s_{i-1} into the new global state s_i. We have defined s_i so that the state of p in it is the final state of e_i. However, for this to be consistent with our original view of e_i as a local event at process p, we expect the state of p in s_{i-1} to be the starting state of e_i. Using the assumption that $\Rightarrow$ is consistent with the sequencing of events in each process, it is easy to show that this is the case.

Besides changing the process states, message sending and receiving events change the state of a channel. There can never be any problem with a sending event; it simply adds its message to the sequence of messages in transit over the channel. However, there can be a problem with a receive event. If e_i receives a message from channel c, then it forms the new state s_i by deleting the first message in c's sequence of in-transit messages. However, for this to make sense, the message deleted must be the message received by e_i. (Recall that the definition of a message-receiving event includes a specification of the message received.) This is the second condition that we make on the $\Rightarrow$ relation. More precisely, we require that if e_i is the event of receiving a message m from channel c, then in state s_{i-1}, m must be at the head of the sequence of messages in channel c.

As an example of such a total ordering and the sequence of global states that it generates, Figure 8.9 shows the sequence of states obtained from the system of Figure 8.8 using the total ordering implied by the positioning of the events on the page, with the higher events being later. (To be consistent with the space-time picture, the sequence of states in Figure 8.9 progresses from bottom to top.) It is easy to see that this condition cannot be satisfied by any total ordering $\Rightarrow$ of the events in Figure 8.7, since in any total ordering consistent with the ordering of events within each process, the first receive event is performed with an empty channel.

8.3.3. Global States in the Space-Time View

The interleaving view is convenient because it allows us to talk about global states. However, not only do we want to talk about global states, we also want to compute them. To construct an algorithm to determine the global state, we must turn to the space-time view. We therefore need some way to talk about global states in the space-time view.

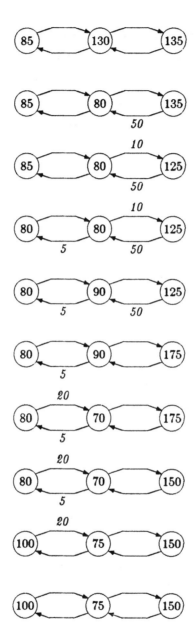

Figure 8.9: A sequence of global states for the system of Figure 8.8.

We begin by investigating the relation between the two views. Given a set of processes and events and a relation → forming a space-time view, how can we construct an interleaving view? The answer is simple. We extend → to any total ordering ⇒, and this total ordering satisfies the conditions for an interleaving view. The proof of this is straightforward and is left as an exercise to the reader. Conversely, given an interleaving view, with its total ordering ⇒, we can construct a space-time view as follows. In constructing the global states corresponding to the total ordering, we can index each message by the event that sent it. Thus, in the global state, the state of each communication line is a sequence of messages indexed by message-sending events. For each message-sending event e that sends a message m, thereby adding m_e to the sequence of messages forming the state of the appropriate channel, we define $\eta(e)$ to be the message-receiving event that removes m_e from that channel. It can be shown that this mapping η satisfies the requirements for the space-time view and, moreover, the partial ordering → that it defines is a subset of the total ordering ⇒. Again, the proof is left as an exercise for the reader.

Note that there is a unique space-time view corresponding to an interleaving view, but there are many interleaving views corresponding to a space-time view since there are many ways to complete a partial ordering to a total ordering. The space-time view contains only information that is derivable from local observations—i.e., from observations of the events at each individual process. The total ordering in the interleaving view contains view contains additional information, namely orderings between events at different processes, that cannot be derived from such local observations—at least, not without the introduction of additional mechanisms such as synchronized clocks. The partial order relation → of the space-time view contains all the information that we can deduce about the temporal ordering of events from local observations.

To define a global state in the space-time view, we define the concept of a *time slice*. Intuitively, a time slice represents the system at some instant of time. However, since we are not assuming any type of clocks, we must define this concept in terms of events. The basic idea is to consider a time slice to be a partition of the events into two sets: those events that happen before the time slice and those that happen after it. Since everything we know about the temporal ordering of events is described by the relation →, the only requirement we can make on this partition is that no event that occurs after the time slice can precede an even that occurs before the time slice. Formally, we define

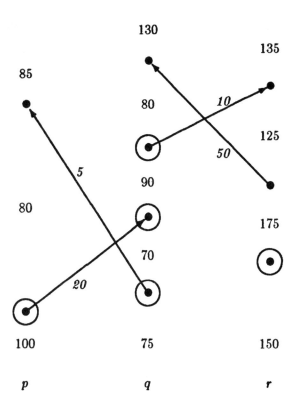

Figure 8.10: A time slice for the system of Figure 8.8

the time slice to be the "before" set, so it is a finite set B of events having the following property:

TS: If $e \in B$ and $f \to e$ then $f \in B$.

Figure 8.10 shows an example of a time slice for the system of Figure 8.8, where the elements of the time slice are circled.

A time slice B is *earlier* than a time slice B' if $B \subset B'$. Unlike clock times, time slices are not totally ordered. However, it is easy to check that the intersection and union of two time slices is a time slice, so the set of time slices forms a lattice, using set "earlier than" as the lattice's ordering relation. Thus, given any two time slices, there is a latest time slice that is earlier than both of them, and an earliest time slice that is later than both of them.

Given a time slice B, we now define the global state $gs(B)$ associated with this time slice. For each process p, The state s_p of each process p in $gs(B)$ is defined as follows. If there are no events of p in B, then s_p is the starting state of p. Otherwise, s_p is defined to be the final state of the latest event of p in B. (This is defined, since, by hypothesis, the events of p form a sequence.) For each channel c, we define the state of c in $gs(B)$ to be the sequence of all messages that are sent by an event in B and received by an event not in B, sequenced by the order of their sending events. (Since the events that send messages on any channel belong to a single process, they are totally ordered.)

The global state $gs(B)$ defined by the time slice B of Figure 8.10 is as follows:

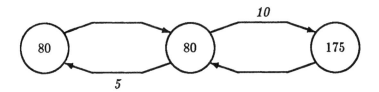

It is easy to see that the following relation holds between the the global state $gs(B)$ defined in the space-time view and the global states of the interleaving view. Let $\Rightarrow$ be any total ordering that extends the partial ordering $\rightarrow$ such that if $e \in B$ and $f \notin B$ then $e \Rightarrow f$, and let e_{max} be the maximal element in B under this total ordering. Then $gs(B)$ is the global state after e_{max} in the interleaving model determined by $\Rightarrow$.

8.3.4. The Snapshot Algorithm

We now derive our algorithm for taking a "snapshot" of the global state.[5] In order to determine a global state of the system, the algorithm must define a time slice. To this end, we add another bit to each process state, which we represent as a color. Each process is initially white, and it will execute a single color-changing event that turns it red. A process's color and its color-changing event are not considered part of the system, but are added solely for the purpose of taking the snapshot. The colors will thus not be part of the state recorded by the snapshot. (The snapshot does not include a picture of the camera.)

Since the color-changing events are not part of the system, a process has a well-defined color at each of its system event. We define that color to be the color of the event. We also define the color of a message to be the color of the event that sent the message.

---

[5] This derivation is based upon a suggestion of Edsger Dijkstra.

Our aim is to make the white events a time slice. For this to be the case, we must insure that no red event precedes (according to the → relation) a white event. The → relation is generated by the following two kinds of precedence events:

- The total ordering of events within a process.

- The sending of a message precedes its receipt.

Since a process makes only one color change, which is from white to red, the first kind of precedence event cannot cause any trouble. We therefore have only to ensure that the receipt of a message sent by a red event is not a white event. In other words, we need only guarantee that a white process never receives a red message.

Each process, when it turns red, will guarantee that the recipient of any red message it later sends is red when it receives the message. The process does this by sending, over each of its outgoing channels, a message warning the recipient to turn red. By the assumption that messages are delivered in the order they are sent, this warning message will arrive before any red messages it sends over that channel. A process that receives such a warning will immediately turn red.

It is easy to see that the set B or white events is then a time slice. What is the global state $gs(B)$ defined by this time slice? The state of each process is just the state of the process when it turns red. (This state is well-defined because the color-changing event does not change the process's actual state.) The sequence of messages in a channel c consists of those messages sent by white events and received by red events—in other words, the sequence of white messages received by red processes. Since a process sends a warning message over each of its outgoing channels when it turns red, the sequence of white messages received by a red process over a channel c is the sequence of all messages received over that channel from the time the process turns red until it receives a warning message over c.

We can now write down the algorithm. First, we define the procedure *turn.red*, executed by any process, to do the following.

1. Set *color* to *red*;

2. Record state.

3. For each incoming channel, begin recording incoming messages on that channel;

4. For each outgoing channel c: send a *warning* message over c before sending any more messages over c.

In step 2, the warning need not be sent immediately. We require only that the warning eventually be sent, and that no other messages be sent on that channel before the warning is sent. The execution of *turn.red* is considered complete, and the next step of the process's algorithm begun, as soon as the commitment to send the warning messages is recorded. The process can resume other activity before those messages are actually sent.

A white process may execute the procedure *turn.red* at any time. Of course, it does so in order to initiate a snapshot. A process takes the following action upon receipt of a warning message on an incoming channel c.

1. If $color = white$, then execute *turn.red*.

2. Stop recording incoming messages on channel c.

A process is said to have finished its part of the algorithm when it has executed *turn.red* and received a *warning* message over every one of its incoming channels. At that time, it has recorded its state and the state of every incoming channel. (The state of a channel is the sequence of messages it recorded from the time it began recording in step 3 of *turn.red* until it stopped recording in step 2 of its actions upon receiving the *warning* message over the channel.)

It is easy to show that if at least one process executes *turn.red*, then every process will eventually finish its part of the algorithm. Moreover, it doesn't matter how many processes initiate the snapshot—two processes concurrently deciding to execute *turn.red* causes no problem.

When all processes are finished, the snapshot has been taken. However, each process has a different piece of the information that comprises the global state. This information must be distributed to those processes that want to know the global state. It is easy to devise an algorithm for doing this, and the interested reader can see how efficient an algorithm he can come up with. However, in practice, one is usually not interested in the entire system state but in some function of it. The method of distributing the information will depend upon just what function of the state is needed by which processes. In our banking example, the main office might want to find out the total amount of assets in the bank. In this case, each process will total the amount of money in its state and in all the messages on its incoming channels, and send this one number to the main office.

8.3.5. Applications

By the time one has recorded the state of the system, further events in the system have probably occurred that have changed the state. Our snapshot is almost certainly out of date by the time it is "developed". What good is such an "obsolete" snapshot of the global state?

An obsolete snapshot may be of use in monitoring the system behavior. Periodically taking snapshots of the system may allow one to determine how well it is performing. However, such applications are of secondary interest. The real use of a snapshot is to determine properties of the system that will not change before the snapshot is developed.

Recall that in Section 2.2 we defined an invariant predicate to be a function P of the system state that satisfies $P \supset \Box P$. An invariant is a property that, once it becomes true, remains true forever. If we find $gs(B) \models P$ for some time slice B, then we know that $gs(B') \models P$ for any later time slice B'. Thus, if P is true on the state shown by the snapshot, then we know it is still true after the snapshot has been "developed".

A global snapshot algorithm is used to detect invariant properties, also known as *stable* properties. The following are examples of such properties:

- In a conservative accounting system (one in which no money enters or leaves the system), the predicate "the total amount of money in the system equals x" is invariant.

- "The system is deadlocked" is an invariant predicate.

- For a token-passing system in which tokens are not created but may be lost, the predicate "there are at most n tokens" is invariant.

Thus, the snapshot algorithm can be used to check that a company's books are balanced, to detect deadlock, and to detect the loss of tokens.

In practice, the predicate being evaluated is not a true invariant. The purpose of detecting deadlock is to break it. What is necessary is that the predicate P satisfy the condition $P \supset P \trianglelefteq Q$ for some predicate Q, where Q will not become false until after the snapshot is developed. For example, if P is the predicate "there is deadlock" then Q would be the predicate which asserts that no action has been taken to break the deadlock. The predicate Q would be made false only by the process responsible for breaking the deadlock, and it is that process which would receive the global state information.

In a realistic situation, the snapshot algorithm would be executed not once, but many times. For example, a waiting process might periodically check if the system is deadlocked. There must be some method for distinguishing successive executions of the algorithm. However, time does not permit us to discuss this here.

8.4. Other Paradigms

8.4.1. Elections

In some countries, leaders are selected by election, along the following lines. Each citizen votes for the candidate he would like to see selected; a citizen can vote at most once, although some don't vote at all. A candidate that receives a majority of the votes is selected. Since only one candidate can receive a majority of the votes, at most one candidate can be selected. It is possible, although rare, that no candidate will receive a majority. Then, some other procedure is employed. For example, candidates that have received only a few votes might be removed from the ballot and the election repeated.

The election paradigm can also be used to make decisions in a computing system, where a set of processes must choose one outcome from among some candidates, any of which is acceptable. Examples of such decisions include:

Choosing a Coordinator:

In some distributed programs, one process coordinates the tasks performed by the other processes in the system. (The Two-Phase Commit protocol of section 8.1.3, for example.) Choosing a coordinator from among the available processes is a decision problem that can be solved by election. The candidates in the election are all processes that can serve as the coordinator.

Resolving Conflicts:

In a distributed database system, an object may be replicated. To update a replicated object, a transaction must obtain an exclusive lock for each copy of the object. If two or more transactions attempt to update the same object concurrently, each might succeed is obtaining locks for some, but not all, of the copies. An election can be used to choose which transaction to abort, since it is pointless to abort both.

Administration of an election among a collection of processes involves three mechanisms.

Election Mechanisms:

Initiation: The mechanism by which processes determine that an election is occurring and what the candidates are.

Tally: The mechanism by which the candidate receiving a majority of the votes is determined.

Announcement: The mechanism by which processes are notified of the outcome of the election.

The requirement that the winner of an election receive a majority of the votes rather than a plurality allows assumptions about process execution speeds to be avoided. Once a majority of the processes have voted for one candidate, no action by any process can change the outcome of the election. This is not true when a plurality can determine the winner of an election because even though a plurality of processes have voted for one candidate, slow processes might eventually cause a different candidate to be elected. When only a plurality is needed to win an election, the tally mechanism must have some way of knowing when no more votes will be received. For example, knowledge of process execution speeds and message delivery delays would allow a fixed time to be set after which no votes would be accepted by the tally mechanism.

Implementing the Election Mechanisms

One way to implement the three election mechanisms enumerated above is based on the state machine approach (section 8.2). The initiation mechanism is based on an agreement protocol. In order to initiate an election, a process disseminates an *initiation message* to all potential voters. The initiation message contains a unique name for the election and may contain the list of candidates, if this information is not already known to the voters.

The tally mechanism is implemented by a state machine called *tally*. Processes vote after receiving an initiation message for election *Ename* by sending a *vote mes-sage* to the *tally* state machine associated with election *Ename*. A vote message *m* is assumed to contain two fields: *m.sender* is the identity of the process voting; *m.value* is the candidate being voted for. In our implementation of *tally* (see Figure 8.11), there are *N* candidates and *SYS* is the set of processes eligible to vote. Notice that in *tally* at most one vote from each process is recorded for each candidate. This prevents a faulty process from subverting an election by voting for the same candidate more than once. However, if enough processes don't vote, no candidate will receive a majority of the votes, and *tally* will never announce a winner. This could be avoided by using a timeout transition that causes *tally* eventually to make an arbitrary choice among the candidates and announce that as the winner. With this strategy, we are exploiting the fact that any of the candidates is an acceptable choice and we are merely concerned with making a decision. Fault-tolerance of *tally* is achieved by replication, as with any other state machine.

Finally, the announcement mechanism in our implementation is a broadcast per-formed by *tally*. Once the outcome of the election has been decided, *tally* sends an *outcome message* naming the winning candidate to every process in *SYS*.

```
tally:  var  votes : array[1..N] of set of process,
            maj_votes : integer;
        maj_votes := (|SYS| div 2) + 1
        forall 1 ≤ i ≤ N:   votes[i] := Φ;
        do  true  →  receive(vote);
                    votes[vote.value] := votes[vote.value] ∪ {vote.sender};
                    if |votes[vote.value]| ≥ maj_votes → forall p ∈ SYS:
                                                      send vote.value to p;
                    ∥ else  →  skip
                    fi
        od
```

Figure 8.11: Tally State Machine.

Voting Rules

Voting rules cause processes to vote in a way that, with high probability, will result in one of the candidates receiving a majority. In short, we "rig" the election. This ensures that an election terminates promptly, rather than because the tally mechanism made a timeout transition. Some useful voting rules for choosing a coordinator from among a collection of processes p_1, p_2, ..., p_n are:

Bully Voting Rule: Vote for the process p_i with smallest i that is available.

Invitation Voting Rule: Vote for the process p_i that initiated the election.

When voting rules are used, additional information is known about how processes will vote. This can be exploited to yield optimized election mechanisms. Consider a system where processor clocks are approximately synchronized, but processors can exhibit arbitrary behavior in response to a failure. The state machine implementation given above could be used in such an environment. To do this, the *tally* state machine would be replicated and a copy of it run on several processors; each process's vote message would be disseminated by using Byzantine Agreement; and the outcome of the election would be determined by each process taking the majority of the outcome messages received from instances of *tally*.

Use of the Bully Voting Rule allows this implementation to be optimized.

Bully Algorithm:

Some processor initiates the election at time τ on its clock by disseminating the message

$$\text{Election } Ename \text{ starts at: } \tau_{start}$$

where $\tau_{start} > \tau + \Delta$ and $Ename$ is the unique name for the election. An agreement protocol that establishes Real-Time Interactive Consistency is used to disseminate the message.

If processor p_k has not received a message

$$\text{The winner in } Ename \text{ is: } p_j$$

by time $\tau_{start} + k\Delta$ on its clock, then it disseminates the message

$$\text{The winner in } Ename \text{ is: } p_k$$

Again, an agreement protocol that establishes Real-Time Interactive Consistency is used.

Upon receipt of a message

$$\text{The winner in } Ename \text{ is } p_w.$$

process p_w is considered to be the winner of election *Ename* by the recipient of the message.

This election algorithm was derived from our state machine implementation (above) by using timeout transitions in *tally*, instead of vote messages. In particular, the absence of messages at various times and the synchronized clocks allow each process to determine candidates processes do not vote for.

Coping with Network Partitions

Failure of communication links in a distributed system could cause the system to be partitioned into two or more disconnected networks. To the processors in each partition, the processors in other partitions appear to have failed, when, in fact, they have not. Allowing processors in more than one partition to continue executing can have disastrous consequences. For example, in a distributed database system with replicated objects, if processors in more than one partition continue executing, then transactions modifying instances of this object might be executed in different partitions. This would cause the copies of the object in different partitions to diverge, perhaps irreconcilably.

An election algorithm can be used to choose one partition to continue executing. The candidates in the election are the partitions; each processor votes for the partition of which it is member. If a partition has a majority of the votes, it is selected to continue processing. Thus, at most one partition will be able to continue processing, since at most one partition can contain a majority of the votes.[6]

Weighted Voting

Thus far, we have tacitly assumed that each process has one vote. In fact, there are advantages to allowing some processes to have more than one vote. By distributing votes among processes, it is possible for a candidate to receive a majority of the votes, without a majority of the processes actually voting. This may allow a decision to be reached earlier than if each process had one vote, since an election is decided as soon as a majority of the votes have been cast for one candidate.

Weighted voting is also useful in constructing systems that are resilient to network partitions. Votes are assigned to processors so that likely communication failures that can partition the network will result in some partition having a

---

[6]In the absence of a majority, making an arbitrary choice to determine the winner is acceptable

majority of the votes. This is illustrated in the graphs of Figure 8.12, where nodes correspond to the processors of a distributed system and the edges to communications links. In the vote assignment of Figure 8.12a a single link failure (link cd) results in formation of two partitions, neither of which has a majority of the votes; no single link failure can cause this to happen in Figure 8.12b.

Related Work

An extensive treatment of election protocols appears in [Garcia-Molina 82]; it is the source of the Bully Algorithm and others. The use of election algorithms for reconfiguration of a system and choosing a coordinator was first discussed in [LeLann 77]. Election protocols have been included in a number of database management systems [Thomas 79, Menasce 80, Stonebraker 79]. Weighted voting was first proposed by Gifford as part of a concurrency control algorithm for distributed database systems [Gifford 79]. A commit protocol based on weighted voting

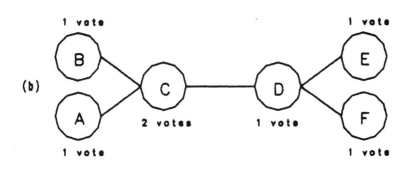

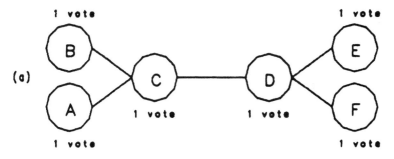

Figure 8.12: Weighted Voting Assignments.

only if every partition makes the same choice.

is described in [Skeen 82]. Garcia-Molina has studied the relationship between assigning votes to processes and defining groups of processes where the intersection of every pair of groups is non-null, and has showed that the two approaches are not equivalent [Garcia-Molina 83].

8.4.2. Wave Algorithms

Wave algorithms allow information known to each processor in a distributed system to be disseminated to all the other processors in the system. They require minimal information about the topology of the communications network. Therefore wave algorithms have application in computing and distributing the topology of a distributed system, as well as assembling the global state of a distributed system after the algorithm of section 8.3 constructs a "distributed snapshot" of the system.

The operation of a wave algorithm is not unlike what is observed when a stone is tossed into a pond. A circular wave forms around where the stone entered the pond and expands outward, until it has traversed the entire pond. Whenever the wave passes an obstruction that penetrates the surface of the pond, another wave is induced—this time, around the obstruction. That wave spreads out until it has traversed the entire pond, causing more waves to be induced as it passes obstructions, *etc.* Eventually, after all the waves have traversed the surface of the pond, everything becomes still again.

In a wave algorithm, the obstructions correspond to processors and the waves to messages carrying local information stored by every processor encountered. Thus informally a wave algorithm works as follows:

Wave Algorithm

A processor broadcasts its local information to its neighbors. Each neighbor receives that information and rebroadcasts it along with its own local information. The algorithm terminates after every processor has received the local information of all the processors.

The hard part in designing a wave algorithm is determining when every processor has received the local information of all processors—a global property—using only the local information available to each processor. If each processor's local information includes the topology of the communications network then it is easy to devise a termination criterion. For example, if for a processor p it is known that there exist paths of length at most t to each other processor, then p need perform at most t relays. In general, we desire a termination criterion that does not require such extensive knowledge about the topology of the network. One such termination criterion is derived below.

Example of Wave Algorithm

We now derive a wave algorithm for a computer network where each processor knows only local information about the topology of the network: in particular, the identities of the processors from which it can receive messages. Thus, such an algorithm can be used to compute and disseminate the topology of a distributed system. In addition to showing how to devise a termination criterion, the example also illustrates how to derive a distributed program by using the assertional reasoning techniques described in section 5.2. A complete derivation and proof of correctness for the algorithm appears in [McCurley 83].

We will model the distributed system by a strongly connected directed graph $G=(V,E)$, where the nodes correspond to processors and the directed edges correspond to communications links.[7] Define

$|j,k| \equiv$ the length of the shortest directed path from processor j to processor k.

$$diam(k) \equiv \max_{j \in V} |j,k|.$$

Note that $|j,k|$ and $diam(k)$ are total because the network is strongly connected,

We will assume that W_i the local information stored at processor i satisfies

W-Assumption: $(\forall i: i \in V: W_i \neq \emptyset) \land (\forall i,j: i,j \in V: i \neq j \supset W_i \cap W_j = \emptyset).$

It is not difficult to make arbitrary sets satisfy the W-Assumption. The set $W_i \times \{i\}$ is used in place of W_i, for all processors i. For each processor i, define[8]

$$Q_i^t \equiv (\cup j: |j,i| = t: W_j) \qquad \text{for } 0 \leq t.$$

Thus, Q_i^t contains those values that appear in set W_j at each processor j that is connected to i by a shortest path of length t.

We desire an algorithm that sets program variable S_i at each processor i to $(\cup j: j \in V: W_j)$, or equivalently, an algorithm that establishes:

$$R_i: \quad S_i = (\cup j: 0 \leq j \leq diam(i): Q_i^j).$$

---

[7]This is consistent with the assumption that communications links are not necessarily bidirectional.

[8]The symbol $-$ denotes set difference.

The Loop at Processor i. Processor i uses a loop to establish R_i. The loop is developed from a loop invariant, which is obtained by generalizing R_i. R_i can be weakened by replacing the constant $diam(i)$ by an integer variable c_i to obtain the loop invariant:

$$PO_i: \quad S_i = (\cup j: 0 \leq j \leq c_i: Q_i^j) \quad \wedge \quad 0 \leq c_i.$$

Replacing a constant by a variable is one of the standard techniques described in [Gries 81] for obtaining a loop invariant from a result assertion. PO_i asserts that S_i contains values in sets W_k for all processors k connected to i by a directed path of length at most c_i.

Our first task is to make PO_i true initially. The multiple assignment

$$c_i, \; S_i := 0, \; W_i$$

suffices for this because $true \supset wp(\,"c_i, \; S_i := 0, \; W_i\,", \; PO_i)$.

Our next task is to choose a guard β_i for the loop. β_i must satisfy $\neg \beta_i \wedge PO_i \supset R_i$, and an obvious choice for the guard is $c_i \neq diam(i)$. If $diam(i)$ were known at processor i then this guard would be suitable; since $diam(i)$ is not known by processor i, we shall have to devise a guard that implies $c_i \neq diam(i)$. We return to this below.

Finally, we develop the body of the loop. Execution of the loop body, in a state in which β_i and PO_i are true must reestablish the loop invariant and make progress towards termination. Progress can be made by increasing c_i (see PO_i). In order to reestablish PO_i, values must be added to S_i. Since $wp(\,"c_i, \; S_i := c_i+1, \; S_i \cup Q_i^{c_i+1}\,", \; PO_i)$ is

$$S_i \cup Q_i^{c_i+1} = (\cup j: 0 \leq j \leq c_i+1: Q_i^j) \quad \wedge \quad 0 \leq c_i+1,$$

which is implied by $PO_i \wedge c_i \neq diam(i)$, the assignment

$$c_i, \; S_i := c_i+1, \; S_i \cup Q_i^{c_i+1}$$

suffices.

It remains to compute $Q_i^{c_i+1}$ from values local to processor i. Let $pred_i$ be a set of processors defined by

$$pred_i \equiv \{p \mid pi \in E\}$$

and assume $pred_i$ is known to each processor i. By definition, $z \in Q_i^{c_i+1}$ if and only if (1) $z \in Q_k^{c_i}$ for some $k \in pred_i$, and (2) there is no $k' \in pred_i$ for which

$z \in Q_k^{c'} \wedge c' < c_i$. That is, $z \in Q_i^{c_i+1}$ if there is a path $(p, ..., k, i)$ of length $c_i + 1$ where $z \in W_p$ and there is no path from p to i (through k or any other predecessor of i) with length less than c_i. Thus,

$$Q_i^{c_i+1} = (\cup k : k \in pred_i : Q_k^{c_i}) - (\cup k' : k' \in pred_i : (\cup j : 0 \leq j < c_i : Q_{k'}^{j}))$$
$$= (\cup k : k \in pred_i : Q_k^{c_i}) - (\cup j : 0 \leq j \leq c_i : Q_i^{j})$$
$$= (\cup k : k \in pred_i : Q_k^{c_i}) - S_i.$$

(The last step follows from $P0_i$.) Substituting this expression for $Q_i^{c_i+1}$ into the assignment in the loop body, we get

$$c_i, S_i := c_i + 1, S_i \cup ((\cup k : k \in pred_i : Q_k^{c_i}) - S_i)$$

which simplifies to

$$c_i, S_i := c_i + 1, S_i \cup (\cup k : k \in pred_i : Q_k^{c_i}).$$

This assignment can be executed at processor i only if sets $Q_k^{c_i}$ for all $k \in pred_i$ are known to i. Therefore, let us postulate a routine $Acquire_i$, specified by

$$\{true\}$$
$$Acquire_i$$
$$\{(\forall k : k \in pred_i : V_i[k] = Q_k^{c_i})\}.$$

Then, the program we have developed thus far is obtained by rewriting the assignment of the loop body using $V_i[k]$ in place of $Q_k^{c_i}$:

$$c_i, S_i := 0, W_i;$$
$$\{P0_i\}$$
$$\textbf{do } c_i \neq diam(i) \rightarrow \{c_i \neq diam(i) \wedge P0_i\}$$
$$Acquire_i;$$
$$\{P0_i \wedge (\forall k : k \in pred_i : V_i[k] = Q_k^{c_i})\}$$
$$c_i, S_i := c_i + 1, S_i \cup (\cup k : k \in pred_i : V_i[k])$$
$$\{P0_i\}$$
$$\textbf{od}$$
$$\{P0_i \wedge c_i = diam(i)\}$$
$$\{R_i\}$$

Termination Criterion. We now turn to the problem of devising a guard for the case where $diam(i)$ is not known at processor i. From the definition of $Q_i^t)$ we have

(i) $t > diam(i) \Leftrightarrow Q_i^t = \emptyset$.

Computation of $Q_i^{c_i}$ by processor i is accomplished by maintaining a set-valued variable T_i defined by

$\quad P1_i:\ T_i = (\cup j: 0 \le j < c_i: Q_i^{c_i}).$

By making $P1_i$ an invariant of the loop, $Q_i^{c_i}$ can be computed during each iteration by evaluating $S_i - T_i$ because

(ii) $P0_i \wedge P1_i \supset (Q_i^{c_i} = S_i - T_i).$

Finally, because $P0_i \wedge c_i > diam(i) \supset R_i$, we are free to choose $c_i \le diam(i)$ as β_i the guard for the loop. This is convenient, because, according to (i), $\beta_i \Leftrightarrow Q_i^{c_i} \ne \emptyset$. And, from (ii) we get $\beta_i \Leftrightarrow S_i - T_i \ne \emptyset$. This last formulation has the additional virtue that it is entirely in terms of variables stored by processor i.

Adding statements to the program to establish and maintain T_i and changing the guard as just suggested yields the following program at processor i.

$$c_i, S_i, T_i := 0, W_i, \emptyset;$$
$$\{P0_i \wedge P1_i\}$$
$$\textbf{do}\ S_i \ne T_i \rightarrow \{S_i \ne T_i \wedge P0_i \wedge P1_i\}$$
$$\qquad\qquad Acquire_i;$$
$$\qquad\qquad \{P0_i \wedge P1_i \wedge (\forall k: k \in pred_i: V_i[k] = Q_k^{c_i})\}$$
$$\qquad\qquad c_i, S_i, T_i := c_i + 1, S_i \cup (\cup k: k \in pred_i: V_i[k]), S_i$$
$$\qquad\qquad \{P0_i \wedge P1_i\}$$
$$\textbf{od}$$
$$\{P0_i \wedge c_i > diam(i)\}$$
$$\{R_i\}$$

Implementing Acquire$_i$. During iteration t of the loop, the sets Q_k^t for all $k \in pred_i$ are obtained by the $Acquire_i$ routine. $P1_k$ is an invariant of the loop at processor k, so k computes $Q_k^{c_k}$ during each iteration simply by evaluating $S_k - T_k$ and broadcasts the value to its successors.

The loop body at processor k is executed $diam(k)+1$ times because c_k is initially 0, it is increased by one each iteration, and the body is no longer executed when $c_k > diam(k)$. Thus, if the loop terminates, $diam(k)+1$ values are sent by k to each processor in $succ_k$.

Now consider a processor i, adjacent to k in G. Assuming messages sent along link ki are delivered in the order sent the successive values received on that link are $Q_k^0, Q_k^1, ..., Q_k^{diam(k)}$. Therefore, we can implement $Acquire_i$ by

> **broadcast** $S_i - T_i$;
>
> **cobegin** $\underset{k \,\in\, pred_i}{[]}$ **receive** $V_i[k]$ from k $\quad \{V_i[k] = Q_k^{c_i}\}$ **coend**
>
> $\{(\forall k: k \in pred_i: V_i[k] = Q_k^{c_i})\}$

where execution of **broadcast** m by processor i causes m to be sent to all processors p such that $ip \in E$.

Unfortunately, our implementation of $Acquire_i$ introduces the possibility of infinite blocking. The **cobegin** terminates only if every **receive** terminates, and a **receive** terminates only if there is a message available for receipt. $Acquire_i$ is executed once per loop iteration, i.e. $diam(i)+1$ times. Therefore, at least $diam(i)+1$ messages must be sent on link (k,i) for each $k \in pred_i$ to prevent infinite blocking at processor i.

From the definition of $diam$ and the fact that i is a successor of k in G, we obtain $diam(k)+1 \geq diam(i)$. Consequently, if k makes a **broadcast** after completing $diam(k)+1$ iterations then the total number of messages sent by k is $diam(k)+2 \geq diam(i)+1$ and infinite blocking at i is avoided. Note that the number of messages sent by k, $diam(k)+2$, can be strictly greater than the number of messages received by i, $diam(i)+1$. When this is the case, some messages on the link connecting k and i will not be received. Upon termination at site i, the unreceived messages contain information already in S_i and can be safely discarded.

Inserting the code for $Acquire_i$ into the program and adding a **broadcast** after the loop yields the finished program.

```
c_i, S_i, T_i := 0, W_i, ∅;
do  S_i ≠ T_i  →  broadcast  S_i - T_i;
              cobegin    ▯    receive  V_i[k] from k    coend;
                       k ∈ pred_i
              c_i, S_i, T_i := c_i + 1, S_i ∪ (∪k: k ∈ pred_i: V_i[k]), S_i
od;
broadcast  S_i - T_i
```

Chapter 9

Issues and Tools for Protocol Specification

A system is said to be distributed when it includes several geographically distinct components cooperating in order to achieve a common distributed task.

The development of informatic networks and telematic services, as well as the access to public data transmission networks raised the question of building distributed applications. However it should be understood that distributed processing is not only the result of the combination of local data-processing and transmission facilities.

- With the introduction of dedicated processors (eg. I/0 processors...), then of multiple-processor systems and finally of local area networks, distributed processing has been introduced inside data-processing systems themselves.
- Simultaneously distributed processing was appearing within intimity of the telecommunication networks themselves, first with packet and circuit networks, second in Common Signalling Systems [CCITT 80] where a separate computer deals with all signalling information.

When programs are running at different locations to achieve a common, distributed task, the set of rules which defines the dialogue part among the cooperating entities is called a protocol. When looking into a complex distributed system executing an application distributed among several multiprocessor data-processing systems communicating through a packet switched network, protocols are used for the internal operation of the network and for the internal operation of the data–processing systems, as well as for the cooperation of the application programs. In other words this complex distributed system is made of the assembly of several distributed systems in a more complex architecture in which one of the systems is used as a vehicle for the protocols of the other.

This clearly shows that the scope of distributed systems and their protocols is not restricted to user–oriented application but also applies to the intimity of data–processing as well as telecommunication systems. The complexity and the globality of this problem indicates the need for a common reference architecture for all distributed systems as demonstrated in [Zimmermann 83].

In these lectures we first present the OSI Basic reference model [ISO 83a] established by ISO (International Organization for Standardization) joined by CCITT (Comité Consultatif International pour le Téléphone et le Télégraphe) as a structuring technique for distributed systems. We discuss the main concepts used for decomposition and try to show their generality for any distributed system. The OSI model is then used as a guideline for presenting some issues and tools in protocol specification. We conclude our first lecture on overview in presenting some problems which, despite of their commonality to all protocol design, are not very well known and understood: flow control, expedited flow, multiplexing.

The second section – corresponding to the second and third lecture – describes a set of tools developed by the Agence de l'Informatique toward a general Telecommunication Software Factory: Design – Specification – Implementation – Testing of communication protocols.

In the next section we present the OSI Transport protocol [ISO 83b] in its internal mechanisms as well as we give some indication about its formal specification validation and automated implementation using the tools previously presented.

Finally, we conclude with some "protocol games" in order to give the reader some flavour of the kind of problems encountered with protocol design and specification.

9.1. Overview

In this section we first present the OSI basic reference model as a common reference architecture for all distributed systems. Along this presentation we define some keywords and concepts which will be used throughout the other sections.

The second part of this overview emphasizes some of the structuring principles which have been used for building the OSI basic reference model and tries to show their generality and their applicability to any distributed system. The last subsection of this part also gives the current limit of the model and the further studies required.

Finally the last part of this overview enlights some aspects common to all protocol specification and testing.

9.1.1. The OSI Basic reference model

From the complexity of distributed systems it is clear that the construction of systems will be facilitated if all distributed systems would refer to the same decomposition principles, called a common reference architecture. The nature of the problem is so complex that the natural selection of the best architecture among all those experimented by users, suppliers and carriers would take years and years, leading to a situation in which the investments made in divergent experiments would make any convergence impossible. Therefore a voluntary process has been started by ISO and CCITT, resulting in the definition of OSI basic reference model.

External visibility versus internal behaviour

In order not to impose useless constraints to systems, the model defines only the communication part of distributed system, and therefore only deals with the communication protocols and their external visibility (i.e. the behaviour of the system viewed from outside, not its internal organization).

Layering principles

Layering is a structuring technique allowing to view a network of open systems as composed as a succession of layers. Each layer performs a set of specific functions which, in combination with those provided by the lower layers provide a new – enhanced – service to the upper layer. The service offered to the upper layers may differ from the service offered by the layer below either in the nature of the service (i.e. new services are added) or in the quality of the service (i.e. the service is only enhanced) or both.

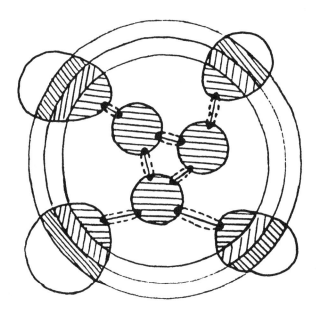

Figure 1: A network of open systems as a succession of layers, each system being viewed as subsystems.

Each individual system is viewed as being an "abstract" open system composed of a succession of subsystems, each corresponding to the intersection of the system with a layer. In other words a layer is viewed as logically composed of all of its subsystems.

Each subsystem is in turn viewed as being made of one or several entities. One entity belongs to only one system and only one layer. All the entities in the same layer are named peer–entities. Since some concepts are layer independent we use the notation "(N)–name" to designate a component or a function which applies to a layer, irrespectively of the actual name of the layer. Application of the above notation leads to the following definition: a (N)-subsystem is the intersection of a (N)-layer with an open system. A (N)-subsystem may contain one or more (N)-entities.

When a (N)-layer communicates with the adjacent layer and higher layer it is also conveniant to use the notation (N+1)- layer and (N-1)-layer.

Objectives of layering – Services – Stability

The goal of layering as a structuring technique is to allow the design of the (N)-protocol to be done in knowing what the (N+1)-layer is expecting and what the (N-1)-layer is providing for, but knowing neither what function the (N+1)-layer is performing nor how the (N-1)-layer is operating. In other words this is to ensure independence between layers. This permits changes to be made in one (set of) layer(s) provided the service offered to the next higher layer remains unchanged. This property is guaranteed if the services provided by the layer are defined independently of how these services are performed.

Communication between the (N)-entities makes exclusive use of the (N-1)-service. In particular direct communication between (N)-entities in the same system is not visible from outside the system and is therefore not covered by the reference model.

The set of rules governing the cooperation between (N)-entities is termed an (N)-protocol: this defines how (N)-entities are working together for offering the (N)-service in using the (N-1)-service and adding their own (N)-functions. The (N)-service is offered to the (N+1)-entities at the (N)-service-access-point or (N)-SAP for short. A (N)-SAP offers service to only one (N+1)-entity and is served by only one (N)-entity, but a (N+1)-entity may use several (N)-SAPs as well as a (N)-entity may serve several (N)-SAPs.

Each layer offers as a common service a way to perform an association between peer SAPs.

The most current association is a bipoint connection between a pair of SAPs. Connection-less-data transmission between SAPs is also now defined as an addendum to the first version of the basic reference model [ISO 82] (multi end—point connection and broadcast are still under study).

For the other concept we encourage the reader to refer directly to [ISO 83a] or [Zimmermann 81].

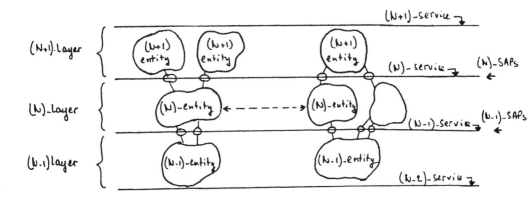

Figure 2: Entities, Services, Protocols, SAPs

The specific layers

The basic model includes seven layers defined as follows:

1. *Physical layer*. The first and well known function of this layer is to be responsible for interfacing systems to the actual physical media for OSI. The physical layer has also the role of relaying bits when necessary (i.e. performing the function of interconnecting data circuits).

2. *Data link layer*. The main function of this layer is to perform framing and possibly error dectection and error recovery.

3. *Network layer*. The network layer relays packets and routes both packets and data circuits.
   Additionally it may perform multiplexing, error recovery and flow control when needed for the optimization of the transmission resources.

4. *Transport layer*. The transport layer performs end—to—end control and end—to—end optimization of the transport of data between end—systems. The transport layer is the last and highest communication oriented layer which purpose is to hide to the users

the peculiarity of the communication facilities and to optimize their use from the viewpoint of the user. No function related to the transport of information (e.g. recovery from transmission error, multiplexing,...) is allowed to be performed above the transport layer.

5. *Session layer*. The session layer offers common functions used by any dialogue between processes: initialization, different variants of termination, synchronization...

6. *Presentation layer*. The presentation layer offers functions for data formats, code and representation of the informations which application wishes to manipulate: the presentation layer takes care of syntactic aspects of information exchange. Therefore application entities are only concerned with the semantic aspects.

7. *Application layer*. The application-layer performs those functions necessary to achieve a specific distributed task using the services provided by the lower layers.

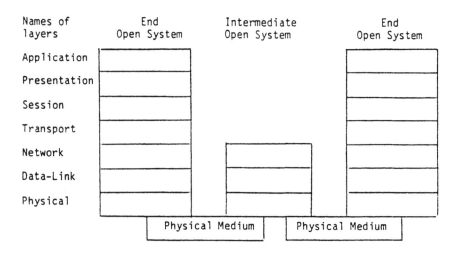

Figure 3: The seven layers of the OSI Reference Model

9.1.2. Basic principles for decomposition

While the previous section presented a brief overview of the OSI Basic Reference Model, this section recalls three basic principles which have been used when building the model and which can be applied for the decomposition of any distributed system [Zimmermann 83].

Separation between data transmission and data processing

The transport service defines a firm boundary between the data-transmission part (layer 1 to 4) and the data-processing part (layer 5 to 7). This is based on the following assumption:

- evolution of technology in both domains should be allowed independently
- the problems to be solved are of different nature:

as an example recovery from error when transmitting is much simpler than recovery in data-processing.

Separation between "end-to-end" and network control

This separation allows to make a clear distinction between

- network control such as routing (finding, changing, reconfiguring routes),
  recovery from line failure or from intermediate mode crash or congestion, controlling flow over network.
- end-to-end transport function managing only simple configuration, based on well known ent-to-end flow control and recovery mechanism.

One could view the network layer as taking into account the interest of the overall community in sharing the telecommunication resources and offering the highest possible availability, while the transport layer offers to its users what they need, on an end-to-end basis without the knowledge of the internal organization of the network – using the network at the lowest cost.

End-to-end transport and network control do not deal with the same kind of optimization, the same kind of resources and therefore do not call on the same kind of functions.

Basic and specific functions in the higher layer

The OSI reference model structures the higher layers (data–processing) as follows:

1. The session and presentation layer contains functions of general use for distributed application. In order to offer this service the session layer [ISO 83d, ISO 83e] contains a set of functions (termed functional units) which can be selected or not on request of the application.

    Those functional units include negociated release, expedited flow, two–way–alternate (TWA) versus two–way–simultaneous (TWS) mode of dialogue, weak synchronization (termed minor marks) or strong synchronization (termed major marks), resynchronization and the possibility to structure a dialogue into phases (termed activities). At session establishment time the application–entities select the functional units they need to achieve their common task. The OSI session sevice and protocol are defined in [ISO 83d, ISO 83e].

    In order to play this role (allow the application entities to share a common view of data without taking care of the syntactic aspects) the presentation layer – which is still under definition – will allow for syntax transfomation and use of predefined types (eg. the structure of a document into pages, windows, graphics,... for a virtual terminal) as well as user–defined types [CCITT 83].

2. The application layer contains the functions which are specific to the application to be executed.

It is clear that this structure has been largely influenced by high level languages (as well as by operating system concepts). The reader will find in [Zimmermann 83] a comparison between some functions in OSI and in traditional data processing.

Despite of the fact that some further study is still necessary both in the session layer (multiparty dialogue, commitments protocol,...) and the presentation layer, we share the view expressed by H. Zimmermann that any distributed system architecture should adhere to the same structure as OSI for the higher layers.

9.1.3. Some basic concepts and terminology for protocol design and specification.

This section introduces some basic concepts and terms as defined in [ISO 83a] which knowledge and understanding is useful for protocol design and specification.

Identifiers

Objects within a layer or at the boundary to the layer above and below need to be identified.

- Each (N)-entity is uniquely identified by a global title in the network of open systems.
- Within a specified domain a local title identifies the (N)-entity in the domain. A domain can be defined geographically or for one layer or any other combinations.
- A (N)-SAP is identified by a (N)-address at the boundary to the (N+1)-layer.
- A directory allows to find the (N-1) address through which a (N)-entity having a given global title can be reached.
- A mapping function gives the correspondence between the (N)-addresses served by a (N)-entity and the (N-1)-address(es) used for this purpose. Address mapping may be done by table or on a hierarchical basis (in which case the (N)-address is formed or the (N-1)-address completed by a (N)-suffix).
- A (N)-CEP (connection end-point identifier) is used to distinguish inside a SAP between different connections.

Data-units

- (N)-SDU (service data unit) is the amount of data whose integrity is preserved from one end of a (N)-connection to the other. In some services the length of the SDU is unlimited (e.g. X25).

- (N)−PDU is an unit of data exchanged between two (N)−entities, using a (N−1)−connection, when operating the (N)−protocol. A (N)−PDU contains (N)−protocol control information and possibly (N)−user data (which is a (N)−SDU or a part of a (N)−SDU or serveral (N)−SDUs. In X25 the network−protocol−data−unit is the packet. A data packet contains either a complete network−service−data−unit or a part of a network−service−data unit. The 'more data' bit allows for the preservation of the integrity of the NSDU

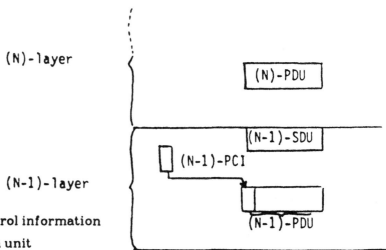

PCI: Protocol control information
PDU: Protocol data unit
SDU: Service data unit

Figure 4: Logical relationship between data units in adjacent layers.

Relationship between (N) and (N−1)−connections

The operation of a (N)−connection requires the use of (N−1)−connection(s).

Three types of combinations are of particular interest:

- One−to−one correspondence where each (N)−connection uses one (N−1)−connection, and one (N−1)−connection is used for only one (N)−connection.

- Multiplexing where several (N)−connections use the same (N−1)−connection.

- Splitting where one (N)−connection uses several (N−1)−connections. (Note that splitting and multiplexing can be combined).

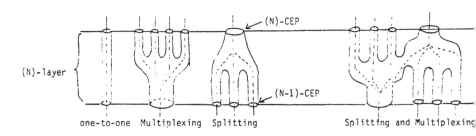

Figure 5: Correspondence between connections

Flow control

Some services offer a flow control service allowing the receiving user to slowdown the rate at which the service delivers to it the SDUs. The service propagates (if necessary) this regulation to the sender.

This flow control service may be offered at the protocol level using different techniques which can be classified in two main categories:

- explicit techniques where the protocol includes its own mechanism for flow regulation.

- implicit techniques where the protocol makes use of the flow control provided by the lower service. In this case there is a risk of long term blocking which may lead to an unacceptable degradation of the service.

Expedited data

Some services offer an 'expedited data' transfer service allowing for the transmission of a short piece of 'fast' data. An expedited data may bypass normal data, in particular when the receiving user exercices flow control on normal data. Experience using expedited data has shown that this is a powerfull service − in particular for forcing resynchronization when the receiving user is not willing to accept normal data any more. However unexpected bypass of normal data by an expedited is a source of errors in protocol design (e.g. an expedited carring a resynchronization request arrives before the normal data carring the synchronization mark referred to in the resynchronization request).

9.2. Toward a telecommunication software factory

This section presents a set of integrated tools developed by the Agence de l'Informatique in France for helping the protocol designers, implementors and users at each stage of the 'life' of a protocol.

At the first stage the protocol is designed by users, suppliers or standardization committees. During this stage the protocol should be specified and validated.

At the second stage the protocol will be implemented, possibily by different teams, in different systems.

At the last stage, the protocol will be put into operation in real networks with possible maintenance of the equipments running the protocol (or of the protocol itself !).

At first glance it appears that specification – validation are tightly coupled. However our methodology proposes a refinement of this stage into two steps:

- The first step includes an initial specification of the protocol in which some details may not be included (like encoding, mapping of $(N)-PDU$ into $(N-1)-SDU...$) and a validation of this specification. The tool for helping during this stage is called LISE and is presented in the first subsection.

- The second step consists in a complete specification of the protocol (including those details which have been missed in the first step) using a formal specification language called PDIL. This also includes simulation, study of properties as well as automated implementation.

From one hand this provides a reference description which can be used by any implementor, from another hand this builds all the environment for conducting real experiments at low cost and provides help for a smooth transition toward easy implementation. PDIL is presented in the next subsection.

Whatever the tools are for helping the implementors —including an automatic translation from the specification into machine executable code — it is likely that a lot of implementors will implement protocols manually in assembler language because of specific performance or environment constraints. Therefore this raises the question of testing equipments which claim to be in conformance with the protocol. The third subsection presents some testing tools which can also be used when the network is operational (i.e. during the third stage).

9.2.1. LISE

LISE is a tool based on extended finite state automata (state automata with predicates). This form has been chosen since it is the more popular in the community of protocol designers (i.e. suppliers, carriers, standardization committes).

The concepts

According to the OSI Reference Model a (N)—protocol is run by peer (N)—entities – 2 or more – using an-(N-1)-service and providing a (N)—service. The behaviour of each (N)—entity is described using an extended automata, by a set of transitions of the following form:

<trans>:: = '('<event> <fromstate> <predicate> <tostate> <action> ')'
<event>:: = nothing | <input-event>

Nothing means that this is a spontaneous transition which can fire at any time provided the state and predicate are as specified in the other part of the transition.

<input event>:: = N−service request or response

|(N−1)−service indication or confirmation

|(N)−PDU

<from state>:: =   state−name

<to state>:: =   state−name

<predicate>:: =   a boolean expression calculated using parameters of the event and variables. The variables are in fact an extension of the state of the process.

<action>:: =   <action−on−variable> <action−to−(N−1)−service>
<action−to−(N)−service>

<action−on−variable> :: =   nothing | set−variables

<action−to−(N−1)−service>::= nothing | send (N)−PDU send | an (N−1)−service request or response.

<action−to−(N)−service>:: =   nothing | send (N)−service indication or confirmation.

Then a model of the (N−1)−service is introduced and the (N)−entities are interconnected through this model.

We have gained from our experience that constructing the model of the (N−1)−service may be more costly than building the model of the protocol itself.

For this reason LISE offers a set of predefined models corresponding to almost all existing networks. The predefined models are listed in the section on "(N−1)−service models", page 498.

After the model has been selected (or constructed by user if none of the preexisting models fit into the (N−1)−service which is to deal with) the properties of the overall communication can be studied. This study may include: validation through global state exploration, simulation, study of properties.

User interface

LISE has been designed to be an interactive tool, therefore it includes an ease−of−use user interface which essential features are:

- A transition oriented editor including functions such as searching or deleting transitions using criteria like:

list all transitions including a specific object as a component ... etc.

- Save−restore a set of transitions into/from a specified file.
- Check the properties of a local state automata: connexity, paths, cycles, sink state...
- List the objects (i.e. the components of the transitions) and their characteristics and check them for consistency (for instance a state and a (N)−PDU shall not have the same name, or a (N)−PDU which never appears as the event of a transition cannot be a (N)−PDU!).

The user interface also includes some facilities which are called on after a validation has been done − they are presented later.

Finally it should be noted that LISE is a bilingual system which proposes to its user to use either French or English.

Validation

We will first consider the case of two (N)−entities and then describe the extension for n. Similarily we first consider the case of a simple (N−1)−service comprising two fifo queues without flow control (i.e. when the queue is full this is an error).

The method is very simple and based on a global state exploration. As proposed in [Zafiropoulo 80], starting from an initial global state in which both processes are in their initial state and the channels are empty, the reachability of the system is build in studying all possible transitions done by the two processes. A data base contains all the global states and when a new global state is computed it is first checked against the already exiting global states in the data base and added to the database only if it does not already exist. The validation stops when the tree has been globally explored (i.e. no new global state can be created).

The method allows the detection of three kinds of errors:

- unspecified reception: Reception of an event ev, head channel $P_i \dashrightarrow P_j$, when the process P_j is in a state S such that there are no transitions

<ev S predicate ...> for which the predicate is true.

- deadlock: The global state of the system is such that no transition can be executed further.
- non executable transition: At the end of the communication analysis a transition has never executed.

In case of errors the system may display upon request of the user a 'history' of the error.

In parallel with the construction of the reachability tree of the communication, the global state automata is constructed (i.e. not only the global states but also all the transitions between these states are put into the data base) and a new part of the user interface is then available:

- Display all or part of the global state automata.
- Study its connexity, cycles ...(note that the deadlock detected by this method has less power than the liveness property in petri-nets, which has to be studied through the connexity of the global state automata).
- Display communication scenarios: a global covering of the state automata is constructed and then the corresponding transition sequences are displayed. This can be further used either for protocol teaching purpose (a special extension of LISE, called a protocol teacher is also available for this purpose) or as test suites when performing equipment testing.

Simulation and properties study

While in validation mode the system fires all possible transitions in every global state, when turning to simulation mode the system selects only one transition. This selection is done on a random basis. This mode is useful when it turns out that a validation cannot be run due to a too high number of global states.

An other feature allows to put low priority to transitions corresponding to error cases (for instance). Therefore when running a simulation, the error cases are considered with a lower probability than the normal operation cases.

It is very well known that absence of deadlock does not proof that the protocol operates properly: it is very simple to build a (so-called) mutual exclusion algorithm which does not fall into deadlock but allocates the resource more than once simultaneously. One key drawback of the state exploration method is that it provides no tool for verifying that the protocol meets certain requirements. Such a feature has been added in LISE in the form of global assertions.

A global assertion is nothing but a spontaneous transition whose predicate can check any component of the communication (including the remote process, and the $(N-1)$-service). In fact the predicate of such a transition is true when the assertion is false and then the process goes into an error state. Global assertions have the highest priority in order to be still detected in simulation mode.

$(N-1)$-service models

The basic $(N-1)$-service model consists of two fifo queues. LISE proposes to the user to build its $(N-1)$-service model in adding to this basic model any combination (except certain combinations which are senseless like datagram and flow control or datagram and expedited data) of the following properties:

- purge: The fifo queue can be purged on request, each direction independently.
- complete purge: The fifo queue can be purged on request, simultaneously, including a purge collision resolution algorithm (like the X25 reset).
- flow control: The receiving process can block/unblock the channel and the channel can block/unblock the sending process.
- expedited data: Each element put in the queue can be characterized as normal or expedited. Expedited elements may bypass normal elements. All combinations resulting from bypassing are

considered by the system.

- datagram: The order in which the elements are delivered is independent of the order they have ben put into the queue (misodering).

- datagram with loss: Similar to the previous one except last that the $(N-1)$-service may also loose any data.

The properties selected by the user are represented in the form of parameters which are used by the validation/simulation algorithm when building the next global state(s). The system also offers global variables which can be used to add user-defined properties to the $(N-1)$-service. These global variables can be checked/set in every transition.

Timers

As an important feature, the system includes a timer management facility. A property is added to the channels which is to define a minimum transit delay and a maximum transit delay for the elements put into the channel.

An actual transit delay is attached to each element in the channel and initialized to zero when a process puts an element into a channel. When exploring the global states the validation algorithm

- does not deliver an element if its actual transit delay is less than the minimum.

- forces the delivery of the element if its actual transit delay has reached the maximum.

- progresses the time if no transition corresponding to a timer which has run out or to the delivery of an element having reached the maximum transit delay can be fired.

    "Progressing the time" means:
    - increment by one the actual transit delay of every element in the channels
    - execute a user-defined action (like decrementing a counter modeling a timer which has been started).

Unlike classical simulation systems there is no 'virtual clock' in the sytem (such a variable would prevent the validation algorithm to ever terminate).

Extension to n processes

Although very powerful, the main drawback of the system is to be limited to the study of the communication between two processes. An extension allowing to interconnect n processes through a (N−1)−service has been recently developed and is currently under test.

While figure 6 gives the general configurations of LISE in the 2−process version, figure 7 gives the configuration of the extension in the n−process version.

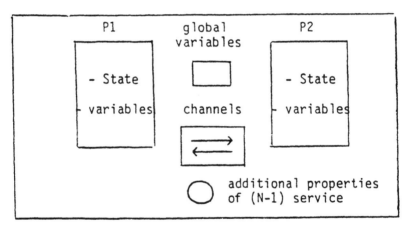

Figure 6: LISE in the 2−processes version (model)

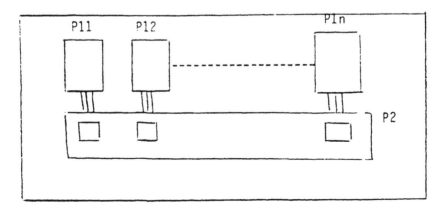

Figure 7: LISE in the n−processes version (model)

In the n–processes version there are still two "processes" P1 and P2.

- P1 is declared as having n instances P11... P1n representing the n (N)–entities to be interconnected. Each instance has its own state and variables.

- Each instance of P1 communicate with P2 through an interface modelled by two channels which are fifo queues P2 has a global state and context–states (one context is attached to each channel). P2 is used to model the (N–1)–service. The validation/simulation algorithm again explores all transitions and builds the global states.

  A global state is a vector comprising

  - the state and variables of P11...P1n
  - the state and variables of P2
  - the context–state and context–variables of all contexts of P2
  - the global variables
  - the content of the interface channels.

It is clear that the number of global state is largely growing with this configuration. Therefore if validation cannot be used, the system automatically turns to simulation mode.

Conclusion

The LISE system is operational under Multics on a Honeywell 68 large main frame computer. It has been used for validating example protocols (HDLC/X25) but also real protocols during their design phase ISO Transport, ISO Session, file transfer.

The format of the input (transistions) facilitates the setting up of the system since it is close to what is used by standardization committees. The global assertion feature has been felt of primary importance when validating the transport protocol [Ansart 80].

The possibility to easy select a complex (N–1)–service model has been largely used when validating a subset of the OSI session protocol [Ansart 83a] and has permitted to conduct a significant validation of this complex protocol in a short time [Ansart 82a, Ansart 82b].

The reader familiar with the french language may find in [Ansart 83b] a complete user's manual of LISE.

9.2.2. PDIL

PDIL (Protocol description and implementation language) is a language developed by the Agence de l'Informatique — and also set of associated tools: a compiler (or more appropriately a preprocessor) which translates a PDIL program into a PASCAL program, a simulator which executes the PASCAL programs produced by the preprocessor and finally a set of run–time environments which allow to integrate the PASCAL programs into real operating systems and execute them as an automatic implementation of a protocol.

Concepts

PDIL allows the description of both services and protocols. For describing a protocol the technique used in PDIL is to describe a (N)–entity running the (N)–protocol. When specifying a service, the corresponding PDIL program describes it as a box. The main difference between these two units of description is that in the case of an entity there are service access point(s) at which the entity is offering service and service point(s) at which the entity is using services, while a service unit of description does not use other services.

In general, a service is not subject to automatic implementation but is only used for simulation purpose. This is the case when we describe a distributed service in the OSI sense (e.g. the transport service). However local services may also be described and therefore implemented (e.g. a memory management service). We will focus on entity description in the remainder of these lectures.

Model and Instances. The unit of description in PDIL is in fact a model of an entity which represents all possible behaviours of a (N)–entity respecting a (N)–protocol. At implementation time a system will support one or more instances of this model, each instance being derived from the model in fixing parameters. The behaviour of each instance conforms to the model.

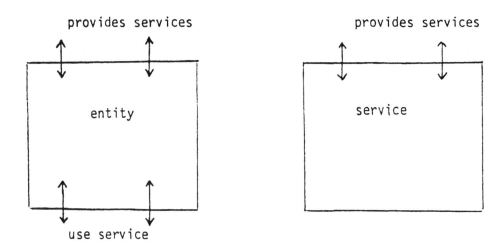

Figure 8: Entity and services unit of description

Parametrization. Four levels of parametrization are offered in the PDIL language in the following way: constants, types, variables and procedures/functions may be declared as "external" with the following semantic: whatever their values are, the behaviour of any instance giving to them the actual values conforms to the behaviour of the model which specifies the protocol.

Machines, channels, contexts. Entities in a system are communicating through channels. Channels are bidirectional fifo queues which can be dynamically allocated and destroyed. Additional intelligence can be attached to channels (for instance resolutions of collision when closing a channel).

An entity can be splitted into several machines. As entities, machines communicate through channels (no shared memory).

An (N)−entity does not need to know the internal structure of the (N−1) and (N+1)−entities (i.e. how they are splitted into machines).

Inside a machine, several contexts can be dynamically created/ destroyed. Therefore, a machine has the capability to multiplex several activities in parallel.

State automata. The behaviour of a machine is described in terms of an extended finite state machine as follows:

- The default context of the machine contains a major state and variables (minor states) for the overall machine. This is used for controlling the general behaviour of the machine. In general only a few states (like not–operational, operational, shutdown–in–progress) are used. Interactions asking for creation of new activities are processed in the default context (e.g. a new connection is rejected in the shutdown–in–progress state).

- Each created context contains also a state and variables. When interactions dealing with an existing activity are received through a channel they are directed to the appropriate context in which they are processed according to the state automata of the context.
  Channels are dynamically attached to context in order to have this association done automatically for all interactions received via channel.

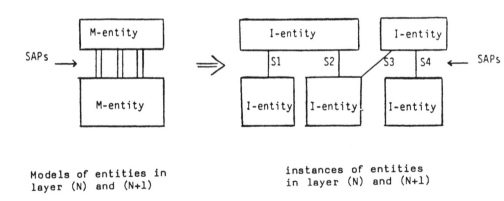

Figure 9: Use of SAPs for addressing instances of entities.

Addresses and service access points. Entities are connected at service–access–points (SAPs). Each SAP is uniquely identified by an address.

When a channel is created the address of the SAP is given as a parameter. This allows several instances to be created in adjacent layers at implementation time, in conformity with the model.

Moreover this allows for separate compilation and implementation of the layers: adding new users only requires to change the SAP table in the system.

Language features

The language used is an extension of Pascal. Pascal has been chosen due to its popularity, good structuration, typing facilities and the fact that it is standardized.

A unit of description starts with a header of the following form:

entity name1 *providing-to* name2 *using* (name31,... name3n);

name1 defines the service which is provided. There could be several descriptions providing the same service. Each instance will use one of those at implementation time.

name2 is only used internally to designate the potential users of the service. This header is used to provide linking information between separate descriptions of entities and services, therefore allowing for separate compilations.

name3i designates other services which are used by the current description. They shall be defined somewhere else as 'name1' of other description.

As is Pascal, labels, constants, and types are then introduced, with the difference that constants and types may be 'external' (i.e. not defined).

The next section gives the components of the entity, mainly:

- the names of the machines composing the entity,
- the name of the channels to be used,
- the structure for the addresses of the SAPs,
- the name of the interactions to be exchanged through the channels,
- the structure of the interactions in the form of Pascal records,
- the structure of the contexts and the state space of each of the state variables.

Then the behaviour of the entity is specified in the form of an extended state machine, through constructs of the following form:

when interaction–name

    from state–name

        provided predicate

           to state–name

           .

           .   action

        provided other–predicate

       .

       .

    from other–state–name

when interaction–name

    .

    .

    .

Undeterminism

One important feature of the PDIL language is that it allows to describe an undeterministic behaviour. This is of prime importance when describing protocols in order to avoid over–specification. Undeterminism can be introduced

- in calling on external functions which return a result having a specified type but an undefined value,
- when more than one predicate (provided clause) is true and one of the actions corresponding to one of those predicates may be executed.
- Spontaneous transitions may also be introduced: they are transitions which are not triggered by any external event. A spontaneous transition can fire at any time, provided a set of conditions based on the internal state of the entity is true.

Other facilities

A state automata description implies that there are well identified events which are received in well known states. The problem in protocol description is that identifying the event itself is a part of the protocol description. Similarily identifying to which state automata instance the event applies is also a part of the protocol.

When a (N-1)-SDU is received, it is first necessary to recognize a (N)-PDU (i.e. identify the event), then find to what connection the PDU belongs (i.e. select the state automata instance) before applying the transition of the state automata.

PDIL contains all the appropriate features for describing this part of the protocol.

When a (N-1)-SDU is received it is first processed in the context attached to the channel to which the interaction carrying the (N-1)-SDU has been received.

Then a special decoding function is called, which allows for recognizing the PDU and selecting the appropriate event.

If necessary, the parameters of the PDU may be used to identify what automaton's instance the PDU belongs to.

Then the appropriate context is selected before the state automata is called. Context can be selected by identifier or by criteria. Other constructs allow to apply one event to several contexts in turn (e.g. all contexts meeting a particular criteria).

Abstract memory management

Additionally, PDIL includes a facility called 'abstract memory management' allowing to describe what happens to the data passed by the (N+1)-entity and the (N-1)entity. A set of system calls (fragment, assemble, copy, forget, create, expand) are offered to the user for describing user-data manipulation. This approach offers tools for an unambiguous description of this important aspect of a communication protocol and has permitted to achieve automatic - and efficient - implementation.

Automatic implementation and simulation

Automatic implementation and simulation both rely on a compiler (a preprocessor) which translates PDIL source into PASCAL programs.

The preprocessor. The preprocessor – operational under Multics – translates a PDIL description into

- a main Pascal program containing one procedure per interaction belonging to the entity.
- a set of Pascal subroutines which may be either complete (i.e. they contain a completely programmed body) or to be completed by the user at impletation time.
- a set of tables containing internal information on the structure (machines, interactions, ...).

The PDIL preprocessor makes the syntax checking and produces a Pascal code independent from the target system.

Automatic implementation. Automatic implementation is the creation of instances corresponding to the model previously described. The Pascal programs produced by the preprocessor should be completed (in order to become executable):

1. with a run time environment offering the system calls used by a PDIL description: mainly abstract memory management and channel management.
2. with some part of the protocol which may not be fully specified (e.g. detailled encoding / decoding).
3. with the parameters and subroutines characterizing the instance.

The run time environment differs depending on the target system on which the automatic implementation is to be executed. But it has to be constructed only once per target system and can then be reused for any protocol implementation in any layer on the same system.

The part 2 referred to above is specific of each protocol and should be coded manually for each new protocol which is implemented.

The part 3 may be reduced to some simple tables or may be comprise some sophisticated subprograms depending on the protocol (like an algorithm to optimize local resources).

Our experience has shown that, when the run time environment has been constructed for a given operating system, more than 90% of the code representing an implementation is obtained automatically.

The simulator. The simulator is nothing but a specific run time environment which executes the code in a controlled manner. Simulation of the (N)−protocol requires that the (N−1)−service has also been specified. A typical configuration of a simulation is given in figure 10.

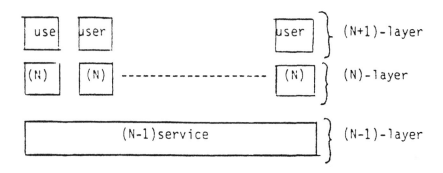

Figure 10: Typical configuration of an (N)−protocol simulation

As can be seen in figure 10, the simulation also requires users in layer (N+1). The users excercise the service provided by the (N)−entities. The users are also written in PDIL as very simple (N+1)−entities. They include spontaneous transitions representing all possible behaviours of the user of a the (N)−service.

Conclusion

From experience it appears that PDIL and the associate tools are really the basis of a protocol software factory. The preprocessor, the simulator and a run time environment on INTEL RMX 86 are operational. A lot of protocols in layer 2,3,4 and 5 have been specified using PDIL [Ansart 83c] and the experiments of the automatic implementation on RMX86 are very promising - more than 90% of the code is produced automatically and the mean time for implementing a protocol is reduced by more than 70% compared with traditional implementation methods for protocols. New experiments are in progress using UNIX.

PDIL is close to the work developed at the Montreal University by the team of G.V. Bochmann [Bochmann 82], at NBS [Blummer 82] and also to the language currently in development by ISO/TC97/SC16 [ISO 83f].

Overview of PDIL in English can be found in [Ansart 83d] and the reader familiar with the french language will find in [Chari 83] a complete specification and user's manual of PDIL.

9.2.3. Testing tools

As soon as a distributed system involves several components built by different parties − e.g. users, suppliers, ... − and communicating using protocols, setting up the system does not end with the protocol design and implementation steps: verifying that the components conform to the protocols − i.e. that the equipments really respect the protocols when running is also an important task.

Purpose of testing and testing tools

First, testing tools should provide help for debugging implementations while building the system. This includes mainly two aspects:

- checking that the equipment correctly run the protocol;
- checking the robustness of the software against abnormal situations: reaction to protocol errors made by another party as well as to transmission errors (i.e. errors signalled by the (N−1)−service).

Secondly, testing tools should provide help for performing acceptance testing: when a component of a network is installed by its user who may have bought it from a supplier, the user should be able to verify that:

- the equipment conforms to the protocol,
- the range of options really supported conforms to what is claimed to be supported by the supplier,
- the equipment has an acceptable degree of robustness,

- the performance meets the user requirements.

Finally, after equipments have been put into an operational network, the experience has shown that there is a need for:

- arbitration facilities: in the case of abnormal behaviour it is of prime importance to be able to designate without ambiquity the faulting equipment;
- online measurement facilities: this covers traffic measurement (in order to anticipate the possible evolution of the network topology) – as well as specific protocol performance measurement (like the ratio between the number of data messages versus control messages) in order to prepare the next versions of the protocols themselves.

Specific constraints for a testing tool in an open environment

For systems under test which have implemented an interface permitting direct access to a specific layer, it will be possible to test this layer, provided that the lower layers have already been tested.

If this is not possible, combined testing of layers will be necessary.

For example, once the transport layer has been tested in this way, the session layer may be tested. Then, after this, it will be possible to test a virtual terminal protocol or a file transfer protocol. Conversely, if the transport layer interface is not available, but the session interface is available, the transport and session layer will be tested together, before the VTP is subsequently tested.

This flexibility is of prime importance, because a system will make the choice not to exhibit a particular interface for performance or architectural consideration e.g. an X25 chip does not provide external access to the layer 2 service interface.

Another fundamental constraint for a testing tool is its ability to accommodate different versions of protocols: if the cost for building the testing tool when changing the protocol is higher than the equipment production cost, then the testing tools will never be used... This aspect is very important when several versions of a protocol are experimented. This property is sometimes referred to as 'protocol independence' of the testing tools [Ansart 81].

Brief overview of some testing tools

In parallel with the development of the OSI protocol, some countries have decided to start an extensive study of testing tools for equipment implementing the OSI protocols. In the USA, the NBS has set up a set of tools for the OSI higher layer (layer 4 to 7) which are now operational for the transport protocol [Nightingale 81, Nightingale 82].

In Germany the GMD concentrated on teletex layer 4 [Faltin 83] . In the UK, the team leaded by D. Rayner at NPL has developed testing facilities for the network layer over X25 [Rayner 82], while in France, the Agence de l'Informatique received the task to study tools for layer 4,5 and 6.

This subsection briefly presents three testing tools developed by the Agence de l'Informatique in France [Ansart 83e, Damidau 82, Bonhomme 83, Ferret 83].

The STQ system. The STQ system is based on two main components

- the reference system,
- a distributed application which uses (and exercices) the service provided by the reference system and the implementation under test.

The distributed application contains mainly two parts:

- a test driver which is the active part executing a scenario,
- a test responder acting as a passive system which responds to the stimuli sent by the test driver via the (N)-service. The test driver and the test responder are cooperating in executing a scenario.

A scenario is a set of commands requiring (N)-services. The test driver transmits to the test responder the commands to be executed in (N)-SDUS of a previously opened (N)-connection. To some extent the responder may be viewed as an interpreter which is remotely loaded by the active tester. Execution of a scenario is splitted into several phases, each of which starting with the transmission of the commands to be executed in the second part of the phase. Since the responder is a quite complicated program, it is important to reduce the cost of its production, as well as to ensure its correctness. In order to achieve these two goals the test responder is splitted into two parts:

- One is the main program comprising the algorithm for command loading, interpretation and execution. This part is written in Pascal and portable. It is given to each potential client of the STQ test system. This part assumes a (N)-service strictly identical to the theoretical (N)-service defined by ISO for the (N)-layer under test.

- The second part deals with the mapping of the (N)-service abstract interface into the real interface available inside the implementation under test. This part is system dependent and shall be realized by the user of the implementation under test. (I..U.T).

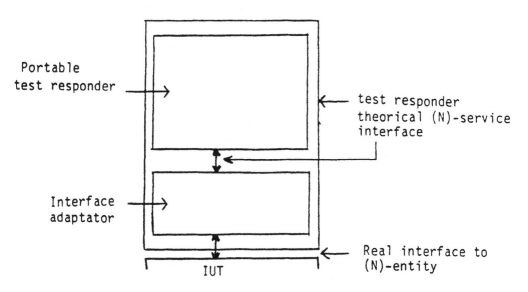

Figure 11: The test responder.

As shown in figure 12, the STQ system contains the following components:

- the reference implementation runs the (N)-protocol;

- the management and configuration module allows for tracing the events, configuring the test (setting parameters and options) and also introducing errors and simulating abnormal behaviour;

514

- the test driver controls the execution of the tests and pilots the remote test responder(s);
- the (N−1)−service implementation runs protocols (N−1) ... to 1 in order to provide the (N−1)−service used by the (N)−entity.

The scenario commands are divided into three subcategories:

- the supervision commands allow the user of the systems (i.e. the operator of the STQ test system) to set up the configuration, and activate/deactivate the trace and log facilities;
- the operator commands for building/modifying, loading/executing, starting/suspending/resuming scenarios;
  automatic as well step by step mode of operation are available;
- the scenario elements themselves: operation of the (N)−service, remote loading of the test responder, and execution of a distributed scenario (send/receive data, synchronize, echo, ...).

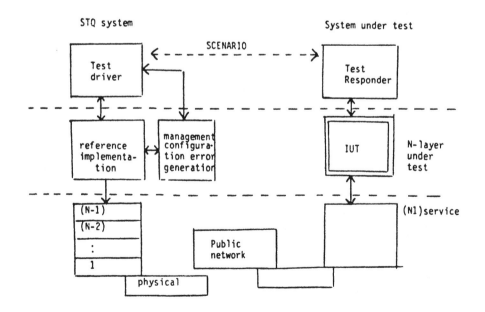

Figure 12: The components of a STQ system.

A traductor based on an syntax analyser translates the external form of a scenario (i.e. a form suitable for the operator) into an internal form (i.e. a form suitable for execution by interpretation).

In order to perform tests starting from elementary tests and increasing the complexity and the completeness, a scenario data base is also available. The tests recorded in the data base fall into four categories: elementary tests for service availability, tests requiring configuration, tests of protocol options and parameters, tests including error recovery and reaction to abnormal situation (error generation). Mono-connection as well as multi-connection tests can be also be run.

The CERBERE tool. CERBERE is a tool designed to be introduced between two equipments running high level protocols. One equipment is the implementation under test, the other one is the reference equipment (i.e. a testing center or an equipment previously tested). The CERBERE cannot provide directly for a complete test system but is only a complementary aid. CERBERE is also useful for arbitration and measurements in an operational network.

CERBERE acts as a relay in layer 3, allowing for

- analysing the user of the network service made by the higher level protocols,
- simulating errors in the network service.

CERBERE offers to its user an interface allowing for decoding/analysing the high level protocols contained in the network service data units. In parallel mode the analysis is done simultaneously with the relay function therefore guaranteeing that the traffic is not perturbed. In serial mode the analysis is performed before the relay function is called on, allowing for 'intelligent' perturbation of the network service (e.g. simulate a network disconnect when the high level commit protocol is in its 'window of vulnerability').

CERBERE also offers a lot of complementary services like: statistic calculation tools, network usage cost computation, sophisticated full screen display of results, traffic storage on disk for deferred off-line analysis ... etc.

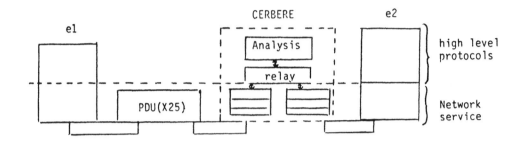

Figure 13: CERBERE as a high level protocol analyser

The GENEPI tool. GENEPI is a protocol data units generator which is indepedent of the protocol: i.e. changing the protocol supported by GENEPI is an easy (and costless) task.

- GENEPI is designed to manipulate conceptual objects involved into a (N)-protocol: (N)-PDUs, access to (N-1)-service, mapping of PDUs into (N-1)-SDUs, encoding/decoding, ...
- The basic software knows neither the format of the PDUs (the syntax) nor of tables and automata that the GENEPI basic software uses to generate the (N)-protocol.

Assuming that GENEPI is designed to generate (N)-PDUs, its basic software contains:

- an implementation of the (N-1)-service
- a set of commands to access the (N-1)-service
- a set of commands to manipulate local variables
- a set of commands to compose and send (N)-PDUs and to decode (access to the fields of) received (N)-PDUs
- a facility for macro-commands
- a state automata-driver
- trace, logging and display functions

In the first stage, the operator introduces the format of the PDUs in two different ways: the logical format describes the PDU's fields as "records" while the physical format deals with the actual PDU's bit strings and the mapping between logical and physical formats.

GENEPI can be run in manual mode: the operator composes logical PDUs with the help of the system (prompting for each parameter), then the system encodes and sends them. When receiving, the system decodes the arriving PDUs und displays them in logical format.

Parameter values can be set to/assigned from local variables for speeding up the protocol operation. This mode allows to set up elementary – but significant – tests of high level protocols in a very few days.

Another mode – termed automatic – is also available: the manual operator is replaced by a set of interconnected state automata, whose events are (N)–PDUs and (N–1)–service indications, and actions are GENEPI commands. Automatic mode permits to build an acceptance test which can be run without the help of any operator. The system includes multiple state automata instances selection/manipulation, therefore complex functions like multiplexing – splitting – error recovery are easy to introduce into GENEPI.

Finally, the system provides for a multilayer testing facility in which PDUs of two adjacent levels (N and (N+1)) can be manipulated simultaneously. The GENEPI package has the network and transport service implemented as standard (N–1)–service: it can therefore be used for testing any protocol in layer 4,5,6 of the OSI architecture. It has been used to test the early implementations of OSI made by French suppliers and PTT.

Conclusion

Testing the conformity of equipments to protocol is one of the key points for the OSI protocols development and use: the objective of OSI will not be achieved unless products are produced in conformance with OSI and tested for this conformance. Although some early testing tools are available – with promising results, there is one main area which has not really been tackled so far: how can the specification tools automatically produce the testing tools:

- deriving the test scenarios automatically from the specification,
- implementing the testing center automatically from the formal specification of the protocol,
- generating automatically analysis programs to be run in an 'observer' (like CERBERE).

Although a tool like LISE produces test scenarios as a result of the validation process, the number of scenarios is too high for being used in practical tests and there is no tool for selecting an useable – and significant – subset offering an appropriate test covering.

Although implementations can be automatically produced from a formal specification, this does not address the problem of error generation and does not help for producing the test scenarios.

The only area in which significant results have been obtained so far is in deriving an automatic observer for the specification of a protocol [Ayache 79].

9.3. Example: The OSI transport protocol

The transport layer is the last layer of the communication oriented layers of the OSI reference model.

Its purpose is to isolate the processing oriented layers from the variation of the quality of service of the network service. It also allows for the optimization the use of the network service on an end-to-end basis.

9.3.1. The transport service

The transport layer provides the transport service [ISO 83c] by adding to the network service the functions supported by the transport protocol.

The transport service offers point-to-point transport connection between transport-service-access points. More than one transport connection may be opened between the same pair of T-SAPs: according to the model they are locally distinguished by means of Transport-connection-end-point identifiers (T-CEP-ID).

A transport connection comprises three phases:

- The connection phase allows for opening the connection   between a
  pair of specified transport adresses. The connection   establishment
  phase provides also for:

  - negotiation of the quality of service;
  - negotiation of the use of expedited data transfer service during
    the subsequent data transfer phase;
  - transmission of a limited amount of user data.

Figure 14 summarizes the transport service primitives for the
connection establishment phase, while figure 15 gives typical operation
of connection establishment.

Primitive	Parameters
T-CONNECT request	Called Address, calling address, expedited data option, quality of service, user-data.
T-CONNECT indication	same as T-CONNECT request
T-CONNECT response	Responding address, quality of service, expedited data option, user-data
T-CONNECT confirmation	same as T-CONNECT response

Figure 14: Parameters for connection establishment.

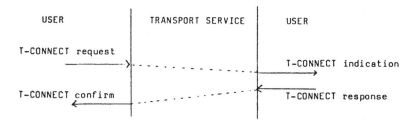

Figure 15: Typical operation of the connection establishment phase.

- The data transfer phase provides for

  - transmission of TSDUs of unlimited lenght in both directions according to the agreed upon quality of service;

- transmission of expedited TSDUs (up to 16 octets in both directions, if negotiated during the establishment phase.

Flow control is offered independently for both, the expedited and the normal flows. An expedited data may bypass a normal data but a normal data cannot bypass an expedited one.

- The release service allows for terminating the connection at any time. Termination is normally invoked by one of the users (or both simultaneously) but may also be invoked by the service itself in case of errors. Termination is an unconfirmed service which may result in loss of data.

Figure 16 shows typical termination cases of a transport connection termination

Figure 16: Typical cases of a transport connection termination

9.3.2. The transport protocol

In order to bridge the gap between the network service and the service to be provided to the users, the transport protocol uses the following functions:

- mapping of transport addresses into network addresses,
- assignment of transport connections onto network connections,
- identification of transport connections,
- segmenting TSDUs into TPDUs and reassembling TPDUs into TSDUs,
- implicit flow control (use of the (N−1) flow control) or explicit flow control by means of acknowledgement and credit mechanisms,
- multiplexing of several transport connections onto one simple

network connection,

- explicit disconnection (i.e. disconnecting the transport connection without disconnecting the supporting network connection) or implicit disconnection (via the disconnection of the supporting network connection),
- recovery from errors signalled by the network,
- detection of errors not signalled from the network.

Due to the variety of network services and the differences in the user's requirements, the transport should be able to dynamically adapt the quantity of functions put into operation over a given transport connection. This is done in negotiating the functions to be used at connection establishment time.

In order to simplify the negociation mechanism, the functions have been organized in classes:

- Class 0 is the simplest class including the minimum functionality:

  - connection establishment,
  - data transfer and segmenting,
  - implicit disconnection.

- Class 1 includes class 0 functions and also

  - explicit disconnection,
  - recovery from errors signalled by the network.

- Class 2 includes class 0 functions and in addition those functions necessary for multiplexing:

  - explicit disconnection,
  - connection identification,
  - explicit flow control.

- Class 3 uses class 2 functions and offers additionally recovery from errors signalled by the network layer.
- Class 4 detects and recovers from errors which are not signalled by

the network.

Therefore, class 4 may operate on top of connection−less network (e.g. datagram network) or split a transport connection onto several network connections (use of several network connections for a single transport connection leads to misordering of TPDUs).

The functions included in the classes demonstrate the possible negotiations (see figure 17).

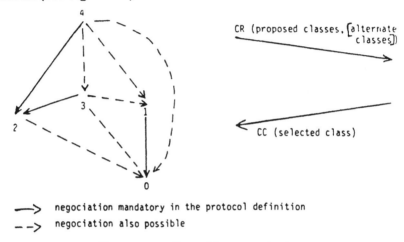

CR (proposed classes, [alternate classes])

CC (selected class)

——> negociation mandatory in the protocol definition
− −> negociation also possible

Figure 17: Possible negotiations.

In order to avoid collision on a given connection identifier when establishing two connections simultaneously (and to simplify the implementations), the connection references are established as follows: each party selects one part of the identifier (see figure 18) and communicates it to the partner during the connection establishment phase. Then both partners keep track of the parts which have been locally selected (local reference) and remotely selected (remote reference).

In the data transfer phase only the remote reference is put in the PDUs which are sent (in the 'destination reference field'). When a PDU is received, the destination reference field is used to match with the local reference in order to associate the received PDU with the appropriate connection. In the disconnection phase, both references are exchanged again in order to perform a more secure exchange. This technique gives to implementations all freedom for allocating/releasing references in the most convenient way and avoids 'cross-generation' of systems.

Figure 19 gives the list of the TPDUs and their eventual parameters, while Figure 20 shows some typical protocol exchanges in classes 0,1 and 2.

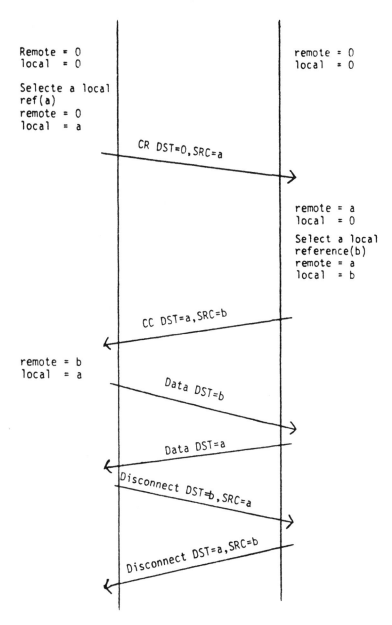

Figure 18: Connection references selection and use.

TPDU's	PARAMETERS
Connection request (CR)	initial credit destination reference, source reference, proposed class and options, alternative class, addresses, quality of service, data
Connection confirm (CC)	initial credit, destination reference, source reference selected class and options, address, quality of service, data
Disconnect request (DR)	destination reference, source reference reason, data
Disconnect confirm (DC)	destination reference, source reference
Acknoledgment (AK)	destination reference, credit, expected TPDU number
Reject (RJ)	=
Data (DT)	destination reference (in class 2,3, and 4) end of TSDU mark, TPDU number in classes other than 0
Expedited data (EX)	destination reference expedited TPDU number, data
Error (ER)	destination reference, reason, text of rejected TPDU.

Figure 19: TPDUS and their parameters.

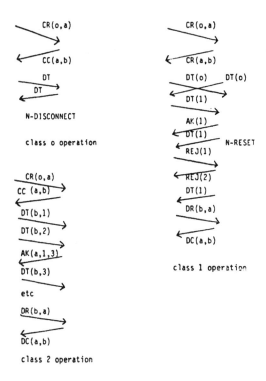

Figure 20 : Typical exchanges on classes 0,1,2.

9.4. Protocol games

This section proposes some "protocol games" based on very simple examples, in order to give to the reader some flavour of the problems which may be encountered when specifying and validating protocols.

For the sake of simplicity, we focus on the following two aspects:

- use of (N−1) flow control service,
- influence of transit delay.

The study is done using a simple protocol invented only for this purpose. When necessary, references are made to existing protocols (e.g. ISO transport and session protocol) where similar problems are found when studying them.

9.4.1. The example

The protocol involves two processes called 'Sender' and 'Receiver'.
On request of its user the Sender sends messages of fixed − (short) arbitrary length. The Sender has a variable called X used as follows:

- At initialization time X is equal to zero.
- Before sending a message X is incremented by one.
- If X reaches a bound called M, the Sender detects an error and stops.
- When the Sender receives from the Receiver a RESET message, it resets X to zero.

The Receiver receives messages and passes them to its user.
The Receiver has a variable called Y used as follows:

- At initialization time Y is equal to zero.
- When receiving a message Y is incremented by one
- If Y reaches a bound called N, the Receiver sends a RESET message to the Sender and resets Y to zero.

M and N are parameters of the communication and have values allocated before the communication starts.

The Sender and the Receiver exchange their messages via a medium without error (no loss, no duplication, no misordering).

9.4.2. Notation

In order to facilitate further reference to this protocol we use the following notation:

The Sender and the Receiver are described by means of transitions of the following form:

<event state (predicate) resulting−state message (variable−setting)>

Using the notation, the Sender's transitions are:

S1 : <U−request normal−state $(X<M-1)$ normal state data $(X:=X+1)$>
S2 : <U−request normal−state $(X=M-1)$ error−state − () >
S3 : <RESET normal−state ( ) normal−state − $(X:=0)$>

The Receiver's transitions are:

R1 : <data normal−state (Y<N−1) normal−state U−indication
      (Y:=Y+1)>
R2 : <data normal−state (Y=N−1) normal−state
      RESET&U−indication (Y:=0)>

We represent a global state of the communication as follows : [West 78a, West 78b]

$$\begin{bmatrix} \text{Sender} & \text{Receiver} \\ \text{M(S<-R)} & \text{M(R<-S)} \end{bmatrix}$$

Where Sender and Receiver are the state (and variables) of the processes and M (S<−R) and M (R<−S) are the content of the medium in the specified direction.

In our case the states of sender and receiver are represented by the X and Y variables respectively.

Using this notation the initial state is:

$$\begin{bmatrix} 0 & 0 \\ \text{empty} & \text{empty} \end{bmatrix}$$

We also give a possible Petri net for the Sender and for the Receiver:

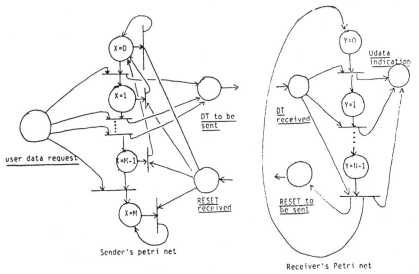

Sender's petri net

Receiver's Petri net

9.4.3. Flow control

Although very simple, the protocol is in fact incompletely specified: nothing is said about flow control.

In fact the following implicit assumption is made:

- the receiving user regulates the rate at which the Receiver delivers massage to it,
- the Receiver regulates the rate at which the medium delivers messages to it,
- the medium regulates the rate at which the Sender may pass messages to it,
- and finally the sender regulates the rate at which it accepts messages from its user

Conversely, it is clear that the protocol cannot operate without this assumption; if the Sender can send an infinite number of messages even if the receiver does not process them (i.e. they are in the medium), then the X variable will reach the bound M and the Sender will detect an error.

In general the protocol specification does not include this flow control aspect for the following reason: protocols include control phases based on handshake in which an entity refrains itself from sending an infinite number of messages before waiting for an acknoledgment, and this mechanism hides the above described 'backpressure' flow control.

It should also be noted that a full specification of the communication cannot be obtained without specifying the maximum capacity of the medium.

We give here a possible model of medium with a capacity of 2 and the flow control property.

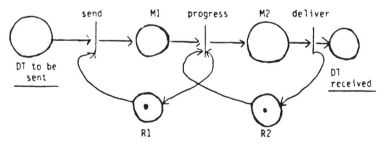

The 'send' transition represents the acceptance of a message by the medium, while 'deliver' models the acceptance of the message by the Receiver.

Places R1 and R2 represent the capacity of the medium, while M1 and M2 model the medium itself (fifo with capacity of 2).

It is now necessary to express the 'back-pressure' flow control between the medium and the Sender (i.e. the Sender shall be refrained to put tokens into the 'DT to be sent' place while the place is busy) and between the Sender and the user, etc... The total capacity of the system is the sum of the capacity of each of its components. Note that, when using Petri nets, a more simple solution is to prevent the sending user to put a new token in the 'userdata request' place until the previous message has not been completely processed by the system.

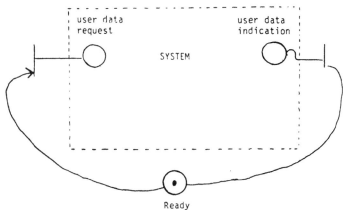

This model is more simple and guarantees an overall capacity of one (or p if we put p tokens in the ready place). However it is far from the real protocol to be modelled and the equivalence of both models has to be proved.

The ISO transport protocol classes 0 and 1, as well as the ISO session protocol use back-pressure flow control during their data transfer phase.

9.4.4. Transit delay

In general the transit delay is neither specified in protocol, nor used by the validation systems.

The semantic behind this absence of specification of time is sometimes unclear, sometimes an event may appear in the interval (0, infinity).

This is at least the case in Petri nets, but also in the perturbation method as developed at the IBM ZÜRICH Lab [West 78a, West 78b].

Let us consider our example, assuming a flow control and a medium capacity of one. In each direction assume also that M is greater than N but lower than $2 \times N$.

Let us consider the following global state

$$\begin{bmatrix} X = N & Y = N-1 \\ - & MESSAGE \end{bmatrix}$$

Since the medium is full the only possible next global state is (transition R2).

$$\begin{bmatrix} X = N & Y = 0 \\ RESET & - \end{bmatrix}$$

Then, the next global state could be either the delivery of the reset message or a production of a new message. The later case will lead to the following global state (transition S1).

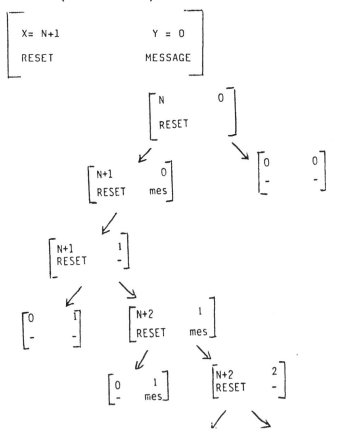

Finally the Sender will detect an error and stop. The problem comes from the fact that, since there is no bound of the transit delay for the messages, it is possible to send an 'infinite' number of messages in one direction (Sender to Receiver), while the RESET message sent by the Receiver is not delivered (i.e. is still in transit). Again, this is due to the absence of a handshake in the protocol: in the case of a handshake, the execution of the handshake implies that a message is sent and another received and this represents a bound for the transit delay.

If we assume for the messages a minimum and a maximum transit delay, then the protocol operates properly (with appropriate values for N, M and the bounds of the transit delay).

A similar problem has been discovered in the OSI session protocol in which, in the absence of transit delay, an infinite number of expedited data may bypass a given normal data....

If we go back to our Petri-net, it would be necessary to add a [tmin, tmax] interval to every transition, tmin being the minimum time the transition will wait after being and staying enabled, and tmax being the maximum time the transition may wait after being and staying enabled before firing [Merlin 76].

All transitions will receive an [0,0] interval except

- production of messages by the sending user and acceptance of messages by the receiving user which receive a [0, infinity] interval,
- transitions for progression of messages in the medium which receives a [tmin, tmax] interval.

The resulting Petri-net can be analysed [Berthomieu 83] and will be found correct.

9.4.5. Side effect in flow control

Let us assume now that M> 2*N, and consider that there is no transit delay specified for the messages.

Assume that the medium capacity is one.

Let us consider the following global state.

```
┌                                           ┐
│  2*N                    N-1               │
│                                           │
│  RESET                  MESSAGE           │
└                                           ┘
```

This global state reached after the Sender has first sent N messages. Then, the Receiver has sent a RESET when receiving the message number N and has set his Y variable to zero. Again the sender has sent N messages before the RESET has been delivered.

Since $Y = N-1$, the protocol specification says that a RESET message shall be sent back. However, the medium is not ready for accepting a new message. There is a lack of specification in the protocol. Depending on the semantic used for the model of specification, the choice may be:

1. Since the Receiver cannot completely process the received message we consider that the receiver does not withdraw the message from the medium (the sending and receiving flow control is coupled in a loop-back fashion).
2. This is an error.
3. The RESET message is produced by the Receiver and put into a temporary queue in which it waits before being sent.

In the case 1 and only in this case the protocol is operating properly.

A similar case has been found in the OSI transport protocol when spurious TPDUs are received and answered (for instance a Disconnect Confirm is sent back for any unexpected received Disconnect Request), regardless of the sending capacity of the network connection.

9.4.6. Protocol correctness versus service conformity

The example below presents a protocol, currently under design by CCITT and called "D-protocol". The protocol is very simple and designed for reliable transmission of messages over an unreliable link which does not signal errors. Only one message is transmitted at a time.

The D-protocol: The model of the D-protocol can be given as follows:

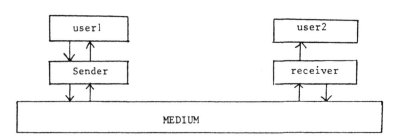

User1 requests of a message in passing to the Sender the DTA request primitive and will eventually receive from the Sender the DTA confirmation which indicates that the Sender is ready for accepting the next request. A parameter of the DTA confirmation also indicates if the message has been successfully transmitted (+ confirmation) or has been (possibily) lost (– confirmation).

At the receiving side there is one service primitive passed by the Receiver to user2: NDTA indication.

The protocol itself makes use of two messages:

DT (Sequence_number, data)   sent by the sender to the receiver

AK (Sequence_number)   sent by the receiver to the sender

The protocol is defined as follows (in pseudo–PDIL)

```
const maxretrans=...;              (* the maximum retransmission *)
      timer_value=...;             (* value to be used for retransmission
                                      timer*)

type sequence_number= 0...1;       (* as for alternating bit *)
     datatype=...;                 (* undefined string of octed *)
     conf_type=(positive,negative); (* confirmation *)

interaction  DT = record
                 seq: sequence_number;
                 data: datatype;
             end ;
             AK = record
                  seq: sequence_number;
             end ;
             DTArequest = record
```

```
                    data: datatype;
             end ;
             DTAindication = record
                    data: datatype;
             end ;
             DTAconfirmation =record
                    conf: conf_type;
             end ;

(* sender operation *)

var retrans: integer;              (* retransmission counter *)
    my_seq: sequence_number;       (* current sequence number *)
    state (ready, waiting);        (* current state *)
    copy_data: data_type;          (* copy of data for retransmission*)
init begin retrans:=0 ;            (* initialize retransmission counter *)
          my_seq:=0 ;              (* initialize sequence number *)
          to ready;                (* initial state *)
      end ;
trans when DTArequest              (* from user *)
  from ready                       (* in ready state *)
     to waiting                    (* next state *)
     send_to_medium_DT(my_seq,
     DTArequest.data);             (* send *)
     copy_data:= DTArequest.data;  (* next copy *)
     set_timer (timer_value);
   endfrom
endwhen;                           (* in other state, this is a user error *)
when AK                            (* from remote entity via medium *)
  from waiting                     (* in waiting state *)
  provided (AK.seq=my_seq)         (* OK *)
     or (retrans = 0);
     reset_timer; retrans:= 0;     (* reset variable *)
     to ready ;                    (* back to ready*)
     my_seq:=1-my_seq;             (* ready for next seq. number *)
```

```
        send_to_user_DTAconfirmation (positive);
     endprov
     provided otherwise            (* not OK *)
        reset_timer;
        set_timer (timer_value);   (* a new timer *)
        my_seq:=1-my_seq;          (* change seq *)
        retransm:=retrans+1;       (* retransmit *)
        send_to_medium_DT (my_seq, cpoy_data);
                                   (* again *)
     endprov
     endfrom
endwhen;                           (* in other state this is an error *)

when time_out                      (* timer runs out *)
   from waiting                    (* in waiting state only *)
   provided (retrans=maxretrans)   (* limit reached *)
      retrans:=0;                  (* reset retrans *)
      my_seq:=1-my_seq;            (* ready for next *)
      send_to_user_DTAconfirmation (negative);
                                   (* may be lost *)
   endprov
   provided otherwise              (* limit not reached *)
      retrans:=retrans+1;          (* incremented retrans *)
      set_timer (timer_value);     (* timer needed *)
      send_to_medium_DT(my seq,copy data);
                                   (* retransmission *)
   endprov
   endfrom
endwhen;

* receiver operation *)

var my_seq:integer;                (* no state needed *)
init  my_seq:=0;                   (* initialize my sequence *)
rans when DT                       (* from medium *)
```

provided (my_seq=DT.Seq)　　　　(* sequence as expected *)
　　send_to_medium_AK (my_seq); (* AK *)
　　send_to_user_DTAindication (DT.Data);
　　　　　　　　　　　　　　　　(* data to user *)
　　my_seq:=1−my_seq;　　　　　(* ready for next *)
endprov

Environment and parameter assumptions: The maxretrans parameter may take any value. The timer−value parameter may take any value provided it is greater than twice the maximum transit delay of the medium. The medium may transmit or loose any message provided the message is either delivered before the maximum transmit delay or never. Provided the above described conditions are respected, there is only one message in transit at a time, therefore, the question whether the medium may deliver the message out of order is irrelevant.

Protocol validation: The validation of the protocol has been done (using LISE) and shows the following:

- There are no deadlocks or unspecified receptions.
- The global state automata is connex and contains no unproductive productive cycles.

Service conformity: Although the protocol validation has been successfully accomplished, it remains to be proved that the protocol provides the service it has been designed for.

The service can be defined as follows:

- For every NDTArequest issued by the user, the data is either delivered at the other end (NDTAindication) or lost.
- A NDTAconfirmation (positive) is never delivered if the data is lost.
- A NDTAconfirmation (negative) may be delivered even if the data has not been lost, but on this case, is passed to the user after the data has been delivered to the remote user.
- If the data is lost a NDTAconfirmation (negative) is always passed to

the user.

- If the data is not lost a NDTAconfirmation (positive) is always passed to the user.

In other words, the only valid sequence of service primitive is defined as:

valid-sequence::= NDTArequest.<result>.<valid-sequence>
result::= NDTAindication. NDTAconfirmation (positive)
      |NDTAindication. NDTAconfirmation (negative)
      |NDTAconfirmation (negative)

The service conformity checking can be done by using "global variables" and one "invariant transition".

A variable is said to be global if it can be accessed by the sender and receiver side. An invariant transition is a spontaneous transition which shall never be enabled, otherwise an error is detected (in other words the predicate representing the guard of the transition is of the form "provided invariant-is-false").

The service conformity can be checked as follows: the two following global variables are introduced.

diff : integer   (* the difference between the number of data sent
                  and the number of data passed to the user *)

receiv : boolean   (* true if a message has been delivered *)

- The transitions are modified as follows:
  - sending DT: diff:=diff+1;
                            receiv:=false;
  - passing data to user: diff:=diff-1;
                            receiv:=true;
  - passing NDTAconfirmation (negative) to the user
                    if (not receiv) then diff:=diff-1;

- The following invariant transition is introduced
                      provided (diff <0 or diff>1) to error-state;

Running the validation with LISE has shown that a service violation is possible (i.e. a message lost and positive confirmation returned).

9.4.7. Conclusion

A number of other "games" can be constructed with these protocols or with variants, but this is not our talk... Our goal was only to illustrate by a few examples the need for:

- A precise specification of a protocol including the relationship between the (N)−protocol and the (N+1)−user, and the use of the (N−1)−service.
- A precise and well known semantic when the validation of the protocol is done. Otherwise problems may be detected only at implementation time.
- A precise definition of the service the protocol should provide.

There exists a large variety of techniques for specifying and analyzing protocols. The most important, from the user's point of view, seems to be how to deal with the four steps of the design procedure: specification − validation − implementation − maintenance. The tools which have been presented along these lectures are probably not the most advanced and efficient for a specific phase, however they present the advantage to be fully operational, to have been experimented with a large number of 'real' protocols and to provide aid for each of the four above mentioned phases. Conversely, we must admit that the techniques presented here have the drawback to work at a "low" level of abstraction and to use validation by enumeration rather than verification by proof....

Chapter 10
Conclusion

10.1. Introduction

This course has addressed the topic of methods and tools for specification of distributed systems. Seven major themes have been discussed:

. Acquisition and the Environment Requirements

. Systems Requirements

. Formal Foundations for Specification and Verification

. Language Constructs for Distributed Programs

. The Argus Language and System

. Paradigms for Distributed Programs

. Issues and Tools for Protocol Specification

This summary of conclusions from the various discussions attempts to indicate their relevance to the three concepts in the title of the course (Distributed Systems, Methods and Tools) and to the practical application of advanced techniques and tools to system development projects.

10.2. Distributed Systems

The major structural boundary for a system is between it and its environment. The environment is almost always distributed in some sense (eg there are usually several users or several interface locations - such as a terminal, a printer and storage devices). Hence a method of identifying the requirement of the environment must allow recognition of the distributed nature of the environment.

The system itself may be distributed, either to match the structure of the environment or for reasons of internal architectural convenience in meeting the overall requirements of the environment for such things as reliability, security or fast throughput.

Once a decision has been taken to distribute the components of a system a number of recurrent problems arise. It is desirable that the developers should not attempt to re-invent the solutions to these problems on each new system.

In this course the CORE method has been used as an example of a method for analysis of the requirements of a distributed environment. It adopts an approach based on the ideas of "real world" modelling. Few other methods exist for analysis of the environment of a computer system, but those which do also use the concept of real world modelling.

The SREM method has been used here to illustrate the examination of the implication of the environment's constraints on the system requirements and their later influence on overall system structure at the level of both the major component design and the detailed module design.

Concepts and techniques from Temporal Logic have been used to illustrate how the developer can prepare for the analysis of complex system behaviour in distributed systems by preparing system specifications which are amenable to formal analysis. This may not always lead to complete verification of the implemented system against its broadest statements of requirement, but is can lead to much greater confidence in the achievement of key qualities such as safety and reliability than is possible with "ad-hoc" development techniques.

The use of paradigms has been discussed, to illustrate that there are a number of recurent problems for which complete or partial formal treatments do exist. In such cases, it is clearly advantageous to recognise that some aspect of a system under development embodies one of the known problems and to adopt the appropriate formal approach to handling it. Here again, the use of formal techniques for specification may be expected to assist recognition of such cases.

Language constructs have been discussed, using existing languages and proposed extensions, to examine the problems of specifying key properties of distributed systems, such as system configuration and re-configuration. The possibility has been assessed of using existing "coding" languages with relatively simple extensions to specify the system and later to implement the specification.

The Argus system has been used to illustrate a practical approach to the specification and implementation of a system which can be distributed in various ways, while retaining properties of fault tolerance and reliability. No claim has been made about speed of operation for "time-critical" systems, but the possibility is shown for achievement of significantly improved recovery from random failure than is normal with complex systems.

Finally, the problems of reliable communication between the components of a distributed system is known to be extremely difficult and has been addressed by many researchers in the computer industry.

The OSI approach to achievement of a standard for transfer protocols has been used on this course to illustrate the problems to be addressed, a philosophy and practical realisation of a usable standard for distributed systems communication.

10.3. Methods

Methods for specification can address two issues: acquisition of information and expression of the information which has been acquired.

Acquisition means more than just provoking a stream of statements about the system and its environment. It means establishing and policing the scope of the information, getting the information in the "best" order, making use of known techniques for handling specific aspects of the system, provoking decisions when they are needed and dealing with forced omissions.

Expression means more than just establishing formatting rules and a consistent terminology. It means use of a terminology which is consistent and permits expression of the full specification. It requires that the adopted terminology has agreed and formally defined semantics. In many cases it may also require that subsets of the full formal expression can be mapped onto one or more equivalent, less complete terminologies for readers with less training in the use of formal notations.

The CORE method has been used to illustrate techniques for acquisition of information and the discussion of paradigms has been used to illustrate the potential for re-use of past experience in handling key problems of specification and design. CORE makes use of a notation of a type which is quite popular, but which is also extremely dangerous, because of its incompletely defined semantics.

The SREM method has been used to illustrate an approach to bridging between the use of acquisition techniques and formal specification terminologies via a combination of mutually consistent diagrammatic and textual terminologies. It has also been used to illustrate an approach to the use of an integrated set of techniques for all stages of specification.

Temporal Logic has been used to illustrate the power and utility of use of a formally defined terminology in conjunction with well defined techniques for approaching the problem of specification in order to maximise the chances of verifying key properties of a system.

The OSI and Argus discussions have been used to illustrate the scope for support of a philosophy of development in a practically realisable set of tools. The OSI protocols have been shown to be realisable in numerous ways, each of which provides support for distributed systems structuring techniques which conform to a common reference architecture for distributed systems.

Finally, the discussion of language constructs, and the more detailed description of the Argus language as a specific instance have been used to indicate some of the key concepts which must be supported by a terminology for specification of distributed systems.

10.4. Tools

Tools for specification, as discussed in this course, can be divided into those which solely support the process of specification and those which support the generation or execution of code which implements the specification. It is probably fair to say that most of the detailed discussion of tools has concentrated on the tools which support generation or execution of source code.

The CORE and SREM methods have both been supported by use of database systems specifically developed to support the process of specification. SREM has gone further than CORE, in that a number of other tools have been built to support SREM specification, the most widely quoted of these extra tools is a simulation facility which can be used in association with SREM specifications.

The discussion of Temporal Logic and Paradigms has not attempted to cloud the issues by discussion of how they might be automated, but it is possible to see from other work on the use of formal techniques that strong tool support is both desirable and possible.

The main discussion of tool support in this course has concerned tools for protocol specification and those associated with the topic of language constructs, of which the Argus language and tools have been discussed in greatest depth.

The main lesson to be drawn from the existence of such tools is that the methods discussed here for the specification of distributed systems can be supported by tools and that the size and complexity of the problem of distributed system specification is such that the users of advanced techniques have found it desirable to build tool support.

10.5. Practical Use

There is a tendency for many technical staff in the computer industry to join one of three warring camps. There are those who believe that attempts to restrict the techniques used or the freedom of expression in the process of specification are not only non-beneficial, but they are actually harmful in some cases. Others think that some restrictions are desirable, but that fully formal techniques are not cost-effective. The rest think that everyone in the industry should be required to demonstrate an understanding of formal techniques before they are allowed to practice.

The fact that there is an element of truth in all three cases makes it difficult to break down their prejudices and achieve constructive progress towards the goals of productivity and quality required by customers, managers and technical staff.

The discussions of the CORE method give an indication that it is possible to use information gathering techniques and psychological techniques to increase the chance that the right information will be gathered at the right time. The example used to illustrate CORE techniques demonstrates the potential for failure when a specification is expressed in some ad hoc form (eg. natural language).

The CORE diagrammatic notation demonstrates that there is some value in using a constrained notation (ie. not free form natural language) which can be discussed with inexperienced end-users and customers. A careful examination of what CORE diagrams do not say demonstrates also the potential danger of using a notation which either fails to express some key properties of a specification or has incompletely defined semantics. Such notations cannot generally form a safe basis for a contractual agreement.

The discussions on formal foundations (Temporal Logic, etc.) indicate that it is possible to use more formal techniques for expression than those used for CORE. Moreover, with appropriate training, those techniques can be applied more systematically than many people believe possible.

Nevertheless, the degree of difficulty of using formal techniques is great enough to suggest that many people will be unprepared or unable to use them directly. A mapping from a formal notation and formal techniques to a "quasi formal" notation and technique such as CORE would ease the problems. The possibility of achieving such a mapping has not been demonstrated on this course. To achieve a mapping, the definers and users of methods such as CORE must be prepared to adjust their notations somewhat, so that a consistent mapping is possible.

The discussion of language constructs gives some indication of some of the key concepts which are not always addressed by quasi formal notations such as that used for CORE, and which must nevertheless be addressed in the implementation of the system. This suggests a possible link between formal and quasi formal notations via use of constructs in high level applications languages and indicates key information which quasi formal languages for specification must be able to express.

There remains the problem that some aspects of systems specification are extremely difficult. The discussions on paradigms, protocol specification and the Argus system indicate that there can be some improvement in the ability of project teams to handle such aspects.

The discussion of the Argus system indicates that some aspects of traditionally difficult problems can be helped by use of a language which permits a degree of automatic support for control of some of the more difficult problems. The use of effective standards for development of reliable communications systems is another example of the scope for removal of some of the traditional problems from the concern of the applications designer/developer.

Greater concentration on the recognition of difficult cases for which there exist formal treatments can both minimise the probability that project teams will continue to derive poor or partial solutions to problems for which a "state of the art" solution already exists. Where solutions do not yet exist, the existing formal treatments may be expected at least to fore-warn of the potential failure modes for partial solutions.

Finally, there is a problem with the scope and compatibility of many existing methods and tools. There is a need to be "methodical" at all stages of a system's life. To produce a high quality requirement according to some criteria and then be unable to relate that to the language for design, or to be unable to relate a high quality design to the language for implementation give few benefits. Moreover, to use methods for requirement and design which do not agree on at which stage information should be specified is a recipe for confusion and contractual disagreement.

The discussion of SREM has been used to indicate the potential for a coordinated approach to system development. It illustrates the potential for use of several mutually consistent notations, which can be demonstrated to be consistent with a theory for which formal treatments exist. It illustrates the potential for use of methods for various stages and for a rationale for transition from one stage to the next.

References

[Ada 82] "Reference Manual for the Ada Programming Language", ACM AdaTEC, July 1982.

[Ada 83] Reference Manual for the Ada Programming Language, United States Department of Defense, Washington, ANSI/MIL–STD–1815A–1983, 1983.

[Alford 77] M. Alford, "Software Requirements Engineering Methodology", Transactions on Software Engineering, Jan. 1977.

[Alford 79a] M. Alford, "Requirements for Distributed Data Processing", Proceedings of First International Conference on Distributed Processing, Huntsville, Al., 1979.

[Alford 79b] M. Alford, "SREM", Proc. of STL Symposium on Formal Design Methodology, 1979, pp. 139–170.

[Alford 80] M. Alford, "Requirements in the 80's", Proceedings of ACM 80.

[Allchin 83] J.E. Allchin, An Architecture for Reliable Decentralized Systems, Technical Report GIT–ICS–83/23, Georgia Institute of Technology, School of Information and Computer Science, September 1983.

[Alpern 84] B. Alpern, F.B. Schneider, Proving Properties of Concurrent Programs, in preparation.

[Andrews 81] G.R. Andrews, "Synchronizing Recources", ACM Trans. on Programming Languages and Systems 3, 4 (October 1981), pp. 405–430.

[Andrews 83] G.R. Andrews, F.B. Schneider, "Concepts and Notations for Concurrent Programming", Computing Surveys 15, 1 (March 1983), pp. 3–43.

[Ansart 80] JP. Ansart, Formal Validation of the OSI Transport Protocol, Research Report FDT 7534 RHIN Project, Agence de l'Informatique, 1980.

[Ansart 81] JP. Ansart, "Test and Certification of Standardized Protocols", in D. Rayner and RWS Hale (editors), Protocol Testing, Toward Proofs, Volume 2, NPL, 1981, pp. 119–126 .

[Ansart 82a] JP. Ansart, Validation de la Session ECMA 75, Rapport de recherche RHIN–FDT7517, Agence de l'Informatique, 1982.

[Ansart 82b] JP. Ansart, Validation de la Session Architel (ISO BC5), Rapport de recherche RHIN, Agence de l"Informatique, 1982.

[Ansart 83a] JP. Ansart, Validation de la Session ISO, Rapport de recherche, Agence de l'Informatique, 1983.

[Ansart 83b] JP. Ansart, Manuel Operateur LISE, Document RHIN-FDT7539, Agence de l'Informatique, 1983.

[Ansart 83c] JP. Ansart, Formal Description of ISO Transport and Session in PDIL, Computer Printout, Agence de l'Informatique, 1983.

[Ansart 83d] JP. Ansart, V. Chari, M. Neyer, O.Rafiq, D. Simon, "Description, Simulation and Implementation of Communication Protocols Using PDIL", ACM Austin, March 7/9, 1983.

[Ansart 83e] JP. Ansart, "STQ, CERBERE and GENEPI Tree Testing Tools for Implementation Testing in EUTECO", T. Kalin (editor), North Holland, 1983.

[Apt 80] K. Apt, N. Francez, W. de Roever, "A Proof System for Communicating Sequential Processes", ACM TOPLAS 2, 3 (July 1980), pp. 359-385.

[Ayache 79] J.M. Ayache, P. Azema, M. Diaz, "Observer: A Concept for On-Time Detection of Control Error in Concurrent Systems", IEEE Int. Symp. on Fault-Tolerant Computing, Madison USA, 1979.

[Balzer 71] R.M. Balzer, "Ports - A Method for Dynamic Interprogram Communication and Job Control", in Proc. AFIPS Spring Jt. Comp. Conf. (Atlantic City, May 1971), vol.38, AFIPS Press, Arlington, 1971, pp. 485-489.

[Balzer 83] R. Balzer, "The Inevitable Intertwining of Requirements and Design", ACM Communications, 1983.

[Barringer 82] H. Barringer, I. Mearns, "Axioms and Proof Rules for Ada Tasks", IEE Proc. 129, Pt. E. No. 2 (March 1982), pp. 38-48.

[Bauer 82] F.L. Bauer, H. Wössner, Algorithmic Language and Program Development, Springer-Verlag, New York, 1982.

[Bayer 81] M. Bayer, et al., "Software Development in the CDL 2 Laboratory", in H. Hünke (Ed.), Software Engineering Environments, North-Holland Publ., Amsterdam, 1981, pp. 97-118.

[Bell 76] T.E. Bell, D.C. Bixler, M.E. Dyer, "An Extendable Approach to Computer-Aided Software Requirements Engineering", Proc. 2nd. Int'l Conf. on Software Engineering, 1976.

[Berthomieu 83] B. Berthomieu, M. Menasche, "Analysis by State Enumeration of Time Petri Nets", Proc. of IFIP Congress Paris, September 1983.

[Bernstein 81] P. Bernstein, N. Goodman, M. Lai, "Two Part Proof Schema for Database Concurrency Control", Proc. of the Fifth Berkeley Workshop on Distributed Data Management and Computer Networks, February 1981, pp. 71–84.

[Birrell 82] A. Birrell, R. Levin, R. Needham, M. Schroeder, "Grapevine: An Exercise in Distributed Computing", Comm. of the ACM 25, 4 (April 1982), pp. 260–274.

[Boehm 81] B. Boehm, Software Engineering Economics, 1981.

[Bloom 83] T. Bloom, Dynamic Module Replacement in a Distributed Programming System, Technical Report MIT/LCS/TR–303, M.I.T. Laboratory for Computer Science, Cambridge, Ma., 1983.

[Blummer 82] T. P. Blummer, R. L. Tenney, "A Formal Specification Technique and Implementation Method for Protocols, " Computer Networks 6, 1982, pp. 201–217.

[Bochmann 82] G.V. Bochmann, et al., "Experience with Formal Specification Using an Extended State Transition Model", IEEE Trans. on Communications, December 1982.

[Bonhomme 83] B. Bonhomme, Le Systeme STQ/ARGOS, Document RHIN NOR 7516.1, Agence de l'Informatique, 1983.

[Brinch Hansen 72] P. Brinch Hansen, "Structured Multiprogramming", Commun. ACM 15, 7 (July 1972), pp. 574–578.

[Brinch Hansen 73a] P. Brinch Hansen, Operating System Principles Prentice–Hall, Englewood Cliffs, N.J., 1973.

[Brinch Hansen 73b] P. Brinch Hansen, "Concurrent Programming Concepts", ACM Comput. Surv. 5, 4 (Dec. 1973), pp. 223–245.

[Brinch Hansen 78] P. Brinch Hansen, "Distributed Processes: A Concurrent Programming Concept", Commun. ACM 21, 11 (Nov. 1978), pp. 934–941.

[Burstall 74] R.M. Burstall, "Program Proving as Hand Simulation with a Little Induction", Information Processing 74, North Holland (1974), pp. 308–312.

[Campbell 74] R.H. Campbell, A.N. Habermann, "The Specification of Process Synchronization by Path Expressions", Lecture Notes in Computer Science, vol. 16, Springer–Verlag, New York, 1974, pp. 89–102.

[Campbell 79] R.H. Campbell, R.B. Kolstadt, "Path Expressions in Pascal", in Proc. 4th Int. Conf. on Software Eng. (Munich, Sept. 17–19, 1979), IEEE, New York, 1979, pp. 212–219.

[CCITT 80] CCITT, Specifications of Signalling System No 7, Rec 0701–741, Yellow Book 1980.

[CCITT 83] CCITT, Special Rapporteur on Message Handling, Draft Recommandation XMSH–4, 1983.

[Cerf 71] V. Cerf, Semaphores and a Graph Model of Computation, UCLA, 1971.

[Chandy 84] K.M. Chandy, L. Lamport, "Distributed Snapshots: Determining Global States of Distributed Systems", submitted for publication.

[Chari 83] V. Chari, D. Simon, JP. Ansart, Manual Operateur de PDIL, Agence de l'Informatique, 1983.

[Cheheyl 81] Cheheyl, Gasser, Huff, Millen, "Verifying Security", Computing Surveys 13, 3 (1981), pp. 279–339.

[Dahl 70] O.-J. Dahl, B. Myhrhaug, K. Nygaard, The SIMULA 67 Common Base Language, Norwegian Computing Centre, Pub. S–22, Oslo, 1970.

[Damidau 82] J. Damidau, JP. Ansart, "CEBERE a Tool to Keep an Eye on High Level Protocol in Protocol Specification, Testing and Verification", Sunshine (ed.), North Holland, 1982.

[Davies 78] C.T. Davies, "Data Processing Spheres of Control", IBM Systems Journal 17, 2 (1978), pp. 179–198.

[De Remer 76] F.L. De Remer, H. Kron, "Programming–in–the–Large Versus Programming–in–the–Small", in H.–J. Schneider, M. Nagel (Eds.), Programmiersprachen, 4. Fachtagung der GI, (Erlangen), Informatik-Fachbericht 1, Springer–Verlag, Berlin, 1976, pp. 80–89.

[Dijkstra 68a] E.W. Dijkstra, "The Structure of the "THE" Multiprogramming System", Commun. ACM 11, 5 (May 1968), pp. 341–346.

[Dijkstra 68b] E.W. Dijkstra, "Cooperating Sequential Processes", in F. Genuys (Ed.), Programming Languages, Academic Press, New York, 1968.

[Dijkstra 74] E.W. Dijkstra, "Self Stabilization in Spite of Distributed Control", CACM 17, 11 (Nov. 1974), pp. 643–644.

[Dijkstra 75] E.W. Dijkstra, "Guarded Commands, Nondeterminacy, and Formal Derivation of Programs", Commun. ACM 18, 8 (Aug. 1975), pp. 453–457.

[Dijkstra 76] E.W. Dijkstra, A Discipline of Programming, Prentice Hall, New Jersey, 1976.

[DIN 66253] DIN 66253, Programmiersprache PEARL, Beuth Verlag GmbH, Berlin, 1982, (in English)

[Dolev 82a] D. Dolev, H.R. Strong, "Polynomial Algorithms for Multiple Processor Agreement", Proc. 14th ACM SIGACT Symposium on Theory of Computing, May 1982.

[Dolev 82b] D. Dolev, H.R. Strong, "Authenticated Algorithms for Byzantine Agreement", to appear SIAM Journal on Computing.

[Dolev 82c] D. Dolev, H.R. Strong, "Requirements for Agreement in Distributed Systems", Proc. 2nd International Symposium on Distributed Data Bases, Berlin, Sept. 1982.

[Dolev 82d] D. Dolev, H.R. Strong, "Distributed Commit with Bounded Waiting", Proc. 2nd Symposium on Reliability in Distributed Software and Database Systems, Pittsburgh, July 1982, pp. 53-60.

[Eswaren 76] K.P. Eswaren, J.N. Gray, R.A. Lorie, I.L. Traiger, "The Notion of Consistency and Predicate Locks in a Database System", Comm. of the ACM 19, 11 (November 1976), pp. 624-633.

[Faltin 83] U. Faltin, E. Faul, A. Giessler, E. Guenther, W. Orth, H. Parslow, The TESDI Manual Testing and Diagnostics Aid for Higher Level Protocols, IFV-IK-RZ, GMD Darmstadt, FRG, 1983.

[Ferret 83] B. Ferret, R. Puch, Le Systeme GENEPI, Document RHIN, NOR 7531, Agence de l'Informatique.

[Fischer 82] M.J. Fischer, N.A. Lynch, M.S. Paterson, Impossibility of Distributed Consensus with One Faulty Process, Technical Report MIT/LCS/TR-282, M.I.T., Laboratory for Computer Science, Cambridge, Ma., September 1982.

[Fischer 83] M.J. Fischer, "The Consensus Problem in Unreliable Distributed Systems (A Brief Survey)", Proc. International Conference on Foundation of Computation Theory, Borgholm, Sweden, August 1983.

[Floyd 67] R.W. Floyd, "Assigning Meanings to Programs" Proc. Symposium Applied Math 19, American Mathematical Society, Providence, R.I., 1967, pp. 19-32.

[Francez 80] N. Francez, "Distributed Termination", ACM Trans. Prog. Lang. and Systems 2, 1 (Jan. 1980).

[Garcia-Molina 82] H. Garcia-Molina, "Elections in a Distributed Computing System", IEEE Trans. on Computers C-31, 1 (Jan. 1982), pp. 48-59.

[Garcia-Molina 83] H. Garcia-Molina, D. Barbara, How to Assign Votes in a Distributed System, TR 311-3/1983, Department of Electrical Engineering and Computer Science, Princeton University, Princeton, N.J.

[Gerth 82a] R. Gerth, "A Sound and Complete Hoare Axiomatization of the Ada-Rendezvous", Proc. ICALP 82, Lecture Notes in Computer Science, Vol. 140, Springer-Verlag, Heidelberg, 1980, pp. 252-264.

[Gerth 82b] R. Gerth, W.P. de Roever, M. Roncken, "Procedures and Concurrency: A Study in Proof", Proc. ISOP'82, Lecture Notes in Computer Science Vol. 137, Springer-Verlag, Heidelberg, 1982, pp. 132-163.

[Gerth 83] R. Gerth, W.P. de Roever, "A Proof System for Concurrent Ada Programs", Technical Report RUU-CS-83-2, Vakgroep Informatica, Rijksuniversiteit Utrecht, The Netherlands, Jan. 1983.

[Geschke 77a] C.M. Geschke, J.H. Morris Jr., E.H. Satterthwaite, "Early Experience with Mesa", Commun. ACM 20, 8 (August 1977), pp. 540-553.

[Geschke 77b] C.M. Geschke, E.H. Satterthwaite, Exception Handling in Mesa, Palo Alto Research Center, Draft, 1977.

[Gifford 79] D.K. Gifford, "Weighted Voting for Replicated Data", Proc. Seventh Symposium on Operating System Principles, Pacific Grove, CA., 1979, pp. 150-162.

[Good 79] D. Good, R. Cohen, J. Keeton-Williams, "Principles of Proving Concurrent Programs in Gypsy", Proc. of the Sixth Annual Symposium on Principles of Programming Languages, Jan. 1979, pp. 42-52.

[Goodenough 75] J.R. Goodenough, "Exception Handling: Issues and a Proposed Notation", Commun. ACM 18, 12 (1975), pp. 683-696.

[Goos 73] G. Goos, "Hierarchies", in F.L. Bauer (Ed.), Software Engineering, An Advanced Course, Springer-Verlag, 1973.

[Gray 76] J.N. Gray, R.A. Lorie, G.F. Putzolu, I.L. Traiger, "Granularity of Locks and Degrees of Consistency in a Shared Data Base", Modeling in Data Base Management Systems, G.M. Nijssen, Ed., North Holland, 1976.

[Gray 78] J.N. Gray, "Notes on Data Base Operating Systems", Lecture Notes in Computer Science 60, Goos and Hartmanis, Eds., Springer–Verlag, Berlin, 1978, pp. 393–481.

[Gray 79] J. Gray, "Notes on Data Base Operating Systems", Operating Systems: An Advanced Course, Lecture Notes in Computer Science, Vol. 60, Springer–Verlag, New York, 1978, pp. 393–481.

[Gray 81] J.N. Gray, et al. "The Recovery Manager of the System R Database Manager", ACM Computing Surveys 13, 2 (June 1981), pp. 223–242.

[Gries 81] D. Gries, The Science of Programming, Springer–Verlag, New York, 1981.

[Guttag 78] J. Guttag, E. Horowitz, D. Musser, "Abstract Data Types and Software Validation", Comm. of the ACM 21, 12 (December 1978), pp. 1048–1064.

[Halpern 83] J. Halpern, B. Simmons, R. Strong, An Efficient Fault–Tolerant Algorithm for Clock Synchronization, IBM Research Report RJ 4094, Nov. 1983.

[Hamilton 76] M. Hamilton, S. Zeldin, Integrated Software Development System/Higher Order Software Conceptual Description, US Army Report ECOM–76–0329–F, 1976.

[Hamilton 77] M. Hamilton, S. Zeldin, "Higher Order Software", Transactions on Software Engineering, Jan. 1977.

[Herlihy 82] M. Herlihy, B. Liskov, "A Value Transmission Method for Abstract Data Types", ACM Trans. on Programming Languages and Systems 4, 4 (October 1982), pp. 527–551.

[Hoare 69] C.A.R. Hoare, "An Axiomatic Basis for Computer Programming", CACM 12, 10 (Oct. 1969), pp. 576–580.

[Hoare 72a] C.A.R. Hoare, "Proof of Correctness of Data Representations", Acta Informatica 4 (1972), pp.271–281.

[Hoare 72b] C.A.R. Hoare, "Towards a Theory of Parallel Programming", in C.A.R. Hoare, R.H. Perrott (Eds.), Operating Systems Techniques, Academic Press, New York, 1972, pp. 61–71.

[Hoare 74] C.A.R. Hoare, "Monitors: An Operating System Structuring Concept", Commun. ACM 17, 10 (Oct. 1974), pp. 549–557.

[Hoare 78] C.A.R. Hoare, "Communicating Sequential Processes", Commun. ACM 21, 8 (Aug. 1978), pp. 666–677.

[Hommel 76] G. Hommel, S. Jähnichen, W. Koch, "SLAN – eine erweiterbare Sprache zur Unterstützung der strukturierten und modularen Programmierung", in H.-J. Schneider, M. Nagel (Eds.), Programmiersprachen, 4. Fachtagung der GI, (Erlangen), Informatik–Fachberichte 1, Springer–Verlag, Berlin,1976, pp. 101–110.

[Hommel 78] G. Hommel, "Computer Science Education with ELAN", Computers and Education, vol.2, 1978, pp. 205–212.

[Horning 74] J.J. Horning, et al., "A Program Structure for Error Definition and Recovery", in E. Gelembe, C. Kaiser (Eds.), Operating Systems (Rocquencourt, Apr. 1974), Lecture Notes in Comp. Science, vol. 16, Springer–Verlag, New York, 1974, pp. 177–187.

[Ichbiah 79] J. Ichbiah, et al., "Preliminary ADA Reference Manual", SIGPLAN Notices 14, 6 (June 1979), part A.

[ISO 82] ISO/TC97/SC16, Working Draft for an Addendum to ISO 7498 Covering Connectionless Mode Transmission, DOC N 1194, June 1982.

[ISO 83a] ISO, Open Systems Interconnection, Basic Reference Model, IS 7498, 1983.

[ISO 83b] ISO, Open Systems Interconnection – Connection Oriented Transport Protocol Specification, DIS 8073, 1983.

[ISO 83c] ISO, Open Systems Interconnection – Connection Oriented Transport Service Definition, DIS 8072, 1983.

[ISO 83d] ISO, Open Systems Interconnection – Basic Connection Oriented Session Service Definition, DIS 8326, 1983

[ISO 83e] ISO, Open Systems Interconnection – Basic Connection Oriented Session Protocol Specification, DIS 8327, 1983.

[ISO 83f] ISO/TC97/SC16/WG1/DFT – Subgroup B.

[Jackson 75] M.A. Jackson, Principals of Programming Design, Academic Press, London 1975.

[Kramer 83] J. Kramer, J. Magee, M. Sloman, A. Lister, "CONIC: An Integrated Approach to Distributed Computer Control Systems", IEE Proc. Part E, vol.130, no.1, Jan. 1983, pp. 1–10.

[Kung 81] H.T. Kung, J.T. Robinson, "On Optimistic Methods for Concurrency Control", ACM Trans. on Database Systems 6, 2 (June 1981), pp. 213–226.

[Lamport 76] L. Lamport, Towards a Theory of Correctness for Multi–User Data Base Systems, Report CA–7610–7612, Massachusetts Computer Associates, Wakefield, Ma., October 1976.

[Lamport 77] L. Lamport, "Proving the Correctness of Multiprocess Programs", IEEE Trans. on Soft. Eng. SE–3, 2 (March 1977).

[Lamport 78a] L. Lamport, "Time, Clocks and the Ordering of Events in a Distributed System", CACM 21, 7 (July1978), pp. 558–565.

[Lamport 78b] L. Lamport, "The Implementation of Reliable Distributed Multiprocess Systems", Computer Networks 2 (1978), pp. 95–114.

[Lamport 80a] L. Lamport, "'Sometime' is Sometimes 'Not Never': A Tutorial on the Temporal Logic of Programs", Proceedings of the Seventh Annual Symposium on Principles of Programming Languages, ACM SIGACT–SIGPLAN (Jan. 1980).

[Lamport 80b] L. Lamport, "The 'Hoare Logic' of Concurrent Programs", Acta Informatica 14, 1980.

[Lamport 82a] L. Lamport, P.M. Milliar–Smith, Synchronizing Clocks in the Presence of Faults, Op. 60, Computer Science Laboratory, SRI International, Menlo Park, CA, March 1982.

[Lamport 82b] L. Lamport, R. Shostak, M. Pease, "The Byzantine Generals Problem. ACM TOPLAS 4, 3 (July 1982), pp. 382–401.

[Lamport 82c] L. Lamport, "An Assertional Correctness Proof of a Distributed Algorithm", Science of Computer Programming 2, 3 (Dec. 1982), pp. 175–206.

[Lamport 83a] L. Lamport, "Specifying Concurrent Program Modules", ACM Trans. Prog. Lang. and Systems 6, 2 (Apr. 1983).

[Lamport 83b] L. Lamport, "What Good is Temporal Logic?" Information Processing 83, R. E. A. Mason, ed., (1983) North Holland, Amsterdam.

[Lamport 84a] L. Lamport, "Using Time Instead of Timeout for Fault–tolerance in Distributed Systems", to appear, ACM TOPLAS, 1984.

[Lamport 84b] L. Lamport, F.B. Schneider, "The 'Hoare Logic' of CSP and All That", ACM TOPLAS 6, 2 (April 1984).

[Lampson 76] B. Lampson, H. Sturgis, "Crash Recovery in a Distributed Data Storage System", submitted for publication, 1976.

[Lampson 79] B. Lampson, H. Sturgis, "Crash Recovery in a Distributed Data Storage System", Xerox PARC, Palo Alto, Ca., April 1979.

[Lampson 80] B. Lampson, D. Redell, "Experience with Processes and Monitors in Mesa", Comm. of the ACM 23, 2 (February 1980), pp. 105–117.

[Lampson 81a] B.W. Lampson, "Atomic Transaction", in Distributed Systems – Architecture and Implementation, Lecture Notes in Computer Science, vol. 105, Springer–Verlag, New York, 1981.

[Lampson 81b] B.W. Lampson, M. Paul, H.J. Siegert, "Distributed Systems – Architecture and Implementation", Lecture Notes in Computer Science, Vol. 105, Springer–Verlag, New York, 1981.

[Lano 77] R. Lano, The N–Squared Chart, TRW Report TRW–SS–77–04.

[LeBlanc 82] R. LeBlanc, A. Maccabe, "The Design of a Programming Language Based on Connectivity Networks", Proc. 4th International Conference on Distributed Computing Systems, Oct. 1982.

[LeLann 77] G. LeLann, "Distributed Systems – Towards a Formal Approach", Proc. Information Processing 77, B. Gilchrist, Ed., North Holland, Amsterdam, The Netherlands, 1977, pp. 155–160.

[Levin 77] R. Levin, Program Structures for Exceptional Condition Handling, Dept. of Computer Science, Carnegie–Mellon University, Ph. D. thesis, 1977.

[Levin 81] G. Levin, D. Gries, "Proof Techniques for Communicating Sequential Processes", Acta Informatica 15, 1981, pp. 281–302.

[Lindsay 84] B.G. Lindsay, et al., "Computation and Communication in R*: A Distributed Database Manager", ACM Trans. on Computer Systems, to appear, 1984.

[Liskov 74] B. Liskov, S.N. Zilles, "Programming with Abstract Data Types", Proc. of the ACM SIGPLAN Conference on Very High Level Languages, SIGPLAN Notices 9, 4 (April 1974), pp. 50–59.

[Liskov 77] B. Liskov, A. Snyder, R.R. Atkinson, J.C. Schaffert, "Abstraction Mechanisms in CLU", Commun. ACM 20, 8 (August 1977), pp. 564–576.

[Liskov 79a] B. Liskov, A. Snyder, "Exception Handling in CLU", IEEE Trans. on Software Engineering SE–5, 6 (November 1979), pp. 546–558.

[Liskov 79b] B. Liskov, "Primitives for Distributed Computing", Proc. 7th ACM Symposium on Operating Systems Principles, (Dec. 1979), pp. 33—42.

[Liskov 81a] B. Liskov, "On Linguistic Support for Distributed Programs", Proc. of the IEEE Symposium on Reliability in Distributed Software and Database Systems, Pittsburgh, Pa., July 1981, pp. 53—60.

[Liskov 81b] B. Liskov, et al., "CLU Reference Manual", Lecture Notes in Computer Science 114, Goos, Hartmanis, Eds., Springer—Verlag, Berlin, 1981.

[Liskov 83a] B. Liskov, M. Herlihy, Issues in Process and Communication Structure for Distributed Programs, Programming Methodology Group Memo 38, M.I.T., Laboratory for Computer Science, Cambridge, Ma., July 1983.

[Liskov 83b] B. Liskov, et al., Preliminary Argus Reference Mand anual, Programming Methodology Group Memo 39, M.I.T., Laboratory for Computer Science, Cambridge, Ma., October 1983.

[Liskov 84a] B. Liskov, "The Argus Language and System", in Proc. Advanced Course on Distributed Systems – Methods and Tools for Specification, TU München, Apr. 1984.

[Liskov 84b] B. Liskov, M. Herlihy, L. Gilbert, "Limitations of Remote Procedure Call and Static Process Structure for Distributed Computing", in preparation.

[Lomet 77] D. Lomet, "Process Structuring Synchronization, and Recovery Using Atomic Actions", Proc. of an ACM Conference on Language Design for Reliable Software, SIGPLAN Notes 12, 2 (March 1977).

[Maccabe 82] A.B. Maccabe, Languages Features for Fully Distributed Processing Systems, Georgia Institute of Technology, Technical Report GIT—ICS—82/12, 1982.

[Magee 83] J. Magee, J. Kramer, "Dynamic Configuration for Distributed Real—Time Systems", Proc. IEEE Real—Time Systems Symposium, Washington, Dec. 1983.

[McCurley 83] R. McCurley, F.B. Schneider, Derivation of a Distributed Algorithm for Finding Paths in Directed Networks, TR 83—586, Dept. of Computer Science, Cornell University, Ithaca, N.Y., Dec. 1983.

[Menasce 80] D.A. Menasce, G.J. Popeck, R. Muntz, "A Locking Protocol for Resource Coordination in Distributed Databases", ACM TODS 5, 6 (June 1980), pp. 103-138.

[Merlin 76] P.M. Merlin, D.J. Farber, "Renoverability of Communication Protocols − Implication of a Theoretical Study", IEEE Trans. on Communications, 1976, pp. 1036-1043.

[Mesarovic 70] M.D. Mesarovic, D. Macko, Y. Takahara, Theory of Hierarchical Multilevel Systems, Academic Press, New York 1970.

[Misra 81] J. Misra, K.M. Chandy, "Proofs of Networks of Processes", IEEE Trans. on Software Eng. SE-7, 4 (July 1981), pp. 417-426.

[Misra 82] J. Misra, K.M. Chandy, T. Smith, "Proving Safety and Liveness of Communicating Processes with Examples", Proc. ACM SIGACT-SIGOPS Symposium on Principles of Distributed Computing, August 1982, pp. 201-208.

[Mohan 83] C. Mohan, R. Strong, S. Finkelstein, "Method for Distributed Transaction Commit and Recovery Using Byzantine Agreement Within Clusters of Processors", Proc. 2nd Annual ACM Symposium on Principles of Distributed Computing, Montreal, Canada, August 1983, pp. 89-103.

[Moss 81] J.E.B. Moss, Nested Transactions: An Approach to Reliable Distributed Computing, Technical Report MIT/LCS/TR-260, M.I.T. Laboratory for Computer Science, Cambridge, Ma., 1981.

[Mujtaba 79] S. Mujtaba, R. Goldman, AL User's Manual, Stanford University, Report, Stanford, 1979.

[Mullery 79] G.P. Mullery, "CORE − A Method for Controlled Requirement Expression", Proc. IEEE 4th. Intl. Conf. on Software Engineering, 1979.

[Nelson 81] B.J. Nelson, Remote Procedure Call, Dept. of Computer Science, Carnegie-Mellon Univ., Ph.D. Thesis, Rep. CMU-CS-81-119, May 1981.

[Nightingale 81] J.S. Nightingale, A Benchmark for the Implementation of the NBS Transport Protocol, NBS Draft Report ICST/H.NP-81-20 NBS, Washington DC, Sept. 1981.

[Nightingale 82] J.S. Nightingale, "Protocol Testing Using a Reference Implementation", in Protocol, Specification, Testing, and Verification, C. Sunshine (ed.), North Holland, 1982.

[Noble 68] J.M. Noble, "The Control of Exceptional Conditions in PL/I Object Programs", in A.J.H. Morell (Ed.), Proc. Informat. Processing 68 (Edinburgh, Aug. 1968), North-Holland Publ., Amsterdam, 1969, pp. 565-571.

[Owicki 76] S. Owicki, D. Gries, "An Axiomatic Proof Technique for Parallel Programs", Acta Informatica 6, 4 (1976).

[Owicki 82] S. Owicki, L. Lamport, "Proving Liveness Properties of Concurrent Programs", ACM Trans. on Prog. Lang. and Sys. 4, 3 (July 1982).

[Papadimitriou 79] C.H. Papadimitriou, "The Serializability of Concurrent Database Updates", Journal of the ACM 26, 4 (October 1979), pp. 631-653.

[Parnas 72] D.L. Parnas, "On the Criteria to be Used in Decomposing Systems into Modules", Commun. ACM 15, 12 (Dec. 1972), pp. 1053-1058.

[Parnas 76] D.L. Parnas, H. Würges, "Response to Undesired Events in Software Systems", in Proc. 2nd. Int. Conf. Software Engineering (San Francisco, Oct. 1976), IEEE Comp. Soc., Long Beach, 1976, pp. 437-446.

[Pease 80] M. Pease, R. Shostak, L. Lamport, "Reaching Agreement in the Presence of Faults", JACM 27, 2 (April 1979), pp. 228-234.

[Peterson 81] J. Peterson, Petri Net Theory and the Modeling of Systems, Prentice Hall, 1981.

[Pnueli 77] A. Pnueli, "The Temporal Logic of Programs", Proc. of the 18th Symposium on the Foundations of Computer Science, IEEE (Nov. 1977).

[Randell 75a] G. Randell, "System Structure for Software Fault Tolerance", in Proc. Int. Conf. Reliable Software (Los Angeles, Apr. 1975), ACM SIGPLAN Not. 10, 6 (1975), pp. 437-449.

[Rayner 82] D. Rayner, "A System for Testing Protocol Implementation" Computer Networks (6) 1982, pp. 383-395.

[Reed 78] D.P. Reed, Naming and Synchronization in a Decentralized Computer System, Technical Report MIT/LCS/TR-205, M.I.T., Laboratory for Computer Science, Cambridge, Ma., 1978.

[Rescher 71] N. Rescher, A. Urquhart, Temporal Logic, Springer-Verlag, New York, 1971.

[Rivest 78] R. Rivest, A. Shamir, L. Adleman, "A Method for Obtaining Digital Signatures and Public–Key Cryptosystems" CACM 21, 2 (Feb. 1978), pp. 120–126.

[Rosenkrantz 78] D. Rosenkrantz, R. Stearns, P. Lewis, "System Level Concurrency Control for Distributed Database Systems", ACM Trans. on Database Systems 3, 2 (June 1978), pp. 178–198.

[Ross 77] S. Ross, "SADT", Transactions on Software Engineering, Jan. 1977.

[Schlichting 82] R.D. Schlichting, F.B. Schneider, "Understanding and Using Asynchronous Message–Passing", Proc. ACM SIGACT–SIGOPS Symposium on Principles of Distributed Computing, (August 1982), pp. 141–147.

[Schlichting 83] R.D. Schlichting, F.B. Schneider, "Fail–Stop Processors: An Approach to Designing Fault–Tolerant Computing Systems", ACM TOCS 1, 3 (August 1983), pp. 222–238.

[Schlichting 84] R.D. Schlichting, F.B. Schneider, "Using Message Passing for Distributed Programming: Proof Rules and Disciplines", to appear ACM TOPLAS.

[Schneider 80] F.B. Schneider, "Ensuring Consistency on a Distributed Database System by Use of Distributed Semaphores", Proc. International Symposium on Distributed Data Bases, Paris, France, March 1980, pp. 183–189.

[Schneider 82] F.B. Schneider, "Synchronization in Distributed Programs", ACM TOPLAS 4, 2 (April 1982), pp. 179–195.

[Schneider 83] F.B. Schneider, "Fail–Stop Processors", Digest of Papers, Spring Compcon 83, San Francisco, Calif., March 1983, pp. 66–70.

[Schneider 84] F.B. Schneider, "Byzantine Generals In Action: Implementing Fail–Stop Processors, to appear, ACM TOCS 2, 2 (May 1984).

[Schwartz 83] R.L. Schwartz, P.M. Melliar–Smith, F.H. Vogt, An Interval Logic for Higher–Level Raesoning: Language Definition and Examples, SRI International Technical Report CSL–138, February, 1983.

[Shaw 77] M. Shaw, W.A. Wulf, R.L. London, "Abstraction and Verification in Alphard: Defining and Specifying Iteration and Generators", Commun. ACM 20, 8 (August 1977), pp. 553–564.

[Shrivastava 78] S.K. Shrivastava, J.P. Banatre, "Reliable Resource Allocation Between Unreliable Processes", IEEE Trans. on Software Engineering 4, 3 (May 1978), pp. 230–240.

[Silberschatz 79] A. Silberschatz, "Communication and Synchronization in Distributed Programs ", IEEE Trans. Softw. Eng. SE–5, 6 (Nov. 1979), pp. 542–546.

[Skeen 82] D. Skeen, Crash Recovery in a Distributed Database System, Ph. D. Thesis, University of California at Berkeley, May 1982.

[Soundararajan 81] N. Soundararajan, Axiomatic Semantics of Communicating Sequential Processes, Technical Report, Department of Computer and Information Science, Ohio State University, 1981.

[Spector 82] A.Z. Spector, "Performing Remote Operations Efficiently on a Local Computer Network", Comm. of the ACM 25, 4 (April 1982), pp. 246–260.

[Stark 84] E. Stark, Foundations of a Theory of Specification for Distributed Systems, Ph.D. Dissertation, M.I.T., Department of Electrical Engineering and Computer Science, Cambridge, Ma., forthcoming.

[Steusloff 81] H. Steusloff, "The Impact of Distributed Computer Control Systems of Software", in Digital Computer Applications to Process Control, Pergamon Press, Elmsford, N.Y., 1981, pp. 529–536.

[Stonebraker 79] M. Stonebraker, "Concurrency Control and Consistency of Multiple Copies of Data in Distributed INGRESS", IEEE Trans. Software Eng., SE–5 , 5 (May 1979), pp. 188–194.

[Strong 83] H.R. Strong, D. Dolev, "Byzantine Agreement", Digest of Papers, Spring Compcon 83, San Francisco, Calif., March 1983, pp. 77–81.

[Sturgis 80] H. Sturgis, J. Mitchell, J. Israel, "Issues in the Design and Use of a Distributed File System", Operating System Review 14, 3 (July 1980), pp. 55–69.

[Tajibnapis 77] W.D. Tajibnapis, "A Correctness Proof of a Topology Information Maintenance Protocol for a Distributed Computer Network", Comm. ACM 20, 7 (July 1977).

[Tanenbaum 81] A. Tanenbaum, Computer Networks, Prentice Hall, New Jersey, 1981.

[Teichroew 77a] D. Teichroew, E.A. Hershey III, "PSL/PSA: A Computer Aided Technique for Structured Documentation and Analysis of Information Processing Systems", IEEE Trans. on Software Engineering, Vol. SE-3, No. 1, 1977, pp. 41-48.

[Teichroew 77b] D. Teichroew, "PSL/PSA", Transactions on Software Engineering, Jan. 1977.

[Thomas 79] R.H. Thomas, "A Majority Consensus Approach to Concurrency Control", ACM TODS 4, 6 (June 1979), pp. 180-209.

[van Wijngaarden 75] A. van Wijngaarden, B.J. Mailloux, J.L. Peck, C.H.A. Koster, M. Sintzoff, C.H. Lindsey, L.G.L.T. Meertens, R.G. Fisker, "Revised Report on the Algorithmic Language ALGOL68", Acta Inform. 5, 1-3 (1975), pp. 1-236.

[Weihl 82] W. Weihl, B. Liskov, Specification and Implementation of Resilient, Atomic Data Types , Computation Structure Group Memo 223, M.I.T., Laboratory for Computer Science, Cambridge, Ma., December 1982.

[Weihl 84] W. Weihl, Specification and Implementation of Atomic Data Types, Ph.D. Thesis, M.I.T. Department of Electrical Engineering and Computer Science, Cambridge, Ma., forthcoming.

[Wensley 78] J. Wensley, et al., "SIFT: Design and Analysis of a Fault-Tolerant Computer for Aircraft Control", Proc. IEEE 66, 10 (Oct. 1978), pp. 1240-1255.

[West 78a] Ch. West, "General Technique for Communication Protocol Validation", IBM J. R & D, Vol. 22, July 1978, pp. 393-404.

[West 78b] Ch. West, P. Zafiropulo, "Automated Validation of a Communication Protocol", the CCITT X21 Recommendation , IBM J. R & D, Vol. 22, January 1978, pp. 60-71.

[Wirth 77a] N. Wirth, " Modula: A Language for Modular Multiprogramming", Softw. Pract. Exper. 7 (1977), pp. 3-35.

[Wirth 77b] N. Wirth, "The Use of Modula", Softw. Pract. Exper. 7 (1977), pp. 37-65.

[Wirth 77c] N. Wirth, "Design and Implementation of Modula", Softw. Pract. Exper. 7 (1977), pp. 67-84.

[Wirth 83] N. Wirth, Programming in Modula-2, Springer-Verlag, New York, 1983.

[Wood 80] W.G. Wood, Recovery Control of Communicating Processes in a Distributed System, Technical Report 158, University of Newcastle upon Tyne, 1980.

[Wymore 76] A. Wymore, Systems Engineering for Interdisciplinary Teams, John Wiley and Sons, 1976.

[Wymore 78] A. Wymore, An Interdisciplinary Approach to System Engineering, ...

[Yau 83] S. Yau, M. Caglayan, "Distributed Software Design Representation Using Modified Petri Nets", Transactions on Software Engineering, November 1983, pp. 733−745.

[Zafiropulo 80] P. Zafiropulo, Ch. West, H. Rudin, D.D. Cowan, D. Brant, "Towards Analysing and Synthetizing Protocols", IEEE Transactions on Communications, Vol. COM−28, 4 (April 1980), pp. 651−662.

[Zimmermann 81] H. Zimmermann, "Progression of the OSI Reference Model and its Applications", Proc. of the NTC'81, December 1981, F8.1.1, F8.1.6.

[Zimmermann 83] H. Zimmermann, "On Protocol Engineering", Invited Paper IFIP 83, Paris.

Index